AMERICAN MOSAIC
SOCIAL
PATTERNS
OF RELIGION
IN THE
UNITED STATES

18·67

AMERICAN MOSAIC

———◆———

SOCIAL PATTERNS OF RELIGION IN THE UNITED STATES

edited by

Phillip E. Hammond
University of Arizona

Benton Johnson
University of Oregon

RANDOM HOUSE   NEW YORK

FOR *SANDRA* AND *MIMI*

First Edition

987654321

Standard Book Number: 394-31009-8
Library of Congress Catalog Card Number: 77-122482

Manufactured in the United States of America by the Kingsport Press, Inc.,
Kingsport, Tennessee.

Book design by Pedro A. Noa

Introduction

The United States is a religious mosaic. Nowhere in the Western world are so many different kinds of religion available to the public. The full range, of course, is more readily available in large cities than in small towns or in the open country, but even in rural America far more religious variety exists than in rural Europe or Latin America. Moreover, American religion, unlike religion in many other lands, can be described neither as moribund nor as an unchanged relic of the past. To be sure, some denominations now find their growth at a standstill, and some theologies are publicly ridiculed. It is true that some faiths, whether viable or not, have changed little for a century or more. But there is another side to American religion, a side that can best be illustrated by a brief reflection on the national past. America was a religious mosaic in 1800, but it was not the same mosaic it is today. There were then virtually no Catholics in Boston, few Jews in New York, and no Mormons anywhere. No Jehovah's Witnesses rang doorbells in the suburbs, and no one had ever heard of Christian Science, Pentecostalism, or the social gospel. The most influential denominations preached a stern predestinarian Calvinism, and the Baptists, of whom there were rather few, used tobacco and drank hard liquor. A glance through the American past reveals elements of continuity in religious life, but it reveals above all that America has been a land of religious change. The pattern of the mosaic has continually shifted as new religious movements have arisen and the heritage of old churches has been challenged from within and from without.

v

We have put this anthology together in the belief that there is a need for a collection of essays documenting and interpreting the changing mosaic that is American religion. It has not been possible, of course, to treat the full range of religious diversity. We have therefore tried to expose the highlights, the major patterns within the mosaic as we see them. We have confined our attention to Christianity and Judaism because these faiths have been and continue to be the dominant ones in the United States. We have paid little attention to the great number of bodies, large and small, outside the mainstream. Within the mainstream we have focused on phenomena of broad rather than limited import, and our concern with change has led us to include several selections on the American past. Most of the essays are about religion itself, the relations between religious bodies, or the impact of religion on everyday life. Though we are well aware that nonreligious factors have constantly influenced the forms and fortunes of American religions, we have chosen not to "explain" religion in terms of these other factors. Instead, we have left our theme—mosaic pluralism—to stand as a largely implicit, chief "causal" factor.

Although both of us are sociologists, and the major orientation of this book is sociological, more than half the readings we have chosen were written by scholars from other disciplines. The selections therefore reflect a variety of perspectives and are largely nontechnical in character. Most of them can be easily read by anyone with at least a modest background in social science, contemporary religion, or American studies. Most of the selections were written recently, but a few were published several decades ago. Several have never before appeared in print.

Of course, a collection of articles such as this one does not achieve the comprehensiveness of many textbooks or anthologies. A few collections of social scientific essays about religion already exist, but they tend to be broad-gauged, containing samples of the whole enterprise known as sociology of religion. Thus, excerpts of Max Weber and Karl Marx are included along with ethnographic reports of little-known religions, demographic accounts of church attendance in the industrial West, and social psychological descriptions of prophets. Such an anthology is fine, needless to say, perhaps even necessary if it is to be the only text used in a class. Our teaching experience, however, indicated the need for a reasonably inexpensive set of readings that could be used in parallel fashion with any of the current texts in sociology of religion [1] or with the wealth of paperback "classics" [2] now available (or with both). Having decided from the

---

[1] One such is N. J. Demerath III and Phillip E. Hammond, *Religion in Social Context: Tradition and Transition* (New York: Random House, 1969).

[2] A number of these are listed in the annotated bibliographies concluding each chapter.

outset, therefore, that the volume should supplement, not supplant, whatever text choice an instructor makes, we then sacrificed one kind of comprehensiveness—the usual textbook kind which claims universality—in return for a more complete, if substantively narrower, focus. Thus, we chose American religion as being of primary interest to students in American universities.

This is not an apology. Most instructors' references to "contemporary" religion are to American religion anyway, and in significant ways the religious pluralism of the U.S. *is* an example of the mosaic pattern developing (or already developed) in much of the rest of the world. We have therefore accented in our selections those features of religion owing to its presence in a society of manifold religious expressions. And we have arranged the selections in such a fashion that the *pluralistic* character of America's religion is accented throughout.

The book is organized into three parts, each part subdivided into three chapters, each chapter containing several reading selections. Part One is devoted to the problem of defining and measuring religion and to delineating some major differences in orientation within the mainstream of American religion, although several of the selections in Part One are also of general theoretical significance. Part Two focuses on the churches as corporate bodies in the American past and present, and Part Three concerns the influence of religion in the lives of individuals and in the national life. We have written introductions to each of the nine chapters. The introductions are intended to highlight the major issues treated in the reading selections, but they have been written as interpretive essays in their own right and may be read without necessary reference to the selections themselves. Questions for discussion and suggestions for additional reading are included at the end of each chapter.

Phillip E. Hammond
Benton Johnson

Contents

Part One

Expressions
of Religion

Chapter I

---◄•►---

Locating
the Idea
of Religion

Knowledge of the destination can aid any
would-be *journey*. As we *journey* toward a social scientific understanding of American religion, therefore, we can profitably look first
at the subject under review, doing so in a manner that conveys not
simply the myriad experiences of religion but especially the rich as-
sortment of schemes for grasping or locating those experiences. That
is, even if every person has a wholly private idea of what religion *is*,
when he wants to communicate meaningfully with another *about* such
phenomena, he must convey the *concept* of religion. How, then, might
religion be conceptualized? What meaning might persons have in using
the idea of religion?

No amount of persuasion is likely to resolve all questions and
"legislate" a single, unambiguous meaning of religion. The most that
can be hoped for is clarity on the one hand and appropriateness on
the other: Can a reasonably precise meaning be inferred? And in a
given context, is that precise meaning the one that yields the greatest
understanding? What is clear and appropriate in the sociohistorical
investigation of religion, therefore, may be less so in sociopsychological
investigations. And neither usage may be suitable for the poet, the
theologian, the philosopher.

Locating the idea of religion is, then, an arbitrary act, justified
simply on the pragmatic grounds that by using one notion rather than
some other, our understanding is enhanced. The present task is to
demonstrate, especially in a context of American religion, that there
exist serious and successful efforts to conceptualize religion. The three
selections of this first chapter perform that task well.

Consider the excerpt from H. Richard Niebuhr's *The Kingdom of*

3

God in America (Selection 1). Eight years before its publication in
1937, Niebuhr had written what was to become the classic *Social
Sources of Denominationalism,* identifying a number of economic and
social forces which led not to Christian unity and brotherhood but to
denominational splintering and distrust. This "sociological" or
"Marxist" view (as he calls it) suggested a notion of religion as
epiphenomenal, that is, as caused by social forces that are secular
in character. Thus, in response to himself, so to speak, he wrote another book (from which the first selection is taken) to show that
religion is not merely subject to external forces to which it reacts; it
can also be faith in motion. Religion, Niebuhr argues, can be dynamic,
creative, and prophetic as well as static, reactive, and complacent.

Most scholars, unless they are still engaged in simplistic debate,
would agree. But it may not be enough merely to acknowledge that
dual nature of religion—as cause as well as effect—if the duality is
thought to exist only in tension, with now one nature, now the other
"winning." Thus, it would be a mistake in our view to interpret
Niebuhr here as arguing that at any point in time religion must be
seen as *either* cause *or* effect, for certainly it is both all the time.

But if religion is always caused and causal, dependent variable and
independent variable, it is also the case that conceptualizing the
phenomenon involves more than seeing its duality in some temporal
sense. Related to Niebuhr's distinction between cause and effect are
at least three other distinctions worth bearing in mind when one is
"locating" religion. Closely akin to the temporal distinction is that of
the degree of religion's institutionalization. For some, religion is a
(certain kind of) idea with potential impact regardless of how many
persons may share that idea. For example, Alfred North Whitehead's
definition of religion as "what a man does with his own solitariness" or
Paul Tillich's concept of "ultimate concern" point to what could be a
very lonely religiousness. In contrast, others discount such possibly
idiosyncratic expressions and regard as religion only those ideas that
are shared, established, and long-lasting. It should not be surprising
that persons more often equate "causal" religion with individual,
"prophetic" religious expressions and equate "effect" religion with
institutionalized religious expressions.

Another distinction related to Niebuhr's has to do with religion as an
individual matter versus religion as a property of collectives. It is
specifically with this point that Richard H. White deals in "Toward a
Theory of Religious Influence," the second selection of this chapter.
Contending that most social theory of religion uses an individualistic
or "psychological consonance" notion, White then suggests instead an
"interaction" model—a notion wherein religion is a social or collective
phenomenon in which individuals participate in varying degrees. No
less arbitrary, of course, than the stance it would replace, White's

interaction model claims validity on the grounds that it better organizes the relevant facts. It is significant, incidentally, that most objections to this kind of position are based on the assumption that even in the abstract some ideas of religion are more real or authentic than others. That is, just as causal religion is regarded as more religious than "effect" religion, and idiosyncratic more than institutionalized, so is individual religion more real than the religion a person shares with a collectivity. White challenges such assumptions.

A third distinction related to religion as cause or effect is an age-old controversy over definitions of process versus definitions of essence, of functional versus substantive definitions. As might be anticipated, those who view religion as process are more likely to see religion as cause, whereas religion seen in terms of essence more likely accompanies "static" religion, which only reacts to the forces around it. It is in this light that Mervin F. Verbit's essay (Selection 3) should be understood. Beginning with six "components" of religion—ritual, doctrine, emotion, knowledge, ethics, and community—he then argues that each of the six can be characterized along the four dimensions of content, frequency, intensity, and centrality. Where the six components represent the essence or substance of religion, then, the four dimensions represent the functions or processes. In the same scheme, in other words, Verbit tries to "locate" religion as both dynamic and static, both cause and effect, both idiosyncratic and institutionalized, both individual and collective.

Such an endeavor is no small undertaking, of course. Measurement, a topic we address in Chapter II, is a stringent criterion by which to judge any idea or conceptualization. We would not minimize that aspect of the locational task. Yet neither Verbit's essay nor the other two should evoke a response of "That's not *my* idea of religion!" The fact is, communication about religion requires some idea of religion. It simply will not do to conceive of religion as some unknowable force and then ask that it be measured or even commonly understood. Nor will it do to pretend that studies of religion—historical or contemporary, sociological or psychological—can successfully take place without attention to the locational task. Whether it is Puritan "religion" in seventeenth century America, merging "denominations" in the twentieth century, or "religious" influence throughout American political life, all require a specification of the concept of religion. Hopefully, such ideas will be clear and appropriate, and if they are, it will be because they have contended with the kind of issue this chapter exemplifies.

Obviously, the question of locating the idea of religion is intimately related to the question of how religion should be measured. That issue—of measuring American religion—will therefore be dealt with in the next chapter.

1

H. Richard Niebuhr

Religion as Cause and Effect

Christianity in its twenty centuries and many lands is a Protean thing and nowhere does it seem to be more diverse and multifarious than in America. Here it has no central organization; it has not even such an institutional core as an established church provides, accompanied though it be by sectarian organizations. Here there is no common system of doctrine nor any distinctly American confession of faith which, like the Augsburg Confession in Germany or the Thirty-nine Articles and the Westminster Confession in Great Britain, emerged out of a great critical and formative period in the past to remain a depository of religious insights painfully won by the fathers and a program of spiritual discipline for their children. Here no national liturgy, no Book of Common Prayer, leads generation after generation to pattern its religious thought upon a classic model or to channel its pious emotions in purified forms of expression. Instead of a history of American Christianity we seem to have here only a series of histories—of Congregationalism in New England, of sectarianism in Pennsylvania, of Anglicanism in New York and Virginia, of Presbyterianism and Methodism and of the Baptist movement upon the successive frontiers, of Lutheranism among German and Scandinavian settlers, of Catholicism in Maryland and among nineteenth century emigrants, of Unitarianism and Christian Science in Boston, of Mormonism in Utah, of the Four Square Gospel in Los Angeles and the Apostolic Overcoming Holy Church of God in Alabama. If one must speak of denominations and sects, of organizations here and there, of movements now and then, how can one speak of Christianity in the

United States? Is not this religious chaos, like Bertrand Russell's world, all spots and jumps?

The impression of diversity and pluralism is increased by any inquiry into the connection of Christianity with the secular institutions and movements of the New World. The relations of church and state, of gospel and church, of Christian and civil liberty, of the faith and democracy, of Protestantism and capitalism, of Christianity and nationalism, of religion and popular education—and slavery, and reform movements, and imperialism, and internationalism, and pacifism, and socialism—these all seem to be ambiguous and confused. When has American Christianity taken a consistent and continuous attitude toward one of the institutions or movements of the secular life so that the historian or spectator was able to say, "There typical American Christianity is at work"? Has it not always been on both sides of every question? Clear-cut, unambiguous, Christian answers to the moral questions which agitated the American generations have been so rare that both the critics of the church, who declare its policy to be one of pure opportunism, and the defenders of Christianity, who reply that the churches cannot be blamed since they are only churches, seem to be right.

Under these circumstances one answer to the search after a pattern in American Christianity obtrudes itself upon us. It is the answer of many a social historian and it is offered in its extreme and most logical form by the Marxian interpreters. Christianity in America—so the theory runs in general—is, like the faith of any other culture, an epiphenomenon. Religion echoes in mystical and high-flown language the voice of political and economic interests. Faith is part of the defense mechanism of racial, sectional and, above all, economic groups. No pattern is discernible in the history of a religion until this fact is recognized; then it is seen that the underlying sociological or economic pattern has been faithfully reproduced in the dogmas and liturgies of faith, and the apparent pluralism of Christianity can be reduced to a fairly intelligible order. With the political and economic map in our hand we may trace the religious boundaries and find our way among confusing signposts. We understand that when New England divines of the first and third generations preached about grace and divine sovereignty they were but speaking in their curiously allegorical fashion about the political questions with which their audiences were preoccupied. We see that the quarrels about antinomianism and the qualifications for communion, infant baptism, free will and determinism were really exhibitions of the class conflict between an old aristocracy and a rising middle class, or between the latter and the poor, or between frontier and settled community, or between early and late immigrations. Instead, then, of looking to religious history for a pattern which will help us to make choices in the present we must look for it in the economic or the total social history. We must say: The challenge of the present is the preservation of American civilization—that is, the preservation of the customs which have been transmitted and particularly of the system of privileges which power has established in the past; or else it is the accomplishment of that economic and political revolution which has been the "American dream" from the beginning. Whether or not we will meet the challenge with symbols of the faith on our banners is a matter of slight concern, though there are social conservatives who connect their interests with the religious forms and revolutionaries who agree with them that religion is an inalienable part of the established system of habits and laws.

The sociological answer, so briefly indicated, is exceedingly attractive to the searcher after the meaning of ecclesiastical culture. It satisfies the demand for a simple hypothesis and explains many of the facts which otherwise remain obscure. When the rifts which political and economic sectionalism and racial and national division have caused in the churches are noted, when it is seen how religious thought-forms and attitudes reflect the habits of industrial or agricultural workers or of creditors and debtors, when the correspondence of the forms of ecclesiastical organization to the forms of political structure is examined, when the behavior of Christian groups in times of political or economic crisis is studied, then the evidence in favor of the sociological hypothesis begins to carry conviction. It is so clearly the true interpretation of so much that happens in religion that the student is ill at ease in seeking to exempt from its scope any part of faith. Even though the extreme form of the hypothesis, which sees only an economic pattern in human culture, be rejected as an oversimplification, more moderate theories of the social basis of religion must continue to receive serious consideration. Bergson, for instance, like Lévy-Bruhl whom he follows, demands attention when he interprets religion as in large part a defense mechanism whereby society protects itself against the dissolvent power of the intellect, against discouragement and the fear of death, and whereby it sustains its claims upon the individual.[1] Whether the society in question be a national, a sectional, a racial or an economic group its religion does appear to be largely dependent upon its secular interests and designed to protect them.

It does seem to be true that the function which the American churches have performed, by and large, differs little from that which religious institutions of any faith, at any time, have performed for the societies of which they were a part. Like primitive, Confucian, Jewish, Hindu or Mohammedan institutions they have transmitted the popular mores, identifying these more or less speciously with the good counsels of the religious founder and adding otherworldly sanctions to them.

Thus they have brought the rising and always somewhat rebellious generations into line with the habits of the past and so helped to preserve the ever precarious balance of social order. They have fortified the morale of individuals and groups by holding up before them in worship a center of reference for their lives and relating their activities to a supremely valuable reality. They have offered consolation and escape when the sacrifices common life demanded of the individual became too hard to bear. Whether in a medical or in a Marxian sense they have given opiate which enabled men to live amid conditions which remained disappointing and difficult despite all revolutions and reorganizations of society and the so-called conquest of nature.

Such faith gave to Pilgrims, Puritans and Quakers the overbelief which enabled them to endure the poverty, despair and peril of life between a savage sea and an ominously unknown continent. Faith enabled pioneers to preserve or to regain their integrity when the social pressure of law and custom was not present to maintain in tolerable unity the centrifugal tendencies in personal life. Through faith emigrants and frontiersmen transmitted to their children some part of that hard-won discipline of the mind and the passions which a raw land, that was all nature with scarcely any culture, could not impress upon the barbarian spirit of youth. Faith in a later time became the defender of the institutions which had been forged in the rude smithy of a new world.

One notes with sympathetic or cynical understanding the stubbornness with which the second generation of Massachusetts Bay Puritans defended their liberties against Andros and Randolph, fortified by the belief that they were a divinely chosen people. One hears with sympathy also the echoing and re-echoing statements that God had sifted a whole people in order that he might choose the best grain for New England and that divine providence had prepared the way for Christian Englishmen by the plague-effected slaughter of pagan Indians. For men who need to meet such ardors and endurances as did the American settlers cannot live by bread alone. When bread is not available they need to feed on faith or else retreat to the fleshpots of their Egypts. When in a later time all the variations on the theme of the chosen people and of the promised land are sounded—particularly in times of crisis—one is tempted again to say that in Christianity Americans found and formed a social faith which nerved them for the task of living, protected their hard-won social unity and justified them in the extension of their conquests. In effect it did not differ from the German belief in race and culture, or the French sense of democratic mission, or the modern Russian gospel of world saviorhood. These all appear to be defenses against the criticisms of the self, against intellectual doubt, against the disillusionments of practiced as well as of suffered cruelty and of victory and defeat, and against the darkness of the surrounding night which envelops all human efforts in futility. What is true of the nation as a whole with its recurrent faith in national destiny, more or less religiously conceived, is then true also of the separate parts, of sections and groups who find and form a faith which enables them to preserve their solidarity and to defend their peculiar institutions.

The kingdom of God in America, so regarded, is the American kingdom of God; it is not the individualization of a universal idea, but the universalization of the particular. It represents not so much the impact of the gospel upon the New World as the use and adaptation of the gospel by the new society for its own purposes.

The obvious pertinence of such a description of the pattern of religious life in the United States makes it very attractive; yet doubt as to its adequacy cannot be quelled. So Bergson finds it impossible to fit the whole of religious development into the pattern of social conservation and defense; for what, on this basis, is to be done with mysticism and all creative, aggressive, dynamic faith? It is difficult if not impossible to fit Amos, Isaiah, Jeremiah, Jesus, Paul, Francis of Assisi, Martin Luther and many another prophet into a system of faith determined by social factors. There is in religion, or in Christianity at least, a revolutionary and creative strain which does not allow itself to be reduced to this pattern. To be sure, one cannot deny the presence of so-called secular interests even in the revolutionary leaders and movements; yet faith does seem to take the initiative in these cases. The poverty of the various attempts which have been made to interpret the prophets and Jesus in sociological and socialistic terms is an indication that something very important is lacking in them. They abstract from life to such an extent that the portraits which they paint are unrecognizable. When we turn to the history of American Christianity in particular we are scarcely convinced by the arguments of social historians that a John Cotton, a Roger Williams, a Jonathan Edwards, a Channing and all the other reputed initiators of new movements were primarily representatives of social loyalties.[2] For the kingdom of God to which these men and the movements they initiated were loyal was not simply American culture or political and economic interest exalted and idealized; it was rather a kingdom which was prior to America and to which this nation, in its politics and economics, was required to conform. We may call the strain which they represented the prophetic one, for one distinction between the Hebrew prophets and their opponents, the false prophets, was that the former began with God and his kingdom, requiring the adjustment of Israel to these while the latter began with Israel and its institutions, which they exalted into a divine kingdom. The prophetic or revolutionary strain demands rebirth rather than conservation; it announces divine judgment rather than divine protection; and it looks forward to God's salvation rather than to human victory. It has been present in American history to an uncommon degree and any interpretation which minimizes it or seeks to explain it in terms foreign to itself is inadequate. It may be conceded that the prophets were closer to nomadic civilization than were their urban opponents, that Paul as a Hellenistic Jew had a smaller stake in the conservation of Jewish culture than had the Judaizers he fought, that the middle class Puritans were in economic revolt against the feudal aristocracy, that there was an alliance between dynamic faith and frontier mentality in the United States; but if we do not presume to reinterpret everything these men and movements have said about themselves or to pretend to a profounder knowledge of their aims and motives than they possessed, we shall find it extremely difficult to squeeze these phenomena into the forms of a purely sociological interpretation.

There is a vast difference, as Bergson has pointed out, between a religious institution or static religion and a religious movement or dynamic faith. The one is conservative, the other progressive; the one is more or less passive, yielding to the influence of dynamic elements in other areas of life, the other is aggressive, influencing rather than being influenced; the one looks to the past, the other to the future. The analysis of religious life which makes only the institution its object and leaves the movement out of account remains very partial and, moreover, cannot do full justice to the institution since this developed out of the movement. Because the sociological interpretation deals with static or passive rather than with dynamic Christianity in America it is unsatisfactory as a complete explanation.

We are put on our guard against this interpretation, furthermore, by the reflection that the instrumental value of faith for society is dependent upon faith's conviction that it has more than instrumental value. Faith could not defend men if it believed that defense was its meaning. The godliness which is profitable to all things becomes unprofitable when profit rather than God comes to be its interest. This ancient dilemma is not solved by any doctrine of necessary fictions but only by the recognition that objectivism rather than pragmatism is the first law of knowledge. Hence if we are to understand American Christianity we need to take our stand within the movement so that its objects may come into view. If we adopt a point of view outside it we shall never see what it has seen but only the incidental results of its vision, which we shall then seek to explain as due to some strange transmutation of political and economic interest.

Every movement, like every person, needs to be understood before it can be criticized. And no movement can be understood until its presuppositions, the fundamental faith upon which it rests, have been at least provisionally adopted. The presuppositions may not be our own; we may find good reason for rejecting them in favor of others;

but we cannot understand without occupying a standpoint, and there is no greater barrier to understanding than the assumption that the standpoint which we happen to occupy is a universal one, while that of the object of our criticism is relative. The political and economic interpreters assume that because political and economic interests are primary for them and in the modern world, they were always primary, that because economic value or political power are their supreme values therefore they were always supreme. They can say with Parrington that "the historian need not wander far in search of the origin of the theocratic principle; it is to be found in the self-interest of the lay and clerical leaders"; [3] but thereby they illuminate their own presuppositions rather than those of the men about whom they are writing.

Such an assumption of the relative standpoint or dogma of our own time or society as an absolute starting place is a begging of the question. We make an arbitrary choice when we substitute the dogma of economic determinism or of human self-determinism for the dogma of divine determinism. Moreover it is a choice which bars us from understanding the thought of the divine determinists and which denies from the beginning the validity of their interpretation of themselves and their world. This-worldliness may seem more objective than other-worldliness to those who have never faced their own presuppositions. When they do face them they become aware that their ultimate dogma is at least as much a matter of faith as is the dogma of the otherworldly man. There is, to say the least, no less of pure assumption in the conviction that human freedom or social condition is the determining force in life than in the dogma that the creative source of existence is the ruler of destiny. There is at least as much of the temporal and passing experience of the nineteenth century in the belief that economic classes are the fundamental social groups as there is of the transient experience of the sixteenth in the thought that religious creeds mark the essential boundaries between societies.

Such considerations urge upon us the desirability of seeking to understand the relation of American Christianity to American culture by making the former rather than the latter our starting point. After we have done this we may compare the results with those yielded by the opposite approach and try to understand the relation between religion and culture more adequately than we can by viewing the scene from a single point of view. But first of all we need to interpret our Christianity out of itself; we need to seek the pattern within it, not to superimpose some other pattern upon it. The ideal needs to be looked for in the real, not imported from without. Is there in this multifarious appearance, we ask, a principle of unity? Is there a law of development in this movement? Is there a guiding idea which unfolds itself and which, without Hegelian presuppositions as to its nature and its law, we can understand vaguely at least and in outline? Of course, every effort to answer these questions is relative to our own situation in this historical process of American faith and can claim for itself no more finality than can belong to that which is itself a part of the moving and shifting scene. Yet the sailor who seeks to find his bearings by consulting the charts his fathers used when they set out on the voyage he is continuing, by noting all the corrections they have made upon them and by looking for the stars which gave them orientation may claim at least that he is trying to be true to the meaning of the voyage.

NOTES ————————————————————————————

1. Henri Bergson, *The Two Sources of Morality and Religion* (New York, 1935), chap. 2. Cf. Émile Durkheim, *The Elementary Forms of Religious Life* (London, 1915), pp. 419 f.; Lucien Lévy-Bruhl, *The "Soul" of the Primitive* (London, 1928).

2. Vernon Louis Parrington, *Main Currents in American Thought* (New York, Harcourt, Brace, 1927–30). Parrington believes we can clear the "fog of biblical disputations" and the "crabbed theology" of Puritans only if "we will resolutely translate the old phrases into modern equivalents, if we will put aside the theology and fasten attention on the politics and the economics of the struggle" (I, 6). The significance of Calvinism becomes clear to anyone "who will take the trouble to translate dogma into political terms" (*ibid.*, p. 13). Roger Williams was "primarily a political philosopher rather than a theologian; religious toleration was only a necessary deduction from the major principles of his political theory" (*ibid.*, p. 66). Jonathan Edwards, interpreted by reference to the social tendencies, was a great anachronism who "followed a path that led back to the absolutist past, rather than forward to a more liberal future" (*ibid.*, pp. 148 f., 156). To social interpreters like Parrington political and economic interests are alone real and the language of politics and economics is the only universal tongue.

3. *Op. cit.*, I, 19.

2

Richard H. White

Toward a Theory of Religious Influence

The authors of a recent article published in the *American Sociological Review* argued that "the relationship of religion to economic and occupational success is the most viable topic of debate in the sociology of religion in the United States."[1] Thus began another contribution to the often confusing and somewhat overflowing file of sociological studies in the "Weberian tradition." It is apparent that much of our theory guiding empirical research in the sociology of religion in the United States has been drawn from Weber's thesis concerning ascetic Protestantism and capitalism. But the results of this research have been confusing.

In an early study of the relationship between religion and economic position, Cantril found that there was a higher ratio of Protestants in higher educational and economic status groups than was the case in the lower educational and economic groups.[2] In another survey reported five years later, Liston Pope found essentially the same relationship.[3] However, in a very recent analysis of survey data, Glenn and Hyland report that "by the mid-1960's Catholics ranked *above* Protestants in most aspects of status."[4]

And there is more confusion. Mayer and Sharp, while they did qualify their interpretation to some extent, found in their metropolitan Detroit sample that there was at least some support for a modern day Weber thesis.[5] On the other hand, Mack, Yellin, and Murphy reported that there is apparently no relationship between being Catholic or Protestant and being upwardly or downwardly mobile.[6] To go yet

Richard H. White, "Toward a Theory of Religious Influence," *Pacific Sociological Review* 11 (Spring, 1968), 23–28. © 1968 by The Pacific Sociological Association. Permission to republish granted by the publisher. Richard H. White was, at the time of his accidental death, a graduate student in the Department of Sociology, University of Oregon.

another step, the data and analysis of Veroff, Gurin, and Feld indicate that Catholics actually score *higher* than Protestants on tests of achievement motivation.[7] Finally, the study of Andrew Greeley[8] and that of Bressler and Westoff[9] report no significant differences between Catholics and Protestants along the lines that Weber suggested many years ago.

Certainly with this accumulation of confusing, if not conflicting, findings, there is some justification for suggesting that we in the sociology of religion are at a theoretical impasse in our analysis of the Weber thesis in particular and our understanding of religious influence in general. In fact, some have even suggested that religion has no real differentiating impact at all in the contemporary United States—that there is no religious factor operating today.[10]

But surely this diagnosis is too sweeping. We do, in fact, have some fairly well established correlations between religion and secular behavior—particulary political behavior. The fact that Jews and Catholics generally vote Democrat while Protestants are typically more oriented to the Republican Party seems pretty well established.[11] However, even these findings, clear and repeatable though they may be, do not seem to be predictable from any kind of theory of religious influence. So then, as in some of the studies of religion and economic success, we are hard-put to interpret the differences which we do find.

The Poverty of Current Theory

We think that this interpretational impasse reflects the poverty of the theoretical model most sociologists use when they study religion—a model which is typically implicit rather than explicit. This model—which, for lack of a better term, we shall call a "psychological consonance" model—is peculiarly individualistic and makes some questionable assumptions concerning the *process* of religious influence. These assumptions are: (1) that theology is the primary source of religious behavior, and (2) that individuals who "believe" seek a consonance between these theological tenets and their attitudes and behavior in other spheres of life. Let us examine these two assumptions more critically.

With respect to theology being the source of religious differences, it is apparent that the Weber thesis is bound up entirely with the idea that the practical rationality of ascetic Protestant theology was the primary force in creating, or at least legitimating, a "spirit of capitalism." However, it is difficult to make the same kind of derivations from Jewish theology. Nevertheless, most studies show that Jews "out-Protestant" the Protestants in manifesting both the spirit and the success of capitalism.[12]

In addition to this problem in the Weber thesis, one is hard-put to determine any connection between the Negro Protestant Democratic vote and any particular theological tenets of Negro religion. Along the same lines, Greeley has noted in commenting on a study of the educational and occupational aspirations of college seniors that *none* of the traits he found to be significantly associated with Protestant, Catholic, or Jewish affiliation are clearly derivable from official religious teachings.[13]

So then, the assertion that theological differences are the only, or even the primary, sources of religious differences in other aspects of the religious person's life is highly suspect.

The second assumption of the theoretical model implicit in most of the research we have reviewed is also suspect. This assumption is that the motive force in religious influence is a "within-the-individual" drive for consonance between religious beliefs and behavior in other areas of life. Although few sociologists would care to admit it, this is the only interpretation possible when an individual identification with a broad theological orientation is all that is reported. That is, when we ask for a self-reported religious preference of the Protestant, Catholic, Jewish, or "Other" variety, we are, in effect, trying to ascertain the theological doctrine of the individual. With no other data present, the only interpretation we can make is that theological conviction directs secular behavior.

Following the same argument, when various indices of theological commitment are introduced as control variables, we are led to believe that theology is the primary source of religious influence *and* that the strength of commitment to that theology leads the individual to discover its implications for other areas of life and to act accordingly. Such an assumption would seem to underlie those indices of religious involvement which measure theological belief or knowledge.

Now, perhaps our implicit acceptance of this kind of "within-the-person" theory stems from the fact that we wish to think of religious influence as something quite different from the other kinds of social influences with which sociologists are concerned. However, our acceptance of this unique kind of influence has led us as sociologists to accept implicitly these two assumptions of religious motivation that we do not generally make in studying other groups.

That the religious factor does not have to be, indeed may not be, a force of psychological consonance stemming directly from theology has been well-demonstrated in the work of Gerhard Lenski.[14] Lenski, much to his credit, set out to measure the religious variable much more closely than any of the other researchers to whom we have referred. Although he still retained the use of the gross theological categories of Protestant, Catholic, and Jewish, his indices of religious involvement reflect not one but at least two different theoretical models of religious influence. Religion may be seen as a set of theological beliefs in his index of doctrinal orthodoxy. It may also be seen as an object of devotion in his index of devotionalism. Unfortunately, neither of these indices predicted terribly successfully, with the doctrinal orthodoxy index being the least efficient. It is significant, moreover, that both of these indices are based on, or at least reflect, the aforementioned theoretical model of "within-the-person" psychological consistency.

However, Lenski's other two indices of religious involvement—communalism and associationalism—proved to be very efficient predictors. In these, religion is seen as a subcultural or group phenomenon. And religion so conceived was found to be at least as efficient a predictor as social class.[15] Now the interesting point here is that these two indices rest on a relatively unknown, or at least unused, theoretical model of the religious factor. This model may be termed an interaction model of religious influence.

An Interaction Model of Religious Influence

The basic principles of such a model are rather well-accepted and time-honored concepts in sociology in general. The first of these principles is that religion is first and foremost a group phenomenon. That is, the religious group, regardless of its specific identifying characteristics is, in the last analysis, a group. That is, it is composed of people in interaction with one another.

The second basic principle in the interaction theory is that the religious group, like any other group, has a particular *normative* structure. That is, the expectations for behavior of any individual member of the group are normative expectations. Granted, these expectations may have the additional force of divine authority; nonetheless, the religious group is characterized by normative expectations, as is any other group. Now, rather than getting bogged down in the issue of just what constitutes a specifically *religious* norm, at this point it would be just as well to study any norm of the religious group —regardless of whether or not it is logically connected to any body of theological beliefs.

The third basic principle of the interaction theory is that these norms are *enforced* by sanctions, ranging all the way from resounding approval to rejection from the group in disgrace. These sanctions may be mild or severe, obvious or not quite so obvious. They are the kind of sanctions associated with group norms no matter what the group.

Finally, and it is in this area that most studies of the religious factor leave much to be desired, the norms of the religious group are enforced by its members, *in interaction with one another*. That is, the normative expectations of religious group living are both socialized into the children (or the adult converts) *and* continually reinforced by the members of the group in interaction with one another.

For all of these reasons, those researchers who attempt to describe a proposed religious influence by categories of theology rather than by groups of people are seeing only a part, and perhaps the most insignificant part, of religion. Although some might argue that all Catholic groups are essentially the same, we have good evidence that they are not.[16] Likewise, there appears to be a greater diversity in the Jewish faith than some researchers would seem to assume. Finally, it is overwhelmingly apparent that about the only thing that most Protestant groups have in common is the name.[17] Now, many sociologists have argued that we should make finer distinctions in religious orientation than we usually do. However, when religious influence is viewed as normative influence, these group-specific distinctions become more than just evidence of scientific precision—they become theoretically necessary.

Bearing in mind that it is the group norm affecting the participating member's attitudes and behavior, not just the contents of theological doctrine, there remains the intriguing question of just where these group-specific norms come from.

It is clear that Weber has argued altogether too convincingly for the sociologist to immediately eliminate the possibility that some norms are, in fact, derivations from, if not theological precepts, then at least theological styles. In this we are referring to the "practical rationality" of capitalism that was shaped, at least in part, by the practical rationality of ascetic Protestantism.

But, how did the detached ethical maxims of ascetic Protestantism become transformed into group-specific norms carrying rather severe interpersonal sanctions? We believe that Weber himself gave us at least part of the answer in his analysis of the types of prophecy. The prophet, whether emissary or exemplary, is more than likely a charismatic leader whose ethical maxims do in fact, through his authority, become group norms. In fact, the authority of any kind of leadership may be enough to make the difference between an ethical maxim and a sanction-carrying norm.

However, a little reflection will indicate that the prophet or leader making his derivations from theology is not the only—and perhaps not even the most important—source of the norms of the religious group. We have already noted that Greeley found that none of the traits significantly associated with religious preference in college seniors were clearly derivable from theological precepts. Greeley has also argued that many of the "effects" of religion reported in Lenski's work are in fact due to ethnic rather than religious differences.[18]

That is a very interesting point. However, when religion is thought of as a "group" phenomenon, the distinction between ethnicity and religion becomes more apparent than real. That is, any given religious group has a history of its own—a history that is affected by the cultural location of its members, by their relative economic positions, and a host of other "so-called" ethnic factors. The point to be made is that insofar as religious groups are characterized by group-specific norms, these norms constitute the "religious factor" regardless of whether they have been logically derived from theology or picked up somewhere on the Italian countryside.

In a similar fashion, we can (perhaps for the first time) put Marx and Weber into the same theoretical model. There can be little doubt that the economic position of the members of any given religious group does have an effect on the norms of that group. Such economic concerns as the dependence of the Southern United States on the tobacco industry have doubtless had their effect in the indifference with which Southern Baptists view smoking—an indifference which their fundamentalist Northern counterparts do not show. In much the same way, the famous Niebuhr hypothesis of the *Social Sources of Denominationalism* can be seen as the effect of economic position on religious group norms.[19]

In fact, we could go on and on for the remainder of this paper and never exhaust the possible influences on religious group norms. But let us not again forget that when we are speaking of the religious factor, we are actually dealing with the normative effects of religious group membership.

The Utility of the Model

Now then, what can we say of the utility of the interaction model of religious influence? It certainly cannot explain less than the confusing psychological consonance model of most contemporary research. However, since the *initial* utility of any given theory in sociology must be evaluated in terms of its fruitfulness in generating testable hypotheses, we would like to suggest four aspects of religion, including the study of religious influence, which could be profitably studied using the interaction model. At the same time, some previous hypotheses and findings will be incorporated into these aspects as they relate to interaction theory.

The first aspect of religion that can be handled in this perspective is the general research question: How is faith acquired? *Doomsday Cult*, a recent book by John Lofland, fits into the interactionist solution to this particular research problem quite well.[20] Although he described other conditions which must be present for the potential convert, he found that the principal influence at work in bringing in converts to this new and rather bizarre cult was precisely the interpersonal influence of cult members on non-members. In fact, a reasonable hypothesis with respect to the recruiting of new members in any religious group, unless of course the members are born into it, would be that the major or deciding factor in religious conversion is interpersonal influence.

A second aspect of religion that "fits" the interactionist perspective quite well is the general research problem: How is the faith maintained? Now although Lofland also notes that interpersonal influence —sanctioning and rewarding—are the key elements in this aspect, the main theoretical breakthrough in this respect came with Bryan Wilson's insightful article on sect development.[21] Sects, which in our terms may be thought of as deviant subcultures of the larger society,[22] can maintain their own distinctive norms and retain their members to the extent that they are able to isolate or insulate their members from the normative expectations of the larger society. Thus, we have the case where a sect can retain its deviant identity by either curtailing interpersonal interaction outside the group or by making such interaction relatively ineffective.

A third area where fruitful hypotheses may be generated from the interaction model is in the area of losing the faith. In actuality, this is the other side of the problem of maintaining the faith. We might, for example, hypothesize that to the extent that an individual receives normative pressures in his interactions with other people to withdraw from the religious group, he will be inclined to do so. Probably the most likely casualty in this respect is the person with strong interactive ties outside the religious group and weak interactive ties within it.

Finally, and more in keeping with the main concern of this paper, the interaction approach is particularly suited to studying the concomitants of faith; in short, the religious factor. Now, regardless of which particular group norm we wish to investigate, it is the main assumption of the interaction theory that any individual will adhere to that norm to the extent that he is in a position to receive sanctions from other members of the religious group. That is, the fact that an individual believes strongly, or even prays, often is not as effective in directing his behavior as are the sanctions he receives from other people.

So then, a modified Weber hypothesis would be: To the extent that an individual ascetic Protestant interacts mainly with other ascetic Protestants, either through formal participation in group meetings or in informal primary groups (thus being in a position to receive sanctions from other people), he will manifest more of "the spirit of capitalism" than will his Catholic counterpart. In addition, the ascetic Protestant whose interpersonal relationships are predominantly with non-ascetic Protestants will be less "capitalistic" than the one with monolithic and supportive relationships.[23] Of course, we could only test such hypotheses as these if we were willing to assume that each ascetic Protestant religious group is characterized by the norms of the "spirit of capitalism" and that each non-ascetic Protestant group is not. It would be better if we could get a norm profile of the specific religious groups in question before we test the effects of these norms on the lives of individuals.

Dealing only with those relatively few norms that are known to be specific to certain broad categories of religious groups, we could suggest that if a devout Catholic interacts primarily with Protestant fundamentalists at work or even within his own family, he might take a dimmer view of drinking and gambling than he would if his interaction were confined to other Catholics. What is more, there might be some tendency for him to vote Republican even though his co-religionists are predominantly Democrats. The hypotheses derivable from the interaction theory can be multiplied almost indefinitely. Of course, once we get beyond the norms that characterize *all* religious groups of a certain type, our hypotheses will necessarily become more restricted in scope. In fact, they might in the final analysis become hypotheses about specific congregations.

Conclusion

In conclusion then, it can be seen that those studies of the religious factor which include only personal adherence to a broad category of theological precepts as their independent variable have no room for what the religious factor may in fact be; namely, the normative pressure of interpersonal expectations. To the extent that religion is any kind of an influencing factor at all on the individual behavior in these studies, it can only be in an individualistic or psychologistic fashion wherein the assumption is that the individual generalizes the specifics of theological belief to other areas of his life. Research that has been generated from this model has proven either contradictory or inefficient at best. An alternative to this conceptualization of religious influence is the interactionist perspective wherein religious influence becomes a category of social influence in general. While many of the details of this particular theory remain to be worked out, we have outlined the basic elements of the theory drawing on rather well-accepted principles of social theory in general and have indicated its relevance to previously isolated and unrelated findings and hypotheses in the sociology of religion. Although many additional hypotheses can be derived from the interaction theory, few have as yet been tested, indicating that the possibilities for future research are relatively unlimited. Finally, and most importantly, when the findings of this kind of research are reported, we will, perhaps for the first time in the sociology of religion, know more precisely what it is that we are calling the religious factor.

NOTES

1. Norval D. Glenn and Ruth Hyland, "Religious Preference and Worldly Success: Some Evidence from National Surveys," *American Sociological Review*, 32 (February, 1967), p. 73.

2. Hadley Cantril, "Educational and Economic Composition of Religious Groups: An Analysis of Poll Data," *American Journal of Sociology*, 48 (March, 1943), pp. 574–579.

3. Liston Pope, "Religion and the Class Structure," *Annals of the American Academy of Political and Social Science*, 256 (March, 1948), pp. 84–91.

4. Glenn and Hyland, *op. cit.*

5. Albert J. Mayer and Harry Sharp, "Religious Preference and Worldly Success," *American Sociological Review*, 27 (April, 1962), pp. 218–227.

6. Raymond W. Mack, Raymond J. Murphy, and Seymour Yellin, "The Protestant Ethic, Level of Aspiration, and Social Mobility: An Empirical Test," *American Sociological Review*, 21 (June, 1956), pp. 295–300.

7. Joseph Veroff, Sheila Feld, and Gerald Gurin, "Achievement Motivation and Religious Background," *American Sociological Review*, 27 (April, 1962), pp. 205–217.

8. Andrew M. Greeley, "A Note on the Origins of Religious Differences," *Journal for the Scientific Study of Religion*, 3 (Fall, 1963), pp. 21–31.

9. Marvin Bressler and Charles Westoff, "Catholic Education, Economic Values and Achievement," *American Journal of Sociology*, 69 (November, 1963), pp. 225–233.

10. For example, Peter L. Berger, *The Noise of Solemn Assemblies*, Garden City, New York: Doubleday and Co., Inc., 1961.

11. Luke Ebersole, "Religion and Politics," *The Annals of the American Academy of Political and Social Science*, 332 (November, 1960), pp. 101–111.

12. Mayer and Sharp, *op. cit.*

13. Greeley, *op. cit.*

14. Gerhard Lenski, *The Religious Factor*, Garden City, New York: Doubleday and Co., Inc., 1961.

15. *Ibid.,* p. 326.

16. John Kosa and Leo D. Rachiele, "The Spirit of Capitalism, Traditionalism and Religiousness: A Re-examination of Weber's Concepts," *Sociological Quarterly,* 4 (Summer, 1963), pp. 243–260.

17. Charles Y. Glock and Rodney Stark, *Religion and Society in Tension.* Chicago, Ill.: Rand McNally and Co., 1965, Chapter 5.

18. Greeley, *op. cit.*

19. H. Richard Niebuhr, *The Social Sources of Denominationalism,* Cleveland and New York: The World Publishing Co., Meridian Books, 1957.

20. John Lofland, *Doomsday Cult,* Englewood Cliffs, N.J.: Prentice-Hall, Inc., 1966.

21. Bryan R. Wilson, "An Analysis of Sect Development," *American Sociological Review,* 24 (February, 1959), pp. 3–15.

22. Benton Johnson, "On Church and Sect," *American Sociological Review,* 28 (August, 1963), pp. 539–549.

23. Athough Lenski tested some similar hypotheses in his Detroit study, it should be pointed out that he did not distinguish ascetic Protestants from other Protestants. In view of this, it is somewhat surprising that he found as much correlation between religion and economic orientation as he did.

3

Mervin F. Verbit[*]

The Components and Dimensions of Religious Behavior: Toward a Reconceptualization of Religiosity

Reifications, like other creatures, beget their own kind. "Religion" is a reification, and what it begat is the concept "religiosity." Fortunately, lineage counts for little in science, so a concept can rise above questionable origins to become a highly useful and valid part of the analytic apparatus of a discipline. This paper will attempt, first, to show briefly how the parent concept has been spoiling its offspring and, second, to nudge the youngster a step closer to a complex maturity in which it can carry a heavier load in the scientific study of religion.

Secular and Religious Meanings of "Religiosity"

Religion is best defined as man's relationship to whatever he conceives as meaningful ultimacy. This definition is inductively sound because the sets of behaviors that we commonly call religions do in fact claim to be elaborations of man's relationship to what is ultimate and further assert that the Ultimate is meaningful.[1]

This is an original essay prepared especially for the present volume. Reprinted by permission of the author, Mervin F. Verbit, a sociologist at Brooklyn College.

* I want to thank Professors Robert K. Merton and Phillip E. Hammond for reading early drafts of the paper and making valuable comments.

God, Brahman-Atman, and the Tao, for example, are all poetic names for Ultimacy with meaning, though the specific delineations of that meaning, of course, vary. As a logical consequence of this definition, atheism is the denial that ultimacy has meaning, and that denial is indeed the essence of mature, sophisticated atheism.

Since the ultimate and the proximate are related, integral religion subsumes *all* of life. Its meanings define life, its rituals sacralize life, its values direct life. Man's relationships to ultimacy involve many kinds of behavior. Man seeks to define its nature, believing certain things about it and questioning others. He attempts to achieve immediacy and response in his contact with it. He expresses symbolically his sentiments regarding it and celebrates the occasions on which it seemed more immanent and salient. He establishes organizations to perpetuate and facilitate implementation of what he believes its implications to be. In simpler terms, he develops theology, rituals, moral values, "churches," and the other component parts of religion.

However, when ultimate meanings become less salient or when the scope of religious influence is narrowed in order to accommodate people of diverse religions within a single political entity, then religion comes to be seen as a separate institutional sphere, that is, as a circumscribed *part* of life. Thus, it is a secularism that reifies religion as a social institution and calls the man who is much involved in that institution "religious." Religious systems themselves call for commitment "with all your heart, with all your soul, and with all your might." Their claims are comprehensive, as logically they must be. They honor the man who conforms to their norms with adjectives like "righteous," "pious," "devout," or—simply yet tellingly—"good."

"Religious" and its nounal sibling "religiosity" are thus seen to be ambiguous. As normally used from a secular perspective, they denote acceptance of a specific array of beliefs, feelings, and ritual practices that constitute "religion" in its narrow sense. If used by religions themselves, these words would imply conformity to *all* the norms of living set forth in a specific religious tradition, and are consequently far more encompassing. The former usage is, religiously speaking, sinful in that it includes only part of life. What is not so readily recognized is that it is also scientifically sinful. Both usages—the religious and the secular—imply a metaphysical conclusion. (Durkheim's classic division into sacred and profane,[2] for example, is a consequence of a particular religious position. A more positive religious stance than Durkheim's would generate dichotomies like actual versus potential sanctity or turning toward versus turning away from awareness of the Ultimate.) Caught, at least for the present, between the Scylla and Charybdis of two kinds of definitions, both of which are value-laden, it seems better on the face of it to work with the one that is phenomenologically true to the substantive matter at hand.

Components and Dimensions
of Religiosity

Most early indices of religiosity in the behavioral sciences were rather simple. Agreement with a few doctrinal assertions, frequency of church attendance, or the feeling of "religious sentiments" were the usual bases on which people were placed along a continuum from non-religious to very religious. A study of how, in light of religion's complexity, such indicators came to be popular in surveys would probably reveal more about the surveyers than they revealed about the surveyed. Happily, such measures are now in disrepute, and social scientists, recognizing the multifaceted character of religious behavior, are engaged in an effort to determine how best to isolate and identify the various aspects of religiosity.[3] What normally happens is that an array of religious expressions (in the narrow sense) gets sorted into several sets, occasionally as a result of a factor analysis, occasionally on the basis of some *a priori* characteristic common to the items in each set, and these sets are referred to as the "dimensions" of religiosity.

These so-called "dimensions," however, lack the primary characteristic of dimensionality in that they are not amenable to a single measurement, and a new terminology is therefore in order. Religion has several *components*, and an individual's behavior vis-à-vis each one of these components has a number of *dimensions*. (A rough analogy can be drawn from the "elements" and "properties" in physical science. Hydrogen, sodium, and mercury are "elements"; their "properties" include nuclear mass, specific gravity, and viscosity.) The use of the word "dimensions" to refer to the classes of religious behaviors rather than to the different ways of measuring an individual's behavior within each class creates verbal blinders that usually keep us from studying —sometimes even perceiving—the rich variety of religious life that exists in complex society. The categories that we impose on our data are thus prematurely limited, and potentially important variables slip through our fingers.

Six *components* of religion can be identified as: (1) ritual, (2) doctrine, (3) emotion, (4) knowledge, (5) ethics, and (6) community. Some religious acts fall wholly within one of these classes; others are characterized by several, perhaps all six, of them. Consider prayer as a case of religious behavior. A praying man, most obviously,

1. recites a prayer; but he also
2. asserts something about the relationship of Ultimacy to the individual (i.e., God to man),
3. feels some level of emotion,

4. demonstrates some ability to read or remember a text or at least an idiom,
5. implies something (perhaps indirectly) about how a man should affect the lives of his fellows, and
6. participates in a community, historically if not in the flesh.

He may not be aware of all that accompanies his act and may even feel differently from those who arranged his liturgy concerning its interpretation and implications, but these aspects of prayer are nevertheless there to be studied.

An individual's behavior with respect to each of the six components of religion can be measured along four *dimensions*, namely, "content," "frequency," "intensity," and "centrality." "Content" refers to the specific elements of a person's religious repertoire: it betokens what he believes, feels, does, knows, and joins. It denotes the *direction* of his religious behavior, indicating participation or non-participation in any item of religion. "Frequency" refers to the *amounts* of various religious behaviors that an individual incorporates into his normal routines. Given any behavior, some people do it more often; others, less often. "Intensity" measures the degree of *determination* or consistency with which a man sticks to his position. Some people never make exceptions; their pattern—whatever its form or rhythm—is unvarying. Others occasionally cut a corner or add a flourish. (Interestingly, colloquial usage recognizes this dimension: "He may not go to church every week, but he goes 'religiously' on every feast day.") The final dimension, "centrality," has to do with the *importance* that a person attributes to a given act or tenet or feeling within the total religious system. The assumption that a man's religious behaviors are an indicator of his evaluations of those behaviors is too facile. Behavior is the consequence of many factors, some of which inhibit performance of an act believed to be important, others of which lead men to perform acts seen as secondary at best. "What I would do, that do I not." In sum, the four dimensions of religiosity measure what a person does (believes, feels, etc.), how often, with what determination, and how important it is to him.

There is one sense in which "centrality" and "content" might at first seem to overlap. Stark and Glock, for example, asked their survey respondents whether they believed that each one of an array of beliefs, ritual acts, and "works" was necessary in order to achieve salvation.[4] In terms of the four dimensions defined here, one might believe that there were two ways to interpret the responses: (1) as indicating the "centrality" of each item in the array for each respondent, or (2) as indicating the "content" of each respondent's beliefs concerning the prerequisites for salvation. The first option, however, makes an assumption which, unless independently confirmed, is unwarranted. It takes for granted that salvation is the central religious goal of the

respondent. Even though salvation *is* the central goal of classical
Christianity, we can no more assume that it is the basic aspiration of
individual Christians than we can assume their acceptance of other
elements of Christian thought and practice. (Needless to say, this
principle applies to all religions, however they define their central
goals and the means of achieving them.) Since one purpose of measures of religiosity is to determine how individuals relate to religious
systems, the measures must not assume conformity at the outset. The
questions in the Stark and Glock study are, therefore, better seen as
indicators of beliefs about salvation, that is, as measures of "content."
"Centrality" in this context could be tapped by a question in the form:
"How important do you believe each of the following to be in what you
consider a good Christian life?"

We turn now to a discussion of how the four dimensions characterize behavior in all six components of religion.

Dimensions of Ritual Practice

The "content" dimension indicates which ritual
acts a person performs. Does he say grace at meals? Does he attend
worship services? Does he take communion? Does he refrain from
eating non-kosher meat?

The "frequency" dimension indicates how often, or with what cus-
tomary regularity, a person does the acts that are part of his ritual
repertoire. The most obvious use of this dimension in past research
has been inclusion of questions about frequency of church attendance,
but other rituals can also be dimensionalized in terms of frequency.
Bigman found in his study of the Jewish community in Washington,
D.C., for example, that 29% of the respondents light Sabbath candles
"always," while 19% light Sabbath candles "sometimes." [5] One might
similarly determine whether a respondent says grace at all meals, at
the big meal of the day, or on special occasions only, and whether he
refrains from non-kosher meat everywhere, only at home, only with his
family, or in some other definable circumstances.

It might be claimed that "content" and "frequency" are really the
same, a negative value on the "content" dimension being merely the
zero point or "never" category on the "frequency" dimension.
However, the gap between inclusion and exclusion is vastly different
from the gap between varying degrees of inclusion. A negative value
on "content" indicates either lack of awareness or purposeful rejection, both of which are different in kind from acceptance, even if
acceptance is minimal.

The "intensity" dimension measures the strictness of a person's
adherence to his normal pattern of observance. One man may pray

daily, but occasionally abridge his prayers or omit them altogether. Another man may pray once a month, but never miss his monthly service, no matter what other pressures or attractions present themselves. The first has higher "frequency," but lower "intensity," of that ritual act than the second. It should be noted that "intensity" as used here is not a description of the feelings that accompany prayer. Those feelings are part of the *emotional* component of religiosity and are subject to measurements independent of the performance of the ritual acts that may induce them. Intensity of action alone is referred to in the present context.

The fourth dimension, "centrality," indicates the importance that a person attributes to a ritual. It might be expected that the "centrality" of an act would be positively correlated with its "frequency" and "intensity," but such is not necessarily the case. A person may believe that an act is important, but be casual about its observance, and yet persist in "religiously" observing another act which he enjoys and wants to preserve for aesthetic, interpersonal, or other reasons. There is no necessary inconsistency in such a position. A person may believe an act to be important, yet not believe that its observance need be as frequent as some formal code prescribes. In any case, since people do not always behave logically, we should not construct our concepts and indicators in a way that necessarily implies logical behavior and thus precludes our tapping the full range of diversity in religious observance.

Dimensions of Doctrinal Adherence

Application of the four dimensions to doctrine makes faith look more dynamic, and consequently more realistic, than do most current indices. "Content" indicates what a person believes about God, man, revelation, the afterlife, and so on. But such doctrinal statements alone are an insufficient measure of belief. Religious literature records not only belief, but also doubt. Indeed, it has often been those who believe most deeply who have had the most vexing doubts. The "frequency" dimension measures the degree of doubt that accompanies any item in a person's belief system. It answers the question, "How certain is he?" Some social scientists, of course, have realized that religious belief is never a matter of simply accepting or rejecting a given assertion, and in empirical studies, Likert-type options from "strongly agree" through "strongly disagree" are sometimes provided for respondents to indicate their positions on an array of doctrinal assertions, a procedure which generates data on both the "content" and the "frequency" of belief.

Faith has two meanings: faith "that" and faith "in." The former denotes acceptance of an assertion; the latter, commitment to it, often in the face of doubt.[6] "Intensity," when applied to doctrine, measures the strength of a person's commitment to an idea or to a claim on his life, and is independent of his doubt concerning its truth. For example, a man may be familiar with all the arguments against the assertion that we can know the will of God and take those arguments seriously enough to live in continual uncertainty, and try nevertheless to behave according to norms to which he has committed himself on the basis that they seem to him most likely to be "what God requires of man." The commitments men make in marriage and friendship, their faith "in" their wives and their friends, are not unlike their religious commitments in this regard.

A question used by Stark and Glock in their recent study of religiosity illustrates how the existence of the three dimensions of "content," "frequency," and "intensity" can be seen in the best empirical work. The options provided for responses to the question, "Which of the following statements comes closest to what you believe about God?" included

1. "I know God really exists and I have no doubt about it."
2. "While I have doubts, I feel that I do believe in God."
3. "I find myself believing in God some of the time, but not at other times."
4. "I don't believe in a personal God, but I do believe in a higher power of some kind."
5. "I don't know whether there is a God and I don't believe there is any way to find out."
6. "I don't believe in God."[7]

In analyzing their findings, Stark and Glock point out that ". . . the greatest proportion of persons who rejected the first statement did not do so because they held a different image of God, but because they differed in their certainty."[8] The difference between the first and second options is a matter of "frequency," and the difference between the second and third would seem to be a matter of "intensity." The fourth option implies a variation in "content," as Stark and Glock recognize: "The fourth response category . . . marks a different conception of God, rather than differences in the certainty of faith."[9] But Stark and Glock do not measure the "certainty of faith"—or what we propose to call the "frequency" and "intensity" of belief—in this alternative conception. The sixth option seems in its context to be a matter of "content," that is, acceptance of the atheistic position, but again there is no measure of the doubt felt by those who hold that position. (The fifth option, depending on how it is read, does not necessarily contradict the others, except the first.) Thus Stark's and Glock's sophisticated understanding of the complexity of belief—too rare among social scientists—has led them to use a far more subtle and sensitive question than is normally found in empirical research. Application of the dimensions identified here would have the merit of treating more systematically and comprehensively the variables only implied—and then fragmentarily—in their instrument. Among other advantages, it would treat less traditional beliefs with the serious detail that is now normally reserved for the more traditional beliefs.

"Centrality" as a dimension of doctrinal religiosity means precisely what it does with respect to ritual and needs no further explication here. In fact, since its application to all components of religiosity is the same, it will not be considered separately in each case. Only one additional observation about "centrality" is necessary. Some men consider specific behaviors important, while others emphasize a class of behaviors and have little concern for the details. To illustrate, some Christians believe that faith in Jesus as the literal Son of God is essential to a good Christian life; others consider it important to "have faith," but do not care about its specific content. Many Jews consider some involvement in the life of the Jewish community essential, but believe that all forms of involvement are equally legitimate; others are quite specific about what constitutes acceptable participation in Jewish communal activity. "Centrality" must, therefore, be studied with respect to both specific behaviors and classes of behaviors.

Dimensions of Religious Emotion

The "emotional" component of religiosity signifies affect, feeling, sentiment. We do not call this aspect "religious experience" for two reasons. As a general word, "experience" includes all forms of behavior and does not differentiate feelings from acts and beliefs. As a technical term, it is usually taken to designate "some sense of contact with a supernatural agency" [10] and thus is only one kind of experience. A term more inclusive than the latter usage, yet less inclusive than the former, is needed, and "emotion" seems as appropriate a word as any.

The "content" of religious emotion has several components, a tentative list of which would include at least the following:

1. setting. Some people feel their deepest religious sentiments in church; others, in a field or a forest. Some thrive in the collective spirit of a congregation; others ascend the mountain in solitude.
2. mood. Some souls are stretched further by the lubricant of tears; others, by the stimulant of song and dance. Sometimes, peace is needed; at other times, passion.
3. involvement in one of the other components of religion. Singing a hymn can release religious emotion; so can holding out the

hand of fellowship and love. Belief can arouse it; so can studying a religious text.

4. the o(O)bject. A man's feelings may be a response to God, to
   nature, to history, to mankind, or to any combination of these
   and other possible objects of feeling.
5. relationship to the o(O)bject. The most useful typology of which
   is perhaps the one suggested by Glock, who describes the con-
   firming, responsive, ecstatic, and revelational experiences and
   their respective negative complements.[11]

The "frequency" and "intensity" dimensions of religious emotion are
self-explanatory. The words are used in their simple literal sense.

Dimensions of Religious Knowledge

With respect to religious knowledge, the dimen-
sions are easily defined. "Content" refers to specifically what a person
knows, "frequency" to how much he knows, and "intensity" to how
much he studies (that is, his commitment to knowledge). These
measures can, of course, be applied separately to the various divisions
of religious knowledge: Bible, later religious texts, systematic theology, religious law, history, and so forth.

Dimensions of the Ethical Component
of Religiosity

For all the major religions, a man's relations with
his fellows are part of his relationship to the Ultimate, and therefore
how a person behaves politically, economically, and socially is part of
his religious life. This segment of behavior is what Glock called the
"consequential" component of religiosity in his earlier formulation.[12]
He drops it in his latest work with Stark, explaining that "although
religions prescribe much of how their adherents ought to think and act
in everyday life, it is not entirely clear the extent to which religious
consequences are *a part* of religious commitment or simply *follow
from it.* . . . For our present purposes, we will assume that the initial
four dimensions [belief, practice, knowledge, and experience] provide
a complete frame of reference for assessing religious commitment." [13]
As has been suggested above, it is probably better to conceptualize
religion in its own terms, and to do so requires that ethical behavior be
viewed as a part—albeit an empirically independent part—of religiosity. The Roman Catholic Church claims hegemony in matters of "faith
and morals." Protestantism's "Social Gospel" is justified as an indispensable accompaniment of faith. For Judaism, relations "between

man and man" are a necessary complement to and test of relations "between man and God." And in this regard, Eastern religions are not different. Of course, we all know people with a fine sense of ethics who are largely uninvolved in the other aspects of religion and for whom religion (in its narrow sense) is irrelevant to ethics. Inclusion of the ethical component of religion in the analytic scheme does not keep us from taking account of these secular humanists (who may not like being called "religious," though in one sense they are), but its exclusion does seriously hamper our ability to chart the religiosity of those whose ethical behavior has religious roots. For the sake, then, of phenomenological integrity and empirical comprehensiveness, the ethical component of religion is included in the paradigm.

The "content" dimension of a person's behavior in the ethical component indicates his definitions of what is right in his interactions with others. The "frequency" dimension measures the number of actions with respect to which ethical considerations intrude into his interrelations. "Intensity," as before, measures the firmness and determination with which a person does what he considers right.

Dimensions of Communal Involvement

Finally, the four dimensions can be used in measuring a person's involvement in the communal aspect of religiosity. "Content" indicates which religious organizations (and/or organizations of co-religionists) a person belongs to, which ones receive his financial contributions, whether he tithes, and the situations in which religion is a criterion in his choice of friends and associates. "Frequency" measures the degree of his participation in "religious organizations," the amount of his contributions, the extent of religious homogeneity in his various primary and secondary groups. "Intensity" indicates the strictness with which a person adheres to his normal pattern of involvement.

Some Remaining Issues

The paradigm proposed here is not presumed to bring the concept of religiosity to full maturity. A number of theoretical and methodological problems still need to be solved. One such problem involves the selection of a base line from which an individual's religious behavior is measured. To use the oversimplified "traditional-liberal" dichotomy for the purpose of illustration, someone whose behavior is distinctly untraditional may be either irreligious or a devout religious liberal. While it is probably true that most people view the traditional forms of religiosity as normative, there is a big and, for our purposes, crucial difference between statistical modes and universal contexts. Granted that deeply involved religious liberals may be a minority, they must still be provided for in our conceptual schemes. Indeed, inclusion of more liberal religious elements in our scales may reveal a higher degree of religiosity than many observers have reported.

In order, however, to select the most appropriate base line, we need some means of determining the order of mutually supportive factors. When does a man's calling himself a Lutheran follow a realization that he accepts that denomination's approach more than others', and when is Lutheranism an *antecedent* referent for his religious behavior? Does a Jew not keep kosher because he is Reform, or does he choose to identify himself as Reform because *inter alia* he rejects dietary laws? If traditional Judaism defines the base line, then not keeping kosher is negatively scored and the ceremony of confirmation is at best neutral. If Reform Judaism is the base, then confirmation is positively scored and neglecting dietary laws is at worst neutral. Similar examples could be drawn around issues like episcopal authority, transubstantiation, and Bible reading, to cite only a few. The base should, of course, depend on the purpose of the research. The traditional form of a religion, the specific official positions of a given denomination or "movement," the modal responses of a defined group, or the positions implied by some "ideal type" are all appropriate—sometimes in combination—from time to time. One item on our current scientific agenda should be the elaboration of a conceptual framework that will handle religiosity relative to each of these bases.

A second need is the development of comparable measures of religiosity for various religions. There is as yet no instrument that incorporates truly comparable items for the major religious groups in America. Many of the doctrinal items that must be included in a sound study of Christian belief, for example, are largely irrelevent to Jews. Many of the rituals that constitute the range of Jewish practice are not meaningful to Christians. When indices that include only items held in common by these two religions are used, such as belief in God and church (or synagogue) attendance, two crucial errors are made. First, a large number of highly significant items get omitted. Second, it is assumed incorrectly that the items that exist in both religious traditions have similar meanings and identical weights despite the differences in their respective contexts. Sound studies of the patterns in each religious group require a research instrument specific to that religion, but in the long run, the many instruments must be made to produce comparable ranges of variation.

A third need is the development of instruments that will independently tap behavior on the one hand and norms concerning behavior on the other. We should not assume without empirical and theoretical justification that the religiosity of two men is the same because their behavior is the same. One may accept far more rigorous standards and consider himself unable to live up to them because of some internal failing or external constraint, while the other may have almost perfect articulation between what he does and what he thinks he should do. Conceptually, we need only multiply the twenty-four categories in our paradigm by two: one set for behavior, the other for norms. However, having two sets of related measures requires a theoretical framework within which their relationships can be systematically expressed.

("Centrality," incidentally, is not an indicator of norms concerning behavior. It is easy to imagine, perhaps to recall, the statement, "I guess I should consider this important, but to tell the truth, I don't.")

Finally, motive must be considered. The seminal notions of "intrinsic" and "extrinsic" motivations for religious behavior that Allport contributed to our thinking,[14] for example, mark two significantly different kinds of religiosity whose observable behaviors need not vary in every case. The issue is further complicated by what O'Dea, in a closely related context, has called "the dilemma of mixed motivation."[15] While O'Dea uses the term to describe the mixture of institutional and charismatic attractions to the clergy (it is a career as well as a calling, and it offers security and prestige as well as an opportunity for service and the implementation of commitment), the same dilemmas *mutatis mutandis* characterize the laity. Theoretical and methodological instruments are needed to deal with the various configurations of motives and their relationships to religious behavior.

Conclusion

The purpose of this paper has been, as was said at the outset, "to nudge the [concept of religiosity] a step closer to a complex maturity in which it can carry a heavier load in the scientific study of religion." That we have left the concept more complex than we found it is apparent—perhaps exasperatingly so. The essential justification for elaborating six components and four dimensions into a twenty-four cell matrix to measure what is usually seen as a single concept rests in the nature of that concept. Religiosity is not simply a matter of more or less involvement in a clearly delimited social institution. It is not even a matter of more or less intensiveness or extensiveness. It is the full range of individual responses to the whole body of religious options available in a culture. To consider less is to ignore the nature of religion or to assume that the part of religiosity that is now usually studied is representative of the whole.

Omitting some of the twenty-four cells in the notion of religiosity is analogous to drawing a sample that purports to be representative of the American people, but systematically excludes everyone, say, between the ages of thirty and forty or all residents of New England. It may be that for some purposes these biases would do no damage. In some ways people in their thirties and New Englanders may be like everyone else; the mechanisms through which they resolve role-strain, for example, are probably the same as those used by people in other age cohorts and regions. However, in other ways—their fertility rates and political attitudes, for example—they are clearly unlike the rest of the population, and their omission from a sample would make it unacceptable. Until it is demonstrated empirically that given parts of a population are like the remainder of the population, it is wise to be inclusive in our sampling. This is true of indicators as well as people.

There are four general ways in which the conceptualization proposed here can bear a "heavier load" in the social scientific study of religion.

First, systematic study of the internal dynamics of religious adherence requires a conceptual framework that differentiates the various types of religious behavior. These types can then be empirically interrelated. To omit any of them at this stage of our knowledge would be to foreshorten the research that is needed to show how different elements of religious life complement one another or serve as alternative means of expression. Consider, for example, the following two equally plausible yet opposite hypotheses. It might be expected that doctrinal doubts generate an inconsistency in observance. On the other hand, scrupulous ritual observance may provide a sure anchor to compensate for lack of doctrinal certainty. One of the tasks of sociology is to determine the circumstances in which each member of such a pair of hypotheses holds true. But the necessary research will be much more powerful when we separate doctrinal "frequency" and ritual "intensity" from the other dimensions of belief and ritual practice. Moreover, additional questions of this kind are generated by the divisions in the component-dimension paradigm.

Second, it may turn out upon investigation that certain cells in the matrix will be found to intercorrelate to produce types,[16] and we shall be able to collapse some of the categories. We would then have a typology of religiosity that is theoretically and empirically derived. It would also maintain comparability through revisions as various forms of religious involvement ebb and flow with social change. Yinger has urged that we ask of a population not only "How religious are they?" but also "How are they religious?"[17] The twenty-four aspects of religious behavior provide a far more comprehensive, schematic, and suggestive framework for both questions, but especially the latter, than has normally been used in past studies.

Third, religiosity is often related to other variables such as age, political attitude, and socioeconomic status. It is not unlikely, however, that these factors are related to religious behavior in more specific ways that can be detected with an overly general research instrument. As one illustration, it has been observed that people in their child-rearing years tend to be "less religious" than during adolescence and in later life. It may be that lack of time and the greater need to respond to unpredictable situations during these middle years leads to lower frequency of ritual, which in the absence of other measures would produce low values on a religiosity scale. However, before we can soundly conclude that people are indeed less religious during their middle years, we would have to know how they score on the other categories in the paradigm. If there is no change with age in most of the other categories, we could hardly assert that young parents really find religion less salient in any substantial degree. A second example is suggested by Allport's observation that while many studies show church-going and prejudice to be positively correlated, we would expect the opposite to be the case, since the major religions frown on prejudice.[18] This contradiction may be accounted for not only by application of the "intrinsic-extrinsic" distinction, but also by correlating prejudice with the different kinds of religiosity in our conceptualization.

Fourth, religious change is a frequent subject of study. But societies are not simply more or less religious. Shiner has suggested six meanings for the notion "secularization,"[19] and the frequently-posed question "Is there a religious revival?" has elicited both affirmative and negative answers. The reason for the debate, of course, is that different indicators of religiosity are used, and the best answer to the question is probably "In some ways, yes; in others, no." The present paradigm has the merit of systematizing and specifying that answer.

A detailed description of the ways in which the conceptualization of religiosity outlined above can be helpful to social science would be tantamount to the larger part of a catalogue of the social scientific study of religion and is beyond the scope of this paper. If the paradigm of components and dimensions proposed here encourages us to turn our attention from "religiosity" as an almost unitary variable to the variety of religious patterns that mark real, breathing, worshipping, and doubting men, then it will have done its work, and at least this particular crisis in conceptual adolescence will have been successfully weathered.

NOTES

1. This definition has been proposed by several students of religion. See, for example, Paul Tillich, *Biblical Religion and the Search for Ulti-*

mate Reality (Chicago: University of Chicago Press, 1955) and Joachim Wach, *The Comparative Study of Religions* (New York: Columbia University Press, 1958).

2. Émile Durkheim, *The Elementary Forms of the Religious Life* (Glencoe, Ill.: Free Press, 1954).

3. Among the articles that deal with this issue are Charles Y. Glock, "On the Study of Religious Commitment," in *Review of Recent Research Bearing on Religious and Character Formation,* a Research Supplement to *Religious Education* (July–August 1962), reprinted in Charles Y. Glock and Rodney Stark, *Religion and Society in Tension* (Chicago: Rand McNally and Company, 1965); Yoshio Fukuyama, "The Major Dimensions of Church Membership," in *Review of Religious Research,* Vol. 2; Morton King, "Measuring the Religious Variable: Nine Proposed Dimensions," in *Journal for the Scientific Study of Religion,* Vol. VI.

4. Rodney Stark and Charles Y. Glock, *American Piety: The Nature of Religious Commitment* (Berkeley and Los Angeles: University of California Press, 1968), pp. 41–54.

5. Stanley K. Bigman, *The Jewish Population of Greater Washington* (Washington, D.C.: The Jewish Community Council of Greater Washington, 1957).

6. A discussion of the relationship of these two kinds of faith can be found in H. H. Price, "Belief 'In' and Belief 'That,'" in *Religious Studies,* Vol. I.

7. Stark and Glock, *op. cit.,* pp. 28–29.

8. *Ibid.,* p. 27.

9. *Idem.*

10. Charles Y. Glock, "A Taxonomy of Religious Experience," in *Journal for the Scientific Study of Religion,* Vol. V, reprinted in Glock and Stark, *op. cit.*

11. *Loc. cit.*

12. Glock, "On the Study of Religious Commitment."

13. Stark and Glock, *op. cit.,* p. 16.

14. Gordon W. Allport, *Religion in the Developing Personality* (New York: New York University Press, 1960).

15. Thomas F. O'Dea, "Five Dilemmas in the Institutionalization of Religion," in *Journal for the Scientific Study of Religion,* Vol. I.

16. Cf. Joseph H. Fichter, S. J., *Social Relations in the Urban Parish* (Chicago: University of Chicago Press, 1954), Part One.

17. J. Milton Yinger, "A Structural Examination of Religion," in *Journal for the Scientific Study of Religion,* Vol. VIII.

18. Gordon W. Allport, "The Religious Context of Prejudice," in *Journal for the Scientific Study of Religion,* Vol. III.

19. Larry Shiner, "The Concept of Secularization in Empirical Research," in *Journal for the Scientific Study of Religion,* Vol. VI.

QUESTIONS FOR DISCUSSION

1. What is an appropriate response for a behavioral scientist to make to the question, "What is the meaning of being religious?"

2. From your knowledge of history, can you generalize about the meaning of "religion" in instances where historians talk of "religious influence"?

3. Does the selection by White suggest a one-sided view of religion, religiosity, and so forth? How do you think H. Richard Niebuhr would have reacted to White's essay?

4. What meaning do you assign to: (1) "He is not a churchgoer, but he is very religious," (2) "Person A is a religious Jew whereas Person B is an ethnic Jew," (3) "Since the Pilgrim landing, the religious mood of America has fluctuated, now higher, now lower."

ADDITIONAL READING

Berger, Peter L. *The Sacred Canopy.* Garden City, N.Y.: Doubleday, 1967. Throughout, but especially in Appendix 1, "Sociological Definitions of Religion," Berger stakes out a position on which his various analyses of religious phenomena are built.

Geertz, Clifford. "Religion as a Cultural System," in Michael Banton (ed.), *Anthropological Approaches to the Study of Religion.* ASA Monographs, 1966. Reprinted in Donald Cutler (ed.), *The Religious Situation, 1968.* Boston: Beacon Press, 1968. Geertz discusses religion in terms of three "intergrading" aspects: the analytic, the emotional, and the moral.

Greeley, Andrew M. "A Note on the Origins of Religious Differences," *Journal for the Scientific Study of Religion,* 3 (Fall 1963), 21–31. Greeley argues that the distinctive values and norms of religious groups do not always have a "religious" origin.

Malinowski, Bronislaw. "Magic, Science and Religion," in *Magic, Science and Religion and Other Essays.* Garden City, N.Y.: Doubleday, 1955. First appearing in 1925, this essay is Malinowski's chief argument for a "psychological" understanding of religion.

Tillich, Paul. *Dynamics of Faith.* New York: Harper and Row, 1957. One of the places where Tillich's notion of religion as "ultimate concern" is discussed, this volume, though not, strictly speaking, social science is nevertheless complementary to much sociology of religion.

Chapter II

Measuring Religion in America

Measuring people's religion would be a fairly simple task if only one religion existed and everyone knew precisely how this one religion was expressed. Measurement would then be largely a technical matter, much like constructing and scoring a test of a person's knowledge of French grammar or of mathematics. It would probably be useful to construct several measures of such a religion, each one corresponding to some distinct aspect or dimension of the overall faith. Just as people who do well in arithmetic may do poorly in calculus, so people who score high on one dimension of religion may score low on another. Not all who can recite their prayers may know their Bible.

Measuring religion is more than a technical task, however, because there is not just one religion, there are many. To be sure, there are places on earth where a single religion predominates, and there are students of religion who concentrate on one faith, but the student of American religion must face squarely the fact of religious diversity. He must find ways to measure several religions, often in a single study. Nationwide surveys, for example, must use questions about religion that are widely understood and that can classify the bulk of respondents with at least some validity. A simple and widely used way of doing this is to ask the respondent to identify himself as Protestant, Catholic, Jew, or "other." Although there is little reason to doubt that most Americans understand what these labels mean and can apply them to themselves, the use of such a simple classification has been justly criticized by sociologists of religion. In the first place, American religion is far more differentiated than this fourfold classification would suggest. Protestantism in particular is divided into dozens of denominational families and theological camps, many of

them radically different from one another. It makes no sense, therefore, to assume that one Protestant is essentially the same as another.
In the second place, a simple measure based on a respondent's
religious self-identification gives the investigator little help in interpreting his findings. If he finds, for example, that Catholics are more
likely to spank their children than Jews are, he can speculate why
this is so, but he cannot prove that there is anything about the
Catholic religion, as opposed to the Jewish religion, that explains why
it is so. In short, religious labels do not tell anything directly about
religious content.

But measuring religious content is not an easy thing to do. In
the first place, it would be a formidable undertaking to construct
valid measures of the content of each of the principal religions in
the United States. Moreover, it would be impossible to administer
all of these measures in ordinary survey research. The measurement
task is made much more complex by the fact that social scientists are
interested in building theories of wide rather than of narrow applicability. They are interested in making systematic comparisons among
religious bodies and among people of various religious traditions. In
order to do this they need common yardsticks, that is, they need to
build their measurements on a set of categories or dimensions that
can be applied to all religions, or at least a large number of them.
When measurements are constructed on this basis, it should be possible, for example, to explain that Catholics spank their children because they score high on some religious dimension on which Jews score
low. Unfortunately, there is little agreement on what the basic
dimensions of religion are and how to measure them. In fact, problems of the conceptualization and measurement of religious content
are among the most difficult in the sociology of religion.

Nevertheless, social scientists have been relying on content-based
measures of religion for a long time. Many different measures are
in use, but most of them have been designed along similar lines.
First, most existing measures of content are based on the principal
American religions. Second, these measures tend to reflect the
officially prescribed, historically based content of these religions. For
example, both Christianity and Judaism prescribe belief in God,
prayer, and attendance at corporate worship. Both acknowledge a set
of sacred scriptures. Accordingly, social scientists often select their
dimensions of religiosity from one or more of these traditional
aspects of Judeo-Christian piety. They ask respondents about church
attendance, prayer, knowledge of the Bible, and so forth. Third,
the problem of religious diversity is "resolved" by selecting only
those dimensions and items shared by all the religions under investigation and by excluding anything they do not share. This procedure,

which can be called the common denominator method, may be simply illustrated by referring to the religions of Springdale, the rural community studied by Arthur J. Vidich and Joseph Bensman (Selection 4). There are only four denominations in Springdale, all of them Protestant. In measuring the local religion it would therefore be appropriate to include explicitly Protestant items, but one would have to be careful to avoid items that give one denomination an "unfair advantage" over another. For example, in measuring observance of ritual obligations, one might ask about church attendance but one should not ask about infant baptism or the observance of Lent because Baptists do not believe in these observances. It would be proper to include items on knowledge of the New Testament, but not knowledge of the Book of Common Prayer, because only Episcopalians use this book. Similarly, in measuring feelings of closeness to God it would not be appropriate to ask respondents whether they have ever had a sudden emotional experience of religious conversion, for this would give Baptists an advantage over all the other denominations.

The common denominator method "solves" the problem of religious diversity by avoiding it altogether. This may not matter greatly in Springdale, where religious diversity is at a minimum, but it begins to matter when one tries to construct measures for use across a wide variety of religious traditions. If Catholics are to be included, one must stick to items shared by Catholics and Protestants. If Jews are to be included one must select items that Christians and Jews share. But how does one broaden such measures to include Moslems, Zen Buddhists, or traditional Navajos? In short, the common denominator method ultimately runs the risk of overlooking the vital content of particular religions by imposing a totally artificial uniformity.

Social scientists are becoming aware that their measures of religious content leave much to be desired. J. Milton Yinger, for one, has objected to the narrow, tradition-based conception of religion that is embodied in most existing measures (Selection 5). He has called for a broader, more theoretically fruitful conception that emphasizes the ultimate concerns men have, the kinds of courage they show in the face of chaos and evil. This conception obviously includes a good deal more than most conventional definitions of religion, but it is very much in keeping with much of the classic literature in the sociology of religion. Yinger believes most current measures utterly fail to tap the ultimate concerns people actually have. They measure the relics of the past, not the living faith of today. Rather than assuming a priori what the basic dimensions of religion are, Yinger would have the social scientist search for them by asking people

to talk about their ultimate concerns in their own words. Universal
dimensions might then be extracted from the diverse content
gathered by investigators in many different settings.

The task of exploring how people actually express their religion is
already under way. Yinger asked his college students four open-ended
questions about their ultimate concerns and extracted a relatively
small number of categories from their answers. In an entirely
different setting, Robert R. Monaghan discovered three basic religious
orientations among the members of a fundamentalist church
(Selection 6). Monaghan's study is of particular interest because
the three orientations he extracts are quite different from anything
one might predict on the basis of that church's official teachings.
Similar studies of religious content are appearing with increasing
frequency. Although these studies have so far yielded rather
dissimilar results, it is much too early to pass judgment on this
approach. Like all new methods this one will need to undergo many
refinements before it can be put to an adequate test. For the time
being it seems the most promising method yet devised for discovering
how people express their religion and what the common dimensions
of religion are. It may lead not only to better measures of religious
content but to a deeper understanding of religion itself.

4

Arthur J. Vidich
and Joseph Bensman

Church Life in a Small Town

The Place of the Church
in Community Life

Church-going is of major importance in the social
life of Springdale simply because it constitutes so great a part of the
publicly visible community activity. Church activities involve relatively large groups of people and occur in conspicuous places at fixed
times. A large part of the attention of the community is captured by
activities centered in the churches.

The major portion of church activity occurs in four Protestant
churches located in the village. The churches and the number of
participants in each are:

1. *Baptist.* 135[1] local members, of whom between 70 and 100 attend
church regularly and participate in other church activities.

2. *Episcopal.* 100 active and inactive[2] communicants. Between 30
and 50 attend regularly and take part in other related activities.

3. *Congregational.* 100 members, of whom 30–50 participate.

4. *Methodist.* 250 members, about half of whom participate.[3]

Sunday morning in Springdale is a time of exclusive devotion to
religious pursuits, to the exclusion of all other public affairs. Each
church, surrounded by cars, becomes a focal point of activity and no
other organized activity exists to compete with the specifically reli-

From Arthur J. Vidich and Joseph Bensman, *Small Town in Mass Society:
Class, Power and Religion in a Rural Community,* revised edition copyright
© 1968 by Princeton University Press. Reprinted by permission of Prince-
ton University Press. Arthur J. Vidich is a sociologist at the New School for
Social Research; Joseph Bensman is a sociologist at City College of New
York.

gious. The Sunday service and schools, however, by no means exhaust the range of church activities.

Altogether, church-related activities constitute approximately 50 percent of all organized social activities in the community. Each church sponsors a broad range of activities and supports a number of auxiliary organizations. These vary slightly from church to church but, on the whole, with the exception of the Baptists, the pattern of activities of any one church is relatively indistinguishable from any other. Characteristically there are a board of trustees or deacons, a ladies' aid, a missionary society, a men's society, youth groups and a choir. All such organizations conduct their own social programs, a fact which again multiplies the number of church-connected activities. Under auxiliary auspices fall the church supper, the ice-cream social, the bake sale, the rummage sale, the men's supper, the hay rides and the picnics. The Baptists explicitly reject such social and money-raising activities —for them there are no suppers, no bake sales and no ice-cream socials. The church for them is an exclusively religious fellowship and money is collected by the direct means of tithing and contributions; women's activities are organized in a missionary society, youth activities in Bible classes and men's fellowship in a tither's association. As an added layer, evangelistic speakers are almost a weekly feature of the Baptist church program.

The range of activities centered in the churches and the extensiveness of the programs offered by the auxiliaries, then, are sufficiently broad to attract people to the church and to appeal to a variety of interests.

The churches are an important part of the life of the whole community because of the public nature of their activities. Most of their social activities are open to anyone who cares to attend. In practice, however, the public social activities of one church—a supper or ice-cream social, for example—are attended only by members of that and other churches. Irrespective of which church is sponsor, the clientele for these activities is much the same. It is for this reason that the churches cooperate with each other to divide the available dates on the social calendar—i.e., Methodists have a Harvest Supper while Congregationalists have the July Fourth Dinner; no two churches have bake sales or rummage sales at the same time, etc.

In consequence, although the churches organize the major portion of the public life of the community, their activities involve only the 300–400 persons who are interested in church activities. This, of course, is only a small portion of the 1,700 adults involved in the life of the community. Nevertheless, the multiplication of the activities of these 400 people, by participation in numerous church programs and social activities, is so great as to give the appearance of dominating the whole of the public life of the entire community.

Class and Church Membership

All of the class groups are not equally involved in church activities and church memberships are not distributed along class lines. The basic core of memberships in all churches is drawn from various segments of the middle and marginal middle classes. All of the churches claim the membership of at least one of the old aristocratic families. The professionals, with the exception of most teachers (who are Catholics and attend church in another community), are perhaps the most thoroughly involved in church life.

Only a small percentage of industrial workers, who are otherwise similar to the professionals in style of living, are church-involved. Prosperous farmers provide the core membership of the Methodist church and are scattered throughout other churches. Businessmen's participation depends on whether they think active participation in one church will have a negative effect on their business chances. About half are active members of churches, equally divided among all denominations.

In Springdale church membership is largely determined by considerations other than class. Kinship, marriage and family tradition all play a part in explaining the mixed class composition of the congregations. Children, with few exceptions, adopt the church of their parents. However, affiliation by kinship does not assure family continuity in a given church. In the Protestant churches, unless the husband is without a church, the wife upon marriage affiliates with the church of her spouse and any children who are products of this mating do likewise. Siblings and first cousins who all trace their descent to a common maternal grandfather can belong to different churches. Except for the Baptist church, where marriage tends to be endogamous, marriage tends to cut across church lines relatively freely. Beyond the nuclear family, kinship groups are not identified with a particular church.

Characteristically, church membership is determined by the husband's church preferences and these preferences are determined by family tradition. New migrants to a community generally enter a local church according to their prior predispositions. These factors of tradition and custom rather than class or theology account for the mixed social and economic composition of the congregations.

Only one class is decisively and completely uncommitted to church life, the shack people. They neither attend church nor participate in the various activities that surround the churches. The traditional farmers are the only other class grouping that stands apart from the religious sphere of community life. Their traditional family church affiliations are to country churches which have fallen into disuse and they have not been willing to shift their membership to a village church. They do not participate because of their incapacity to adjust to the 20th century trend to centralized churches.

Although there is preponderantly a mixture of class and church membership, there are a few points at which class and church meet. The membership of the Baptist church consists largely of members of the marginal middle class, but this does not mean that all members of this class are church participants. Although all churches include a few prosperous farmers, the majority of these farmers are Methodists. The historic 19th century appeal of Wesleyanism to farmers is reflected in the social composition of the contemporary church. The Congregational church commands the greatest percentage of the professional class, but does not monopolize this group. There are no professionals in the Baptist church. Outside of these tendencies, no one church is exclusively monopolized by any one class group.

.   .   .

Church Competition and
the Unchurched

The competition for church membership is geared only to newcomers and the already churched, those who have a church affiliation. The bulk of the population which is not church-going is not the object of missionary work. The thousand individuals who are not members of a church, excluding a small number who go to church in other communities, are made up of two distinct groups:

1. Those who have been approached by one or more ministers and have consistently resisted; these are people who outwardly give the impression of being good prospects, but who turn out not to be. They become known as intransigents by all the ministers, none of whom attempt any longer to involve them in church activities.

2. Those who are simply known to be non-church-going people: the immoral, the irresponsible, those without self-respect, the "unreliable." Proselytizing activities are never aimed at this group; church programs are not designed to appeal to them and ministers never visit them.

In the face of inter-church competition for membership, this absence of missionary effort requires explanation.

Psychologically, for the first group, it means that the effort required to gain these persons as new members is so great that the ministers feel they do not have the time or the persuasive skills necessary to "sell" them religion and active church participation. For the second group, the explanation lies in the fact that the ministers and their laymen are often simply unaware of the existence of the traditionally unchurched. They either do not see the unchurched or they have no desire to pollute the church membership with socially undesirable types. This attitude results in an almost total neglect of local missionary opportunities.

While the mission opportunity on the local scene goes unseen, each church carries on an extensive missionary program for non-Christians in remote places. Collections of mission funds, clothing, books, missionary speakers and the adoption of a distant mission church make up an important part of the churches' programs. The community of the damned still exists, but it is not noticed in one's immediate environment.

In spite of inter-church competition and in spite of *sub-rosa* ecumenicalism, formal ecumenicalism is still celebrated by a number of church programs which have at least symbolical significance. The ministerial council exists, the joint summer Bible classes meet and the community choir sings from time to time. This means that at the public level, in any case, the relations among the churches are carried on in a civilized manner.

The Place of Theology in Ecumenicalism

The tensions and problems raised by ecumenicalism and by the similarities in the social programs of the churches are partially solved by differences in theology. The previous discussion which has focused on church programs has emphasized the similarities in the activities of the different churches. Theology, as used, emphasizes the differences and helps to preserve the jurisdictional boundaries between the churches.

On theological grounds no minister completely commits himself to ecumenicalism, keeping, as it were, a theological ace in the hole to prevent the ecumenical absorption of his own church. The Episcopal minister refuses to participate in any joint activity of a sacramental nature; the sacraments signalize the identity of Episcopalianism. The Methodists and Baptists decline participation in any joint activity which implies an historical attitude to the Bible and to Christ; their badge of distinction is the apocalyptic Biblical literature, *Revelation, Ezekiel* and *Daniel*. The Baptists, in addition, distinguish themselves by the adult baptism. The Congregationalists and Baptists refuse participation in any activity which acknowledges a worldly hierarchy of religious officials; for them the church is and can only be the living Church of Christ in which each man has a direct, unmediated tie to God.

Such theological differences play an important part in maintaining the identity of each church. For the membership they provide a way of justifying their commitment to a given church: "I wouldn't want to be a member of a church that had a bishop." "If you look at *Revelation*, you can see this is an apostate age." "In our church you have a definite book of prayers." "What I like about my church is that the minister can't tell me what to do." For the minister they represent sales points that competitors cannot meet: only the Baptists can offer baptism by full immersion; the Episcopalian minister alone administers sacraments in church and home; if you are a Congregationalist you have the liberty of conscience and belief—no one tells you what to believe; when you are an Episcopalian, you know there is a strong organization of like-minded behind you; the Baptists give you the truth of the Bible, the only undeviating truth, the word of the Lord. All ministers emphasize the theological points that distinguish their doctrine from the others and highlight these differences as the badge of their church. Theology itself, then, becomes an organizational device for holding and recruiting members and, as such, it becomes a branch of administration.

However, it must be recognized, in order not to give a distorted perspective, that no matter what other activities occur at say a social or organizational level, theology, no matter how imperfectly practiced, is a central part of the framework of rhetoric and discussion surrounding church-centered activities. Of course, this is neither new nor startling. When contradictions in alternatives are available, all parties to a discussion can phrase their position in at least bad theological terms. Thus a church supper is no different from any other supper in any other context except that (a) it is sponsored by the church and takes place in a church building, (b) church-like words are used, (c) a distinctly religious atmosphere prevails: conversation is subdued and behavior is formal and restrained.

But theology in the past has had other meanings, has signified more than a rhetoric. It has defined an attitude to life and to God. It has defined specifically religious attitudes and values. It has placed a premium on certain psychological states and feelings as being desirable and exalted and has created frameworks within which ethical and moral codes are meaningful in other spheres of life. From a social-psychological point of view, it has provided the theoretical foundations for sets of perspectives which for a particular theology can be defined as "the religious."

The Baptists and Theology

Theology, in the above sense, is important for only one group in the community, the Baptists, who in Springdale form an exclusive religious community of their own. In the Baptist doctrine the church is conceived as a living church—"a company of believers in Jesus Christ, linked with him in baptism and associated for worship, work and fellowship." The official position of the Baptist church in relation to the rest of the community is derived from this definition of the living church. In practice it means that the church is a "fellowship of people based on a fellowship of faith, it is a fellowship separated from the larger community, it is a community in itself." A Baptist is a person who "is called out of the secular community into the church" and his "primary loyalty is to the fellowship of Christ." The organization of the Church community takes its cue from the New Testament and attempts to make itself a model of the Early Christian Church. Within these terms the Baptists have become a "spiritual community" within an alien secular society to which they refuse to accommodate.

The contemporary world is regarded as apostate; Baptists remove themselves from it, not wishing to have anything to do with it. The religious way, while unsuccessful in this world, provides salvation for those who duly prepare themselves in the present. To the Baptist the emotional religious experiences of conversion to the way of Christ, of being publicly saved and of adult baptism by total immersion are the central personal experiences of life that give him a sense of pride, distinction and self-esteem, whatever his worldly position. The combined consequences of this orientation lead to a theological abnegation of this world wherever possible under the conditions of modern living.

In this theology, accommodation is replaced by evangelization, but for "practical" reason (of *sub-rosa* ecumenicalism), the missionary attitude is reduced to "neighborliness." Stemming from this attitude, the Baptists have become a social enclave within the secular community, while the doctrine provides the justification for controlling the religious and social actions of its members in relation to specific issues as they arise in the community.

The doctrine requires Baptists to abstain from all community functions except the political and educational. Voting, holding political office, teaching and belonging to the P.T.A. are permitted on grounds that this is the only way to keep civil government out of the church and to keep education directed to inculcating the virtues of "obedience and respect for authority." The esteemed Baptist boycotts all other forms of community activity. Since the conception of the "Baptist community" is linked with the pietistic morality of Baptist theology, members are prohibited from all participation not directed to "fellowship and pressing business." This prohibition specifically excludes association for entertainment, secret lodges, idle sociability and gossip. Organizations which condone drinking, dancing or recreation are prohibited. Organized charity drives are boycotted on grounds that they are not administered and controlled entirely by Christians (in the

Baptist sense of the term). In special instances the minister and
deacons of the church have explicitly permitted participation in certain community affairs where it is felt the ends of the activity are in
consonance with Baptist doctrine.

No other church assumes such a monastic attitude toward the community. The Congregational church, whose organizational structure is
patterned on the living church of the New Testament, adapts itself to
the changing circumstances of secular life and encourages secular
action within the secular framework. Episcopalians and Methodists
freely engage in community affairs and feel their engagement remains
consistent with religious belief. For these groups no sharp line distinguishes sacred from secular activity. By its exclusiveness and by the
moral and ethical imperialism of its members, the Baptist church
stands out as a peculiar group in the life of the community. By his
theology and his social isolation from the secular, the Baptist appears
to others to be "queer"—non-cooperative, unsociable, fervently religious.

The distinctive feature of Baptist religious practice is that it is not
ordinary—i.e., it is removed from the non-religious. It is "peculiar" in
the sense that the religious attitude and perspective are distinct from
the non-religious.

The Place of Religion
in Community Life

The characteristics of other religions in Spring-
dale do not have this Baptist quality of peculiarity. They are ordinary
—i.e., similar to the regular activities of people acting in public social
activities. The religious halo for these people is one that surrounds
activities which in their intrinsic qualities are not religious, i.e., not
peculiar.

Church life, then, is an added layer of social activity which merely
thickens the public life of the four hundred people who participate.
Since all persons in the community do not participate equally, it is not
a mere replication of the total behavior of the community. It is
characteristic only of that portion which is the most social and most
external in its activities. Church activities afford an opportunity
whereby these social activities can find expression in additional ways.
Church activity, then, lends quality and depth to the external and social
aspects of the public life of the community. The multiplication of
church activities and the duplication of church programs give the community the appearance of greater domination by these public social
activities than is actually the case when one views the total population
of the town. But since these other groups do not participate, the

activities of the church participants magnify the appearances of one segment of the community almost to the point where all others are obliterated from the public view.

NOTES

1. The official total membership of this as well as other churches is about 25 percent higher than the figures given here. This results from the practice of retaining names on membership rolls after people have moved from the community.

2. Those who have not taken communion for one or more years. They are still members of the church, but not in good standing.

3. In addition to the village churches, there are seven others (two Methodist, two Baptist, one Episcopal, one Seventh Day Adventist and one Catholic), all located in rural parts of the township. The Seventh Day Adventists are situated on the fringe of the community and appeal to a small regional membership which includes few Springdalers. The Catholic church, also located on the geographical fringe, was built by and serves about 20–30 local Polish families. Catholic activities are physically and psychologically segregated from the life of the community, whose religious tone is given by Protestantism. Non-Polish Catholics attend churches in other communities. In this sense the Catholics are socially invisible.

The other country churches are officially or informally linked to their village counterparts. They represent a 19th century phase of rural religious decentralization and are now supported by small congregations and do not retain a minister. One exception should be noted: of the two Baptist churches, only one is affiliated to the village church. The other is a schismatic group which absorbs elements hostile to the aggressive theology of the minister in the village.

The village churches are made up of persons from all parts of the township and include the bulk of the church-goers. The membership figures given do not include the rural affiliates and this study deals only with the village churches.

5

J. Milton Yinger

A Structural
Examination of Religion

I would propose that we set aside the questions of who is religious and who is not, how far secularization has proceeded, whether there is a return to religion, and the like. In my judgment, examination of those questions has been carried about as far as it is profitable to carry them. I suggest that we adopt a research model analogous to that of structural linguistics. Rather than asking *if* a person is religious, we ask *how* he is religious. How does he define "chaos"? What concerns him most fundamentally? What actions follow as a result of these definitions and concerns? How widely shared are they? What groups form around them? We may discover that there are many hidden religions around us which haven't been apparent because we expected all religions to look like the most familiar ones. I find it helpful to think of everyone—or nearly everyone—being religious, just as nearly everyone speaks a language. This is an assumption, not a demonstrated truth. The question is: What can one do with such an assumption that will advance our understanding of human action? It does not imply that all persons are equally interested in or involved in religion, just as not all persons find language equally important. Some are highly "lingual," others inarticulate.

In structural linguistics, the various elements or dimensions of language have been identified—phonology, semantics, grammar, etc. One determines whether or not any given system of sounds is a language by the presence or absence of these constituent elements. We can observe the shifts from Beowulf to Chaucer to Shakespeare to Tennyson

From J. Milton Yinger, "A Structural Examination of Religion," *Journal for the Scientific Study of Religion*, **8** (Spring 1969), 88–99, reprinted by permission of the author and publisher. J. Milton Yinger is a sociologist at Oberlin College.

to Eliot without saying that the latter forms are a nonlanguage, that they have been "secularized." In the same manner, let us design measures of continuity and change in religion without presuppositions that some efforts to deal with man's ultimate problems—those new and only slightly institutionalized, for example—can be disregarded. Let us ask our respondents to "speak their religion" to us, uninstructed by our own preconceptions.

Those who have pointed to and begun the measurement of the several dimensions of religion have taken an important step toward a structural examination of religion. I am suggesting another step, involving the search for more analytic categories that are less closely identified with the major institutional systems we have labelled religions. In such a search, I propose the following operational definition: Where one finds *awareness of and interest in the continuing, recurrent, "permanent" problems of human existence*—the human condition itself, as contrasted with specific problems; where one finds *rites and shared beliefs relevant to that awareness which define the strategy of an ultimate victory;* and where one has *groups organized to heighten that awareness and to teach and maintain those rites and beliefs*—there you have religion. (The term "victory" in this definition may be too western a concept. It should be read to mean "achievement of that state in which the fundamental problems of the human condition have been brought within the frame of an ultimate order.")

Each of the three parts of this definition is a variable, not an attribute. We will do well, I think, to speak in terms of a religious quality, present to greater or lesser degrees in many situations, rather than of religions. What I have described is a three-level definition combining an individual character aspect (awareness and interest), a cultural aspect (shared rites and beliefs), and a social structural aspect (groups). Each is vital in my judgment. Where one is lacking, religion is not present in the full meaning of the term.

Following this line of argument, one does not start out by identifying the highly visible religious traditions among a group, and then measuring individuals' relationships to them, in terms of belief and participation. Important work has been done in this way, but it cannot deal with the problems mentioned above—bringing the new and "invisible" religious expressions into the analysis and distinguishing between religious change and religious decline.

In many ways, such measures of religiosity as those designed by Glock and Stark, for example, are better designed to determine the religious views and practices *not* performed, rather than those which are. Some standard is set—usually a conservative one—as a benchmark from which departures are recorded. Those who share fewer of the traditionally stated beliefs or practice fewer of the designated rites are "less religious."

From the benchmark, however, one can move in at least three directions. The measures being used indicate only whether one has left point A, not where he has gone. One can, by these procedures, say that certain individuals are still close to point A, others have departed significantly from it. But where have they gone? One traditionally-trained and formerly practicing Presbyterian may drop out of all "religious" groups, become individual and family oriented, play golf on Sunday, and drift a long ways from the beliefs he once shared. Another joins the Unitarians or the Quakers. Still another drops from the church but joins the American Civil Liberties Union, supports the National Association for the Advancement of Colored People, gives to CARE, and develops strong faith in the possibilities of the United Nations and the long-run potentials of science as the way to solve man's problems. Measured against his Presbyterian background, each gets a "low" score. He engages in few of the established rites. If he is asked whether "miracles actually happened," "the devil actually exists," "there is life beyond death," each answers no. Measured positively, however, in terms of their ultimate concerns, they are quite different.

If we are to understand religious trends, it is not enough that these three individuals all be recorded as having moved from point A. The need is to determine positively what the beliefs and practices of various segments of a population *are*, not simply what they are not. I am suggesting that the range of religious beliefs and actions might better be allowed to emerge from research, not imposed on it, by letting individuals and groups speak for themselves. Let us approach them "blind," and inquire about the ways they view the human condition in its most fundamental aspects, and what responses they make to that viewing.

After such data have been collected from a wide range of persons, we can look for patterns and relationships. We can compare different times and places. We can chart the changes in religion through a person's life. College students, for example, are often identified as irreligious. I propose that we examine *their* ultimate concerns, the groups which form around them, and the activities which flow from them. We may discover that they are simply differently religious.

I have a friend with such a keen ear for human sounds that he can record, in a phonetic script, the flow of a language he does not understand, that he cannot name. After recording a large number of statements from persons speaking a language, he studies them for pattern. He isolates the phonemes, then the words, the phrases, the grammar, and the semantics. I have sometimes wondered what would happen if a group of informants teamed up on him to play a trick, uttering a continuous flow of sounds in which there was no pattern—

no words, in the sense of sounds with established meaning, and therefore no grammar and no possible meaning. I suspect that rather
quickly he would see what was going on; he would note that the
structural models of languages with which he was familiar furnished
him no guidance for this pattern of sounds; and he would decide that
this was either a wholly new kind of language, requiring an enlarge-
ment of the categories of structural linguistics, or was a very private
language, or else not a language at all.

Can we follow the same procedure in research on religion? Can we
ask people to speak their religions to our unknowing ears? We record
what we hear, and then look for patterns of belief and action among
our respondents, properly classifying them, of course, by age, sex, race,
region, class, educational level, society, and other sociological characteristics.

Some Experimental "Listening"

The first research task in the preparation of a
cross-cultural measure is to design a way to elicit such religious
"sounds." My efforts along this line are just beginning, hence my
suggestions are tentative and subject to extensive revision. It is my
hope that others will be encouraged to try modifications and new
approaches to the task of isolating and measuring the generic quality
of religion.

I have recently asked several groups of college respondents to answer the questions and respond to the statements noted below. They
were given a minimum of instructions. The word religion was not
used in the introduction, and in some versions of the questionnaire, did
not appear until the last page. I did not explain what I was trying to
do until after they had completed the task.

Non-doctrinal religious questions/ Seven statements were presented
to respondents who indicated degree of agreement or disagreement
"by placing a check in the appropriate column." Table 1 summarizes
the answers of two sets of respondents. The first, a pretest group, is
broadly representative of one college student body, but is not a formal
sample. The second and larger group is a carefully drawn sample
from the student bodies of ten Middle Western liberal arts colleges.

Disagreement with questions 1, 3, and 5, and agreement with the
remaining four questions were construed as representing a "religious"
response. Over two-thirds of the responses were "religious." (These
are in bold face in Table 1.)

TABLE 1 RESPONSES OF TWO SAMPLES OF COLLEGE STUDENTS TO NON-DOCTRINAL RELIGIOUS QUESTIONS

(in percent)

Sample A, N = 96 Sample B, N = 1325		Fully Agree	Partly Agree	Partly Dis- agree	Fully Dis- agree	Un- certain	Percent "Reli- gious"
1. Efforts to deal with the human situation by religious means, whatever the content of the beliefs and practices, seem to me to be misplaced, a waste of time and resources.	A B	6 5	16 22	44 37	30 33	4 4	74 70
2. Suffering, injustice, and finally death are the lot of man; but they need not be negative experiences; their significance and effects can be shaped by our beliefs.	A B	26 39	41 39	15 10	15 8	4 3	67 78
3. In face of the almost continuous conflict and violence in life, I cannot see how men are going to learn to live in mutual respect and peace with one another.	A B	13 16	25 32	29 27	23 23	11 3	52 50
4. There are many aspects of the beliefs and practices of the world's religions with which I do not agree; nevertheless, I consider them to be valuable efforts to deal with man's situation.	A B	44 46	32 37	14 10	7 4	3 3	76 83
5. Somehow, I cannot get very interested in the talk about "the basic human condition," and "man's ultimate problems."	A B	3 9	12 17	11 22	73 48	2 4	84 70
6. Man's most difficult and destructive experiences are often the source of increased understanding and powers of endurance.	A B	32 40	42 38	9 10	8 5	8 7	74 78

TABLE 1—Continued

Sample A, N = 96 Sample B, N = 1325		Fully Agree	Partly Agree	Partly Dis- agree	Fully Dis- agree	Un- certain	Percent "Reli- gious"
7. Despite the often chaotic conditions of human life, I believe that there is order and pattern to existence that someday we'll come to understand.	A B	23 27	32 35	8 17	13 12	24 9	55 62
Percent of "religious" answers, total						Sample A 69 Sample B 70	

Open-ended questions/ Four open-ended questions were asked of just the smaller sample A.

1. In your most reflective moments, when you are thinking beyond the immediate issues of the day—however important—beyond headlines, beyond the temporary, what do you consider the most important issue mankind has to face? Or, to put the question another way, what do you see as the basic, permanent question for mankind?

2. What do you believe with regard to the issue stated above? By belief, I mean not simply something you can clearly support by evidence, but statements you are ready to affirm as almost certainly true even if evidence is lacking?

3. Are you a participant in or member of some group, whether large or small, for which the "basic, permanent question" and the beliefs connected with it are the focus of attention and the most important reasons for its existence? If so, please characterize the group briefly. By what kinds of activities does the group express its concern for this most important issue noted on page one? (This question appeared on a second page, and the respondents were asked to answer the first two questions before turning the page.)

4. In what ways do you think your behavior is affected by your appraisal of the basic issue and your beliefs associated with it?

The students were strongly interested in the problem; they responded to the questions seriously; they left few of the items blank. Every respondent indicated at least one "permanent" question. Only half, however, stated that they were members of, or participated in, a group that was primarily concerned with that question (and only 15% indicated a church).

Without taking time to examine the full range of the data, let us explore some of the implications of the answers of this group of 20-year-old middle and upper class American students.

Basic, permanent question/ Although the first question asks for their view of *the* most important, permanent issue, some gave two responses. I tabulated them all, a total of 118 from the 96 respondents. The answers can be classified into eight varieties, which in turn might be consolidated, in an informal way, into four categories. (See Table 2.)

TABLE 2 IDEAS OF "THE BASIC, PERMANENT QUESTION FOR MANKIND" AS SEEN BY STUDENTS

	Separate themes N
Major social issues	
Establishing peace; insuring survival	35
Overcoming poverty; reducing population pressure	19
Interpersonal relations	
Removing barriers between people; understanding others	24
Individual creativity and happiness	
Promoting individual creativity and happiness	9
Balancing needs of individual freedom and social order	4
Using technology creatively	7
Meaning, purpose, relationship of man to God	
What is the meaning of life; what are basic purposes; where are we going	17
What is the relation of man to God; what is the soul of man	3

It is highly problematic, of course, whether a formal factor analysis of more adequate data would reveal such a clustering; but the pattern revealed here can serve the purpose in hand, namely, to indicate the basic religious issues for the respondents. They emerge from our examination of the students' ultimate concerns. If we were engaged in developing cross-cultural measures, the responses given here could be compared with those given by persons of different age, class, cultural training, and religious tradition, much as a linguist might compare the phonemes of a series of languages to see how much they overlapped and the ways in which they differed. The relationship of these themes to beliefs, knowledge, and action could be studied both among individuals and among groups.

Group relationship/ On the basis of question three, the respondents can be separated into three categories: those who indicated that they belonged to or participated in a church group; those who noted a relationship to some other group primarily concerned with "the basic, permanent question"; and those who listed no group with such a concern. (Since some students gave more than one answer, there are, again, a few more items than there are respondents.) Since some who listed no group later described group actions in which they had participated, the question is clearly an inadequate one. But I believe it can be useful to employ the answers to it, tentatively, as a sorting variable while we analyze the responses to question four.

Although no close parallel appears, it is tempting to relate these indications of the effects of beliefs to Geertz's observation that religion appears at those points where chaos threatens to overwhelm our analytic capacities, our powers of endurance, and our moral insights. Perhaps few in this group of respondents have been pushed to the limits of their powers of endurance, although it would be a mistake to minimize the accumulating weight of perpetual crisis. The three most frequently noted consequences of beliefs listed in Table 3 (responses 1,

TABLE 3 BEHAVIORAL EFFECTS OF BELIEFS, TABULATED BY GROUP IDENTIFICATION

	I Church group (N = 14)	II Other group (N = 34)	III No group (N = 48)	Total
1. Engages in various activities designed to bring about peace, improve race relations, reduce poverty	4	4	10	18
2. Attends formal group meetings	1	1	0	2
3. Affects interpersonal relations; strengthens efforts to be thoughtful of others	5	10	7	22
4. Tries to practice beliefs	0	3	0	3
5. Leads to efforts to find understanding; influences thinking	2	10	17	29
6. Increases faith and hope	0	1	3	4
7. Miscellaneous effects	2	7	7	16
8. Little or no effect	0	1	6	7
9. No answer	1	1	3	5

3, and 5), however, seem clearly to relate to efforts to struggle with the limits of our analytic powers and moral insights.

Non-doctrinal religious statements by groups/ Somewhat clearer differences among the students, sorted into three categories by their answers to the third question, appear in their responses to the statements given in Table 1. We have noted that for the whole group, 69 per cent of the responses are "religious," but there are some interesting differences between those who do and do not indicate group participation (Table 4).

TABLE 4 RESPONSES TO NON-DOCTRINAL RELIGIOUS QUESTIONS, BY GROUP IDENTIFICATION

Statements	I Church group (N = 14)		II Other group (N = 34)		III No group (N = 48)		Total (N = 96)	
	n	%	n	%	n	%	n	%
1	14	(100)	27	(80)	30	(63)	71	(74)
2	12	(86)	24	(71)	27	(57)	63	(66)
3	10	(70)	16	(47)	24	(50)	50	(52)
4	12	(86)	28	(82)	33	(69)	73	(76)
5	10	(70)	25	(74)	45	(94)	80	(83)
6	10	(70)	28	(82)	36	(75)	74	(77)
7	10	(70)	23	(68)	20	(41)	53	(55)
Total	78	(80)	171	(72)	215	(64)	464	(69)
Total religious answers possible	98	(100)	238	(100)	336	(100)	672	(100)

Religious responses predominate in all three groups, but there is an exact progression from Group III (64 per cent) to Group II (72 per cent) to Group I (80 per cent), and the differences are significant ($X^2 = 9.79$, p < .01). It is interesting that the most religious response is made to question five, and that the "no group" category is significantly *more* religious on this issue than are the other two ($X^2 = 7.82$, p = .02). Although they mention no church, indeed no group of any kind as important to their interest in the "basic, permanent question" of mankind, they indicate very strongly an interest in man's ultimate problems. There are other differences among the three categories, some of them statistically significant, but the data are not good enough to deserve further analysis. I believe that they do indicate, however, the presence of many "invisible" religious beliefs and actions that we must learn how to measure.

Validity and Utility

The results of this small study ought to be treated lightly, since they are reported in this preliminary form only to illustrate problems of measurement. The approach used is patterned, in an analogous sense, more after structural linguistics than more usual forms of sociological study of institutions. I believe that this may yield measurements of greater validity, through space and time, than more traditional approaches. Validity, of course, means that one is measuring what he thinks he is measuring; or, in another sense, is measuring something that will give him predictive power. I am expressing it as my judgment that if I had a choice between the following two bodies of knowledge, I would select the latter:

A. Knowledge of the range of beliefs in a population with reference to the traditional or institutionalized or established religions, with knowledge of memberships, participation in rites and other activities, and extent of individuals' formation about these religions, with knowledge of changes in these items through time and comparative information about other such cultural systems.

B. Knowledge of the range of perceptions concerning man's most fundamental problems, the beliefs related to those perceptions, the groups that form with reference to them, and the activities that flow from the perceptions, beliefs, and groups, with knowledge of changes in these items through time and comparative information described in terms of structural categories.

There is no need, of course, to choose between these bodies of information. I am simply suggesting that we have been pursuing the relatively less valuable part. Or perhaps it is enough to say that we have been giving most of our attention to one approach and need better balance. We shall move more rapidly toward a comparative science of religion when we move beyond the study of unique cultural traditions and begin to explore structural categories.

Let us suppose that the four themes emerging from the questionnaires I have reported on (those referring to the "basic, permanent question for mankind") proved to be inclusive and universal categories. (This is unlikely to be the case; but I would guess that the list would not be long and that there would be common elements in many societies.) We could then search for the patterns in ways analogous to the work of structural linguists who describe the shared and variant use of the sixty phonemes they have found to be the outside limit for a language. We could ask: In what various combinations do we find concern for (1) major social issues, (2) interpersonal relations, (3) individual creativity and development, and (4) questions of meaning, purpose, and relationship of man to God? How are these blended in the beliefs of adolescents of a society, compared with those of the middle aged, or the old? How do middle class persons in one country view these matters as compared with those in another? Are the various combinations associated with different group structures?

All of this is to say that in religious studies we are still at the "natural history" level of research, trying to describe all the wonderful beasts of the jungle. Only by isolating analytic categories of religious facts that permit comparisons and contrasts, despite the variations in cultural expressions of those categories, can we move from basically descriptive natural history to analytic natural science. I think we shall discover, for example, that knowledge of the distribution of a belief in some fundamental orderliness to the universe, as a religious category, is a more important datum for a science of religion, more predictive of behavior, than knowledge of the several forms by which that belief can be expressed. Or, knowledge of the distribution of the range of agreement with the statement "Man's most difficult and destructive experiences are often the source of increased understanding and powers of endurance" may prove to be of greater value than knowledge of the range of agreement with the more culture bound statement, "All things work together for good for them that love the Lord."

6

Robert R. Monaghan[*]

*Three Faces of
the True Believer:
Motivations for Attending
a Fundamentalist Church*

Why does a person attend church? What are his needs or motives? What aspirations and gratifications does he associate with church membership? Are such functions the same for all persons, or are there characteristic differences among individuals or types of individuals? This study proposes to answer some of these questions in relation to individuals within a theologically conservative church—an institution which might, by its very insistence on a clear-cut, unambiguous, "fundamental" religion, be expected not only to elicit fairly well-defined attitudes, but also to satisfy relatively strong needs in its members.

Orientation

Representatives of a regional council of churches were asked to identify a theologically conservative church in the area for the purposes of this study. The council officials described the selected

From Robert R. Monaghan, "Three Faces of the True Believer," *Journal for the Scientific Study of Religion,* **6** (Fall 1967), 236–245, reprinted by permission of the author and publisher. Robert R. Monaghan is in the Department of Speech at Ohio State University.

* Special appreciation is expressed for the help and criticism provided by Mr. Thomas Danbury of Foote, Cone and Belding in New York, by Professor Malcolm MacLean, Jr., of the University of Iowa, and by Professor Iwao Ishino of the Sociology and Anthropology Department at Michigan State University.

church as being large, active, significant in the community, and
as having strong fundamentalist or supernatural leanings.
"Fundamentalism" was defined by two criteria: adherence to an
anthropomorphic concept of God and to a literal interpretation
of the Bible. All persons interviewed held both concepts.

The minister of the church was born into a laboring class,
fundamentalist home in Georgia forty years ago, and at eighteen
married a local girl. He has a long history of church activities,
largely due to the influence of his mother. Neither he nor the
church is formally affiliated with any denomination or convention,
although an informal relationship exists with the Southern
Baptist Church. He has held his present position for fourteen
years.

The church is located at the outer edge of a midwestern industrial
metropolis. The interior is spacious, light, and full of color, with
stained windows and an enormous picture of Christ on the wall
behind the altar. The basic design of the four-year-old building
incorporates the traditional steeple style with the modern slanted
roof architecture. The large sanctuary easily accommodates the
900 or more regular worshippers who meet each Sunday for
the main service.

The minister (perhaps cautiously) estimated that 45 to 50 per
cent of his congregation was from small southern communities.
Most of the persons interviewed considered themselves
Southerners, in some way identified with small community living
below the Mason-Dixon line, or at least expressed favorable feelings
toward the South. Apparently, there are no Negro members of
the church.

The church originated in 1934 when a small group of persons
began worshipping together without a regular church edifice.
Soon the small congregation arranged to meet in a local community
hall, and still later, in one of the buildings of a nearby elementary
school.

The church is located approximately three city blocks from the
community school, which was annexed to the city school system
two years previous to this study at the time the community itself
was annexed. One of the local elementary school teachers
estimated that about half of her pupils were in some way affiliated
with the church. The teachers report that parents still tend to
consider the school as "their" school, rather than as part of
the city.

The surrounding community might be described as somewhat
ethnocentric. An experienced teacher from the local school, who
had taught in other systems and other states, described the
community as "tight-knit." Other teachers supported this observation. An informal estimate of socioeconomic status (based
on education, estimated income, and observation of general living
conditions) might place the members of this church in the
"lower-than-middle" class. None of the respondents had gone

beyond high school. One-half were not high school graduates. Some had left school before high school.

In the pulpit the minister has the capacity for great exuberance, dynamism, and activity, and there are frequent audible responses from the congregation during his sermons. Members punctuate his points in partial unison with "hallelujah," "amen," "yes, suh," *etc.* Members of the congregation sing in full and enthusiastic participation.

There is an "altar call" or "invitation" following each formal service, during which the minister remains on the platform, although he may step forward from the pulpit. A response to the "call" may be indicated with nothing more than a quickly raised hand while all persons are supposed to be in an attitude of prayer.

During the early part of the regular Sunday morning service, the minister builds rapport with the congregation by calling for any visitor to stand—in the midst of the entire congregation—and identify himself. He welcomes each visitor individually with a friendly comment. There is also a five-minute hand-shaking ceremony early in the service. The minister steps down from the platform for this ritual, while all members of the congregation shake hands and greet each other. The church buys time for a weekly Sunday morning radio broadcast on a local radio station.

In addition to regular services, there are such individually planned events as concerts, evangelistic meetings, family suppers, and Sunday school class parties. There is activity in the large church building every evening of the week.

Five trustees and five deacons constitute the official decision-making board of the church. The minister reports that "routine" matters, such as salaries (including his own), are determined in the semi-private board meetings because ". . . the board members know what can and cannot be done." "Major" matters, such as the choice of color when painting the sanctuary, are presented to the congregation for vote, after being discussed by the board. When the board presents a matter to the congregation, it is likely to be, in the minister's words, "for their approval." Congregational voting is by acclamation, and it is necessary for a disapproving voter to rise before the entire congregation and state the reasons for his objection. Although the minister is an ex officio member of the board, he seems to have a vote in case of a tie, and has a great deal of personal influence generally. He decides, for example, who is qualified and who is not qualified to serve on the board.

Although the church is not officially affiliated with other organizations, it does support some foreign missions. However, it is clearly a locally autonomous system.

Method

After the church was tentatively selected, the minister agreed to endorse the interviewer and to recommend him to members of his congregation. In an extended interview the minister supplied information about the organization of the church, details of the belief structure, and his perceptions of members' motives in attending. He also, in effect, became the first respondent, answering questions of attitude regarding the church, the minister, explanations of morality, free vs. limited interpretations of the Bible, the church as a social change organization, definitions of God, self-concepts, feelings about authority, enjoyment during church services, leisure time use patterns, mass media use, reading habits, and other topics. All respondents were questioned according to a memorized interview guide. The usual demographic information was also obtained.

Respondents were selected from church records by a stratified-quota system that provided equal proportions of males and females, of two age groups (20–39 and 40–65), and of three categories of participation (officers, regular attenders, and non-attenders). This provided $2 \times 2 \times 3 = 12$ combinations.

Focused interviews (Merton 1956) of at least one hour were conducted with one set of twelve respondents. From the tape recordings of these interviews statements were developed which provided a fifty-six item Q-sort. These were administered to the minister and twenty-six other persons matching the sample design. Respondents were asked to sort the statements along an 11-point scale (with a fixed near-normal distribution), according to how well the items described their own feelings about the church. Comments about the items were then invited.

These data were then analyzed by the Q-method (Stephenson 1953). The rank scores for each respondent were correlated with the rankings of every other by the Pearson product-moment formula. The intercorrelation matrix[1] was then factored using a principal axis factor analytic program with varimax rotation. This procedure generates a number of multi-factor solutions. The solution containing the largest number of significant factors accounting for the greatest amount of variance constituted the selection criteria. For each factor the estimated factor array was computed. That is, the responses for each subject were assigned weights proportional to his correlation with the factor. The more closely a respondent's scores resembled the factor, the more weight was given to his rank order in computing the array for that factor. The totals of all such weights for every person on a factor were then converted to standard Z-scores. The full rank-order of items emerging in this way, then, is called a factor array. Since an array represents a systematic composite, or "typical" order, from those subjects having responses which identified them on a factor, the array for that factor represents the expressions of a hypothetical person.

Results

Three such factors emerged, as reported in Table 1. Each factor represents a specific and distinct array, representing a hypothetical type of person who may be described by the items most weighted on that factor. The items suggest these labels for the three types: the *authority-seeker*, the *comfort-seeker*, and the *social participator*.

The Authority-Seeker/ The first factor represents the kind of person who seeks to submit himself to authority. It does not imply a loss of self-direction simply by default, but rather, a strong and consistent desire for a submissive relation toward authority. This orientation is so basic that its implications are seen to touch the central belief system, the training of children, the interpretation of the Bible. The authority-seeker wants his authority boldly imposed, even to include criticism. See the wording of the first item in Table 1—a statement which distinguishes the authority-seeker most sharply from the other types, particularly from the comfort-seeker.

The authority-seekers do not want the minister to be *more* outspoken. Apparently he is outspoken enough for them.

This type of person likes the minister because he has authority. He prefers to depend upon the authority of the minister for an interpretation of the Bible, rather than interpret it for himself. He is not eager to open up religious questions for discussion. (Some of these respondents were reluctant to set appointments for an interview, and were very difficult to interview.) He prefers a one-way, direct line of communication from the pulpit. During the depth interviews each respondent was given a hypothetical and contrived case of conflict between his own personal interpretation of the Bible and the minister's, a kind of verbal forced-choice. Typically, as the authority-seeker was painted into a corner in this way, the most satisfactory solution for him seemed to be something like:

> Well, there is only *one correct* meaning of the Bible: God's Word. The minister is educated, and of course he knows more about these things than I do.

Frequent comments indicated that the minister provides meaning for church members where none existed before. Throughout all the interviews his authority regarding such matters was never questioned, except by the interviewer.

As might be expected, a person whose predominant orientation toward the church is authority-based is also authoritarian in non-theological matters, such as his domestic and personal affairs, particularly the rearing of children. See the third item of Table 1. Some authority-seekers related this statement to patriotism. Others accepted the statement because they wanted children to learn to get along socially through church training.

The authority-seeker associates church attendance with harmony in the home. One young married person in this type said, "A family that goes to a Bible church, and lives like the first family—Adam and Eve—will not be split." Another said that family church attendance helped family members to "think alike" and made them "more understanding." Some mentioned the slogan: "The family that prays together, stays together." One respondent said he could tell from working in a gas station that church-going families were happier.

This type of church-goer also considers the church as the best possible place for a young person to meet friends, and specifically, to meet a future mate. He considers others in the church—the minister, the deacons, and other members—as friendly and gregarious, and feels these persons are genuinely interested in him.

The church services provide him with an inner peace that contrasts with personal troubles. He endorses the following statement even slightly more than the comfort-seeker:

I feel peaceful being in the church building during a service.
Whatever troubles I might have, they seem to slip away while I am there.

One woman commented that her husband had a terrible temper, and both he and the children were very demanding. The church service provided her with one hour during which she could escape them and the rest of her usual world. She said the church service ". . . helps me forget a lot of my troubles. I'm calmer. I don't worry too much. It's about the only time I get to relax."

Nationalism is another recurring theme for the authority-seeker. Although it would be difficult to discern which cause serves which, there is little separation between church and state in his context. Again, submission and obedience to authority seem to characterize this type:

This church helps mold persons into the kind of God-fearing people who are the backbone of our country.

One woman who placed this item on the extremely favorable end of the distribution explained, "The best people in the country have faith in God, and the church tells people to obey God."

This type of person strongly rejects a statement emphasizing the reality and fear of Hell. The authority-seekers seem to somehow avoid this concern, while both of the other types, particularly the comfort-seeker, most clearly express worry and fear.

The authority-seeker is apparently nonchalant about death. While both of the other types clearly indicate that death and damnation are major concerns, the authority-seeker does not. This was further substantiated by the open-ended interviews. One said:

> I am not scared of death. If she happens tomorrow, or next week, or next year, or in the next five minutes, I don't care. I'm not scared of it. Too many people are, and that's the damn trouble. They're scared of it.

The Comfort-Seeker/ In sharp contrast is the comfort-seeker, who expresses satisfaction that the church provides the way to eternal life, the attainment of which he believes is everyone's primary goal. He seeks peace of mind. His orientation appears consistent with the need for peace, identified as a strong factor by Webb (1965). Persons represented on this second factor were most inclined to assume that everyone is justifiably afraid of death, particularly those who have no church-affiliation "insurance" against the frightening possibility of going to Hell. Religion, which they see as being the simple and readily available way to Heaven, provides them with reassurance. The two highest factor items for the comfort-seeker reflect this strong orientation.

The second statement, suggesting fears of Hell, may help explain why the comfort-seeker does not question the sincerity of those who respond to "altar call" at the end of the service. He is persuaded that other members really believe in the rules and practices of the church. He is fully convinced that persons who walk forward to "accept Christ" at the end of the service are sincere in their actions. This may be somewhat reminiscent of Allport's (1951) notion of the extrinsic-oriented member. If so, the notion has support here, in addition to the supporting evidence and elaboration provided by Brown (1964).

The comfort-seeker apparently feels a strong need to protect his belief. He believes that his own particular church is on the right track and offers insurance against the persuasions of any new belief to which he might be exposed. He strongly supports the concept that the church helps him know the Bible so he can protect himself from others who may try to persuade him toward some other belief. He wants those around him to hold the same beliefs he does. Thus while the two other types reject the idea of religious indoctrination as a prerequisite to church membership the comfort-seeker believes that all persons should go through the same training and study of the Scriptures in order to become members.

He also thinks that the church is a good place for young people to meet friends and begin courtship, although he expresses this view less strongly than the authority-seeker.

Stronger than that of the other types is the comfort-seeker's expressed desire for intimate, personal relationships. He would prefer the church to be smaller, more intimate, so he could see more familiar faces. Although he does not consider the church hostile, neither does he find it as friendly as he would like. He does *not* endorse the statement that both the authority-seeker and the participator agree to: "The minister, the deacons, and just about everyone in this church is friendly to me . . ."

Although the comfort-seeker's specific motivation to belong to the church is important to him, his interest in the church as a whole is more limited, less varied than that of the others. He embraces the church less fully than they do. He is less inclined to feel that church attendance is important or beneficial to family relations than the other two types. He does not feel that his life would become dull or less interesting if he failed to participate in church activities. He may feel that the church is letting him down. It is at least reasonable to infer that he seeks greater satisfaction from the church than he is now getting. While his major orientation seems to be characterized by a need for peace of mind he only mildly accepts the statement about feeling peaceful in the church building during a service.

This further suggests that he is in search of long-range or permanent security rather than temporary reduction of anxiety. The church service itself does not appear to be highly important to him. He does not reject the notion that a person can be "saved" outside the church, while both of the other types clearly agree that church membership, or attendance, is essential for a person to "accept Christ."

It is not surprising that a person apparently in search of tranquility is not as receptive to blunt and direct criticism as are those in the other two groups. The authority-seeker is most extreme in his receptiveness to criticism from the pulpit, and the participator very clearly approves of such criticism. This does not fit the pattern or scheme of things for the comfort-seeker, however, whose predominant desires are for peace. A strong and consistent preference for entertainment, particularly music, may be seen as compatible with this orientation.

This type of person seeks his own kind of peace and tranquility in the church, and approves of the church services and activities as long as they provide for this need. In some areas he feels the church is failing, or at least is not essential. It is possible that some of the solace he seeks may be found elsewhere, outside the church. However, his strongest need—insurance against damnation—is still the specialty of the church, and is not readily available from any other source. Consequently, he has little choice. In order to get his first-class ticket to Heaven, he must listen to criticism, and must tolerate the other features of the church which do not appeal to him. But this does not mean that he must then support the church in general, or embrace the entire system. It is more likely that he takes what he needs and avoids the rest as best he can.

The Social Participator/ This type of person likes the church for "its own sake," finding satisfaction in participation as an end in itself. The person in search of peace of mind finds his satisfaction in the comfort and efficacy of religious teachings which show him the way to Heaven. The person in search of authority finds his in the clarity and decisiveness with which the church lays down guidelines for his religious, social and political attitudes and actions. The participator, however, enjoys the church intrinsically. His experiences in the church rest upon a wider base than those of the other two types. Perhaps he is best portrayed by the breadth of his relationships with the church.

The participator feels at home in the church. There is something friendly and predictable about its people. He feels a strong personal rapport with the minister and has great trust in him. See, in Table 1, his two highest ranking statements. The second statement suggests resistance to change as well as loyalty to the church. He likes conformity for others and he likes to conform himself. He does not feel, however, that new members should be required to undergo indoctrination of any kind.

This type of person enjoys the drama of the church. He likes a lively, dynamic sermon. He enjoys the minister because "His voice is powerful, his gestures are dramatic, and he delivers a fast-paced message." He particularly enjoys such special ceremonies as Baptism and The Lord's Supper. He considers these very impressive, moving and vivid. He prefers hearing the Bible interpreted orally to reading it himself.

The participator sees himself as a leader, and feels that the church provides him with an opportunity to use his talents through participation in Sunday School teaching, visitation, and other activities. He also feels it is his religious obligation to serve the church. One of his high ranking statements expresses the view that God wants him to serve in the church. Another asserts the honor of being an officer. He also sanctions the notion that an established member may lead others who have been Christians for a shorter time, those who may seek help.

The participator likes a sense of involvement with others. He very strongly rejects the idea that one should keep his religious beliefs to himself, preferring instead discussion of religious issues with others. This may represent a desire for social, rather than strictly intellectual or theological, interaction, since the participator expresses a desire for activities involving him in human relationships, but indicates that he

TABLE 1 ITEMS MOST DISCRIMINATING THREE TYPES

	Authority-Seeker	Z Scores Comfort-Seeker	Social Participator
Items most accepted and rejected by authority-seeker			
I like the minister because he is not afraid to criticize the congregation. He is not afraid to lay it on the line and tell you what you should and should not do.	2.24	.05	1.21
I like the minister because he has a wonderful talent for interpreting the Bible. He can make the Bible much clearer for me, much better than I can by reading it alone.	1.98	.57	1.02
I like the training this church gives to children because they, more than anyone, need to learn God's word.	1.69	.59	.17
I feel peaceful being in the church building during a service. Whatever troubles I might have, they seem to slip away while I am there.	1.57	.12	1.22
This church helps mold persons into the kind of God-fearing people who are the backbone of our country.	1.32	1.22	.95
By attending Sunday School classes at this church, children gain the experience of playing and working in a group.	1.25	.43	−.58
The minister, the deacons, and just about everyone in this church is friendly to me. They smile, say hello, shake my hand, and show a genuine interest in me.	1.23	.08	1.06
I think a family is much more likely to live in peace if they attend this church together.	1.17	−.33	1.01
Young people who attend this church can meet friends. I think it is the best place to take a date, and the best place to find your future mate.	1.10	.96	.74
I like the minister because he has authority. When he takes over, things will be done.	.81	.26	.09
I think this church is bound by rules and practices that nobody really believes in.	−1.88	−1.64	−1.40
This church permits too many of its members to behave in a way that dishonors God. I am in favor of asking these people to leave the church if they will not change.	−1.77	−1.13	−1.51
The minister needs to be more outspoken in his sermons. Too often he just straddles the fence when he should be scolding the congregation.	−1.61	−1.22	−.65

TABLE 1—Continued

	Authority-Seeker	Z Scores Comfort-Seeker	Social Participator
The church helps me to recognize those people who try to distract a Christian from practicing God's word. Such people are sinful and should be punished.	−1.55	−.25	−.80
This church should be more friendly. There are too many cliques, and too many insincere people.	−1.44	−.12	−1.11
I think the importance of this church is over-rated. I feel that some people can accept Christ without joining, or attending the church. They might be able to do as much for Him outside the church as inside it.	−1.19	−.35	−1.15

Items most accepted and rejected by comfort-seeker

	Authority-Seeker	Z Scores Comfort-Seeker	Social Participator
When a person is ill, or when he approaches the end of his life, I think he gets a lot of comfort from his religious beliefs and his friends at this church.	.70	1.91	.86
To me Hell is real and its tortures are awaiting those who ignore God's commandments. The church helps me avoid this fate.	−1.11	1.71	1.51
The only thing our church needs is the Bible. Its doctrines are simple and definite and any person can understand them.	−.33	1.63	.76
I would prefer this church to be smaller, more intimate, so you could know everybody.	−.44	1.46	−.77
Congregational singing is a wonderful part of the services.	.30	1.45	−.38
This church helps me to know the Bible so that I can protect myself from anyone who tries to persuade me to accept their beliefs.	−.48	1.23	1.03
I appreciate the special musical numbers at the services.	.43	1.20	−.21
I like to sit quietly before each service and listen to the organ.	.76	.96	−.38
If a man believes what most of the members of this church believe, he cannot be far from wrong.	.42	.90	−.16
I think some people in this church who walk forward to accept Christ at the end of the service are just showing off.	−1.38	−2.20	−1.40
The minister is often too emotional. I prefer a more calm and quiet service.	−1.03	−1.92	−1.56
Sometimes I think this church has too much flashy entertainment at its services.	−1.28	−1.57	−1.03

TABLE 1—Continued

	Authority-Seeker	Z Scores Comfort-Seeker	Social Participator
Many of my friends do not go to this church and I sometimes feel uncomfortable with them. It is not that I am embarrassed at being a church-goer, but I somehow feel different.	−.70	−1.57	−.03
I am a Christian, and I want to do the right thing, but I sometimes think this church puts too many restrictions on members.	−.58	−1.33	−1.12
It does me good to get out of the house and participate in activities of this church. My life would be rather uninteresting and dull without it.	−.27	−1.12	.29
By being close to other members during the worship service, I feel much closer to God.	−.74	−1.00	−.34
By striving to be a good member of this church yourself, you are able to lead other people who have been Christians for a shorter time. They often turn to you for help.	.05	−.52	.24
I know that God wants me to serve Him in this church. If I neglected my duties, I could never feel comfortable.	−.08	−.51	1.15

Items most accepted and rejected by social participator

	Authority-Seeker	Z Scores Comfort-Seeker	Social Participator
I feel free to talk to the minister in private and receive his guidance at any time. It is nice to know there is someone with whom you can discuss confidential matters.	1.37	−.41	1.65
I feel very much at home in this church. It continues to serve God and His people in the sure, unchanging way.	.12	−.01	1.56
In his sermons and Bible studies the pastor shares with us his wonderful knowledge of the scriptures and theology. I really want to know more about these things.	1.39	1.42	1.51
The minister does an excellent job of keeping my attention during the sermon. His voice is powerful, his gestures are dramatic, and he delivers a fast-paced message.	.58	.86	1.34
This church provides an opportunity to use whatever talents we might have for a good cause. There is usually a need for more people to participate in Sunday School teaching, visitation, or some other activity.	.51	.51	1.15

TABLE 1—Continued

	Authority-Seeker	Z Scores Comfort-Seeker	Social Participator
I know that God wants me to serve Him in this church. If I neglected my duties, I could never feel comfortable.	−.08	−.51	1.15
I particularly enjoy the church's special services. The ceremony of Baptism, and the observance of the Lord's Supper, are very impressive, moving, and vivid.	.28	.34	1.08
If I were to be an officer in this church, I would consider it one of the highest honors I could receive.	−.02	−.03	.79
I prefer to keep my religious beliefs to myself rather than to discuss them with others in this church. Discussion often ends up in arguments, and it is senseless.	.05	−1.22	−1.75
It seems to me the more you attend this church the more other members try to put pressure on you.	−.86	−.67	−1.46
This church makes it difficult to have my own individual interpretations of the Bible. After all, we all see things differently and no single interpretation is "true," so we should respect each other's beliefs.	−.92	−1.38	−1.39
There is too much conformity in this church. I try to rely on my own judgment, instead of being influenced by what others think. What might be wrong for me, might not be wrong for someone else.	−.66	−.84	−1.39
All the members of this church should go through the same training and study of the Scriptures in order to become members.	−.87	.80	−1.16
Frankly, I sometimes wish our minister would discuss religious matters more deeply. I think the doctrines of this church are too simple to be meaningful.	−.58	−.51	−1.07

does not want the minister to discuss religious matters more deeply. This is similar to Brown's (1966) religious belief factor which strongly relates to social variables within a religious context. The social participation factor suggests more "social" than "religious" emphasis.

Most of these participators have limited their social relationships entirely to persons within the church. In some cases they systematically and deliberately avoid social contacts outside the church. To the extent that this is the case, it is assumed that social contacts within the church would become all the more meaningful and important. One person highly represented on this factor works at his job in close, intimate contact with a small crew. All the others on the crew (non-members of his church) eat lunch together while he goes off by himself each day and eats alone "because they are not Christians." Social relations *within* the church are most important for the participator. More strongly than the other two types, he supports the statement:

> It does me good to get out of the house and participate in activities of this church. My life would be rather uninteresting and dull without it.

Other statements suggest that this church member type would like to participate even more than he does.

NOTE ——————————————————————————

1. This has been deposited with the American Documentation Institute. Order Document 9579 from the Chief, photoduplication service, Library of Congress, Washington 25, D.C., Auxiliary Publications Project, remitting $1.25 for microfilm (35 mm) or $1.25 for photocopies.

QUESTIONS FOR DISCUSSION

1. There are many possible objections to Yinger's proposal for a broadened definition of religion. How do you react to it?

2. If one were studying attendance at worship among Roman Catholics, one might ask, "Did you go to mass last Sunday?" How would you revise this question for use in Springdale? How would you revise it again in order to use it on a group of people that included Catholics, Protestants, and Jews?

3. Examine Yinger's four open-ended questions carefully. Do you think they would mean the same thing to people with a sixth-grade education that they meant to Yinger's college students? If you think they would not, how would you reword them so that they would?

4. Monaghan used the method of factor analysis to discover his three religious orientations. Yet factor analysis cannot provide names for the factors it reveals. The naming process, which is really an exercise in abstraction or concept-formation, is dependent on the judgment of the investigator. Look over the three parts of Table 1 in Monaghan's article and make your own judgment as to whether Monaghan has given the best names he could to his factors. As a guide to doing this, look at the first five items under each factor and ask whether the factor name accurately captures the content of all the items.

ADDITIONAL READING

Glock, Charles Y., and Rodney Stark. "On the Study of Religious Commitment," Chapter 5 in *Religion and Society in Tension*. Chicago: Rand McNally, 1965. The authors propose that religious commitment be conceived of as multidimensional. They propose five such dimensions, drawn largely from the Judeo-Christian tradition.

Glock, Charles Y., et al. *To Comfort and To Challenge*. Berkeley and Los Angeles: University of California Press, 1967. Using survey data the authors present evidence that the search for comfort and consolation is one of the major motivations for church attendance in contemporary American society.

Lenski, Gerhard. *The Religious Factor*. Garden City, N.Y.: Doubleday, 1961. A classic survey of the relation of religious involvement to a variety of secular beliefs and behaviors. Lenski uses several different measures of religiosity, including two measures of religious content based on the common denominator method.

Luckmann, Thomas. *The Invisible Religion*. New York: Macmillan, 1967. Luckmann argues that the basically religious concerns of people in modern industrial society are not expressed in conventional institutionalized ways. Modern religion is therefore "invisible" in a way that traditional religion was not.

Chapter III

---◆►►---

Dimensions
of Religious
Differences

There has never been religious uniformity in the United States. Well before the American Revolution the colonies were a veritable hodgepodge of independent denominations and diverse religious outlooks. Moreover, as the country has grown, religious diversity has increased. Today Americans have a far wider range of religious orientations to confront than their grandfathers had. And this range is not limited to the Jewish or Christian traditions. Oriental religions enjoy a new burst of popularity, and millions of Americans have an active interest in such parareligious subjects as astrology, extrasensory perception, the occult, and the otherworldly significance of Unidentified Flying Objects.

It is true, of course, that the great majority of Americans are tied in one way or another to religious bodies in the Christian traditions. And it is also true that most Christians belong to one of a relatively small number of denominational families. Yet there is great diversity of belief and practice within this Christian mainstream. It is possible, however, to make sense of much of the diversity in American Christianity if we have a clear understanding of the single most influential religious movement of modern times. This movement has been variously referred to as liberalism, modernism, or the quest for religious relevance in the modern world, but the name we give the movement is not so important as correctly identifying its major orientations. At the risk of considerable oversimplification, these orientations can be defined in terms of two distinct but complementary themes. First, Christian liberalism has progressively de-emphasized the *otherworldly* or *supernatural* aspects of the Christian faith. This means that personal salvation is no longer the chief goal of Christian activity or the chief motivation for being a Christian.

Secondly, liberalism has enormously upgraded the significance of this *present world* and the *natural dignity* of man. To the liberal, the major aim of Christian activity is to honor man's dignity by making it possible for everyone to be fully human. Liberalism strives to liberate men from the physical and mental suffering and oppression of this world.

The liberal movement obviously represents an orientational shift of major proportions, a shift fully as radical as the shift brought about by the Protestant Reformation of the sixteenth century. But it has provoked no confrontation or rupture quite as dramatic as the break that Luther and Calvin made with the Catholic Church. Liberalism has no single founder. It is a flexible rather than a creedal or dogmatic tradition. It has created very few new denominations, but it has profoundly influenced the religious outlook of many existing denominations. It has brought a new unity of outlook among great numbers of clergy and laymen in denominations of quite diverse historical backgrounds. In fact, it has made many churchmen feel more at home with liberals in other denominations than with traditionalists in their own.

The liberal movement has made uneven headway. In principle, it reigns supreme in the Unitarian-Universalist Church, but some denominations have scarcely been touched by it. Its greatest impact has been in Protestant denominations and congregations that have a high proportion of well-educated clergy and laity. It is stronger among Congregationalists than it is among Baptists, and it has made greater headway in suburban parishes in the Northeast than in rural churches of the South. But it has met with considerable resistance. Indeed, a great many of the controversies that have taken place in American religion over the past few decades have been inspired by the liberal movement or by reactions against it. The best known of these reactions is Protestant fundamentalism. The article by C. C. Goen (Selection 7) traces the history of this bitter controversy between liberals and fundamentalists and makes it clear that fundamentalists saw in liberalism a threat to the very foundations of historic Christianity. Fundamentalists, or conservatives, as many now style themselves, have responded by laying stress on those traditional doctrines that they feel liberals deny. Among these doctrines are the depravity of man, the atonement of Christ, and the inerrancy of the scriptures. So widespread has this controversy become that many observers consider the liberal-conservative distinction to be the single most important religious difference within contemporary Christianity.

Liberalism made little headway in the Catholic Church until very recently. In fact, the Catholic Church had managed to insulate itself rather effectively from most new intellectual currents since

the Council of Trent in the sixteenth century. But now the Second
Vatican Council has signaled a change in all that. The liberal
spirit of many of the council documents has inspired a strong
movement for basic reform in the church. But as Selection 8 by
Douglas Roche shows, much Catholic liberal sentiment takes the form
of challenging the way authority is exercised in the church. For
centuries most important church decisions have been made by
ecclesiastical authorities; the laity, like private soldiers in a vast
army, have rarely been consulted on anything. They have been told
what to believe and how to behave. Now the movement for the
enfranchisement of the Catholic laity is well under way. Laymen are
questioning the arbitrary exercise of ecclesiastical authority and
demanding the right to participate in the shaping of a new church.
They and their clerical allies are reopening questions that have
long been regarded as settled. But they are not likely to win an
early victory. Although the bishops were responsible for the liberal
tone of the Vatican Council documents, and they have recently
asserted their own right to share in the authority of the Pope and his
administration, many of them tend to be conservative on other basic
issues, including the right of the laity to a meaningful voice in
church affairs. Moreover, many laymen are not in full sympathy
with the liberal spirit. An organized Catholic conservatism has come
into existence in the last few years. Like Protestantism, American
Catholicism is rapidly dividing into liberal and conservative
camps. It is much too early to predict what the outcome of the
liberal movement within the church will be, but it seems destined
to play an increasingly influential role in church affairs, and it seems
certain that many Catholics will no longer accept without question
the teachings and directives of their ecclesiastical superiors.

No one is surprised that people of widely differing religious backgrounds should disagree with one another on religious matters.
But why do people who share a common heritage so often disagree
with one another? Some of their disagreement reflects the simple
fact that the doctrine or scripture of their tradition does not provide
answers to all religious questions. On some issues, for example,
the Bible has nothing to say, and on others its language is vague.
But experience has shown that people are often unable to agree on
the meaning of texts that seem perfectly clear by the standards of
ordinary discourse. As the research by Sanford M. Dornbusch and his
associates shows (Selection 9), people tend to explain away the
"plain sense" of scripture when that plain sense contradicts other
values to which they subscribe. Dornbusch selected simple,
concretely worded Bible passages that contradicted American
middle-class values and found that college students who considered
themselves to be religious tended to agree with these passages but

to interpret them metaphorically, that is, to allege that the words do not really mean what they appear to mean. They tried to make the passages conform to American values. This research helps us understand how serious-minded people can accept the elements of a religious tradition and yet interpret them quite differently. It also suggests that people's understanding of their religion is *always* based on an interpretation, on a criterion, so to speak, by which the various elements of the religious heritage are related to one another, assigned relative importance, and given meaning. Religious conflicts are generally conflicts over interpretations. How systems of religious interpretation come into being and change over time is a major theoretical problem in the sociology of religion.

7

C. C. Goen

Fundamentalism in America

Fundamentalism is sometimes erroneously identified, especially in the Southwest, with the anti-convention agitations of a schismatic group of Baptists. This has caused some to lose sight of the larger aspects of the Fundamentalist-Modernist controversy in American Christendom. In an effort to broaden the perspective, this article presents a survey of Fundamentalism in terms of the developments which provoked it, the course of the controversy, and the issues involved. It is no more than a simple summary description of the movement as viewed in the total context of American Christianity.[1]

Liberal Theology and the Social Gospel

Between 1865 and 1914 the United States became the most highly industrialized nation in the world. This period also brought vast numbers of Europeans, who quickly found their places in the expanding economy. Industrialization and immigration made for a phenomenal rise in the population of American cities, with all the social problems which inevitably attend such a development. Not the least of these was the relation of the capitalist to his workers, a problem which was aggravated by the unscrupulous methods of many businessmen to amass more and more wealth. Free in this period from governmental restraint, protected by high tariffs, and unhampered by any powerful labor organization, many of the industrial magnates grew rapacious in the extreme. Social and economic abuses were rife.

Soon the more sensitive churchmen began to criticize this turn of

Adapted by the author from C. C. Goen, "Fundamentalism in America," *Southwestern Journal of Theology*, 2 (October 1959), 52–62, reprinted by permission of the author and publisher. C. C. Goen teaches church history at Wesley Theological Seminary.

events. The classic critique was that of Walter Rauschenbusch (1861–1918), who pointed out that a social crisis was being precipitated because most of the wealth and property were concentrated in the hands of a few who were exploiting the masses and thus destroying the solidarity of society. Out of his experience as a Baptist pastor at Hell's Kitchen in the slums of New York City, Rauschenbusch boldly declared that individual personal religion was not sufficient to meet the needs of an industrial society. That this sort of faith was professed by many of the business men, who were also church members, was a factor which encouraged many churches and pastors to remain content with the *status quo*. In contrast, Rauschenbusch sought to show that sin has an organic nature, that it affects groups as well as individuals, that it manifests itself primarily as selfishness. The cure, he declared, was to revitalize society through the ethic of the kingdom of God, which kingdom he defined as "society ordered according to the will of God." This is the so-called Social Gospel.[2] Although Rauschenbusch himself insisted on the necessity of personal regeneration, and taught that the kingdom was to be wrought by divine power through the efforts of dedicated men, his followers became more self-sufficient and spoke of "building the kingdom" much as if it were to be their own doing.

This fitted in quite well with the evolutionary philosophy which had won fairly general acceptance in the latter part of the nineteenth century. Under its influence, the focus of interest in religion had shifted from transcendence to immanence: the doctrine of man stressed now his likeness to God in goodness rather than his alienation from God in sinfulness, while historical and rational criticism of the Bible had turned it from an inspired revelation of God into a human story of man's religious development. The new ethical ideal seemed now to point the way toward further progress, and a new confidence in man and his future was born. Respect for science and the scientific method was rising rapidly, and already men like William James had engaged in empirical analyses of religious experience in an attempt to develop a "science of religion." In such an atmosphere the traditional metaphysical doctrines of Christology, hamartiology, eschatology, predestination—all resting on infallible, propositional revelation—would naturally find hard going. Besides all this, the country was imbued with democratic ideals. "God cannot remain an Autocrat," Rauschenbusch exclaimed, "while the world is moving toward democracy!"

In spite of sporadic resistance to the new trends, a general breakthrough of liberal thought in America came at the close of the nineteenth century. Between 1890 and 1900 there arose a whole new generation of religious leaders who had made peace with the new scientific and social outlook, thus creating in the United States a new theological *Zeitgeist*. There was thenceforth a determined effort to come to realistic terms with the contemporary world through freedom of inquiry, openness to new truth, and tolerance of variant beliefs, while continuing to retain the authority of Christian experience and the centrality of Jesus Christ in nominal loyalty to historic Christianity. With this two-fold heritage of nineteenth-century scientism and the evangelical tradition, the liberals directed their rising social concern to the amelioration of the problems delineated so trenchantly by Rauschenbusch. But a reaction was already aborning.

The Fundamentalist Controversy

Fundamentalism is the name which came to be applied to the most extreme form of orthodox opposition to the new forms of thought. There were, of course, wide ranges of belief among the conservatives; some were concerned primarily to resist radical biblical criticism and naturalistic reductions of the gospel, while others were opposed to all innovations. This latter group represents the reactionary fringe of Fundamentalism, whose militant anti-intellectual bias prevented any constructive conversation with the liberals. But of primary concern here are developments as they shaped up around the central issue—which was the supernatural nature of biblical Christianity. The course of the controversy may be divided into three periods.

Early protests, 1865–1910/ This period is characterized by various Bible Conferences which met to decry a growing number of departures from the faith once and for all delivered to the saints. The faith to be defended was defined in the biblicistic terms of the seventeenth century, when elaborate Protestant creeds unequivocally identified the Scriptures with the Word of God, verbally inspired and infallibly preserved from all admixture of error. . . . Because many of the leaders in these conferences had adopted the dispensational notions of J. N. Darby and the Plymouth Brethren (later popularized in this country through the Scofield Bible), the dispensational interpretation of the Scriptures became standard for large numbers of Fundamentalists.[3]

During this period numerous Bible schools were founded, all set for the defense of this faith, and all in more or less conscious opposition to the liberalism of most of the established seminaries. The first was in 1882 at Nyack, New York, and was followed by Moody Bible Institute in 1886; there were twenty-three such schools by 1910. The period also witnessed numerous heresy trials in those churches whose polity and doctrinal standards would admit such a procedure. Notable examples are those in the Presbyterian Church, which dismissed Professors C. A. Briggs and H. P. Smith from its service, while A. C. McGiffert resigned from the ministry before he was unfrocked as a heretic.

Widespread controversy, 1910–1929/ In this period the conservatives made herculean efforts to capture control of the schools and mission organizations of the various embroiled denominations.[4] The method usually resorted to was the proposal of doctrinal tests and creeds to which teachers and missionaries must subscribe. In every instance, however, the conservatives lost their case and began to see that their only alternatives were surrender or schism.

In 1910–1912, twelve paper-backed pamphlets entitled *The Fundamentals: A Testimony to the Truth* were published and distributed at the expense of the Stewart brothers (laymen) in California.[5] Edited by A. C. Dixon and R. A. Torrey (other contributors included James Orr, B. B. Warfield, E. Y. Mullins, C. B. Williams, G. Campbell Morgan, A. T. Pierson, and Charles R. Erdman), these little volumes gave sober and serious explication to the tenets of orthodox Christianity. Some 300,000 copies were sent free to pastors, evangelists, missionaries, theological students, Sunday School superintendents, and youth workers. Such wide circulation did much to bring the issues clearly into the open.

In 1919, the World's Christian Fundamentals Association was formed. Led by the Minneapolis Baptist minister, William Bell Riley, whose widespread and indefatigable labors in behalf of orthodoxy had already brought him into national prominence, this organization sought to bring together for cooperative action all those opposed to liberalism and the Social Gospel. Riley served as president of the Association until 1930; afterwards it declined and finally merged with the Slavic Gospel Association in 1952.

In 1922, a highly inflammatory sermon entitled "Shall the Fundamentalists Win?" was preached by Harry Emerson Fosdick, a . . . Baptist preacher then supplying the pulpit of the First Presbyterian Church of New York City. This daring message flung down the gauntlet, as it were, challenging a fight to the finish. In the uproar which followed, Baptists demanded Fosdick's resignation from the ministry, while Presbyterians agitated for his removal from their pulpit and the censuring of those who had permitted him to preach there. The Fundamentalists won in none of these demands.

In 1925 came the famous "monkey trial" in Tennessee. After the state legislature had passed a law against the teaching of evolution in any of its public schools, John T. Scopes, a young teacher in Dayton, decided to provide a test case. In the ensuing litigation, he was prosecuted by William Jennings Bryan and defended by the brilliant agnostic, Clarence Darrow. The trial, a farce in many respects, degenerated into a haggling argument between Bryan and Darrow over the literal historical accuracy of the Genesis account of creation. The only ones to profit from the sorry spectacle were the merchants of Dayton, who catered to the large crowds of curiosity-seekers, and Scopes, who received from friends funds to complete his Ph.D. in Geology at the University of Chicago.

In 1929, Princeton Seminary entered a crisis which was the turning point of the controversy as far as the Presbyterians were concerned. A last-ditch effort to control the Seminary, led by J. Gresham Machen, was defeated. The conservatives withdrew to establish Westminster Seminary in Philadelphia; later, dissatisfied to contribute through the missionary organizations of the denomination, they formed their own mission board. In 1935 they constituted themselves a separate body, the Orthodox Presbyterian Church.

Northern Baptists were exercised almost as much as the Presbyterians. Within their ranks were formed in 1921 the National Federation of Fundamentalists and in 1923 the much more militant Baptist Bible Union. The former was led by such moderates as A. C. Dixon and J. C. Massee; the latter by reactionaries like W. B. Riley, T. T. Shields, and J. Frank Norris. Dissatisfaction with liberal trends in the seminaries led to the founding of Northern Baptist Seminary (Chicago) in 1913 and Eastern Baptist Seminary (Philadelphia) in 1925. In 1922 a determined effort to pledge the Convention to the New Hampshire Confession of Faith (1833) was averted only by a substitute proposal to declare the New Testament as the all-sufficient rule of faith and practice. Although in 1925 a split was avoided by the narrowest margin, the issue of modernism continued to be agitated until the conservatives finally withdrew in 1947.[8]

Perhaps the most familiar figure in Fundamentalism among Southern Baptists was J. Frank Norris (1877–1952), whose vitriolic tirades aroused Texas Baptists before the denomination as a whole was concerned with the controversy. Making effective use of pulpit and press, he launched a belligerent attack against evolution in the colleges and "ecclesiasticism" in the Convention. His ultra-conservative doctrines and extreme premillennialism brought him into the sympathies of other Fundamentalist leaders; he became active in the World's Christian Fundamentals Association about 1922, and was instrumental in the formation of the Baptist Bible Union. Norris' own denomination, the Fundamental Baptist Fellowship, was organized in 1934, and its scope was greatly expanded when he assumed the pastorate of the Temple Baptist Church in Detroit the next year—without, of course, relinquishing his leadership in Texas. It is scarcely necessary to observe that there is as much difference between Fundamentalists of this type and conservatives of the Machen-Mullins variety as between these latter men and the radical modernists, though many liberals label them all as "Fundies." [7]

Interdenominational associations, 1930–present/ It is not strange that both liberals and conservatives found more fellowship with kindred spirits in other denominations than with antagonists in their own. This last period has seen the formation of two major Fundamentalist groups, besides a number of smaller provincial organizations, which are interdenominational in composition. They are the American Council of Christian Churches, led by Carl McIntire (1941), and the National Association of Evangelicals (1942). Both of these publish periodicals, transcribe religious programs for radio, lobby in Washington (on matters affecting the chaplaincy, radio regulations, and foreign missions), and actively oppose the National Council of Churches—which is to them the most insidious voice of liberalism in the nation. Fundamentalism of this type maintains itself chiefly by negation of everything that does not coincide with its own peculiar views.[8]

An outstanding phenomenon of the present period, which also cuts across denominational lines, is the activity of a group of men who are sometimes styled neo-evangelicals. Repudiating the Fundamentalist extremists who are theologically uninformed and socially unconcerned, they are led by such men as Carl Henry (editor of Christianity Today), E. J. Carnell (Fuller Theological Seminary), and Bernard Ramm (California Baptist Theological Seminary). This group belittles neither education nor modern science, is possessed of a good historical sense, accepts the most assured results of textual and historical criticism, and participates readily in contemporary theological conversation. Quite articulate in their position, they have authored several vigorous doctrinal and apologetic works which seek to present historic Christianity in terms understandable by and acceptable to the modern world.[9]

The Issues Involved

Many efforts have been made to define Fundamentalism in terms of sociological factors. Some see it as a symptom of the conflict between the unsophisticated agrarian population and the urban intelligentsia. Others see it as part of the economic struggle between the proletarian desire for social betterment and the bourgeois effort to preserve the status quo. Some would find it a further manifestation of the cultural differences between certain geographical sections of the country. Evidence, if it is carefully selected, can be adduced to support any or all of these theses.[10] It would seem more accurate, however, to characterize the whole movement as the eruption of a basic ideological conflict, a protest that sooner or later was bound to come against the romanticized humanism that had captivated theology since the days of Schleiermacher. One can admit the influence of social factors without positing them as primary causes. The simple truth is that denials of the central affirmations of the Bible in the name of modernity could not have gone unnoticed in *any* society. Such protest movements—whether Pietism or Wesleyanism or Kierkegaardianism or Barthianism or confessionalism of one sort and another—seem to be an inevitable part of the dialectic in the historical process which bears along the Christian tradition.

Failure to penetrate to the heart of this controversy has resulted, in too many cases, in an unfortunate stereotyping of the whole conservative reaction to radical modernism. Fundamentalism—because it is often an umbrella term covering all opposition to modernistic emasculations of Christian faith—must not be dismissed as either naive uncritical pietism or militant reactionary fideism. These are on the fringe, and biblical Christianity has profited little from their fierce but futile efforts to perpetuate the clichés of a forgotten century.[11] *The central issue is the supernatural nature of Christianity.* This was given classic formulation by a man of unquestioned erudition and theological intensity, J. Gresham Machen.

In summary, his formulation amounts to this: Christianity must be defined in terms of doctrine derived from the Bible rather than in terms of life growing out of religious experience. It is a message rather than a movement. It presents a great saving fact, not merely the description of a feeling. Life is important, to be sure, but doctrine is prior to life; that is, doctrine is not derived from religious experience but is what conditions and determines such experience. This is why much must be made of biblical authority: the Bible represents the essentially trustworthy transmission of the message—it is the Word of God. Its central truths are the transcendence of the living God, the special creation of man as a moral personality, the universality and power of sin, the historical redemption provided by Jesus Christ the Son of God, the need of every person for cleansing and quickening by the Holy Spirit, the incompleteness of time forms and the necessity for a final consummation.[12]

Obviously, this is a supernaturalistic conception all the way, and the conservatives felt that to deny any portion of it was to imperil the whole structure of saving truth—not because one must believe every jot and tittle in order to be saved, but because to call into question any essential affirmation was to endanger the entire concept of biblical authority and to vitiate the very essence of Christianity. Thus biblical inerrancy was always the storm center of the controversy, because an infallible Bible seemed to be the only guarantee of a sure word from God; and any relaxing of this conviction would lead inevitably to a hopeless relativism. The end of liberalism, it was feared, was to humanize God and deify man, thus exposing Christianity to the criticism of the psychologists that religion was merely a construct of the human imagination.[13] That is why the Fundamentalists felt that they were fighting for the very soul of Christianity.

The danger implicit in their approach, which many of them scarcely avoided, is another sort of perversion of Christian faith and fellowship.

> For the vital experience of personal faith in Jesus Christ, fundamentalism has often substituted intellectual acceptance of the doctrine of his deity, undergirded by a series of rational proofs. For a body of Holy Scripture which is interwoven with the saving acts of God in history, fundamentalists substituted a static book of doctrines and precepts, which is liable to all kinds of schemes, eschatological charts, and creedal "tests of fellowship." [14]

The recognition of this danger—a real debt to the insights of the liberals—is what distinguishes evangelical conservatives from the reactionary fringe. It permits both a broader appreciation of the total Christian tradition and a deeper fellowship with those who serve the Savior in somewhat different ways.

The central conviction of the less reactionary Fundamentalists regarding the supernatural nature of Christianity has certainly been justified by the course of recent history. Theologians once again are centering their attention on the God who acts in history to reveal himself and redeem sinful men. The social upheavals of the twentieth century—wars, depressions, constant crises—have completely destroyed the former confidence in the goodness of man and the inevitability of progress. The old liberal doctrines of immanence and perfectibility have had to be discarded. In their place has come a new realization of the perversity of men in sin, a new emphasis on the transcendence and sovereignty of God, a new category and locus of revelation in Jesus Christ the Word, a new sense of the eschatological dimension of historic existence. And once again the God who is God, who in Christ has reconciled the world to himself, is seen as the great Fundamental Fact.

NOTES ───

1. The earliest study of Fundamentalism was by Stewart G. Cole, *The History of Fundamentalism* (New York: Richard R. Smith, 1931). Although out of date in some respects, this is still a helpful work. For a survey of more recent literature, see Norman H. Maring, "A New Look at Fundamentalism," *Foundations; A Baptist Journal of History and Theology*, I (October, 1958), 82–88. Provocative, though brief, is Carl Henry, *Evangelical Responsibility in Contemporary Theology* (Grand Rapids: Eerdmans, 1957).

2. Rauschenbusch's critique of society was *Christianity and the*

Social Crisis (New York: Macmillan, 1907). His mature convictions found best expression in *A Theology for the Social Gospel* (New York: Macmillan, 1918).

3. A recent account of the Bible Conferences may be found in C. Norman Kraus, *Dispensationalism in America* (Richmond: John Knox Press, 1958). Kraus views the transplantation to America of Darby's dispensationalism (in the 1860's) as the "vanguard" of Fundamentalism in this country. This is important because dispensationalism is, by definition, anti-ecclesiastical.

4. Perhaps the best factual study is by Norman F. Furniss, *The Fundamentalist Controversy, 1918–1931* (New Haven: Yale University Press, 1954). Separate chapters are devoted to developments in each of seven denominations.

5. It was the title of these works that gave the movement its name. They were republished in four small volumes by the Bible Institute of Los Angeles in 1917. A new reprint, in two volumes, is now in progress: Charles L. Feinberg (ed.), *The Fundamentals for Today*, Vol. I (Grand Rapids: Kregel Book Store, 1958); the second volume is scheduled for this year.

6. See Chester E. Tulga, *The Foreign Missions Controversy in the Northern Baptist Convention, 1919–1947; Thirty Years of Struggle* (Chicago: Conservative Baptist Fellowship, 1950).

7. Brief surveys of several splinter Baptist groups may be found in *The Quarterly Review*, XIX (April, May, June, 1959), 6–38. The evolution controversy within the Southern Baptist Convention is treated tangentially (in connection with its impact on ecclesiological issues) by W. W. Barnes, *The Southern Baptist Convention, 1845–1953* (Nashville: Broadman Press, 1954), pp. 257 f.

8. See Carl McIntire, *Twentieth Century Reformation* (Collingswood, N.J.: Christian Beacon Press, 1941). The story of the N.A.E. is told by James DeForest Murch, *Cooperation Without Compromise* (Grand Rapids: Eerdmans, 1956).

9. See the symposium by Carl Henry (ed.), *Contemporary Evangelical Thought* (Grand Rapids: Baker Book House, 1957).

10. See Furniss, *op. cit.*, pp. 26–30, and the literature there cited.

11. If this seems too broad a definition, it is provoked by those who consider everything to the right of themselves as "Fundamentalist." For a narrower view, see the definition essay by E. J. Carnell, "Fundamentalism," *A Handbook of Christian Theology* (New York: Meridian Books, 1958), pp. 142–44.

12. J. Gresham Machen, *Christianity and Liberalism* (New York: Macmillan, 1923). A more recent treatment from the same perspective is by Samuel G. Craig, *Christianity Rightly So Called* (Philadelphia: Presbyterian and Reformed Publishing Co., 1946). Notice the sharp alternatives posed by these titles. Some conservatives of the present day, profiting from historical insights recently achieved, would not divorce kerygma and church quite so radically as Machen.

13. This thrust had already been made by Feuerbach.

14. Wayne E. Ward, "Fundamentalism," *Encyclopedia of Southern Baptists* (Nashville: Broadman Press, 1958), I, 516.

8

Douglas Roche

The Challenge to Authority in the Catholic Church

In little mannerisms and big policy statements, the mood, style, and character of the laity in the Catholic Church are changing in the biggest transformation of relationships since the Reformation. They are no longer happy sheep, willing to be blindly led by their shepherd pastors and bishops. Not all the laity know enough about the Vatican Council to react to its intellectual challenge, but sufficient numbers are reasonably well informed to provoke a storm of criticism and creativity. Docility has given way to assertiveness.

Very few laymen have mastered the sweeping outlines of a new Church in the 700 pages of Vatican II's sixteen documents, but a sentence in paragraph 37 of Chapter 4 of the Constitution on the Church has constituted a beacon light to nearly everyone: "An individual layman, by reason of the knowledge, competence, or outstanding ability which he may enjoy, is permitted and even sometimes obliged to express his opinion on things which concern the good of the Church."

From the Lay Congress in Rome to the parish precincts of Missouri, the laity have taken the bishops at their word. As a result, educated, informed, articulate men and women are challenging traditions in a way that would have been considered outrageously presumptuous before the Council began.

Where does the money go and why isn't there full public accounting? Why are we building more big churches when underdeveloped countries need all the help we can give them? Why weren't the liturgical

Excerpted from Douglas Roche, *The Catholic Revolution*, New York (1968). Reprinted by permission of the publisher, David McKay Company, Inc. Douglas Roche, a journalist, is the editor of *The Western Catholic Reporter*, Edmonton, Alberta.

changes better explained? Why can't we practice birth control if our consciences tell us it's all right? Why can't the Church operate along democratic lines? These are only a few of the urgent questions being propounded today by thinking and concerned Catholics in all walks of life.

The sudden rush to open season for the tongue after generations of free speech being off limits is a large factor in the present turmoil of the Catholic Church. The clergy and hierarchy interpret such questioning as challenging (which it is), and too often they respond defensively. The criticisms do not admit of easy answers, and the questioners themselves are frequently divided in their premises and the kinds of answers they want.

Despite repeated attempts by the Pope and the bishops to assert their teaching authority, the tones of authority echo from another age. A few conservatives among the laity are still manning the ramparts in behalf of ecclesiastical judgment, but the great majority are confused about what the Church is, should be, and will be.

After being drilled since childhood in the "timeless qualities of a changeless Church," men and women by the millions were swept up in the conciliar hurricane. Although much more change is needed to speed the updating of a Church falling farther behind the needs of modern man, the simple fact is that change has struck too quickly for immediate adaptation, not to mention digestion.

Catholic experts have stopped counting their crises (of faith, of culture, of authority), but at the very least there is a crisis of confidence in the leadership of the Church, and one needs considerable courage to hope that the hierarchy and the laity will get off their collision course.

For thoughtful laymen, the entire Vatican Council can be boiled down to one word: *freedom*. Freedom from an artificial conformity, freedom from an overbearing clericalism, freedom from the fear of asking pointed questions about the Church. But there is one word that has stayed uppermost in the minds of the bishops: *control*.

The bishops control the Church's vast holdings, including church and school properties and a myriad of welfare institutions: This administrative function is in addition to their principal role as teachers of the faith with a divine commission. The bishops made an important legislative advance at the Council by informing the layman that he is a first-class member of the Church and that his advice is needed in the governing of the Church. But both in the academic atmosphere of the Council and especially in the personal encounters of their home dioceses, they have shied away from anything that looks like a surrender of their considerable power to the laity.

The bishops have put themselves in the position of legislating open-ended change ("continual reformation," the Council said) and yet retaining power over even the minutiae of change. It is an impossible position. When the laity, in their new spirit of freedom, move too close to the cutting edge of an issue, the bishops claim their authority is being watered down. Where, in fact, does lay freedom impinge on hierarchical control? That is the great question that embraces every facet of the Catholic revolution. The question becomes more strident as the tensions between laity and bishops bubble to the surface.

"When the bishops unleashed the desire of contemporary Catholics to really get with the world, they unleashed a force which they could not control," says Dr. Eugene Fontinell, a philosopher at Queens College, New York. "When people get more freedom, they get more impatient with even the more advanced structures that replace the old ones." Thus, even though the Church advanced more in the conciliar years than in the previous fifty, "the gap between the attitudes of the younger and more reflective people in the Church and the bishops is so great that it is hard to see how it can be bridged."

In fact, adds history professor Thomas P. Neill of St. Louis University, the bishop/people gap is the most serious problem in the American Church. And instead of being resolved, it is festering as the bishops continue to safeguard episcopal authority at the expense of developing a dynamic, charismatic laity.

The Catholic Church is squeezed in a revolution of rising expectations. The bishops, who enjoyed a world spotlight on their progressive legislation, feel cheated when they are now accused of resisting reform. The resentful attitude of the laity, however, is too clear to mistake, and it is attested to by qualified observers.

"The Catholic people of the United States are restless, dissatisfied and angry," declares the *Critic*, an influential Catholic monthly.

Priest-sociologist Andrew Greeley sees American Catholicism approaching the 1970s "with a restless liberal elite, a vaguely dissatisfied liberal mass that wants more rapid change but does not understand either the theories or dynamics of change, a youthful population that is bored and apathetic about many religious questions, and a clergy and religious caught in a crisis of ambiguity for which it was not trained."

All these elements are clearly visible, but the total mood of the laity —at least, as I found it on my journey through the United States—is positive as well as negative. It is concerned with growth and progress, as well as with criticisms. It seeks revolutionary change, but has by no means given up hope that it can achieve it by peaceful means.

The new self-awareness of the Catholic laity should not be seen as an isolated phenomenon, but rather as part of the worldwide awakening of the common man to a sense of his power and destiny, an awakening in which modern communications have played a decisive part. What the Vatican Council did was to serve as a catalyst. But the rapidity of the reaction to its initiatives shows that all the elements were already in position, that there would surely have been an explosion if the Council had not provided safety valves.

In the United States, the impact was felt with particular force. Catholics previously had a tradition of following the orders of the priest unquestioningly. They sent their children to the school he recommended. They brought up their families the way he told them. They went to Sunday Mass because he warned them that they'd go to hell if they missed it. In all of this, however, they were running counter to the general mood of the society in which they lived, a fluid and mobile society in which the external pressures to conform are minimal.

Once the Council told them that as laymen they were full members of the Church, called to an active role in performing its mission, obliged to make their own judgments on the basis of general moral principles presented to them by the Church, the social attitudes around them came into play to enable them to apply immediately in practice the newly offered principles.

The communications media quickly responded to the newly awakened interest in religious matters. The general press, radio, and television provided the basic information to permit the formation of a new public opinion on the Catholic Church. Independent Catholic publications were established in response to the need, including the aggressive and astute *National Catholic Reporter,* which serves a broad middle-class readership from coast to coast. Old liberal standard bearers, such as *Commonweal,* were joined by a renewal-committed coterie of a dozen diocesan newspapers in building a climate of reform. The conservative Catholic publications, highlighted by a new entry, *Twin Circle,* have never been a match for the professionalism of the liberal Catholic editors. Though under the control of the bishops, the progressive diocesan weeklies responded to pressure from their readers to give all the religious news and views, knowing that to the extent that they failed, the general news media in their area would supply the deficiency.

Tension between the bishops and the Catholic press, however, is marked. Bishops who dwell on the crisis of obedience have been extremely bitter in their criticisms of Catholic publications. Bishop Bernard Topel of Spokane, Washington, for example, charged that some Catholic publications should not be found in Catholic homes. Cardinal Shehan of Baltimore added that almost wholesale negative criticism has been the stock in trade of some Catholic journalists. For Cardinal Krol of Philadelphia, they are undermining the authority of the hierarchy.

One of the most professional and progressive-minded Catholic editors, John O'Connor, was squeezed out of the Wilmington, Delaware, diocesan newspaper in 1967 because his views were too advanced (though not an inch beyond Vatican II) for the policy-making group in the diocese. His colleague at the *St. Louis Review,* Donald Quinn, put in words the widespread lay reaction to the O'Connor incident, which became a celebrated test case of the new freedom within the Catholic press: "Here was a case that should have worked: good planning, professional skill, creative purposes, lots of energy and zeal went into the project—and it failed. The questions raised by the failure are immense."

Although there are failures, delays, and incidents along the way, the laity are, in fact, gradually moving closer to the power centers of the Church. It is not power for its own sake they want, but an honorable share in the decision-making process. A resolution presented to the Lay Congress in Rome by the United States delegation synthesizes very well the views of thinking American Catholics on their place in the Church. The resolution called for a basic change in the structure of the Council of the laity set up earlier by the Vatican. This body, it said, should be "truly representative of the laity," with its officers and members freely elected by the laity. Truly representative councils of the laity, it added, should be formed at all national, diocesan, and parish levels, with officers and members freely elected by the laity. In addition, national and diocesan pastoral councils, consisting of clergy, religious orders, and laity, should be set up in such a way that the "lay members will be truly representative of the laity and freely elected by the laity."

· · ·

The rising insistence on lay rights within the Church—for both men and women—combined with the new trend among the laity to make their own decisions without waiting for the approval of the Church authorities would seem to spell the dissolution of the character of the Church as it has existed historically. Some Catholics are, in fact, considering such an eventuality, but they are more numerous and more vocal in Europe than in North America. They have even been given a name—the "third man"—meaning one who is personally committed to moral values and to faith in Christ, but who is detached from or unconcerned with institutional structures that cannot keep pace with new modes of thought. He is called "third" to distinguish him from the conservative who wants to defend traditional Church structures, and from the progressive who wants to update them.

In North America, it is the progressive who is most vocal. His ultimate aim is the creation of integrated institutions that will give all the members of the People of God a voice in making policy and supervising its execution. Most progressives would justify the present trends to unapproved liturgical experimentation and to the use of artificial methods of contraception as the result of an abnormal situation in which the institution has become frozen and must be prodded into activity. And many of these would feel that, since they are starting from a historical situation in which all the power structures are under the effective control of the bishops, the first step has to be the creation of parallel but independent organizations of priests, of members of religious orders of men and women, and of the laity. As a matter of practical politics, it is only when such power bases have been formed that it will be possible to take the final step of forming integrated institutions in which all the members will have the voice to which the Vatican Council said they were entitled.

9

Sanford M. Dornbusch

Two Studies in the Flexibility
of Religious Beliefs

Introduction

This is a two-part report[1] of collaborative research
built on the conception that people who apparently share religious
beliefs may, in fact, have different religious perspectives. We assume
that in the American religious context:

1 Americans have numerous religious beliefs which are not well
   articulated, and in some instances are mutually contradictory.
2 Social forces influence which beliefs will be emphasized and
   which ignored.
3 Many secular beliefs in America contradict many traditional
   religious beliefs.[2]
4 A person will tend to select from the set of religious beliefs those
   which are consonant with his social experience. Insofar as his
   selection is "handed down" to him, he will also *interpret* his
   religious beliefs and attach *more or less importance* to them in
   order to make them compatible with his social experience.
5 These processes of interpreting and attaching relative importance
   to religious beliefs can be studied as instances of general social-
   psychological processes.

This is an original essay prepared especially for the present volume, re-
printed by permission of the author. Sanford M. Dornbusch is a sociologist
at Stanford University. His collaborators, Malcolm McAfee, H. Laurence
Ross, Phillip C. Smith, and Karl E. Taeuber are sociologists at Hayward
State College, University of Denver, University of Utah, and the University of
Wisconsin, respectively.

I. Metaphorical Interpretations of
Religious Beliefs
by
Sanford M. Dornbusch,
Malcolm McAfee,
H. Laurence Ross, and
Karl E. Taeuber

This first study was stimulated by a casual remark by the late Louis Wirth. "The trouble with the Bible," he said, "is that it is written and cannot adjust to changing social circumstances." The senior author of this paper strongly disagreed, and this paper represents a response twenty years later to that passing comment. Just as the Supreme Court can interpret the Constitution in ways that would shock our Founding Fathers, so men living in the twentieth century can take advantage of the uses of ambiguity.

Our central hypothesis is that metaphorical interpretations of the Bible permit Americans to accept Biblical injunctions when a literal interpretation would produce apparent conflict with current American secular themes. To put it bluntly: If one wants to agree with the Bible, and the Bible contradicts American values, then one must interpret the Bible so that it does not contradict American values.

We selected twelve passages from the King James Version of the Bible which we believed, if literally interpreted, contradict American middle class values. Our critics might argue that sociologists are not at all sure what *are* American values, and so it is not possible to select quotations contradictory to these values. Therefore, we also selected two placebos, the equivalent of the inert pill in medical research. As a check on our suppositions, we predicted in advance that, since these two did not contradict American values, the cognitive processes posited for the other twelve quotations would not operate for the two placebos. The fourteen passages were:

Thou shalt not suffer a witch to live.

EXOD. 22:18

I say therefore to the unmarried and widows, It is good for them if they abide even as I. But if they cannot contain, let them marry; for it is better to marry than to burn.

I CORIN. 7:8,9

Train up a child in the way he should go: and when he is old, he will not depart from it.

PROV. 22:6

For I the Lord thy God am a jealous God, visiting the iniquity of the fathers upon the children unto the third and fourth generation

*of them that hate me.   And shewing mercy unto thousands of them
that love me, and keep my commandments.*

Exod. 20:5,6

Lay not up for yourselves treasures upon earth.

Matt. 6:19

*And again I say unto you, It is easier for a camel to go through the
eye of a needle, than for a rich man to enter into the kingdom of
god.*

Matt. 19:24

Repent: for the Kingdom of Heaven is at hand.

Matt. 4:17

*But I suffer not a woman to teach, nor to usurp authority over the
man, but to be in silence.*

I Tim. 2:12

*And all things, whatsoever ye shall ask in prayer, believing, ye shall
receive.*

Matt. 21:22

*Wives, submit yourselves unto your own husbands, as unto the
Lord.*

Eph. 5:22

*But I say unto you, That ye resist not evil: but whosoever shall
smite thee on thy right cheek, turn to him the other also.*

Matt. 5:39

Whatsoever thy hand findeth to do, do it with thy might.

Eccl. 9:10

*Take therefore no thought for the morrow: for the morrow shall
take thought for the things of itself.*

Matt. 6:34

*All they that had any sick with divers diseases brought them unto
him; and he laid his hands on every one of them, and healed them.*

Luke 4:40

Our sample for this report consists of 89 students in sociology
courses at a private university, 179 students in sociology courses at a
state college, and 101 students drawn from a random sample at that
state college. The use of the random sample at the state college is to
assure that our data are not biased by the selective processes involved
in registering for a sociology course. Another possible bias is our use
of a student sample. Some people have defined the behavioral sciences as the study of college sophomores, thus doubting the generaliza-
bility of studies on so limited a population. We believe that we are
studying basic social-psychological processes, that college students are

human, and so the same findings would occur in other populations in modern industrial societies (in fact, separate studies of Presbyterian adult males in the San Francisco Bay Area and even of Christian college students in Nigeria show the same fundamental pattern of response which we are examining). We are studying the resolution of conflicts in belief systems, and the processes found here, we believe, are generalizable to other groups and other sets of beliefs.

The questionnaire was introduced as follows:

> We are interested in how laymen interpret the *Bible*. There are many studies of how theologians and religious leaders interpret Scripture, but we need to know what these passages mean to you.
>
> After each quote, write in your own words what these passages mean to you. Then, check whether you agree or disagree with the passage as you have interpreted that passage. Leave out no interpretations and be sure that you always state your agreement or disagreement.

The fourteen quotations were then presented, and the written interpretations and the agreement or disagreement provided the basic data for this research. Since the order of presentation of the quotations might influence the responses, it was necessary to use four different forms of the questionnaire. Each form used a different order, selected from a table of random numbers. Analysis of the responses showed no statistically significant effect of these different orderings of the quotations, so the results from the four forms were combined.

A five-point scale was then used to code each interpretation on its metaphorical content. An interpretation which was considered "literal" we scored (1). For example, for the passage "Thou shalt not suffer a witch to live," the response "This means you kill witches" would receive this score. A "literal-historical" interpretation was scored (2), indicating that the passage was read literally but assigned to the no-longer-existent past. For example, clauses like "But there aren't any witches any more," or "That used to be true," would lead to a "literal-historical" score when combined with a literal interpretation. Scores (3), (4), and (5) referred respectively to "slightly metaphorical," "moderately metaphorical," and "very metaphorical" interpretations. Thus, the respondent who wrote that "Every society must find a way to punish deviance," scored a (5) on the passage about witches.

Content analysis of interpretations of complex material is never likely to yield unequivocal agreement among coders. Therefore, it was necessary to determine the degree to which the data could be reliably coded. Every one of seven coders had among his questionnaires a randomly selected group of questionnaires which, unknown to him, were separately coded by another research assistant. These double-coded questionnaires provided the basis for assessing the reliability of the coding.

The reliability was acceptable. The middle category, "slightly meta-phorical," was not reliably coded, as it was just as likely to be associated with literal interpretations as metaphorical ones. Nor were the coders able to make reliable distinctions between the first and second forms of literal interpretations or between "moderately metaphorical" and "very metaphorical" interpretations. But when categories (1) and (2) were combined as "literal," and categories (4) and (5) as "meta-phorical," the reliability of coding was good. If one coder saw an interpretation as either "literal" or "metaphorical," the other coder was nine times more likely to agree than to code it in an opposite fashion. Stating the same idea operationally, when we eliminated the passages coded (3) and dichotomized all other interpretations into "literal" and "metaphorical," the mean reliability was 90 per cent. We can therefore conclude that reliability of coding was high for the general distinction between more literal and more metaphorical inter-pretations. Thus rough agreement between coders was nine times more likely than strong disagreement.

We are now ready to summarize the findings of our research. To simplify the presentation, we will combine the sociology classes at the state college with the random sample at the same school, since no appreciable differences appeared in the pattern of responses for the two groups. All results can thus be presented as observed in two samples: 89 students at a private university and 280 students at a state college.

Our first task is to show that the placebos were, in fact, handled on a cognitive basis different from that of the twelve passages which were believed to contradict some aspects of American values. The placebos are, as one could probably guess, "Train up a child in the way he should go: and when he is old, he will not depart from it," and "Whatsoever thy hand findeth to do, do it with thy might." We will now show that the placebos differed from the other passages in the perceived difficulty of interpretation and the likelihood of agreement.

At the end of the questionnaire, each respondent was asked, "Which two quotations were the *easiest* for you to interpret?" and "Which two quotations were the *hardest* for you to interpret?" Since we assume that difficulty in interpretation often arises from cognitive conflict, the placebos should have been named more often as easy to interpret and less often as hard to interpret. We computed the ratio of the number of times a passage was voted one of the two easiest to the number of times it was voted one of the two hardest. The higher this easy-to-hard ratio, the easier the passage was perceived to be. Therefore, it is pleasant to report that, for both the private university and the state college samples, no other pair of passages had so high an easy-to-hard ratio.

Since the placebos do *not* contradict other American values, they should also be more likely to have respondents agree with their message. Once again, the data confirm the difference between the placebos and the other passages. In the state college sample, the two placebos are first and second in the proportion of respondents who express agreement. For the private university, they are first and fifth in proportion of agreement, with the average agreement for the two placebos remaining higher than the average for the second and third ranked passages.

Since the placebos are more frequently agreed to and found easier to interpret, it is not surprising that both samples reveal a positive correlation for the other twelve passages between the proportion of agreement and the easy-to-hard ratio. An easy passage is one which, in terms of our conception, can be agreed to without too much reinterpretation. For those skeptics who wonder if easy passages may be short and have few difficult words, we merely note here that the shortest passage with the simplest words, "Thou shalt not suffer a witch to live," was voted the hardest passage of all and agreed to less than any other passage.

We now turn our attention to the use of metaphor as a basis for finding a way to agree with a passage from Holy Scripture. Those persons who, faced with a cognitive conflict, wished to agree with the Biblical passage were more likely to employ metaphorical interpretations. To test this hypothesis, we counted for every respondent the number of times he is scored either (4) or (5) on the twelve non-placebo passages. The number of metaphorical interpretations, we reasoned, should be positively correlated with the proportion of the twelve passages with which he agreed. For both samples, we indeed found this positive correlation between the use of metaphor and agreement.

Although all members of both samples are living in a Judeo-Christian culture, we expected religious persons to be more inclined to agree with the Bible despite cognitive problems. But we checked this conception by examining the responses of those persons who were least likely to be feeling cognitive conflict. Operationally, we asked each respondent to give his religious affiliation. For those who described themselves as atheist or agnostic, we predicted less pressure to agree with the Bible and thus less pressure to give metaphorical interpretations. The data show atheists and agnostics agree with Scripture less and give literal interpretations more than any other religious grouping. It is as if, faced with the conflict between secular and religious values, atheists and agnostics are more content to note their disagreement with the sacred, thus having less need to reinterpret.

We also analyzed our data by considering each passage as a sample of responses in which we expected those agreeing with each passage to use metaphor more than those disagreeing. Dichotomizing the interpretations at the median on the literal-metaphorical scale, we tested whether there is an association between the degree of metaphor used and the likelihood of agreement. The chi-square test, with a one-tail test of significance, provided a simple indication of the existence of such a relationship for each question. Since the same respondents answer every question, these were obviously not independent tests of the hypothesis. Yet the results did show the power of this relationship. For the private university, 10 out of 12 passages showed statistically significant differences in the predicted direction and, for the state college, 11 out of 12. Finally, for the placebos, where no such relationship between the use of metaphor and agreement with the passage was cognitively necessary only 1 out of 2 placebos for the private university and 0 out of 2 for the state college showed such a relationship. The data are very orderly.

We noted above that atheists and agnostics were less likely to use metaphor than were other religious groupings. Yet, since they too participate in this Judeo-Christian culture, they may sometimes wish to agree and find metaphor an appropriate mechanism for resolving conflict. Similarly, persons who say they have attended no religious services in the past month and persons who report that they never read the Bible may nevertheless exhibit the same linkage between metaphor and agreement. The relationship, if our theory is adequate, should thus be less strong, but we should still be able to predict the direction of relationship between the use of metaphor and agreement for these less religiously involved groups. The results are striking. There were no exceptions to the pattern that metaphorical interpretations are linked to agreement, but the relationship is often very weak. A simple directional test was employed for the two samples of twelve passages each. For atheists and agnostics, for non-attenders at church, and for those who never read the Bible, the pattern was consistent. These three groups, for two samples, on twelve passages, provided 72 non-independent sets of data which were always in the predicted direction.

Finally, using the passages themselves as the unit of analysis, we correlated the use of metaphor for each passage with the proportion of agreement with that passage. We predicted that those passages with which many people disagree are more likely to be metaphorically interpreted. If there is a relatively low level of agreement with a literal interpretation, more people find it necessary to use metaphor in order to agree. Unless the metaphor becomes the conventional interpretation, we are led to a prediction of a *negative* relationship between the proportion of persons agreeing with a passage and the proportion who reinterpret it. Our predicted negative correlation was, in fact, present, although weak, in both samples.

We can conclude this report of the first study by again noting how a simple model of cognitive conflict, investigating one specific method of resolution, reveals great consistency in the responses of persons facing difficult religious issues. A second method of resolution will be treated in the second study.

II. Religious Commitment and the
Perceived Importance
of Religious Beliefs
by
Phillip C. Smith and
Sanford M. Dornbusch

Once again we can apply some basic conceptions from social psychology to the study of religious belief. In this study our dependent variable is the respondent's perception of the relative importance of various items of religious belief. We shall show that this importance is related to the subject's commitment to his church or to his religious associates.

Lenski has distinguished between the commitment of an individual to a religious group and his commitment to the tenets of a religious belief system.[3] We apply both conceptions of commitment to situations in which the respondent may face cognitive conflict. Specifically, we hypothesize that religious perspectives which are: (1) in opposition to the orthodox view, or (2) in opposition to the majority view within a church, will be considered less important by church members than those perspectives which are consonant with orthodox or majority opinion.

Our sample consists of 50 Presbyterian adults drawn from a traditional parish and 50 Presbyterian adults drawn from a liberal parish. The 100 persons in the sample were selected at random from lists of members of each parish. Accordingly, some persons in the sample are regular attenders in church and others attend irregularly.

Each respondent was asked 68 questions which tapped many different religious perspectives. For example, he was asked whether he agreed or disagreed with the statement that "God accepts each one of us no matter what we do." Subjects were told to respond to every question, either agreeing or disagreeing with it. They were cautioned to respond to the question as it applied to them, rather than in terms of how it *should* apply to them. This instruction was repeated in the preamble of the questionnaire. Anonymity was stressed, and subjects were reminded of the importance of accurate and honest responses. They were told that the questionnaire is not a test; the "right" answer is the one that best applies to them. Once they began the question-naire, pains were taken to give no other instructions. Respondents who raised questions were told to do the best they could.

After answering the 68 items, each subject was given the opportunity to rate the religious perspectives according to their importance to him. It was reasoned that agreement or disagreement with a question indicates only that a subject takes a particular position with respect to its substantive meaning. We wanted further to see if, apart from the meaning of the question, a subject felt that the issue contained in the question was important to him.

Determination of importance was made as follows: Each subject was given a stack of 3 by 5 cards. Each card restated the issue reflected in each of the 68 religious perspective questions. Subjects were asked to separate the cards into three piles, depending on whether the issue expressed on the card was: (1) of great importance, (2) of moderate importance, or (3) of little or no importance to them. After the responses of each subject were recorded, the cards were shuffled so as to eliminate the possibility that one subject might influ-ence the responses of the next.

Classifying a religious belief as unimportant, we would assert, is one way of reducing cognitive conflict. We can, therefore, operating from that social-psychological position, set forth a group of interrelated hypotheses:

1 Those persons who take a non-orthodox position with respect to a particular religious issue are more likely to state that the issue reflected in that particular perspective is unimportant than are those who take the orthodox position. (Orthodox responses were labeled in advance by the authors in consultation with a Pres-byterian minister.) All of our respondents are members of the Presbyterian Church and have committed themselves to some extent to its theology. Insofar as they differ with particular tenets of that theology, they tend to view those tenets as less important.

2 Those persons who take a position differing from the majority in the sample of 100 with respect to a particular religious issue are more likely (than those in the majority position) to state the unimportance of that particular religious perspective. The mem-bers of these parishes, in other words, are likely to share reli-gious perspectives, so parishioners with deviant beliefs are led to reduce their inner conflict by reducing the perceived importance of the issue.

3 *Within* each of the parishes, we again expect that those whose religious perspectives differ from the majority in the parish will be likely to label their own perspective as unimportant.

4 Because their group interaction gives the members of each parish a clearer sense of majority opinion within that parish, the dif-

ferentials in importance under Hypothesis (3) are likely to be greater than under Hypothesis (2).

5 Similarly, regular church attenders are more likely to have knowledge of which perspectives are orthodox than are irregular attenders. Accordingly, regular attenders, more than irregular attenders, will exhibit greater differences in importance attached to unorthodox positions, as in Hypothesis (1).

6 Finally, regular church attenders are more likely to have knowledge of majority positions than are irregular attenders. Accordingly, regular attenders, more than irregular attenders, will exhibit greater differences in importance attached to minority positions, as in Hypothesis (2).

The data support every one of these six hypotheses. A t score is computed for each difference between the means of importance for the 68 items. The t takes into account the variability of importance of these items. Since the data are based on the same individuals repetitively answering each of the 68 questions, it is not appropriate to do any test of the significance of differences. But, using the t as a rough measure of differentials in importance, we are struck by the order in these data; that order supports the entire set of hypotheses.

Conclusion

These two studies suggest that a major religious distinction among people (at least in religiously heterogeneous societies like our own) is the degree to which they reinterpret and attach differential importance to various tenets of their religious traditions. This distinction calls into question the common practice in social research of asking items on religious dogma, summing the responses, and then concluding that religious perspectives have been adequately measured. Since the actors in the religious drama hold their convictions with considerable flexibility, molding them to accord with personal commitments to groups and ideologies, the study of individual religiosity necessarily requires more depth.

NOTES ───

1. These studies were supported by the Institute of Strategic Studies, Board of National Missions, United Presbyterian Church. Coders at the Laboratory for Social Research at Stanford University included John W. Hanley, David P. Morin, Harold B. Oliver, Anna Romanski, Eoin Ryan, and Rissa White.

2. A previous empirical study using these three ideas is Louis Schneider and Sanford M. Dornbusch, *Popular Religion: Inspirational Books in America* (Chicago: University of Chicago Press, 1958).

3. Gerhard Lenski, *The Religious Factor* (Garden City, N.Y.: Doubleday, 1963), p. 18.

QUESTIONS FOR DISCUSSION

1. Of the many new Protestant denominations that have been formed in the past 100 years, why have almost none of them been organized by Protestant liberals?

2. What impact has the liberal movement had on American Judaism?

3. Why is religious liberalism especially attractive to people with a high degree of formal education?

4. Assume that the author of the Gospel According to St. Mark and the author of the Gospel According to St. John were in sharp disagreement with each other on the events of Jesus' life and on the meaning of these events. Now read the two Gospels with this assumption in mind. How does this assumption change your understanding of what these two Gospels contain?

ADDITIONAL READING

Braden, Charles S. *These Also Believe.* New York: Macmillan, 1949. A readable survey of some well-known and some not so well-known American religious movements outside the Christian mainstream.

Carnell, Edward John. *The Case for Orthodox Theology.* Philadelphia: Westminster Press, 1959. A scholarly Protestant conservative argues the case for a theology based solely on the Bible and certain assumptions about what the Bible actually teaches.

DeWolf, L. Harold. *The Case for Theology in Liberal Perspective.* Philadelphia: Westminster Press, 1959. A noted Protestant liberal argues the case for an open-ended theology that is not based on scripture alone.

Glock, Charles Y., and Rodney Stark. "The New Denominationalism," Chapter 5 in *Religion and Society in Tension.* Chicago: Rand McNally, 1965. The authors' questionnaire data from a cross-section survey of the Christian laity strikingly document the existence of a basic liberal-conservative cleavage on many religious issues.

Greeley, Andrew M. *The Hesitant Pilgrim, American Catholicism After the Council.* New York: Sheed and Ward, 1966. A perceptive analysis of the contemporary ferment in American Catholicism by a self-styled liberal Catholic who is both a sociologist and a priest.

Part Two

———◆———

American
Religion
in Organized
Form

Chapter IV

The Church in the American Past

The United States was the first nation in the Western world to place all religious denominations on a legally equal footing. This was a radical break with tradition. Historically the major Christian faiths had insisted on a legally guaranteed monopoly of religion and had felt justified in persecuting those who held other views. But it is not hard to understand why the young American republic abandoned this tradition so easily and why most denominations accepted its abandonment with good grace. British law had recognized a limited form of religious toleration for almost a century before the American Revolution, and the great English philosopher John Locke, whose writings were so often cited by leaders of the Revolution, had provided an appealing justification for the right of freedom of conscience. But as Willard L. Sperry shows (Selection 10), the most compelling reason for religious equality in America was political. For years before the Revolution, British North America had been in fact religiously heterogeneous. The men who had made the Revolution could not afford to favor one religion over another; the price of American unity was the equality of all religious bodies at the national level.

One of the important legacies of the Revolution and its aftermath has been the virtually unanimous endorsement by the American churches of the principle of religious freedom, the American system of government, and the political and social ideals this system has implied. This does not mean that the churches came to see eye-to-eye with one another on everything. They have sometimes cooperated and sometimes bitterly competed, but they have generally recognized one another's right to exist. In this they have resembled American political parties, all of which have competed with one another but most of which have recognized each other's legitimacy and accepted the legal framework of the American system (see, in this connection, Selection 25, "American Sacred Ceremonies").

Nevertheless, the waves of immigration discussed by Edwin Scott Gaustad (Selection 11) brought to the American system of religious liberty several severe tests. The gravest of these tests concerned the rights of Roman Catholics. As long as there were few Catholics in the United States, Protestants had little cause for alarm, but when large numbers of them began immigrating to this country in the first half of the nineteenth century, many Protestants reacted with apprehension. Their traditional anti-Catholicism was reinforced by the fear that the presence of a strong Catholic population would place the entire American system in jeopardy. These fears were not entirely ground-less, for Roman Catholic teaching had not yet recognized the legiti-macy of popular government or the principle of religious liberty. Some Protestants were sure that Catholics would place loyalty to the Pope above loyalty to the United States. Anti-Catholic movements sprang up, and in several cities mobs attacked Catholics and destroyed church property. These movements were not able to attract a reliable national following, but they achieved local victories that helped shape the policy of the American Catholic Church for years to come, making it essentially defensive in character, aimed at safeguarding the rights and integrity of the Catholic faith in a basically hostile environment. One facet of this policy was to make it clear that American Catholics did indeed accept American democracy and had no intention of abridging the liberties of others. In short, Catholic leaders insisted with evident sincerity that Catholics were loyal Americans. The other facet of this policy was to insulate Catholics wherever possible from aspects of American culture that were deemed antagonistic to the faith. The church set about building a separate system of schools and colleges for its members; it successfully resisted efforts of laymen to democratize the governing of local parishes (see Roche, Selection 8); and it maintained its ancient doctrinal position in the midst of the monumental controversies and changes going on within American Protestantism. Moreover, it was successful in preserving its unity in the face of many conflicts among the diverse ethnic groups that make up the American Catholic laity. And perhaps most important, it was able to retain the undivided loyalty of the vast majority of Catholic laymen. To this day American Catholics are far more likely to be faithful churchgoers than their Protestant neighbors.

Some Protestant bodies have adopted a posture not too different from that of the Catholics. Certain Lutheran denominations, for ex-ample, have held fast to their historic witness by erecting barriers between themselves and the outside world. But other Protestants have had far more ambitious aims. They have sought to minister to the nation at large, to help form the national conscience on significant public issues they believed had a moral dimension. The impetus for this movement came initially from men with deep roots in the New England tradition with its Puritan ideal of a commonwealth made up of actively committed Christians whose consciences were molded in large measure by an educated and well-respected clergy. To implement this ideal in the nation at large required an aggressive strategy rather than a purely defensive one. It also required the efforts of men from several denominations. An informal, interdenominational alliance of Protestants came into being in the first years of the nineteenth century. Originating in the Northeast, its early nucleus consisted of clerical and lay leaders of the older, predominantly Calvinist denominations, whose constituency tended to be both well-educated and well-to-do. Over the years this alliance has gained important strength and suffered important defections, but it remains the single most influential force in American Protestantism. Today it is roughly made up of the denominations having membership in the National Council of Churches.

Leaders of the Protestant alliance have been more interested in building bridges to others than in defending the traditions of their own past. For example, many persons who were brought up in the strict Calvinist orthodoxy of New England abandoned this theology when they realized that most people held it in contempt, and they adopted a frontier-style revivalism when it proved a popular and effective method of converting large numbers of people.

One of the most notable examples of this Protestant flexibility is the shift in policy toward the poor that took place following the Civil War. Always intensely interested in the lower classes, leaders of the earlier Protestant alliance had sought to convert them and improve their personal habits. The temperance movement was one of the fruits of this policy. But soon after the Civil War it became clear to many Protestant leaders living in urban or industrial areas that the traditional approach to the poor would no longer bear fruit. For one thing, many urban working men were Roman Catholic and therefore not receptive to a narrowly Protestant appeal. But more important, the industrial system had created material problems for the working class that could not be solved by improving their morals. This insight, described in this chapter's third selection by Clifton E. Olmstead, profoundly altered the whole social and political outlook of urban Protestant leaders. It gave rise to the social gospel and the current commitment of a major portion of Protestantism to the cause of liberal social reform.

Protestant flexibility has enabled church leaders to continue to speak with relevance on a variety of important issues. But each major shift of policy has provoked opposition and led to defections from the

Protestant alliance. The new Protestant position toward labor and the
poor was partly responsible for the rise of fundamentalism (see Goen,
Selection 7), a movement that has adopted a defensive posture toward
the whole Protestant tradition. Moreover, the liberal policy toward
social reform has inspired little enthusiasm among the laity. In the
twentieth century the price of Protestant social awareness has been
the loss of the kind of lay support the church once enjoyed (see
Introduction to Chapter VII).

10

Willard L. Sperry

The Separation of Church and State: Its Causes

Thomas Jefferson's tomb carries as an epitaph an inscription which he had written: "Here was buried Thomas Jefferson, author of the Declaration of Independence, of the Statute of Virginia for Religious Freedom, and father of the University of Virginia."

The statute in question was passed by the Virginia Legislature in 1786. At the time Jefferson was in France. The letter of the Act is, perhaps, the work of the Legislature, but the spirit of it, and its substance, derived from prior drafts which Jefferson had already made. His epitaph is unequivocal, and the fact that he eventually included the text of the Act as an appendix to his *Notes on Virginia*—first edition, 1784—would seem to confirm his general claim to its authorship.

Since this Act is said to be 'the first law ever passed by a popular Assembly giving perfect freedom of conscience,' it deserves citation at some length.

> Well aware that Almighty God hath created the mind free; that
> all attempts to influence it by temporal punishments or burdens, or
> by civil incapacitations, tend only to beget habits of hypocrisy
> and meanness, and are a departure from the plan of the Holy
> Author of our religion, who being Lord of both body and mind, yet
> chose not to propagate it by coercions on either, as was in his
> Almighty power to do; that the impious presumption of legislators
> and rulers, civil as well as ecclesiastical, who, being themselves
> but fallible and uninspired men have assumed dominion over the
> faith of others, . . . hath established and maintained false religions
> over the greatest part of the world and through all time; that to

Excerpted from Willard L. Sperry, *Religion in America,* by permission of Cambridge University Press. Willard L. Sperry was Dean of the Divinity School, Harvard University.

compel a man to furnish contributions of money for the propagation
of opinions which he disbelieves is sinful and tyrannical; . . . that
our civil rights have no dependence on our religious opinions,
more than our opinions in physics or geometry; that therefore the
proscribing of a citizen as unworthy the public confidence by laying
upon him an incapacity of being called to offices of trust and
emolument unless he profess or renounce this or that religious
opinion, is depriving him injuriously of those privileges and
advantages to which in common with his fellow citizens he has a
natural right; that it tends also to corrupt the principles of that
very religion it is meant to encourage; . . . and, finally, that truth is
great and will prevail if left to herself, that she is the proper and
sufficient antagonist to error. . . .

Be it therefore enacted by the General Assembly, That no man
shall be compelled to frequent or support any religious worship,
place or ministry whatsoever, nor shall he be enforced, restrained,
molested, or burthened in his body or goods, nor shall otherwise
suffer on account of his religious opinions or belief; but that all
men shall be free to profess, and by argument to maintain, their
opinions in matters of religion and that the same shall in no wise
diminish, enlarge, or affect their civil capacities.

The precedent set by Virginia was followed by the makers of the
Federal Constitution. The VIth Article of the Constitution provides
that, "No religious test shall ever be required as a qualification to any
office or public trust under the United States." Two years after the
Constitution had been adopted Madison proposed ten amendments,
known as the Federal Bill of Rights, which were in turn accepted and
appended to the original document. The first of these amendments
says, 'Congress shall make no law respecting an establishment of
religion, or prohibiting the free exercise thereof.' From these two
pronouncements the formal separation of church and state in America
has followed.

The Constitution provides for national procedure by the United
States in their entirety. It does not concern itself with domestic state
practices. As a matter of historic fact, local church establishments
lingered on in certain instances for some years after the adoption of
the Constitution. Thus, Connecticut continued support of its Congregational Churches, by means of taxes applied to clergy stipends, until
1818; New Hampshire made similar appropriations until 1819. The
established churches of the colonies passed finally from the scene in
Massachusetts in the year 1833, when Orthodox Trinitarian Congregationalists demurred to paying further taxes for the support of such of
the original Congregational Churches, with their ministers, as had
become Unitarian. Separation of church and state in America was a
federal fact from 1789 to 91, and became the fact in every single
constituent state of the Union, a little over forty years later. It is

inconceivable that the issue should ever be reopened in this country.

Since the precedent set by America has been followed in a number of modern democracies, and by certain members of the British Commonwealth of Nations, the problems involved deserve due consideration. The formal separation in America of these two historic institutions has, it is true, solved certain difficult administrative problems in our society. But it has not solved the age-old problem of the interrelation of religion and citizenship. All that America has done is to restate a problem which may be theoretically insoluble, and which persists in thrusting itself upon us constantly in spite of such tentative and expedient solutions as we may devise.

. . .

It is true that during colonial times the idea, and, to a greater or less degree, the actual fact of an establishment came as a matter of course to America. The establishment in Puritan New England was a formidable reality, conceding nothing in the way of preeminences and powers to the Established Church at home. The non-theocratic type of life in the proprietary provinces made the Episcopal establishments open to the presence and therefore the active opposition of the sects. Each of the middle and southern colonies had its own local church-sect situation to deal with, the sects in question having been determined by the cosmopolitan type of colonization sought by the proprietors. The Episcopal Establishment had to reckon with the nonconformity of more than one sect, usually with that of a number of sects making common cause against it. On this basis it was often outnumbered, and politically was fighting a rearguard action.

Why was it, then, when the colonies had perpetuated here, each in the terms of its own life and earliest citizenry, the tradition of an established church, that this idea, and with it the fact itself, vanished off the scene when the national independence was won?

Surely, the first and most obvious answer to the question is this—it would have been impossible for the colonies to have agreed upon any single church as that which should become a national church. New England had been as aggressive in fighting the Revolution as it had previously been active in forwarding it. The only church which New England would have accepted as a national church would have been that of the Congregational order. She would never have accepted the Episcopal establishments which had been in nominal force from New York southward.[1]

Apart from New England the one other colony most to the front in the making of Revolution and in the subsequent framing of a Constitution was Virginia. Many Virginians would undoubtedly have welcomed a nationally established Episcopal Church. They were not, however, in a position to press any such proposal. They knew that New England would never conform, and were reconciled to that fact. Moreover they were themselves despoiled of many of their stronger religious leaders. Indeed, it is an open question how strong those leaders had been. There are many references to the Virginian clergy of pre-Revolutionary years which seem to suggest that an appreciable number of them had become, if not sporting parsons, at least easy-going churchmen of the Woodford type. In any case, by the time the Revolution was over, three-quarters of the Episcopal clergy in Virginia had gone back to England, and the church was left shorn of its leadership.

One would have supposed, given the strong Church of England tradition in Virginia and the relatively close connection of its churches with the mother country, that the laity of the colony would not have been so seditious. Much Virginian life at that time was, in a necessarily restricted form, that of the modest country estate in England. To this day every visitor to Mount Vernon, a few miles down the river from the city of Washington, is expected to say how like the English countryside the place was—and still is—and that George Washington was, *au fond*, a late eighteenth-century English country squire. There is no small measure of truth in these reassuring platitudes.

However, the strong Tory or Loyalist element in the colonies was as a whole made up of merchants, traders, and large landowners. It was for the most part the moneyed people who deplored the Revolution and tried to stave it off. Virginia had no sizable cities, and therefore no considerable commercial class. As for its landed proprietors, not a few had drifted into debt to backers in England. The old and ever renewed struggle between the planter-debtor and his creditor inclined many harassed Virginians to welcome revolution as an easy way of dodging their obligations. And as for the Anglican Church in Virginia, the fact that it had been able to live for over a hundred and fifty years without a single bishop in residence had satisfied it that, if need be, it could carry on its own life independent of England. Local vestries had run the church, and their procedure was to all intents and purposes congregational in its methods. Furthermore, with the success of the Revolution, the Episcopal Church was under the shadow of the defeat suffered by the mother country. Episcopalians in Virginia were not in a position to suggest that their church should be an establishment for the emerging nation.

The two oldest churches in the colonies, therefore, the Congregational in New England and the Episcopal in Virginia, which might conceivably have pressed in theory for an American establishment, cancelled each other out. Neither would have agreed to accord the other national recognition, and neither was strong enough to override the other before a Congress and in the making of a Constitution.

If for political and military reasons the Congregational Churches of New England were left, when the Revolution ended, in a stronger and more strategic position, they were by no means as strong as they may appear to have been. Massachusetts had lost her original charter in 1688, and though she was granted a new charter in 1691, this second charter required religious toleration for all except Roman Catholics and non-Trinitarians. The excesses of the earlier theocracy became impossible thereafter. With the coming of the eighteenth century liberal ideas began to invade the Puritan stronghold of the Calvinistic theology. This movement, which was to become explicit Unitarianism at the beginning of the nineteenth century, was implicit in much of the preaching and writing being done by pre-Revolutionary ministers. The laymen of Massachusetts who went to the second Continental Congress and the Constitutional Convention, first to declare American Independence and then to fashion the Constitution, were of the liberal rather than the conservative party, theologically. They would have had no interest in trying to foist the passing theocracy of an earlier time upon the country as a whole. If the Episcopal Church in Virginia was weakened by the exodus of its loyal clergy, the Puritan Church in New England was weakened by theological controversies within its own borders. Neither was in as strong a position in the 1780s as it had been in earlier times.

As for other religious bodies in the country: none of them aspired to become establishments, and most of them repudiated the very idea of an establishment. In this respect they were frankly sects; they asked, not to be accommodated to the order of this present world, but merely to be quit of the hostile attitudes and acts of that order as addressed to themselves. All they wanted was to be let alone and allowed to go their own way.

The Quakers, who had been numerous and influential in colonial times, centered in Pennsylvania, had withdrawn from open participation in the politics of that province by about the middle of the eighteenth century, acting under an impression that their political activities up to that time had injured their integrity as a spiritual society. What was true of them was true of all the scattered pietist groups in the middle and southern colonies. They had no aspirations to sit on worldly thrones beside temporal rulers. They were separatists by a conviction which had been matured out of bitter experience in the Old World.

The Baptists were undoubtedly the most aggressive and also the most effective single religious body in the colonies, so far as the demand for religious liberty was concerned. Roger Williams in Rhode Island had conditioned the thinking of Baptists on these problems and had long before prepared their minds for the separation of church and state. He lived only some forty miles from Boston; but between Providence and Boston a great gulf was fixed, theologically and ecclesiastically. Williams believed that the sources of the state should be sought and found in the secular rather than in the spiritual order. The right of magistrates is natural, human, civil, not religious. The officer of the state gains nothing and loses nothing by being a Christian, or by not being. Likewise, the Christian merchant, physician, lawyer, pilot, father, master are not better equipped for fulfilling their social function than are the members of any other religion. There can be no such thing as a Christian business, or a Christian profession of law or medicine. These vocations stand in their own right. No state may claim superiority over any other state by virtue of being, or professing to be, Christian. The state is not irreligious; it is simply non-religious. As for the church, Williams said it was like a college of physicians, a company of East India merchants, or any other society in London, which may convene themselves and dissolve themselves at pleasure. Roger Williams's ideas in these matters were and still are overstatements and oversimplifications of the problem. Indeed, he followed the logic of his own thinking so far that he outgrew the visible organized church, even of his own independent kind, and finally parted company with all institutional religion. Yet his overstatements were so true to Baptist convictions that one can readily see how this strongest single sect in the colonies, advocating religious liberty for all, was in entire good conscience prohibited by its own faith from any slightest interest in a union of church and state.

Given a situation as complex as that which we have briefly described, it is difficult to see how the makers of the American Constitution could have done otherwise than they actually did in providing for the separation of church and state. The men who framed the Constitution were all laymen; no priest, clergyman, minister, or rabbi had any part in it. James Madison voiced what must have been the common sense opinion of the meeting when he said, "In a free government the security for religious rights consists in a multiplicity of sects." One can only add that, if multiplication of sects beyond the numbers already on the ground in the 1780s is a further guarantee of religious rights, such rights are even more secure today than they were a hundred and fifty years ago!

Meanwhile it is difficult not to read out of the records of the time the layman's familiar impatience with theological controversy, and his readiness to invoke a plague on all their houses. For these laymen who cut the tangled knot were the rather emancipated, if not sophisticated, type of person who was much to the front, the world over, in the latter half of the eighteenth century. For the want of any more accurate term it is the custom of our historians to describe them as 'Deists.' The term presupposes belief in a divine creator to whom reverence is due, but disallows many, if not most, of the orthodox beliefs of the Christian Church. In particular the God of the Deists was, so far as the course of man's affairs was concerned, a non-interventionist. He left his servants largely to their own devices. They were upright, conscientious, moral men. There was among them no cult of atheism or connivance in lowered moral standards. They built no altars to the goddess of reason in their capitols, but they were not theological zealots, since the virtues of tolerance which they praised and practised forbade excess of religious zeal. Washington was a formally devout Episcopalian, but it is said that there is no record of his ever having taken the Sacrament. Thomas Jefferson belonged to no Christian body, though he attended church regularly and thought highly of the ethical teachings of Jesus. Benjamin Franklin said that religion is a private affair which right-thinking men do not care much to discuss. John Adams of Massachusetts belonged to the liberal wing of New England Congregationalism, and had parted company with his Calvinist forbears. There seems to have been abroad, among such men, a weariness with the sophistications of theology and an unwillingness to invite further ecclesiastical rivalries. In the attempt to understand them one is reminded of Professor Whitehead's remark about the Wisdom literature of Israel, that is religion, but "religion at a very low temperature."

More than one of our historians admits, therefore, that our federal government took form at a time when men of affairs were determined to avoid the earlier excesses of religious zeal, and were honestly persuaded of the merits of toleration. If so, their frame of mind was clearly reflected in their pronouncements. The absence in their documents of any references to the Bible is most marked. The name of God does not appear in the Constitution. More than one pious group has attempted over subsequent years to get the name written into the text, but to no effect. It may well be an overstatement to say, as one writer says, that 'the new republic was born in as secular a spirit as the later French republic,' but there is a measure of truth in the words. A more guarded statement is, perhaps, nearer the fact:

> At no period of our history, probably, were organized religion and social idealism so divided as at the time of the formation of the Federal Government.
>
> The whole atmosphere of the entire literature is secular. When one remembers that the Puritan principle, so far as it was Calvinistic, recognized the Jewish theocracy as a model for all time for all governments, the fact that the Old Testament is never alluded to as an authority by the principal authors of the Constitution should give some pulpit rhetoric pause. . . . The republic's ablest group of statesmen, in defending the proposed constitution in appeals to the widest public, and using skilfully every argument that would make the new document palatable to the greatest number of people, saw fit to ignore the whole subject of religion. It is not that it is attacked, or made little of, but the fact that it is entirely ignored, that marks the disappearance of the Puritan

theocratic idea. . . . The purely negative character of this attitude
appears on the face of the instrument.[2]

The liberal Deism of the Constitution makers, with its honest concern for religious liberties, was primarily English in its origin. The
writings and utterances of the time, whether political or theological,
constantly cite John Locke and acknowledge their indebtedness to
principles he had pronounced. The French Encyclopaedists were not
wholly unknown, but prior to the Revolution our colonists were far
more closely in touch with liberal thinkers in England than with those
in France. English books, rather than French, were the literary stock
in trade.

With the 1790s there was, it is true, a brief theatrical outburst of
popular enthusiasm for France. Civic feasts were held in celebration
of the success of the French Revolution; many a house showed the
liberty cap; many a hat carried the cockade. Formal titles, such as Sir
and Mr., Dr. and Rev., were discarded as survivals from an effete
English culture. They were replaced by the 'social and soul-warming
term Citizen.' The Citizen's wife was greeted as Citess, though there
was some doubt as to the accuracy of this designation and certain
purists preferred Civess.

For fifteen or twenty years following the Revolution the country was
patently at a moral and religious low water. This state of affairs was
in part merely a matter of normal post-war reaction. Even while the
Revolution was in process, Thomas Jefferson had been preparing for
friends in France his *Notes on Virginia,* in which he said, 'The spirit of
the times will alter. Our rulers will become corrupt, our people
careless. From the conclusion of this war we shall be going downhill.'
These were sober words from our most distinguished apologist for the
inherent excellence of human nature and the virtues of the average
man, but they were amply fulfilled at the time as, alas, they were to be
fulfilled again in 1865 and 1918.

The decline in public morality was matched by a brief popular cult
of rationalism, as against all orthodoxies. Allusions to Greek and
Latin authors tended to supersede the old conventional citations from
the Bible. Classical place-names—Rome and Athens, Syracuse and
Utica—were sown over the countryside without the slightest concern
for their relevance to the scene. Deistical societies were founded in
the larger cities, addressed by lecturers who were prepared to prove
that the Deluge was physically impossible, that the dimensions of the
ark precluded its carrying its alleged cargo, and that such stories have
an adverse effect on the Moral Temperament of Man. A journal
known as the *Temple of Reason* was launched, but was from the first
embarrassed by subscribers who did not even 'pay the Postage of their
Letters, when they order the Paper,' let alone paying for the paper

itself. Proposals were afoot for building a Temple of Nature in New York City, to be used 'for worship of One God Supreme and Benevolent Creator of the world; and for other purposes of a literary kind.' Persons of talent who wished to celebrate the moral and civilized character of mankind were invited to join an Ancient Society of Druids.

What is more to the point, the colleges of the country were passing through a period of extreme religious indifference. Channing, who was to become the great spokesman for New England Unitarianism, said that Harvard was never in a worse state than when he entered it in 1794, that the French Revolution had diseased the imagination of students and encouraged a general scepticism. Dartmouth reported its students as unruly, lawless, and without the fear of God. At Princeton there were only three or four students who made any profession of piety. The College of William and Mary was said to be a hotbed of infidelity. Timothy Dwight, the president of Yale, complained of the profaneness, drunkenness, gambling and lewdness of his charges, as well as their contemptuous indifference to every moral and religious subject. These comments have a familiar post-war ring, but for the last decade of the eighteenth century the cult of irreligion was undoubtedly accentuated by an adulation of republican France. The cultural prestige of France was, however, soon ended by the self-defeating course of affairs in that country, and by a general reassertion of the traditional concern of Americans for religion. The forces of moral decency, if not of formal faith, rallied to the defence of the cause, and by 1810 the country was beginning to be once more on an even keel.[3]

It is impossible, however, to resist the conclusion that in its date the framing of the Constitution of the United States coincided with the late eighteenth-century cult of rationalism, and that the prevalence of enlightened deistic ideas among educated classes was in part responsible for the studied silences of the document as to the existence of God, and its unwillingness to commit itself, even in the most general terms, to any Christian ideas. One can only say that, given the prior history of colonial times and the subsequent record, the framers of the Constitution must be credited with religious understatement, rather than with overstatement. There had been and there was to be more religion in American life than the Constitution would seem to suggest. But it is probably true that the deliberate silences of the document upon the whole matter, and its understatements, were the price which had then to be paid for a vindication of the principles of toleration and liberty in matters religious. Indeed the word toleration was already in process of being outmoded, since tolerance implies the existence of some authoritative body which exercises that virtue. The refusal of the federal government to assume and to exercise any religious authority whatsoever precluded all opportunity for toleration on its part, and cleared the ground for religious liberty in the broadest conceivable terms of that ideal.

NOTES

1. In 1775 there were formally established churches in three of the New England colonies; these were Congregational. The Anglican Church was established in four counties of New York and in five of the southern colonies. It should be added, however, that these Anglican establishments were technically imperfect, since they had neither bishops nor ecclesiastical courts.

2. *The Religious Background of American Culture,* by Thomas Cuming Hall, pp. 184–6. Little, Brown, and Company, Boston, 1930.

3. On this whole period, cf. *Republican Religion* (The American Revolution and the Cult of Reason), by G. Adolph Koch. Henry Holt and Company, New York, 1938.

11

Edwin Scott Gaustad

The Making of America:
Immigration and Assimilation

"The Homeless, Tempest-tost"

The history of the United States is a history of
immigration. Colonial immigrants set the pattern followed and inten-
sified during the nineteenth and early twentieth centuries. From 1815
to the First World War, a century later, approximately thirty million
persons sailed for American shores. Affecting the nation's history and
culture in every respect, the immigrant transformed that culture even
as he was transformed by it.

. . .

From 1815 to 1860 five million immigrants settled in America, the
largest bloc coming from Ireland (2 million), the next largest from
Germany (1.5 million). England, Wales, and Scotland also dispatched
sizeable numbers in the pre-Civil War period, with smaller groups
coming from Switzerland, Norway, Sweden, and the Netherlands.
Between 1860 and 1890 the number of new arrivals rose to ten million,
and in the brief period from 1890 to World War I the figure zoomed to
fifteen million. In this third period the majority emigrated from
southern or eastern Europe—Italy, Austria-Hungary, Rumania, Greece,
Turkey, and Russia.

In the tumult of transplanting, religion often provided personal
security and ethnic cohesion. In a new land and among strange
people, removed from ancestral home and family ties, the uprooted

Taken from pp. 202, 206–209, 211–214, 216–221, 224–226, "The Making of America: Immigration and Assimilation" in *A Religious History of America* by
Edwin Scott Gaustad. Copyright © 1966 by Edwin Scott Gaustad. Reprinted by permission of Harper & Row, Publishers, Inc. Edwin Scott
Gaustad is Professor of History at the University of California, Riverside.

immigrant turned to the synagogue and church for the comfort of the familiar, for the assurance of continuity in a life severely disjoined. When so much was different, when so many adjustments were demanded, when one's whole world had been turned inside out, calm confidence was found—if at all—in an enduring faith.

Strangely, however, those elements that granted security to the first-generation immigrant often took it away from the second generation. Those born in America found security more by identifying with their new nation than by retreating to liturgy or life distinctly "old world." Second-generation immigrants therefore faced a hard choice: abandon a foreign worship for an "American faith," or accommodate that exotic religion to its new environment. Both courses were taken. While some sons and daughters turned away from old-country ways to prove that they too "belonged" in America, others modernized or Americanized their synagogues and churches. Both groups found themselves opposed not only by the older generation but even more vigorously by newly arriving immigrants who instinctively, hungrily reached for the familiar, the tried, the trusted.

· · ·

The great wave of Irish that arrived before the Civil War posed special problems for Roman Catholicism. The very magnitude of the influx taxed resources to and beyond their limits. The urgency of spiritual needs, moreover, could not be divorced from physical needs obvious in every seaboard city, in every malignant slum. To alleviate the serious social ills Archbishop John Ireland of St. Paul promoted Irish colonization in the uncrowded interior of America. Though some feared that scattered immigrants might be lost to the Church, Ireland successfully planted several colonies in southern Minnesota in the 1870's and 1880's. The Irish Catholic Colonization Society, which he helped found, arranged for cheap railroad transportation from the seaboard as well as for easy payment on land settled and farmed. Archbishop Ireland provided a priest in each colony to aid and advise the settlers in every aspect of their new life.

Despite the energy and devotion poured into this venture, most of the Irish, recalling the dreary, impoverished farm life behind, remained in the cities. There the major crises of immigration and assimilation were squarely met, as church and parochial school took up their ponderous tasks. The Church's ministry to the Irish, while demanding enough, soon expanded to include Germans, French (especially from Canada), Italians, Poles, Austrians, Hungarians, and many others. With greater membership came graver problems.

· · ·

Judaism in America, augmented before the Civil War by an influx of German-speaking Jews, received after that war even greater numbers from eastern Europe. Again the challenges to the religious leadership were momentous, but no central organization directed the immigration, colonization, or preservation of the Jewish people. Instead a myriad of organizations, some religious and some secular, sprang up. Wherever a *minyan* (ritual group of ten men) was found, at least a synagogue could be organized and Judaic worship begun. Apart from the cities, however, Jews frequently lacked even that much spiritual direction. Though some wished to lose themselves in American culture, many were anxious to save themselves and their ancient faith from that absorbing culture.

While nineteenth-century immigration brought dramatic increases to both Catholicism and Judaism, Protestant ranks were also swelled by Lutherans from Germany and Scandinavia, Reformed from Holland and Switzerland, Episcopalians from England, and a variety of sectarians from most of Europe. Protestants carried on vigorous missionary and benevolent activity among co-religionists and non-Protestants alike, dispensing charity, increasing literacy, and seeking converts fervently. For all American religion, immigration constituted a momentous challenge. To some, however, it loomed as a horrendous threat.

"America for Americans"

When a normal fear of the strange and foreign becomes an abnormal hatred of the strange and foreign, then American democracy receives its severest test. The nineteenth century saw two such severe testing times, one shortly before the Civil War and the other near the end of the century. In both periods nativism fed on fears, biases, and aspirations that marched under the banner of religion. And in both periods the American dream almost turned to nightmare.

• • •

As long as Roman Catholics were few in number, they aroused little direct animosity and harassment. The Catholicism of Spain, the prelates of France, the pronouncements of the pope—these could be and were roundly denounced. But the Catholics living in America? Well, there weren't many, and the good patriot John Carroll seemed to have everything under control. From the 1830's on, however, Catholic membership rose rapidly, making the Roman church by 1850 the largest religious group in the United States. The creation of new parishes, the promotion of schools and seminaries, the publication of newspapers and journals proved that Catholicism in America was on the move.

Where would the expansion end?   Were men's liberties in danger?
Was America's destiny secure?

· · ·

Anti-Catholicism moved from intemperate propaganda to violent
attack. An Ursuline convent in Massachusetts was burned in 1834. A
decade later riots broke out in Philadelphia, resulting in the total
destruction of St. Michael's and St. Augustine's Churches. While mob
action was everywhere deplored, oratory and press kept passions high
and rumors rampant.

Of all the printed testimonies to this hysteria, the most scurrilous
(and now thoroughly discredited) was a small book entitled *Awful
Disclosures of the Hotel Dieu Nunnery of Montreal,* first published in
1836. Purporting to be by an ex-nun, Maria Monk, the book seemed to
confirm every suspicion ever harbored by non-Catholics. That three
hundred thousand copies of this lurid volume were sold prior to the
Civil War testifies both to its influence and to the broad base of
anti-Catholic, nativist sentiment.

Though reactions to the influx of Catholic immigrants took many
forms, three areas of searing friction appeared. The first was economic. Cheap Irish labor threatened to undercut native American
labor. When the local brickmakers of Charlestown, Massachusetts,
felt trapped by the competition of Irish labor, they responded by
burning the convent. The financial panic of 1837 resulted in a shortage
of jobs which in turn produced greater resentment against increased
competition in the labor market. As complaints and bitterness grew,
"native American" associations multiplied and resistance became reso-
lute.

Second, Catholicism appeared peculiarly vulnerable in the political
area, both for its tight hierarchical organization and for its alliance
with anti-democratic governments abroad. The opinion prevailed, occasionally buttressed by a Church pronouncement, that the American
pattern of religious liberty was theoretically and ultimately unacceptable to Roman Catholicism. Moreover, the "trusteeism" controversy
(concerning the right of Catholic laity to control parish finances and to
select their own ministers) persuaded many non-Catholics that the
Church was fundamentally undemocratic and *ipso facto* un-American.
This prolonged dispute, extending throughout the first half of the
nineteenth century, created temporary schisms within Catholic parishes themselves (e.g., in New Orleans, Charleston, Norfolk, Buffalo)
even as it fed the flames of nativism.

Education constituted a third area of tension. Both Germans (Lutheran as well as Catholic) and Irish found the American public school
either (1) inadequate in its religious instruction or (2) biased in that
instruction. Controversy waxed hottest in New York and Philadelphia

as ecclesiastical authorities sought to obtain public funds for the Catholic schools. Failing in this, Church leaders sought permission for Catholic children in public schools at least to hear scripture from a Catholic Bible. John Hughes, bishop (later archbishop) of New York, led a vigorous fight for a share of public school monies, contending that the city's Public School Society was really Protestant and that public school texts were openly anti-Catholic. Failing to win major concessions, the Church began to build its own ambitious and expensive separate school system. Far from quieting all criticism, however, the establishment of the parochial schools appeared to cast reproach upon the public schools themselves. The nation's main agency of assimilation and Americanization was being bypassed. Was it being undermined? Was unity still possible? Was America still one?

. . .

These deeply disturbing questions, widely discussed in pulpit, press, and political assembly, led to the major political expression of American nativism: the Know-Nothing or American party, created in 1854. Exercising real power only briefly, the party won quick successes at the polls. But on the critical issues of slavery and secession, Know-Nothingism lost so much relevance and appeal that by 1860 it was politically dead. Moreover, its denial of the democratic faith moved men to seek saner solutions for problems that proved as persistent as they were complex.

. . .

Following four bitter years of war, the nation busied itself for a time binding its own bleeding wounds. But in the 1880's resistance to immigration mounted again. In California, for example, the influx of Chinese provoked resentments that ultimately cut off further immigration from China. The Irish Catholic immigrant opposed cheap Chinese labor in much the same way he had been opposed in the East a generation earlier. To be anti-Chinese was to be pro-Irish, pro-Catholic, pro-organized labor. To be pro-Chinese was to be aligned with Protestantism and the business community against Irish Catholicism and the Workingmen's Party (led by Dennis Kearney). Gradually, however, when the need for cheap labor declined and the Protestant vision of ten thousand Chinese converts dimmed, defense of continued immigration all but disappeared. As mob violence grew and anti-Oriental feeling soared, the federal government in May 1882 passed the first of a series of Exclusion Acts, halting all further immigration from China.

Meanwhile, Easterners again resisted the growing "foreignness" of urban population. Political fears of the radicalism, socialism, and

anarchism found or suspected among new arrivals aggravated the
religious fears. Riots, strikes, and intemperate words convinced many
Americans that revolution was being smuggled into their very midst.
Anti-Catholicism erupted once more, with parochial schools and organized labor again becoming battle stations. The appointment in 1893 of
Cardinal Satolli as the first Apostolic Delegate to the United States
spurred rumors of papal designs on American liberties.

Anti-Semitism likewise increased in proportion to the growing Jewish population. Jews, resented as either too expert at capitalism or
too crafty in socialism, incurred greater resentment when they joined
Catholics in protesting Bible reading in the public schools.
International intrigue, notably in the world of finance, was laid at the
door of the Jewish banker, merchant, or even pawnbroker. The evils
of the big city—and there were many—were too readily attributed to
the Jewishness of the city. Finally, racist theories used against the
Negro and the Oriental now proved useful against the Jew, as preju-
dices mounted and stereotypes hardened.

• • •

As eastern European immigration swelled, doctrines of Nordic supremacy and Anglo-Saxon superiority drew attentive audiences.
Blond, blue-eyed Protestants would save America; dark, sloe-eyed Slavs
would ruin it. Slavic strikers were shot in Pennsylvania, Italians were
lynched in New Orleans, and anti-Jewish riots broke out in the South.
In 1894 the Immigration Destruction League, formed in New England,
urged that only the better "stocks" be henceforth admitted to America.
Early in the twentieth century some social scientists supported restric-
tionist demands, and shortly after World War I a revived Ku Klux
Klan intimidated the "foreigner" in general—the Negro, the Catholic,
and the Jew in particular.

Some nativist drives were unmistakably religious in origin and motive. The American Protective Association, founded in Clinton, Iowa,
in 1887, directed its propaganda specifically against the "Catholic menace." Unlike the Know-Nothings, the A.P.A. solicited and obtained
foreign memberships, most of its support coming from immigrants of
German, Scandinavian, Canadian, and British background. A.P.A.
members swore to resist the growth of Catholicism, pledging that they
would not employ Roman Catholics, nor help build their churches, nor
vote for any Roman Catholic, nor "countenance the nomination, in any
caucus or convention, of a Roman Catholic for any office in the gift of
the American people." Within a decade the A.P.A., having reached the
peak of its power, rapidly declined; yet the mood it represented
endured for decades—indeed, for generations.

World War I widened social fissures that could in calmer days be
ignored. Ties with the old country were still strong, and new loyalties

were compromised by old memories. Theodore Roosevelt spoke impatiently of "hyphenated Americans," and in 1916 Woodrow Wilson wrote intemperately to a pro-German Irish agitator: "I should feel deeply mortified to have you or anybody like you vote for me. Since you have access to many disloyal Americans and I have not, I will ask you to convey this message to them."

A nation at war now saw ethnic diversity as a threat to its security. Furthermore, social reformers and city planners argued that the spiraling problems of poverty, sanitation, education, slums, disease, immorality, and crime could not be solved as long as thousands of immigrants annually poured off the ships into the overburdened cities. In 1921, therefore, Congress passed the first of a series of acts restricting immigration both in number and in kind. With the adoption of the National Origins Act of 1924 a quota system favorable to northern and western European countries was the official federal policy until 1965. The mighty river of immigration that for three hundred years had cascaded into the United States now became a tiny trickle. Freedom's lamp still burned brightly on Liberty Island, but on nearby Ellis Island, where so many immigrants had been received, the gates closed at last in 1954. As they swung shut, a magnificent chapter of American history, even of world history, came to an end.

"And Crown Thy Good"

For the long-established citizen the assimilation of newcomers proceeded slowly. Differences of dress, speech, custom and diet constantly called attention to the strangers sojourning "with thee in your land." But for the immigrant, Americanization and assimilation seemed much too fast—not nearly slow enough! Dutchman, Pole, or Russian hastened from the boat to the nearest church or synagogue only to discover an unfamiliar institution. The Lutheran sat down to a service conducted in English—a language he hardly knew. The Polish Catholic found himself surrounded by sculptured saints he never heard of, preached to by Irish clerics he could not understand. Jews from Russia were first perplexed, then angered by the novelties confronting them in the Ashkenazim (German) congregation. For all these America was too quickly embraced, ancestral ways too lightly forsaken.

• • •

Among the Reformed Protestants from Holland, for example, those arriving in mid-nineteenth century felt little kinship with their co-religionists long in America. The latter sang hymns (not psalms), permitted choirs, ignored revered creeds and doctrines, abandoned the Dutch language, and even tolerated membership in Masonic lodges. The church they found in America was not the church they left behind in Holland. Yet both were Dutch Reformed Churches. What to do except start a True Dutch Reformed Church (1864) which would be what every pious Dutch immigrant expected his Church to be?

Coming from so many contrasting cultures, Catholics sometimes found the ethnic pull stronger than the ecclesiastical one. German Catholics wanted German priests and bishops as well as the use of their own language wherever the vernacular was permitted. To a lesser degree the Portuguese, the French, and the Italians voiced similar sentiments. Wisely resisting that normal desire, the Roman Catholic Church promoted the Americanization and assimilation of the whole. Polish Catholics, chafing under this policy, in 1907 established their own organization: the Polish National Catholic Church.

The problems facing the eastern European Jews were severest of all. The older Jewish immigrants, predominantly German, had begun a major reform in Judaism's doctrine and practice when the flood of newer immigrants arrived. These Jews found little community among their German co-religionists. Services in English were held on Sunday, not on the Sabbath; children attended Sunday Schools, not Talmud Torah Schools. Dietary and other regulations of the Torah (Law) were modified, ignored, or interpreted symbolically. Instrumental music was introduced, and seating by families rather than by sexes practiced. The eastern European Jew happening into a reform German synagogue might fear that by mistake he had stumbled upon a Protestant church.

•   •   •

While part of the Germanic reform was conscious Americanization, the movement was broader than that. Ghettoized Judaism had, of necessity, held itself rigid and unchanging for centuries. In the liberalism of nineteenth-century western Europe, however, Jews breathing a freer, cleaner air began to take their legitimate place in the modern world. Modernizing Judaism—making it relevant to an urban, industrial, secularized world—had already begun in Germany before the major migrations to America. Rabbis coming from this atmosphere simply carried on the program in America, adjusting it to the challenges and freedoms offered in a ghettoless land. By 1873 a Union of American Hebrew Congregations was formed with Hebrew Union College of Cincinnati founded two years later. Under the direction of a native rabbinate the twin task of reformation and Americanization could be carried forward.

For Jews as for so many others America was a great new laboratory for social and spiritual experiment. There one might, with God's help, perfect a product so awe-inspiring, so unmistakably superior that all the nation, indeed all the world, would be enthralled. America was still a place where old men could dream and young men behold visions. Isaac M. Wise, who went to Cincinnati as rabbi in 1854, was wholly American in his high hopes, his heady optimism. Judaism, reformed of its archaic limitations, ennobled in its ethical ideals, cultured in its every fiber, could elevate all America. Such a religion could become, Wise believed, the religion of all mankind.

. . .

But then came the flood of immigrants not tuned to western Europe's reform, not partners in Wise's dream. Fleeing the ghettoes or the brutal pogroms, these Jews asked only to pursue peacefully their ancient faith in all its purity and strength-giving familiarity. Each ethnic group, if not each ship's company, preferred its own synagogue, its own cantor, and, when available, its own rabbi. As a measure of the growing diversity, New York City had only fourteen synagogues in the 1850's, but by the end of that century some three hundred separate congregations were scattered about the city.

. . .

Religious life demanded more than the synagogue. Funeral associations, benevolent societies, and above all, schools were required to maintain the traditional life. Schools presented the hardest problem, as resources both in leadership and money were meager. A school providing only Hebrew language and literature was not enough, since it failed to meet the standards set by state law. A school competing with public education was, on the other hand, too much, since it exceeded the resources of immigrant Jewry. Varied experiments at every level resulted in Jewish religious education being largely a part-time, after-public-school activity. Only a minority, however, met even this minimum in the education of their children.

. . .

Synagogue life itself took one of three paths. Orthodox Judaism maintained the ritual laws of behavior (*kashruth*) in a tightly knit communal society, where food was properly prepared, the Hebrew language carefully preserved, and the Law strictly interpreted. Reform, as noted above, moved rapidly toward a reinterpretation of Jewish doctrine and a modification of Jewish practice. Between these two, Conservative Judaism arose. Conservatism, which was less rigid than Orthodoxy and more traditional than Reform, served as a bridge between newer and older immigrants and maintained the Jew's religious life across much of suburban America.

Under the early leadership of Rabbi Sabato Morais and the later leadership of such men as Solomon Schechter and Cyrus Adler, the

Conservative movement gained great influence. New York's Jewish Theological Seminary, over which Schechter presided from 1902 to 1915, trained an English-speaking rabbinate that saved many eastern European immigrants from a radical abandonment of their faith. Conservative Judaism also saved many second- and third-generation suburbanites from a too easy exchange of religious peculiarity for cultural conformity. In the campaign to keep Americanization from becoming absorption Solomon Schechter emerged with the clearest, most commanding voice. "We must leave off talking about Occidentalizing our religion," he wrote, remembering that the "Torah gave spiritual accommodation for thousands of years to all sorts and conditions of men . . . and it should also prove broad enough to harbor the different minds of the present century." A sermon in English is fine; a renunciation of history is folly.

As Americanization proceeded, Judaism adapted to its new culture and assisted that culture toward richer expression. Though much about American civilization was novel and strange, at its very center stood something marvelously familiar and old: the God of Abraham, Isaac, and Jacob.

What, after all, did Americanization mean? Must one surrender his beard, his beads, his shawl, his crucifix to become an American? Must he forget the Irish songs he knew, the Hungarian music he loved, the Mosaic laws he honored, the Norwegian bread he brought, the Italian holidays he celebrated, or any of a dozen more festivities, fashions, or mores? How much must the melting pot melt?

• • •

The immigrants' answers to these questions were not uniform—not for Protestants, Catholics, or Jews. And answers imposed from without tended to be unhelpful and unavailing. Gradually, the immigrants, by actions more than words, revealed what they thought it meant to be an American. In the most general terms it meant a share in the national dream, as inheritors of the American past and as stockholders in the American future. In economic terms this suggested the right to property, employment, and investment enjoyed by other citizens. In political terms it meant the privileges of suffrage and the protection of constitutional liberties.

In religious terms it involved at least three things. First, it meant something about freedom in religion, a freedom that in law and in fact exceeded what most nineteenth-century arrivals had ever experienced. Americanization meant accepting, enjoying, and ultimately defending this freedom. It could be accepted initially as a simple acknowledgment that in the United States no official religion had the protection and support of the state. The Swedish Lutheran, the Italian Catholic, the Greek Orthodox could perceive the difference immediately. And strange and radical though it was, they accepted it. (To enjoy it took a little more time, as it had for Lyman Beecher.) The recruitment of members, the gathering of support, the competition against heresy, heterodoxy, and indifference—these might not look like rare joys. But after a time few were willing to trade this purifying effort for the corrupting patronage of government, the malignant hatreds bred by persecution, or the adulterating confusion of political with spiritual. Ultimately what may have been accepted as an onerous necessity came to be defended as the dearest liberty.

Second, Americanization had some relevance to language. English enjoyed no special sanctity, just currency. To participate fully in America one must learn English. This simple fact was readily perceived and readily acknowledged—except in religion. Though the battle for the ancestral tongue might be fought in the market place, assembly, or school, the issue was religion: its preservation and its perpetuation. Yet on these very grounds—religion's survival and growth—the argument for English was won. For only the first-generation immigrant found strength and appeal in maintenance of the older tongue. Some churches and synagogues went through the motions for another generation or more, aided by the church schools; gradually, however, the language wall began to crumble. Prayers were translated, hymns received English words, and in at least one service the sermon would be in English.

Language was widely considered the key to ethnic unity and cultural cohesion. But other old-world ties persisted: holidays, parades, dances, special rites, fraternal or military orders, even social and personal habits. In this last category of public and private morality Americanization made its third demand on the nineteenth-century immigrant. A kind of frontier, frugal, aggressive "Methodist Puritanism" permeated much of American life. Lutherans accustomed to friendly picnics on Sunday afternoons, with beer and wine for all, found their midwestern neighbors shocked and scandalized. Temperance and strict sabbath observance, the norm in many regions, became the law in some. "Blue laws," elaborately detailed, demanded a moral conformity often in the narrowest terms.

A concert pianist from Paris, on tour in the United States in 1846, lit a cigar on the streets of Boston. He describes his experience:

> I had not proceeded ten feet when a constable stopped me, shocked.
> "Sir, smoking is forbidden."
> "You are joking, constable."
> "Not at all. Smoking in the streets is forbidden. If you cannot contain yourself, go home to smoke. . . . Your infraction is all the more shocking and blameworthy on Sunday, the day consecrated to the glory of God."

I could not help but consider this taboo, in the land of all the liberties, tyrannical. But I had to obey.

While one need not surrender cigar-smoking to be Americanized, immigrant institutions generally sought the favor and good will of the older population. In this way a pervading Anglo-American morality infiltrated the moral and religious codes of many old-world settlers. As Archbishop Ireland noted in 1891, "An honest ballot and social decorum among Catholics will do more for God's glory and the salvation of souls than midnight flagellations or Compostellan pilgrimages."

If church and synagogue membership were voluntary, then it ought to be meaningful: discipline was demanded, moral achievement was expected. The immigrant's religion, it was assumed, would be a power for reform and reconstruction in America—otherwise it was not religion. All liberty's children were invited to shape their nation's destiny.

12

Clifton E. Olmstead

Social Religion
in Urban America

One of the marvels of American life in that restless, ebullient era which spanned the administrations of Grant and McKinley was the extraordinary growth of the big cities. In 1870, little more than one-fifth of the country's population lived in urban areas; by 1890, the proportion had risen to one-third. This drive toward the city continued apace until 1910, when it was somewhat offset by a trend to the suburbs. By this time, however, the age of the metropolis had dawned, in which the cities reached out and irresistibly drew the surrounding communities into the vortex of urban life. This influx into the cities was made feasible principally through the rise of great industrial corporations, which, by 1919, were employing 86 per cent of all wage earners.

No social panacea resulted from the trend toward urban civilization. The visitor to a typical East Coast city in 1890, New York for example, would have walked through traffic-congested, litter-strewn streets lined by bleak narrow structures in which "cliff-dwellers" carried on lonely existences in a fellowship of the unconcerned. He might have inspected the grimy tenements, breeding grounds for disease and crime, or he might have looked into the steaming sweatshops where refugees from eastern Europe labored long and dangerous hours for a mere pittance. There were advantages in the city, but there were also hazards and a host of new social problems to be resolved.

Motivated by numerous forces, organized religion sought in varied ways to minister to the social needs of the time. Always to be

From Clifton E. Olmstead, *Religion in America: Past and Present*, © 1961. Reprinted by permission of Prentice-Hall, Inc., Englewood Cliffs, New Jersey. Clifton E. Olmstead, at the time of his premature death, was a historian of religion at George Washington University.

considered was the activistic spirit of the churches, the desire to be doing something for the Kingdom of God. Also important was the triumph of mass evangelism which nurtured a passion to defeat sin wherever it might appear. Still another factor was the mounting interest in the new psychology and sociology, which sought to deal scientifically with society's problems. Christians were by no means one in their approach to contemporary issues. Some adhered to the pattern of ameliorating social evils by fighting sin and practicing charity; some advocated a reconstruction of economic and political organization along socialistic lines; others were dissatisfied with the social structure but were more conservative in their advocacy of change.

The Gospel of Wealth

The unprecedented fiscal opportunities of the Gilded Age seemed to confirm the view of many that unrestricted personal initiative would lead to rewards commensurate with acumen and industry as well as to maximum economic stability. If theological support for this conviction was sought, it was most likely to be found in the doctrine of God's providence. The most representative apologist for this philosophy was Andrew Carnegie, who presented it in a manner clearly reminiscent of Charles Darwin. As Carnegie propounded the theory in 1889, where there was free competition in business it was inevitable that there should be a higher standard of living. Of course, the process would involve painful social readjustment as the weak gave way before the strong, but the survival of the fittest was the way of life.

A majority of the clergy, while concerned over the problem of mass poverty, carefully avoided any criticism of laissez-faire capitalism and continued to prescribe evangelism as the remedy for social ills. Russell H. Conwell, the most popular lecturer of the day, told his audiences that "money is power and you ought to be reasonably ambitious to have it. You ought because you can do more good with it than you could without it."

During the years of revolutionary economic and social change, a striking transformation took place in the churches. Membership in the large Protestant bodies became almost exclusively the property of professional men, businessmen, white-collar workers, and farmers. While at one time denominations such as the Methodist and Baptist prided themselves on their ministry to the poor, they could now note with satisfaction that they were becoming churches with status, with soaring budgets made possible by millionaire communicants.

With increasing affluence came a demand for external splendor. Gothic and Romanesque structures embellished with beautifully designed stained-glass windows became standard in Protestantism. Some congregations patterned their churches after existing models in Europe, while others sought to outdo them through the achievement of more solid construction and greater beauty.

Church-related colleges also entered into an unprecedented building program made possible by the gifts of philanthropists. Leading universities such as Cornell, Stanford, and Duke originated through the munificent gifts of wealthy industrialists. John D. Rockefeller gave a fortune to the University of Chicago. It was not long before every college in the country was looking for some grand benefactor who would solve all its financial woes.

As churches and colleges looked increasingly to business for support, they came to interpret their own activities more frequently from the standpoint of a business enterprise, emphasizing administration and finance. Successful ministers of large city churches were expected to have all the skills of an oil magnate, while college presidents gave up teaching in favor of administration and fund raising. At denominational conventions there was a tendency to treat the communication of the Gospel much as a corporation might treat the promotion of its product. An aura of professionalism and machine-like perfectionism settled over the churches, leading to the charge that organized religion was becoming concerned more with goals than souls.

The Labor Issue

During the 1850's, American labor began to experiment with what came to be a powerful weapon for bargaining with management: the union. While there were only some 300 unions in the country at the close of the Civil War, unionism mushroomed during the ensuing years. One of the more important unions was the Knights of Labor, founded in 1869 to protect workers' rights and advance education and morality. Somewhat more conservative was the American Federation of Labor, a trade union founded in 1886, which stressed collective bargaining as a means of negotiation.

In September 1873, the nation entered a period of financial depression, hastened by the failure of the leading banking firm, Jay Cooke and Company. Drastic wage cuts brought labor unions into conflict with capital, but the unions were notably unsuccessful. In July 1877, violence broke out between striking railroad workers and militiamen sent to restore order at the Pennsylvania Railroad's Pittsburgh depot. Similar violence in other cities led authorities to take sharp measures against strikers in order to stamp out what appeared to be a labor revolution. In 1886, another series of strikes swept the nation as workingmen agitated for an eight-hour day.

Since the membership of Protestant churches during this period was composed chiefly of persons in the middle class, it is not surprising that ordinarily they failed to see social problems through the eyes of labor. Most were at least nominally concerned over the problem of poverty, but fear of socialism, which they associated with labor, prompted them to oppose the unions.

Nevertheless, an occasional voice spoke in behalf of labor. Episcopal Bishop Frederick Dan Huntington of Central New York admonished his fellow clergy for their indifference to social concerns, and William Jewett Tucker of Andover Seminary maintained that the labor question is a legitimate concern of Christianity. Yet despite the efforts of socially minded Protestant leaders, there was no notable influx of laborers into the churches. A partial explanation for this situation could be found in a statement by Samuel Gompers of the American Federation of Labor in 1898: "My associates have come to look upon the church and the ministry as the apologists and defenders of the wrong committed against the interests of the people, simply because the perpetrators are possessors of wealth . . . whose real God is the almighty dollar."

The Roman Catholic Church had particular reason to be concerned with the problems of labor because much of its membership potential lay in the immigrant labor class. At the same time the church was somewhat embarrassed by the situation, for conservatives within its midst adhered strictly to a policy of non-interference in social issues. Nevertheless, liberals such as Cardinal Gibbons did what they could to abet the cause of labor unions. When Cardinal Taschereau of Quebec obtained from the curia an official disapproval of the Knights of Labor in his province, Gibbons reported to the Prefect of Propaganda that condemnation of the Knights of Labor would have harmful consequences for the church in America. A year later Propaganda ruled that the Knights might be tolerated. Gibbons had won an important victory.

Christian Social Service

To the impressive number of church members whose social and economic views were of conservative bent, the task of organized Christianity was to provide instruction and worship; for the more unfortunate elements in the community there was the obligation to grant charity and evangelization, since in order to rebuild society one would first have to rebuild men. Firm in this conviction, many

Christians inaugurated programs for the amelioration of social conditions.

Among Protestants, the institutional church, designed to render a broader ministry in urban areas, became a standard outlet for the expression of philanthropic concern in the post-Civil War era. St. George's Episcopal Church on the East Side of New York, during the 1880's, opened a parish house and offered courses in industrial education. In Philadelphia, Russell Conwell's Baptist Temple offered gymnasiums, sewing classes, manual-training courses, reading rooms, day nurseries, and social clubs.

Closely related to the institutional church program was the work of the nondenominational city mission. The movement was patterned after the Water Street Mission of New York, founded by Jerry MacAuley, a converted drunkard and burglar, shortly after the Civil War. This rescue mission offered derelicts not only food and shelter but fervid preaching which guided them to reclamation and a life of usefulness. Within a few years many cities had missions of identical character.

After the Civil War, the Young Men's Christian Association began to devote itself increasingly to activities among middle-class youth, particularly to their physical development; in this way bodily exercise became Christianized. For several decades, however, the Y.M.C.A. in certain cities maintained services principally for the poor. In many respects the Young Women's Christian Association, founded in England in 1855 and organized in Boston in 1866, was the feminine counterpart of the Y.M.C.A. While the local associations offered basic services such as providing food and lodging and operating employment bureaus for those in need, their chief emphasis became the cultivation of the "physical, social, intellectual, moral and spiritual interests of young women."

The last twenty years of the nineteenth century witnessed an effort by evangelical Protestants to relate religion to social life through the activities of cooperative organizations such as the Evangelical Alliance and the Convention of Christian Workers. The Alliance brought prominent religious leaders together to discuss the evils of society and seek a solution to them. By 1889, such alliances had been formed in more than forty cities. The Convention of Christian Workers, established in 1886, was an organization of mission workers. Its purposes were to provide classes and reading rooms, to train theological students and laymen in social work, to help individual churches found missions in impoverished areas, and to raise funds for missions.

Prior to 1890, the principal activities of the Roman Catholic Church in the area of social betterment were along charitable lines. One of the most important agencies was the time-honored Society of St. Vincent de Paul, a lay missionary movement which endeavored to bring both physical aid and spiritual sustenance to unfortunates. A leading benevolent fraternal society was the Knights of Columbus, founded for Roman Catholic laymen in 1882. Its original goal was to protect families of its members by means of a system of insurance; after 1885, the society rapidly developed into a national movement which continued to emphasize beneficence and education.

One of the most remarkable religious and philanthropic organizations was the Salvation Army, founded in England in 1878 by William Booth, a former Wesleyan Methodist preacher. Its program stressed witnessing to Christ by informal preaching and outdoor evangelistic meetings which featured brass bands. After its reorganization along quasi-military lines, the movement became highly centralized and authoritarian. Its theology was conservative, with an accent on sin, redemption, and growth in holiness. The Army was introduced to the United States in 1880; within a few months twelve local units and an official newspaper, the *War Cry*, had been established. The organization was possibly best known for the work of its Slum Brigades, which went into run-down sections of the cities, held services in saloons and halls, brought relief to the destitute, and preached against vice.

The Social Gospel

While the main stream of Protestant Christianity in the United States followed a pietistic and doctrinally conservative position which conceived social progress in terms of organized charities, a group of clerical leaders, small at first, began to ask searching questions about the ethics of the social and economic structure of American life. They saw man as a child of God with infinite capacities for moral improvement. They saw Jesus as a prophet of social righteousness. Their Gospel began with men and moved out to God. It was a typically nineteenth-century faith, but one which had been baptized in the life and thought of the Old and New Testaments.

One of the leading voices at the beginning of the Social Gospel movement was that of Washington Gladden (1836–1918), Congregationalist pastor in Columbus, Ohio. He regarded the competitive basis of laissez-faire capitalism an un-Christian. A proper goal was cooperation between capital and labor, which would be realized if the worker owned a share in the business. But what was needed most of all in industry was the "power of Christian love." Through the power of love and moral persuasion, a more ideal order was bound to be achieved. Another important contributor was Josiah Strong, Congregational pastor, who stunned the nation by his penetrating analysis of its problems in his book, *Our Country* (1885). It was Strong's contention that greed for money and power was corrupting the country. By sounding a note of crisis, he awakened many ministers and congregations to a vital concern over the social situation and gave a powerful impetus to the cause of the Social Gospel.

Decidedly influential in spreading the Social Gospel was the widely read novel by Charles M. Sheldon, entitled *In His Steps: What Would Jesus Do?* Within a few months after its publication in 1897, one hundred thousand copies had been sold. The story concerned the membership of an average American church and its efforts for an entire year to ascertain and do the will of Jesus in every situation which arose. It was a highly sentimental, romantic account, but it touched the hearts of the public and well nigh brought on a national movement for social reform.

Meanwhile, a ferment of more radical character was welling up under the leadership of an Episcopal clergyman, William D. P. Bliss, who organized a Society of Christian Socialists in Boston in 1889. Insisting that the teachings of Jesus lead inevitably to some type of socialism, the society called for the gradual abolition of competition in business and the introduction of profit-sharing, trade-unionism, and municipal ownership. A vigorous proponent of Christian Socialism was George D. Herron, professor of Applied Christianity at Iowa (later Grinnell) College. The redemptive mission of the church he found to be the erection of a just social order, where the public would own the sources and means of production. This could be accomplished only by willing sacrifice for the interests of others.

The chief prophet of the Social Gospel was Walter Rauschenbusch (1861–1918), German-American Baptist, who adorned the chair of church history at Colgate-Rochester Seminary. Unlike leaders such as Gladden, whose heritage lay in New England Congregationalism, Rauschenbusch was a product of German piety, doctrinal orthodoxy, and social concern in the tradition of Ritschl. He is best known for *A Theology for the Social Gospel* (1917), a frank attempt to find a theological basis for social reform. The author propounded the thesis that it was social sin that was most devastating to morality, whether in the form of war, oppression, or intemperance. Men could not hope to build the Kingdom of God until they made a frontal attack on the Kingdom of Evil. This could come through moral, economic, and social reform, involving the overthrow of capitalism and the establishment of a system not based on a competitive struggle for property and power. As for the progress of the Kingdom, Rauschenbusch was restrained in his optimism; he believed in God's immanence and in progressive perfection but never separated these ideas from his concept of human sinfulness. In this he reflected not so much the thought of his own time as that of a somewhat later time, which was hospitable to neo-Orthodoxy.

The principal educational center for the heralding of Social Gospel

doctrines was the University of Chicago, which featured such celebrated representatives as Albion W. Small, Charles R. Henderson, and
Shailer Mathews. Graham Taylor, professor of Christian Sociology at
Chicago Theological Seminary, was also well known for his courses on
the social teaching of Jesus and his work at the Chicago Commons
settlement. Soon a number of seminaries followed the example of
Chicago and established chairs in Christian sociology and ethics.

The Social Gospel enterprise met opposition upon its inception from
at least two sources. Big business attacked it as a mortal foe and tried
unsuccessfully to drive it from the churches. It was also rejected by
groups with a strong revivalistic emphasis upon personal redemption
from sin. Nevertheless, the movement gradually gained momentum in
the great evangelical churches such as the Baptist, Methodist, Congregational, Presbyterian, and Disciples, all of which adopted social
creeds and established agencies to put them into practice.

The capstone of the process was the issuance by the newly founded
interdenominational body, the Federal Council of Churches, of a Social
Creed of the Churches in 1908. This creed, modified by the Council
four years later, called for equal rights for all men, child labor laws,
laws against the liquor traffic, protection for workers in their places of
employment, old age benefits, labor arbitration, reduction of working
hours, guaranteed living wages, and "the application of Christian principles to the acquisition and use of property." Thus official ecclesiastical approval was given to a crusade which for more than a generation
had been in the process of development. Even so, it seems unlikely
that a majority of the laity were won to its cause. With the advent of
"normalcy" in the 1920's, the movement declined; more than ten years
passed before it enjoyed another revival.

Experiments in Cooperation

A salient feature of the American religious enter-
prise in the late nineteenth century was a trend toward greater cooperation and unity. Estranged families of faith, once given to intercom-
munal polemics, found it increasingly possible to join forces in a
common effort to further the Kingdom of God. Contributory to this
development was the growing liberal spirit, which placed more emphasis on a maturing Christian life than on the acceptance of right doctrine. Complex social problems in the great urban areas also seemed
to call for the combined efforts of the denominations for a solution.
The rapidly expanding world missionary program likewise necessi-
tated a pooling of denominational resources in order to achieve optimum results. To a lesser extent Christian unity was fostered by the
community church movement which featured the gathering of local

congregations composed of communicants from various denominations but not organically bound to any communion.

With the organization of the Federation of Churches and Christian Workers of New York City in 1895, a positive step in the direction of interdenominational cooperation was taken. The goal of the Federation was to relate "the gospel to every human need," and to so readjust and direct "its agencies that every family in the destitute parts of our city shall be reached." It was not long before federations with similar purposes were founded in other cities.

Five years after its founding the New York federation called a joint meeting with the Open and Institutional Church League, an organization which had opposed pew rentals and had furthered the work of institutional churches. The result was the formation of a National Federation of Churches and Christian Workers. Local churches and city federations comprised the bulk of its membership. Its inordinate size, however, rendered efficient functioning impossible and suggested the need for a more practical system. Thus at a meeting in 1902, General Secretary Elias B. Sanford called for the establishment of a federation officially endorsed by the denominations. So it came about that the Interchurch Conference on Federation, with official denominational representation, convened in New York in 1905. Out of its deliberations came a plan for the formation of the Federal Council of Churches.

The organizational meeting of the Federal Council of Churches of Christ in America was held in 1908, the constitution of the new body having already been approved by twenty-eight denominations. Thereafter the Council was to meet quadrennially. Its five objectives were to express the Catholic unity of the Christian Church, to foster cooperative endeavor on the part of the churches, to promote mutual counsel in spiritual matters, to broaden the moral and spiritual influence of the churches, and to encourage the organization of local federations. That the Council appealed to denominations of both liberal and conservative theological orientation was due to the fact that it focused attention on practical problems and refrained from making theological pronouncements.

While the Federal Council was building unity on a national level, various state and city federations unrelated to the Council arranged for interdenominational cooperation within a more limited geographical area. On a city level the federations were usually staffed with an executive secretary and directors of specialized ministries such as Christian Education, the Institutional Ministry, Research and Church Planning, and Social Welfare. Some fifty city federations could boast paid executives on their staffs by 1936; by midcentury the number was even greater. The federations contributed significantly to the work of church planning by arranging for comity agreements among denominations in the establishment of new churches. In the realm of religious education and related fields, both state and local federations often encountered difficulty inasmuch as local churches were ordinarily committed to denominational programs. As the twentieth century progressed, many federations found solutions to this vexing problem and made important gains in the enterprise of interdenominational religious education.

QUESTIONS FOR DISCUSSION

1. How has the posture of the American Catholic Church changed since the recent Vatican Council?

2. Why have most Protestant denominations not felt it necessary to maintain their own school system or to restrict the organizations their members can belong to?

3. The social gospel was developed in order to improve the condition of the underprivileged in American society. Yet the social gospel never took root in denominations that cater chiefly to poor farmers and working-class people. Why do you think this is so?

4. Do you think the religious development of America would have been significantly different if the country had originally been Roman Catholic and if the new immigrants of the nineteenth century had been mostly Protestants? How might it have been different?

ADDITIONAL READING

Billington, Ray Allen. *The Protestant Crusade, 1800–1860.* Chicago: Quadrangle Books, 1964. A study of the origins and development of the anti-Catholic, antiforeigner movement in the United States.

Ellis, John Tracy. *American Catholicism.* Chicago: University of Chicago Press, 1956. A Catholic scholar offers an interpretation of the history of the Catholic Church in the United States.

Glazer, Nathan. *American Judaism.* Chicago: University of Chicago Press, 1957. A Jewish scholar offers a historical survey of the Jewish religion in America.

Hudson, Winthrop. *American Protestantism.* Chicago: University of Chicago Press, 1961. A Protestant scholar surveys and interprets the development of Protestantism in the United States.

Smith, James Ward, and A. Leland Jamison (eds.). *The Shaping of American Religion.* Princeton, N.J.: Princeton University Press, 1961. A group of noted scholars contribute to the understanding of the religious development of the United States.

Chapter V

The Church as Bureaucracy

Social scientists have not paid much attention to the subject of churches as formal organizations. To be sure, there are a few good organizational studies of ecclesiastical bodies, but scholars with an interest in American religion have preferred to study what the clergy and laity believe rather than how their churches operate.

Yet there is much about American religious life that cannot be understood without knowing something about the way churches are organized. Churches hold property, they have budgets, they employ people, they operate projects, and they have procedures for making and carrying out decisions. Their major activities may serve a religious purpose, but the way they carry out their activities often bears a close resemblance to the way secular organizations operate. And the issues that engage the attention of churchmen are often issues that are at base organizational in character.

For example, one of the most sharply debated issues during the course of Christian history has been the question of how authority should be exercised in the church. It was a key issue in the Protestant Reformation. From very early times the Roman Catholic Church had organized itself along bureaucratic lines. It developed a centralized administration, a professional clergy dependent on the church for its livelihood, and a uniform set of rules laid down in canon law. The Protestant denominations, by contrast, adopted various modes of church government, all of them giving the laity some voice in church affairs and limiting the authority of ecclesiastical bureaucrats. In fact, some Protestant bodies so thoroughly rejected the concept of centralized authority that they made the local congregation the supreme governor of its own affairs. No denominational authority could require it to do anything. The Baptists and a few other denominations adhere to this principle of church government.

149

The Baptist principle of church government is hard to maintain, however, if a denomination decides to undertake projects that need the cooperation of its local churches. It has therefore been placed under an increasingly heavy strain as a result of the vast growth of new administrative structures that has taken place in most Protestant denominations during the past century and a half. These structures are the many boards, commissions, and agencies set up to direct foreign and domestic missions, to publish Sunday School materials, and to do a host of other jobs ranging from managing pension funds for pastors to planning social action in the urban ghetto. These agencies do much of the day-to-day work of the modern denomination and are run by full-time executives with ample authority over their own staff. But as the essay (Selection 13) by Paul M. Harrison shows, Baptist agency executives, having no formal authority over the local churches, are obliged to enlist the churches' support by other means. The more charismatic among them are able to build a large following among the laity by the sheer force of their personalities. On the other hand, the agency without this kind of leadership is an easy target for hostile power blocs within the denomination. The pressure of agency executives for more authority over church affairs is a major source of organizational changes in the churches today. And resistance to these changes is a major reason why many local Baptist, Congregational, and Disciples of Christ churches have severed all relations with their national denomination.

Like all organizations, churches have their share of people whose viewpoint is not endorsed by the majority. If they are clergymen, they may find it hard to locate a parish where their views will be appreciated (for example, see Marshall Sklare, Selection 16). But most denominations have jobs for clergymen that insulate them from direct pressure from the laity. Those who are theologically more conservative than the majority often volunteer for foreign mission work, and many of the more liberal go to work for one of the denominational agencies. As the reading (Selection 14) by Phillip E. Hammond and Robert E. Mitchell shows, since campus pastors are more likely to be liberal than the clergy in general, no doubt the existence of these segmented, insulated positions keeps many pastors from leaving the church altogether, but perhaps more importantly, it may enable their opinions to exert a leavening influence over the whole church. For example, more and more young people are going to college; perhaps the religion of tomorrow's church-goers is being shaped by today's campus pastors.

Recently much attention has been given to the ecumenical movement, an attempt to bring the various Christian churches closer together with an eye to eventual organic union. No one seriously expects all major Christian bodies to unite in the foreseeable future, but in recent decades there have been several important mergers of Protestant denominations, and proposals for even larger mergers are under study. Most of what has been said and written in favor of the ecumenical movement has stressed the theological principle of a unified Christian witness. Ecumenical spokesmen often call attention to the scandal of division in the body of Christ, a division that produces hostility and competition instead of love and cooperation. Peter Berger, however, advances a more prosaic reason for the interest some denominational officials take in the ecumenical movement (Selection 15). Drawing an analogy from the business world, Berger observes that much ecumenical activity resembles the efforts of businessmen to build monopolies that restrict competition. Church mergers, like business mergers, enable leaders to manipulate the market more effectively. Moreover, as Berger points out, agreements among churches to restrict competition are already more widespread than many realize. Many will argue with Berger's analysis, but no one can dispute the important part played by purely organizational factors in the life of the American churches.

13

Paul M. Harrison

The Subversion of Ideology in a Democratic Church

The Power of the Professional Executives

In many respects centralization and rational bureaucratic organization are in conflict with the current Baptist theology of the church. The tendencies toward impersonalization, the premium placed on technical knowledge, and the removal of the formulation of important decisions from the aegis of the local churches which accompanies rational and centralized social systems are necessary for the achievement of the common goals of the denomination. But they are all equally opposed to the ideals of the Baptist ideology. The organizational needs were too pressing to deny the drive toward centralization of administrative, financial, and policy-making operations. The need for a coordinating organization with an established leadership resulted in an informally organized Baptist elite, a group of leaders whose authority has never been fully legitimated. The influence of certain members of the elite sometimes reaches inordinate proportions because, for the most part, the power of the leadership is veiled and was neither intended nor recognized by the founders of the denominational structure. The creators of the Convention's charter left the boundaries of responsibility and influence poorly defined, and the resulting social relationships are so fluid that the layman or local minister is left in a hopeless quandary when he attempts to understand the mechanism of the Convention or act intelligently within it.[1]

From *Authority and Power in a Free Church Tradition: A Social Case Study of the American Baptist Convention,* by Paul M. Harrison (Copyright © 1959 by Princeton University Press). Reprinted by permission of Princeton University Press. Paul M. Harrison is a member of the Department of Religious Studies at Pennsylvania State University.

152

It is difficult to explain the rationale of the Convention because of the ambiguous nature of the power of the professional executives. *Within* his own society an executive's authority is legally legitimated and his duties are delineated with a reasonable degree of clarity. A bylaw of one of the societies is worded as follows: "The Executive Secretary shall be the executive officer of the Board and shall have general charge and oversight of the work of the board; all divisions and departments shall report to him for instruction and advice, and he shall be kept informed constantly by the heads of all divisions and departments of the condition and progress of the work for which each head is responsible. . . ."[2]

On the other hand, the official authority of the executive secretaries is non-existent with regard to inter-organizational affairs. The autonomous nature of every church, association of churches, and national agency within the denomination precludes the possibility of official inter-organizational authority. Even the General Secretary of the Convention has limited authority in inter-agency affairs. He is called the "principal administrative officer of the Convention and of the General Council," and he "shall act as representative of the Convention in accordance with its Bylaws. . . ."[3] But this does not confer upon the General Secretary any authority in relation to the societies or the local churches or the local or state associations. He is merely the administrative officer of the Convention, "under the direction of the General Council,"[4] and it must be recalled that "The American Baptist Convention declares its belief in the independence of the local church, and in the purely advisory nature of all denominational organizations."[5] This is strictly defined in order to indicate that the Convention cannot exercise any ecclesiastical authority over the affairs of the autonomous agencies of the denomination.

The executive secretary of a society is officially responsible to his board of managers. The constitution of one society reads as follows: "The Board of Managers shall have the management of the corporate affairs; shall have the power to elect its own chairman and recording secretary, and the executive secretary and treasurer of the Board of Education . . . and to define the powers and duties of each. . . ."[6] It should be noted that the boards of managers of all the societies are always elected by the delegates to the American Baptist Convention.[7] Therefore, through the delegates to the annual conventions and boards of managers of the various agencies, the professional executives are indirectly responsible to the constituency of the local churches. Because the executives are responsible to the churches only through their boards of managers, the boards serve as a shield or buffer between the executives and the "vagaries of the local constituency." Actually, the executives often attempt to maintain the fiction that the real creators of policy are the delegates to the annual conventions. In the words of one executive: "We merely implement the policies which the delegates formulate for us from year to year. This is the only way that our claim to democracy can be upheld." [8] This is the direction that conversations with the executives usually take. However, only a few executives maintain this theme throughout an extensive interview or series of interviews. When they are asked how the delegates make policy, how the local churches direct the delegates, how the delegates know which issues are significant, which needs are greatest throughout the denomination, etc., it develops that "a certain amount of direction from the top is necessary in every modern religious body." [9] The delegates to the annual meetings, an associate secretary said, "cannot be expected to know all the problems involved in far-flung missionary activities," or, he could have added, even in the city mission in the nearby area of urban disintegration, or even in the more familiar area of fund-raising and public relations.

Within our modern technological environment a central, rationalized organization is essential for the achievement of the goals desired by a larger number of local groups. The making and implementing of policy, the problems of financing and budgeting, the various kinds of specialized knowledge necessary for foreign and home mission work, publicity problems and problems of education and research, the administration of a large force of sub-executive and office secretaries—all of these require a higher degree of centralized planning and a greater investment in centralized authority than was anticipated when the Baptists formulated their ideology within the milieu of the eighteenth and nineteenth centuries. Leadership by experts is primarily the result of the technical specialization that is the unique characteristic of rationalized organization. [10] In the American Baptist Convention the result is that the power of policy initiation and determination no longer rests with the local church, but rather with the technically experienced, full-time leadership. [11] The professional leaders of the agencies are no longer—if they ever were—the passive executors of the will of the churches expressed through the boards of managers of the various agencies. The officials not only initiate the policies, they implement them as well. There are times when they do encounter opposition to the formulation of their plans, but they are still able to control the implementation of policy, a power which enables them ultimately to determine the nature of the policies even if they do not originally formulate them. Robert Michels noticed this phenomenon in relation to democratic political parties: "The technical specialization that inevitably results from extensive organization renders necessary what is called expert leadership. Consequently the power of determination comes to be considered one of the specific attributes of leadership, and is gradually withdrawn from the masses to be concentrated in the hands of the leaders alone. Thus the leaders, who were at first no more than the executive organs of the collective will, soon emancipate themselves from the mass and become independent of its control." [12]

Reasons will be given in a subsequent section to indicate that within the American Baptist Convention this condition is not so clear-cut as described by Michels with regard to secular democratic politics. But it is true that "organization implies the tendency to oligarchy." If Michels is correct, even in a general sense, whatever residue of democratic procedure remains within the Baptist denomination is due to disappear almost entirely, because "the increase in the power of the leaders is directly proportional with the extension of organization." [13] There is no reason to suppose that the tendency toward more complex organizational forms which has been present within the Baptist movement since its earliest days in America is going to be curtailed. However, there is no necessary reason why organization *qua* organization must be aristocratic or oligarchic in nature. It seems clear that some kinds of organization, e.g., representational, are more "democratic" than other kinds, such as a monolithic structure. However, a lack of awareness on the part of the leaders concerning the possibilities of different degrees of representation, and a general assumption on the part of leaders that the denomination is democratic because it is Baptist, offers no relief from oligarchic tendencies. Baptist leaders have done little critical thinking along these lines. The general assumption of the leaders is illustrated by the phrase, often repeated, "We are proud of our democracy." One executive said, "We may not be as efficient as the Roman Catholics but one of the men from the American Institute of Management, who was a Catholic, admitted that his church could learn a lot from our democratic procedures." [14]

The general tendency of the leadership of the Convention is to convince themselves as well as the laity that the Baptist denomination knows nothing of "leaders" in the bureaucratic or oligarchic sense. The denomination merely has "executive employees" and managerial boards, which are sensitively responsible to the desires of the grass roots. But this only serves to conceal from everyone, leaders and laity, the danger which threatens the cherished democracy.

Although recognized by many people, it has not been publicly admitted that the executive secretaries and their staffs, who officially are confined to the implementation of policy, have also become the initiators of the policy. The establishment of an administrative staff to implement the decisions of the churches leads to a policy-making authority not originally intended by the founders of the Convention organization. But this cannot be classified as an "unanticipated consequence," [15] since it was this circumstance which was most feared by the fathers of the American Baptist Convention. However, the need for an established and full-time leadership is too great to be overcome

merely by anticipating its undesirable effects. If the Convention refuses to legitimate on a formal basis the leadership necessary for the
achievement of its concerns, a group of leaders with tremendous
informal power will appear. There is no easy way to prevent this. In
fact, because the power is unintended and veiled it is oftentimes
considerably greater than the official ecclesiastical authority of the
Episcopalian or Methodist bishop, or the Presbyterian moderator.

In the first place, there is no way for the constituency to know who
has the power. There can be little effective check upon the power of
the leadership when most lay people have no knowledge of Convention
affairs, never attend a national, state, or even a local associational
meeting, do not know the names of their officials nor anything about
the policies they are making, and are not represented in any way at
these meetings if they fail to attend in person.

In the second place, an executive leader may possess charismatic
authority, a phenomenon which is familiar within all types of social
organization. But in the American Baptist Convention, where the
pragmatic is the only form of rational authority, an unbearable burden
is placed upon the limited legitimacy of the Convention officials if they
confine their activities to the formal system of authority. Therefore,
the charismatic type becomes a requirement for the continuing work
of the organization. Many of the leaders deplore the presence of the
charismatic type but are resigned to a necessity for such leadership
since it lends so much support to the functioning of the informal
system. But it is much more difficult to control the power of the
charismatic personality when the formal rules within the official
charter of the Convention are unrealistically conceived with respect to
the power needs of the denominational leaders. A calculated balance
of power is essential for every democratic order, but an attempted
elimination of power merely establishes a condition which is conducive
to social chaos and a greater likelihood of the emergence of charismatic personalities. The Convention has been fortunate in the appearance of charismatic leaders who have contributed positive and dynamic guidance to the denomination in times of crisis, but these
leaders have been restrained by the internal conflicts which have
plagued the Convention for the past three decades.[16] No leader has
been able consistently to unite a majority of the forces by attracting
the allegiance of the fundamentalists, the liberals, the executives, and
others. However, the executive leader who possesses charismatic authority enjoys a unique power within the informal structure of the
Convention.

An executive secretary of one of the major societies may gain the
support of an extensive agency on the basis of his administrative skill
and his official or rational authority, but if charismatic qualities are
added to this formal authority the executive will gain the support of

the active lay constituency at the local level. His personal appearances through his field contacts, his mediation work with the conflicting forces of the denomination, his sensitivity to the needs of widely opposed groups and his ability to attract their loyalty, will all contribute toward the creation of a grass-roots support which evinces primary dedication to him and his concerns.[17] Once this kind of support is obtained it can never be ignored in the policy-making counsels of the other leaders. Just as there is no possible way for such an individual to obtain this kind of power by official means, there is no official road which the other leaders of the Convention can follow to restrain this power. It has been the experience of the Convention that the denominational organization is wedded to the hopes and desires of the charismatic leader until sickness or death do them part. One of the reasons is that while the non-charismatic executives might attempt to coordinate their informal power to restrain or remove the charismatic personality, there is always a critical need within the hierarchy for a man who can exercise the power to mediate between the power blocs of the denomination. One charismatic executive of recent years, who enjoyed the respect but not the general affection of many of the other executives, was periodically on call by these men to mediate conflicts which threatened their organizations, not his own. He was passionately dedicated and had the ability to enthrall the conservatives on one day, the liberals on the next. Such a man is not readily disposed of, even though several leaders reported that their tolerance level reached the breaking point when he exerted this same kind of authority in executive meetings.[18]

Therefore, although informal, the power of the executives may reach startling proportions. Modern Baptist emphasis upon ultimate authority of the individual believer, the authority of the local church, and the corresponding "containment" of the authority of the executive professionals resulted in unanticipated consequences. Being permitted nothing more, at least at the official level, than an instrumental function with no ecclesiastical authority, the executives were forced to substitute informal power for official authority. In individual cases, this can far exceed the power of many executives or ecclesiastical officers of the "authoritarian" religious orders. This has occurred for several reasons, some of them having been mentioned in the preceding paragraphs.

The founders of the Convention did not anticipate the *impossibility* of policy formulation by autonomous churches. They did not anticipate the fact that the system of direct representation could not work within an organization so large and widespread as the American Baptist denomination. . . . If every church in the denomination sent its official quota of delegates, the annual meeting would contain an absolute minimum of 12,744 voting representatives.[19] (With 430-odd delegates, the House of Representatives of the United States government has been characterized as "unwieldy.")

In the second place the founders of the Convention did not recognize the inter-dependent or organic nature of the denomination and the fact that a denominational publication or missionary activity controlled by full-time professional workers would affect the dynamics of the most remote local communion. Because the work of every local church is important to the life of the Convention, it is incumbent upon the executives to see that these churches act and believe in a way which the leadership of the denomination feels is healthy for the Convention. Thus it was not anticipated that the executive leadership would feel a constant need to strive for that informal power which they were not officially given. This refers to an organizational rather than an individual need. While it is true that some leaders strive for power because they do not gain enough personal satisfaction from their official status, it has been necessary apart from this personal motivation for the executives to gain a degree of power which is commensurate with the extent of their responsibility.

In the third place, the founders did not anticipate the potential influence of the executives when they utilized nothing more than the limited official authority that was given them. The right to direct the affairs of an agency whose capital value may exceed by two or three times the yearly budget of the entire Convention has obvious implications for the power of the executives of that organization.[20] When such administrative authority is combined with charismatic authority, as in the case of the executive mentioned above, the power of the individual may attain almost irresistible proportions.

There appears to be an interesting disjunction at this point. On the one hand, the various executives may achieve extreme power over the affairs of the Convention; on the other, there is no one who possesses the kind of authority for coordination which is necessary for the work of the denomination and for the guidance of the leaders. Because their official authority is limited to the administration of their agencies and is not supposed to flow over into the work of any other organization of the Convention, the structural form of the denomination resembles what one executive called "a hydra-headed monster."[21] Like the beasts of mythical literature, the heads are often found in conflict with one another at the expense of the body.

It will be noted in more detail below that no executive obtains unmodified power. In their daily activities they tend to check and balance one another. There has been a change in degree, but there has been no material change since the inception of the Convention in their conflicts for their "rightful" portion of the "unified budget."[22] The constant strife over the budget apportionment is reflected in many of the decisions of the secretaries. Cooperation is a desirable thing between the agencies but only so long as the successful work of one agency does not detract from the program of the others. Because of this competitive tension, it requires an unusually gifted personality to rise above the level of his peers. However, this has happened in the past and several executive leaders believe there is another "personality boy" appearing in the higher reaches of the second echelon.[23]

There are other powerful forces which tend to restrain and limit the activities of the secretaries. The action of the executives is kept in bounds by their fear of group pressures. Actually, these pressures can be very great, or even oppressive, from the point of view of the executive leadership. The result is that countervailing pressure groups are formed to balance the original forces, until the denomination consists of a myriad of power blocs of national executives, state secretaries, conservative ministers, liberal ministers, wealthy laymen, rural church workers, city secretaries, social action advocates, political reactionaries, and many others.

Most people who are active within the denomination will belong to more than one of these groups, thus complicating the inter-group relations. But there is a tendency for the groups to form sympathetic constellations as particular issues arise; and, by virtue of this fact, larger power blocs will be formed on a temporary basis. For example, during critical phases of a theological conflict the groups will probably coagulate around the "conservative" and "liberal" nuclei. On the issue of "Churches for New Frontiers," tension arose between those who wanted funds to be used for areas of slum disintegration and those in favor of middle-class churches. In this case, the blocs would assume a new alignment, perhaps some of the executives uniting with proponents of social action and city mission men, as against those who believed the denomination should be strengthened with new, higher-status churches before it extended its benevolent activities. All of these political relations are informal but essential for the work of the denomination because there exists no official means for supporting the activity of the executives when they are met by an effective opposition bloc. From one point of view denominational politics becomes the basis for reinforcing or opposing the decisions of the leaders, decisions which are made in the national offices during the year and confirmed by the gathering of the delegates at the annual Conventions. It is because this process of approval is necessary for the continued activity of the denomination that the claim is generally made that the Baptists are a democratic group. But if an informed constituency is one of the requisites of a democratic order, the Baptists can make no strong claim at this point.

NOTES ———————————————————————————————

1. This was discovered through conversation with many ministers and lay people within the Convention, but it was most dramatically illustrated at two of the Annual Conventions in 1956 and 1957. At the first Convention the leaders were proposing a reorganization of the Convention structure; at the second a proposal was brought to the floor of the Convention to move the denominational headquarters to Chicago or some other city in the midwest. In both cases it was clearly indicated by the constituency that they had an inadequate comprehension of the nature of the issues. Many of them had some grasp of the problems involved if the outcome were to have an effect upon their local situations. For example, a discussion with a group of ministers from West Virginia revealed that reorganization would be poorly received in their churches. Therefore, they were opposed to it although they seemed to be in favor of some kind of reordering of the structure of the Convention. But there were many lay people and ministers who had no opinion on the subject and felt morally constrained *not* to vote because of their lack of knowledge.

2. *The Board of Education and Publication of the American Baptist Convention,* 44th Annual Report, 1955 (Philadelphia: The Judson Press), p. 90.

3. *Yearbook of the American Baptist Convention,* 1957 (Philadelphia: The American Baptist Publication Society), p. 13.

4. *Ibid.,* p. 13.

5. *Ibid.,* p. 11.

6. *The Board of Education and Publication, op. cit.,* p. 83.

7. *Ibid.,* pp. 82, 83. Cf. also *Yearbook,* 1956, p. 23.

8. Interview with an executive secretary.

9. Interviews with an executive secretary and an associate secretary.

10. Robert Michels, *Political Parties* (Glencoe, Ill.: The Free Press, 1949), p. 31.

11. For example, Hudson observes that "It must be confessed that most Baptists, as yet, would not be willing to admit that their witness in the contemporary world is being crippled by an undue emphasis on the independence of the local church; nor would they readily acknowledge that they are confronted by the necessity of developing appropriate means for achieving a wider church order." (Winthrop S. Hudson, "Are Baptists So Peculiar?" *Christian Century,* LXX, 2 (November 18, 1953), pp. 1324.)

12. Michels, *op. cit.,* pp. 31–32.

13. *Ibid.,* p. 33.

14. The reference was to the "Management Audit" of the American Baptist Convention made by the American Institute of Management in 1954. Of the three men who attended the sessions of the General Council one was a Roman Catholic who was apparently impressed by

the fact that the Council members were free to speak as they pleased within the sessions, a freedom which does not necessarily indicate the existence of a democratic procedure throughout the entire Convention.

15. Merton, *Social Theory* (1949), *op. cit.,* pp. 50–51.

16. Willingham, *Background Material, op. cit.,* p. 10.

17. Three persons who were interviewed, a member of the General Council, an executive, and an associate secretary, each had the same particularly effective leader in mind while discussing this issue.

18. *Ibid.*

19. This figure is based on the number of churches cooperating with the Convention in 1956, namely 6,372, and on the basis of the bylaw which states that "voting members shall consist of two delegates and one additional delegate for every one hundred members above the first one hundred, appointed by any cooperating church from its own membership. . . ." (*Annual,* 1956, pp. 13, 41.)

20. For example, The Home Mission Society listed $26,047,706 on the asset side of their balance sheet in 1956. The unified budget for the Convention for 1957 was $8,764,527. (*Annual,* 1956, pp. 310, 63.)

21. Interview with an assistant secretary.

22. Interviews with a member of the Budget Research Committee and an executive secretary.

23. Personal interviews.

14

Phillip E. Hammond and Robert E. Mitchell*

Segmentation of Radicalism:
The Case of the
Protestant Campus Minister

        In pursuit of their goals, all organizations face a dilemma: how to adapt to changing environments without sacrificing organizational integrity. The dilemma may be thought of as a problem in balancing the commitments of members to the purposes of the organization, on the one hand, and to (their roles in) the organization's structure, on the other. Too inflexible a commitment to the organizational structure by some members can result in the defection of other members who claim that the goals have been forsaken. Too inflexible a goal commitment, however, can produce insensitivity to changing pressures, with a resultant lowered ability to achieve the organization's goals.

Whether viewed as a conflict between means and ends or between idealism and compromise, the dilemma is real. Organizations grow, die, barely struggle along, or change into other entities; and each response reflects some degree of viability. Viability, as an attribute of any organization, refers therefore to its degree of stability in the face of change.

Church organizations do not escape the dilemma. They have goals to achieve and personnel variously committed to those goals. They have environments to adapt to and an identity to maintain. That many of their goals are otherworldly may make it difficult to define

* Phillip E. Hammond and Robert E. Mitchell, "Segmentation of Radicalism: The Case of the Protestant Campus Minister," *The American Journal of Sociology,* **71** (September 1965). Copyright 1965 by The University of Chicago. Reprinted by permission of the publisher. Phillip E. Hammond and Robert E. Mitchell are sociologists, the former at the University of Arizona, the latter at Florida State University.

"adaptation" and "commitment," but viability is no less a property of religious organizations. Indeed, the voluminous literature on church and sect attests to the importance of the dilemma for these organizations. In general, it seems, there have been two responses, neither of which yields optimum viability: the sect response, which maximizes goal commitment at the expense of adaptation, and the church response, which adapts at the expense of goals.

Forces toward breakdown or disintegration can come, then, from the outside in the form of environmental pressures or from the inside in the form of redefined goals, changes in role commitment, or efforts to alter the organization's boundaries. Inside pressures for change might be called "radicalism," and agents for such change "radicals." In every instance they are potential threats to organizational integrity, but they may also anticipate needed adaptation. The viable organization, therefore, finds room for its radicals, but typically does so by segmenting them, thereby minimizing disruption that radicals might create without sacrificing their potential insights by excluding them altogether. A common feature of organizations is thus the differentiation of radicals—a social structure serving two functions: a "safety valve" function of draining off dissidence and a "leavening" function of providing a source of new ideas.

Many organizations have social structures that function in these two ways, whether recognized or not. They may be called "research-and-development groups" in industrial corporations, "institutes" at universities, or "war colleges" in the military. In churches, the safety valve and leavening functions are typically served by such structures as monasteries, seminaries, and special orders. Our purpose in this paper is to discuss another of these structures—the ministry to higher education. We shall argue that for Protestant churches the campus ministry serves as an organizational device for segmenting radicals. Although that is not its manifest purpose, it siphons off potentially disruptive personnel, thus serving the safety-valve function; and, especially, it contributes to organizational change, thus serving the leavening function.

These consequences are not automatic, however; the channels through which they flow can also be identified. Following a discussion of the organizational effects of the campus ministry, therefore, we shall comment on a number of structural mechanisms which permit segmentation to serve the organization.

The Churches' Dilemma

At least since Troeltsch's monumental work on the impact of religious ideology on church structure, the organizational importance of many mansions in the religious house has been recognized. It is now generally recognized that church organizations atrophy unless regularly renewed but that the forces for renewal may also destroy. An *organizational* problem for religion, no less than for other organizations, is therefore one of segmenting the radical element, thereby containing and using it. The medieval church, in Troeltsch's words, "controlled this [radical] tendency by allowing it to express itself in the formation of new Religious Orders and confraternities." [2] At the same time "from this ascetic class the primitive Christian energy once more radiates fresh vitality into all merely relative approximations to the Christian standard." [3]

MacMurray, who goes so far as to claim that the two forces of modernity—the Renaissance and the Reformation—stem from the medieval pattern of monasteries, says of them:

> It is here that the creative forces of the spiritual life are to be found; and here that the ferment of Christianity is most powerful and most difficult to deal with. If the will to power in the church is to maintain itself, it must suppress the spiritual creativeness within its own bosom. . . . The fuction of the monastic system [therefore] is to segregate the creative forces which would seek to realize Christianity and in so doing destroy the dualist structure of society.[4]

The medieval church, in other words, is cited as an example of a viable religious organization. "The church of the thirteenth century was relatively successful in finding a place . . . for the expression of the radical-individualizing tendencies of Christianity." [5] But, as Yinger and other observers of church and sect are quick to point out, the *degree* to which religious organizations "contain and use" their radicals is variable. They differ in their provisions for meeting the safety valve and leavening functions.

> It is commonly observed, for example, that the proliferation of religious divisions is far more extensive under Protestantism than under Catholicism. . . . Protestantism, with its greater emphasis on individual experience . . . encouraged the development of *different* religious structures. Catholicism reflects the variations in religious needs *within* its pattern.[6]

The Campus Ministry as a Radical
Segment in Protestantism

Though by no means the only Protestant social structure for segmenting radicals, the campus ministry is one that has consequences, we shall argue, which exceed its numerical size. Dating from the turn of the century as a self-conscious separate ministry, the

TABLE 1 PERCENTAGE OF CAMPUS MINISTERS AND OF PARISH MINISTERS WHO AGREE WITH VARIOUS STATEMENTS

Statement	Campus Ministers ($N = 997$)	Parish Ministers ($N = 4{,}077$)
Political attitudes:		
1. Strongly approve of the purposes of the United Nations..............................	73%	57%
2. Strongly approve of the purposes of the AFL-CIO....................................	21	11
Breadth of interest:		
3. Regularly read *Christian Century*........	67	33
4. Regularly read *Christianity and Crisis*....	44	6
5. Very interested in news of national and international affairs......................	75	62
6. Very interested in news of own denomination...............................	35	68
7. Very or quite interested in news of other denominations.............................	57	68
The church and social action:		
8. Would very much like to see church-sponsored examination of major ethical issues*.......................................	66	57
9. Agree own denomination is too conservative in the field of social action..........	53	17
Ecumenical attitudes:		
10. Agree own denomination is not sufficiently ecumenical-minded................	42	10
11. Strongly approve of the National Council of Churches..............................	51	42
12. Strongly approve of the World Council of Churches..............................	59	44
Miscellaneous:		
13. Agree own denomination does not have clearly defined policies....................	27	15
14. Have a Bachelor of Divinity degree......	84	65
15. Have a Ph.D. degree......................	13	2
16. Choose, as closest to own belief regarding the Bible, "An infallible revelation of God's will" †...........................	8	24

* The question to campus ministers read ". . . see greater social action by Protestants."

† Other options: "Inspired by God, but subject to historical criticism," and "a great history of religious experience, but not necessarily inspired by God." These two were chosen by 84% and 7%, respectively, of campus ministers, by 70% and 3%, respectively, of parish ministers.

churches' work on college campuses has grown steadily. Currently it contains about 1,300 full-time workers, which is about 1 per cent of the ministerial force of the ten denominations supporting almost all of the full-time campus clergy. Although many schools of higher education, especially junior colleges and teachers colleges, are without campus ministers, large private or state universities may have as many as a dozen, and increasingly the small liberal arts colleges are hosting chaplains. Some of these persons are employed by the school as worship leaders, religious counselors, and teachers. The great majority, however, are employed by a denomination (or a regional division thereof) and, as directors of "foundations" ringing the campuses, administer programs that include study groups, social events, theological discussions, social action, and so on.

Evidence that the campus ministry contains "radicals" is seen in the comparison of results from two studies, one of parish clergy, the other of their campus counterparts. The data on campus ministers were collected in the Spring of 1963 by mail questionnaire sent to all known full-time Protestant campus clergy. The return from this population universe was 79 per cent for an N of 997. The parish-minister data were collected three years earlier, by mail questionnaire sent to a 10 per cent random sample of eight denominations which are members of the National Council of Churches. Smaller samples were taken of two non-member denominations. The return rate in this study was 68 per cent for an N of 4,077. The projected reports cited in the first footnote contain full discussions of the samples.

Table 1 contains evidence of radicalism. There it can be seen that, relative to parish ministers, campus clergy are more liberal in their attitudes toward labor unions and the UN, more critical of their denominations, more favorable toward ecumenical affairs, better educated, and have wider interests. These data are convincing. Although too cumbersome to show in tabular form, the differences are maintained across ten denominations and, within denomination, across three age groups.[7] This latter point is especially worth emphasizing because, although the "radicalism" of campus ministers might be widely acknowledged, it might also be attributed solely to their youth. Yet, in fact, campus and parish ministerial differences persist in all age groups.

Organizational Consequences of the Campus Ministry

Because of the differences between campus and parish ministers in attitudes and values, some consequences of their being a campus ministry can be inferred. Here are several which seem to have strategic importance for organized Protestantism:

1. *More persons are recruited and kept in the ministry than otherwise would be.*—Probably any increase in the diversity of jobs offered by an organization will attract and hold more diverse persons, but careers in education and religion have a special affinity. The job

anticipated by the second largest number of seminarians, for example (the largest number expect to be parish ministers), is teaching.[8] An investigation of 111 former ministers discovered that no fewer than 72 were "teachers or administrators in universities, colleges, or public schools."[9] Campus ministers report that, were they to leave the campus ministry, they would prefer (by a two-to-one ratio) full-time teaching over the parish ministry. Not only does the campus ministry represent a different career possibility for clergymen, therefore, but also an especially important one. An educational occupation that is contained *within* the church and that can be pursued without forsaking a "call" stands to attract and hold persons who might otherwise be in education *outside* of the church.

2. *Radicals are removed from the parish structure.*—Campus posts not only represent an *added* attraction to persons who otherwise would not enter the ministry but also serve as locations for ministers who might otherwise leave the parish. More than seven in ten campus clergy have experience in a parish setting. Leaving, of course, is not always a result of conflict, but Table 1 makes it clear that those who leave are more radical than those who stay, and radicalism does explain some of the moves. One campus minister, for example, had been a parish minister in a border state and intended to remain so. But he was "eased out" by his superior over the question of civil rights. Rather than continue with the tensions created by this man, his administrator urged him to take his denomination's ministry at the state university. Another told of his inability to communicate liberal theology to primarily non-college-educated congregations. He then asked to be assigned a campus ministerial post.[10]

Insofar as these ministers' experience is common, it suggests that liberal agents are removed from parish settings. Thus the campus ministry not only provides a "retreat" for dissident clergymen but also supplies some insulation for the larger segment of the church—insulation from potential disturbance. If the foregoing is essentially true— that an outlet is created for ministers frustrated by the constraints of the parish—then the *extent* to which this is true should differ by denomination according to their degree of constraint. Churches in which "radical" sentiment is relatively rare have greater need for an outlet. To test this hypothesis we have classified denominations by the proportions of parish ministers expressing certain liberal-conservative attitudes. This classification serves as a measure of the constraint a liberal may feel. A comparison of the answers by campus and by parish clergy to various items indicating criticism of the church reveals that in more restrictive denominations the difference is greater between the two groups. For example, in the United Church of Christ (a denomination in which liberal sentiment is common), campus ministers, compared with parish ministers, are more critical, by 15 per cent, of their denomination for being too conservative in social action. In contrast, Missouri Synod Lutheran campus ministers are 53 per cent more critical than are *their* parish counterparts. Table 2 supplies the evidence on three such issues for all ten denominations.

TABLE 2 RELATIONSHIP BETWEEN DENOMINATIONAL CONSTRAINT AND DIFFERENCES BETWEEN CAMPUS (C) AND PARISH (P) CLERGY IN THREE ISSUES INDICATING CRITICISM OF THEIR DENOMINATIONS

Denominations Ranked by Degree of Constraint *	Percentage Who Criticize Their Denominations for									No. Cases		Percentage of Parish Ministers Who Strongly Approve of the	
	Being Too Conservative in Social Action			Not Being Ecumenical Enough †			Not Having Clearly Defined Policies †						
	C	P	Difference	C	P	Difference	C	P	Difference	C	P	UN *	WCC
Least:													
United Church........	22	7	15	12	6	6	27	30	− 3	71	228	61	54
Disciples..............	70	17	53	46	13	33	45	39	6	32	291	60	50
Episcopal.............	50	28	22	29	17	12	26	19	7	125	467	65	38
Presbyterian, USA.....	28	9	19	10	5	5	7	4	3	113	585	54	48
Methodist.............	37	9	28	49	10	39	27	15	12	273	1,566	57	44
Lutheran..............	66	16	50	54	7	47	26	8	18	79	273	57	43
American Baptist......	77	19	58	70	16	54	63	25	38	68	330	49	33
Presbyterian, US......	69	20	49	68	16	52	37	6	31	43	188	40	33
Southern Baptist......	77	20	57	48	17	31	29	9	20	133	62	36	5
Most:													
Mo. Synod, Lutheran..	71	18	53	65	14	51	3	1	2	31	87	19	2

* Denominations are ranked on the basis of *parish* ministers' combined strong approval of the United Nations and the World Council of Churches. Greatest approval = least constraint. Had different items from Table 1 been used, the ordering of denominations would change but little.

† Percentages are non-weighted averages of the three age groups (20–29; 30–39; 40+) in each denomination.

Table 2 does not indicate however, that radicalism (defined above as "inside pressures for changing the organization") is less of a factor in liberal denominations. It merely means that, for them, radicalism regarding *political-theological* issues is less of a factor in creating conflicts. Were the data available, they would probably indicate that campus ministers in politically and theologically liberal denominations are radical in other ways, perhaps in regard to ecclesiastical arrangements, salaries, or routine parish duties. The point is that a campus ministry segments "radicals," providing them with a legitimate base and insulating them from the parish.

3. *The campus ministry serves to sustain radicalism.*—If the short-run consequence of removing some persons to the campus ministry is to leave the parish structure less radical, probably the long-run effect

is quite the opposite. One reason for such a speculation stems from the known differences in radicalism between academic communities and the general public.[11] The campus minister, surrounded by university personnel and having a clientele that remains perpetually young, is in a location that nurtures and sustains intellectualism in general and perhaps radicalism (as defined here) in particular. Certainly it supplies him with a context in which questioning traditional procedures is less frowned upon. Insofar as this radicalism is linked to the "intellectualist–anti-intellectualist" conflict in Protestantism (which Niebuhr has maintained is its primary theological conflict),[12] the campus ministry may represent a strategic realignment of forces within the church. Seminaries no doubt remain the commonest battleground for this issue, but the creation of still more university-based positions might well have a radical effect on how the issue is fought.

4. *Radicalism is returned to the church through ministers who themselves return to the parish.*—The turnover of campus ministers is quite high, estimated at 14 per cent annually. The majority of those who leave go back into a local parish, although some move to college teaching, hospital chaplaincies, church administration, and so forth.[13] Granted, the more conservative are more likely to return to the parish, but even these persons' answers to the items of Table 1 are far more radical than those of parish ministers. Furthermore, not only conservatives return to the parish. It is reasonable to speculate, therefore, that those resuming parish duties are more likely to serve as agents of change in the church because (1) they are more radical to begin with than ministers who never were campus ministers and (2) they come from their campus ministerial years having had that radicalism supported.

5. *Radicalism is returned to the church through campus ministers' clients who become church members.*—Given the difference between campus and parish clergy in such matters as those contained in Table 1, it probably is the case that campus ministers' influence on the church via their clients is a radical one. It is true that little is known of the effects on the clients of campus ministers. But we reason as follows: most, if not all, of the persons *who become church members* following campus ministerial contact are of two kinds. First, there are students from active church backgrounds whose attitudes will more nearly reflect a parish ministerial viewpoint. Insofar as their attitudes are altered, they will probably change in the radical direction. Second, there are persons who, because of their radical attitudes, would not affiliate with the church were it not for campus ministerial contact. Both cases represent additions to the radical sector of church membership.[14]

6. *Radicalism is returned to the church by campus ministers' greater leadership potential in radical causes.*—At mid-twentieth century, two

of the major forces impinging on the church are the civil-rights movement and the move toward ecumenicism. Either issue stands to force
organizational change. The campus ministry has been dispropor-
tionately involved in both movements, a fact not widely known among
church laymen and known hardly at all by the public.

In the case of civil rights, Chaplain Coffin of Yale and Reverend
Klunder (campus minister to Cleveland colleges) have been visible
examples owing to the one's early arrest and the other's death under
the tracks of an earth mover. These are only two instances, however;
many of the clergy—Protestant and Catholic, Christian and Jew—involved in protest demonstrations are ministers on campus. The reason their activity is greater than that of parish ministers is easily
understood. They are more radical to begin with, it is true, but also
they are more strategically located in that they have immediate access
to a major source of manpower for many demonstrations: college
students. The recruitment and training of these students frequently
have been under the auspices—or at least with the counsel—of the
religious ministry on their campuses.

Whereas the civil-rights movement challenges the church at the level
of goals, ecumenicism not only challenges goals but also is a rather
direct threat to denominational integrity or organizational boundaries.
That it may prove to be an organizational necessity if such goal
challenges as civil rights persist only accents the leavening function of
those persons in the church who are at the ecumenical forefront. In
disproportionate numbers here, too, campus ministers have been active.

Visser'T Hooft, as the first (and until recently only) general secretary of the World Council of Churches, had his ecclesiastical experience in European student work, and this fact has often been noted.[15]

Less dramatic but organizationally more significant is the fact that
his is no isolated case.

> It is . . . to the student Christian movements . . . that tribute must
> be paid for aggressive and radical ecumenical pioneering.
> Existing in the different countries of Europe, Britain, the United
> States, and the Far East . . . [they] met together on a world basis,
> and kept in contact with each other through their speakers and
> their literature. Not a part of the churches officially, the student
> Christian movements . . . have regarded themselves in both a
> spiritual and a functional sense as close to the churches, indeed as
> the representatives of the church on the university campuses of the
> world. Free from ecclesiastical control, with the imagination
> stimulated by the intellectual climate of the great universities and
> the small colleges as well, they have been able to point the way. . . .
> It is from the student movements that some of the greatest of
> ecumenical leadership has come and continues to come.[16]

This account has the value of focusing on more than the motivation for ecumenicism; it suggests the importance of facilities such as communication networks and available candidates for leadership through which motivation can be channeled. And this, it seems, is where campus ministers have entered. They have been in a position to assume leadership, and they have had ecumenical experience and prior access to communication networks across denominations.

Some reasons for this availability and experience are clear. First, many campus ministers are chaplains to entire student bodies and therefore cannot appropriately restrict their ministry to persons of their own denominations. Second, like that of the military chaplaincy, the campus ministry's situation has spawned change in an ecumenical direction when, for example, it has felt the need to relax rules for giving and receiving communion. Third, many of the (especially monetary) concerns of parish administration are minimized because they are assumed by college administrations or regional or national offices of the denomination. Fourth, the very lack of structure for many campus ministers encourages interdenominational co-operation, for example, in negotiations with college administrators over matters such as visitation privileges in dormitories, obtaining church preference lists at registration time, and so forth.[17]

In brief, campus ministers, as seen in Table 1, are less interested than are parish ministers in news of their own denominations but more interested in and more concerned with the purposes of the National and the World Council of Churches. As in the case of civil rights, however, campus ministers not only *favor* the changes implied but their segmentation puts them in a better position to *act* on those changes.

Structural Mechanisms Involved in the Segmentation of Radicalism

Control over channels of communication in an organization are of crucial significance if that organization is to contain and use its radicalism. In the case of the safety-valve function, expression of radicalism is restricted to places and times where it is thought to be least disruptive, in other words, where communication can be allowed to go unpunished. Physical isolation—in monasteries, for example—is perhaps the clearest device of this sort. (Of course, the "isolation" must be rewarding or else it is more likely to be defined as punishment.) Provision for selective target audiences along with selectively decreasing visibility to other audiences would seem to be the structural mechanisms through which the safety-valve function operates. Examples include a monk charged with translating esoteric palimpsests, a researcher in industry or university assigned to laboratory or institute, or a campus minister permitted his radicalism in the particular company of academics and young adults. In each case, one result from the organizational standpoint is the selective segmenting of potentially disruptive communications.

But if the structural devices for providing an outlet for radicals (so their commitment is maintained and their communication is selectively directed) are readily understood and practiced by many organizations, the structural means whereby the segment leavens the whole are not. The case of the campus ministry suggests several mechanisms, however, whose applicability would seem to extend beyond church organizations.[18]

Here again the focus is on communication, but this time on its use more than on its containment. The first mechanism is quite obviously a *recruitment* mechanism. Called "co-optation" in some contexts, or quota hiring in others, the practice of attracting more heterogeneous personnel, if only by offering a wider range of positions, is one device for seeing that innovation is more likely *brought into* the organization.

A second structural device for enhancing the leavening function of radicals is implied in the term "segment"—radicals are clustered for mutual reinforcement. Among ministers on campuses with more than one minister, for example, fully 86 per cent report at least weekly contact with one another. A series of separate questions relating to formal and informal relations with clergy of their own and other denominations was asked of the *parish* ministers, although here the time period was not a week but a month. Sixty-five per cent reported that they met informally with clergy of their own denomination at least once a month, whereas the second highest percentage, 57 per cent, was reported for informal contact with clergy of other denominations. (The respective figures for formal contacts are 51 per cent for own denomination and 38 per cent for other denominations.) It would seem clear that parish clergy have less contact with one another than do campus clergy.

Medieval monks were located *together* in monasteries, and research scientists typically *collaborate* in their "isolated" divisions. Whatever may be the difficulty of sustaining "deviance" alone is alleviated to some extent by regular interaction with others likewise predisposed to innovative thoughts.

The campus ministry exemplifies a third structural mechanism: the routine location of the radical segment in or alongside populations with particular characteristics. Whether intended and/or recognized or not, the alignment of radical clergymen with the university community serves to maintain the former's propensity to change. The practice of locating professional schools in universities would seem to be another example of the importance of this mechanism, as would its antithesis—the practice of isolating novitiates from any contact other than with planned echelons of the parent organization.

A fourth mechanism for increasing the probability that a radical segment will have a radical effect is the designing of a position with freedom from routine duties, which is to say freedom from the *usual* constraints impinging on other sectors of the organization. Campus ministers, like junior executives sent to training institutes, would probably object to the statement that their duties are *less*. The significance, therefore, is that the duties are *different* and may include the tasks of leading civil-rights protests or assuming ecumenical leadership. The fact, for example, that most campus ministers need not assume major responsibility for their salaries but may rely upon the denomination's support quite clearly allows them certain extraordinary freedoms that the great majority of parish ministers do not have. The effort to "serve" college populations is at least not contingent upon evoking their financial support.

The radicalism of the campus ministry is used through a fifth structural mechanism which might be called the "circulation of radicals." Granted, in the case of campus ministers, the habit of returning to the parish after a term of serving higher education is not typically anticipated by either the church administration or the campus clergyman, and yet this is the path usually followed. As such, it is structurally analogous to a corporation's practice of electing board members regularly from all its divisions, or of a university's "handing around" its administrative offices to persons from various disciplines. The chance of infusing new ideas increases with the circulation of different types of individuals.

The sixth mechanism is similar to the fifth in that carriers of radical communication are circulated. However, in this case the circulation is of the *clients* of radicals and not of the radicals themselves. The argument was presented above that the impact of the campus minister on would-be church members in most cases would have to be radical, given the differences between campus clergymen and their parish counterparts. The *content* of those differences is irrelevant to the operation of the mechanism, provided only that differences systematically exist. In similar fashion, the mechanism operates in the case of executives-in-training who circulate from department to department thereby being influenced (to the extent that they are) by agents representing various concerns within the organization, all potentially different from each other and from the concerns of current executives. Likewise, the practice of relegating children to elementary instruction from unmarried females, of Catholic young people to college instruction from members of certain orders, or professional trainees to academic rather than to practitioners in an apprentice-craftsman relationship, all exemplify the circulation of clients. The result, as in the case of the other mechanisms identified, is an increased probability that use will be made of a radical segment.

It should be clear from the discussion that the mechanisms through which the "leavening" function operates are not contingent upon particular substantive communications. If an organization typically moves in a certain direction, a "radical" element is any element that would alter that direction. The discussion of these last few pages, then, might be useful in explaining the *inability* of an organization to adapt, just as it might explain the opposite.

Conclusion

Every organization has its potential "radicals"—persons whose commitment to the organizational structure and/or its goals is unusual. Just as these persons can be disruptive if located randomly throughout the organization, so also can they be prophetic. If there exist structures for their segmentation, however, radicalism is more likely to be contained and also more likely to be used. Such segmentation not only serves as an escape valve for disruptive forces, therefore, but also may serve as a source of organizational change.

The mere isolation of the radical segment (perhaps epitomized in imprisonment) can do no more than serve the escape-valve function, however. Simple banishment, firing, or defrocking removes the radicals, but it does not allow use of their possible leavening effect. For this function to operate, certain mechanisms must be associated with segmentation so that radical communication can flow back into the organization. The campus ministry illustrates both these functions—the safety valve and the leavening—and it illustrates also a number of the mechanisms by which they operate. These include devices such as heterogeneous recruitment, mutual reinforcement, location of the radical segment alongside populations with known characteristics, freedom from usual duties, circulation of radicals, and circulation of the clients of radicals.

It is unnecessary to argue that the Protestant campus ministry is only functional, and not at all dysfunctional, for Protestant denominations. The future is contingent on other factors than just the segmentation of radicals. If the analysis here is correct, however, that future will have resulted in part from the presence of the campus ministry—a radical segment with consequences for its parent organization.

NOTES

1. This paper may be identified as publication No. A-50 of the Survey Research Center, University of California, Berkeley. It is based on data from two studies, one of campus ministers by Hammond, with the support of the National Institutes of Health (Grant M-6179) and the Danforth Foundation, the other of parish ministers by Mitchell, with the support of the Russell Sage Foundation. Though independently carried out, the two investigations were planned to contain many items in common, most of which are shown in Table 1 below. Full reports on the two studies are in process: Hammond, "Clergy on Campus: A Study of a Developing Occupation," and Mitchell, "The Professional Protestant."

2. Ernst Troeltsch, *The Social Teachings of the Christian Churches*, trans. Olive Wyon (2 vols.; New York: Macmillan Co., 1931), p. 701. See also pp. 237-45, 700-703.

3. *Ibid.*, p. 272.

4. John MacMurray, *The Clue to History* (London: SCM Press, 1938), pp. 155-56.

5. J. Milton Yinger, *Religion in the Struggle for Power* (Durham, N.C.: Duke University Press, 1946), p. 21.

6. J. Milton Yinger, *Religion, Society and the Individual* (New York: Macmillan Co., 1957), p. 134. (First emphasis added.)

7. With three age groups in ten denominations, a total of 480 comparisons are possible. Of these 480, 89 per cent reveal the difference contained in Table 1 and 11 per cent do not, although a quarter of this last group involves cells containing fewer than ten cases.

8. See the study of 17,565 seminarians by K. R. Bridston and D. W. Culver, reported in *Seminary Quarterly*, V (Spring, 1964), 2.

9. H. G. Duncan, "Reactions of Ex-Ministers toward the Ministry," *Journal of Religion*, XII (1932), 101-15.

10. Examples are from case interviews with campus ministers. A similar problem is discussed by Marshall Sklare in *Conservative Judaism* (Glencoe, Ill.: Free Press, 1955). He speaks of the difficulty faced by seminarians who are trained by the churches' best intellects only to be sent into parishes with no provision for fulfilling their intellectual aspirations.

11. For example, compare the civil libertarianism of social scientists, community leaders, and the general public as reported in P. F. Lazarsfeld and W. Thielens, *The Academic Mind* (Glencoe, Ill.: Free Press, 1958), pp. 391-92, and S. A. Stouffer, *Communism, Conformity and Civil Liberties* (New York: Doubleday & Co., 1955), pp. 40-43.

12. H. Richard Niebuhr, D. D. Williams, and J. M. Gustafson, *The Advancement of Theological Education* (New York: Harper & Bros., 1957).

13. Estimates are based on answers to questions asked of campus ministers regarding where they *would* go if they leave. See also Donald Bossart, "Leaving the Campus Ministry" (unpublished Ph.D. dissertation, Boston University, 1963), in which it is reported that 50 per cent of former campus ministers are in parish work. This is more than double the proportion going into any other occupation.

14. The disconfirming cases—persons made so radical by campus ministerial contact that they leave the church and others who react

to campus ministers by becoming less radical—we assume are rare. This is only assumption, however.

15. "Certainly his experience in the World's Student Christian Federation stood him in good stead, giving him personal contacts and the knowledge of how to take initiative" (Mackie, in R. C. Mackie and C. C. West [eds.], *The Sufficiency of God* [London: SCM Press, 1963], p. 8). On the history of ecumenicism see also R. S. Bilheimer, *The Quest for Christian Unity* (New York: Association Press, 1952); R. Rouse and S. Neill (eds.), *A History of the Ecumenical Movement* (Philadelphia: Westminster Press, 1954); Robert Lee, *The Social Sources of Church Unity* (New York: Abingdon Press, 1960).

16. Bilheimer, *op. cit.*, pp. 81–82. "By 1895 the Student Christian Movements . . . had already coalesced in the World's Student Christian Federation. This was the movement which was destined to produce the great bulk of leadership of the modern ecumenical movement . . ." (Rouse, *in* Rouse and Neill [eds.], *op. cit.*, p. 341).

17. Thus, fully 70 per cent of campus ministers would like to see "the merger of various denominational campus ministers on the same campus whenever possible." The propensity for the campus ministry, from its beginnings, to be interdenominational is discussed in Clarence P. Shedd, *The Church Follows Its Students* (New Haven, Conn.: Yale University Press, 1938), p. 67, chap. v.

18. A similar discussion, although in different terms, is found in Eugene Litwak, "Models of Bureaucracy Which Permit Conflict," *American Journal of Sociology*, LXVII (1961), 177–84. Litwak identifies several "mechanisms of segregation," procedures "by which potentially contradictory social relations are co-ordinated in some common organizational goals."

15

Peter Berger

A Market Model for the Analysis of Ecumenicity

The contemporary period in church history has been repeatedly described as an era of ecumenicity. Within American Protestantism this contention is easily borne out by looking at the most obvious organized manifestations of ecumenicity, such as the development of a variety of cooperative agencies across denominational lines and a marked tendency for denominations to merge. In addition, one can observe the transformation of the ecumenical idea from a concern of fringe theological groups into a concern of the most respectable concern and activity of the denominational organizations and their functionaries. Yet, side by side with this development of a new ecumenical spirit there has occurred a resurgence of denominationalism which has been marked by a renewed emphasis on the historical heritage and peculiar theological position of each denomination in question.

This paradoxical coexistence of ecumenicity and denominationalism has been generally noted, although it has been interpreted in different ways. Some have simply interpreted the two phenomena as antagonistic and antithetical, with denominationalism usually cast in the role of the villain with regard to the achievement of church unity.[1] Those close in their thinking to the official positions taken by the World Council of Churches have stressed that, in theological terms, ecumenicity need not be antithetical to the rediscovery and re-affirmation of one's denominational identity.[2] Whatever the theological merits of these two positions, neither offers an explanation of the emergence of the paradox in the first place. Robert Lee, in his detailed sociological study of ecumenicity in the United States, has listed denomination-

From Peter Berger, "A Market Model for the Analysis of Ecumenicity," *Social Research*, **XXX**, 1 (Spring 1963), 77–93, by permission of the author. Peter Berger is a sociologist at Rutgers University.

alism as one of the "countervailing movements." But beyond also
suggesting that this need not involve an antithesis, he does not offer an
explanation of this paradox.[3] Quite apart from the theological and
ecclesiastical vexations of this situation, the paradox poses a sociological problem that ought to be investigated. Needless to say, the sociological problem will have to be tackled in sociological terms.

A Social Psychological Approach

One possible avenue of approach would be along
social psychological lines. Increasing contacts between denominations
bring about an increasing number of situations where denominational
representatives, both clerical and lay, face each other in a variety of
committees, conferences, consultations, and so on. These situations
are commonly defined explicitly in terms of this interdenominational
confrontation: That is, each representative is expected to play a role
appropriate to the denomination he represents. At this point some
fundamental social psychological processes are set in motion that
could be summarized somewhat pithily by saying that, if a denominational identity does not already exist, it will have to be invented in
accordance with the role expectations of the situation.

For instance, a Lutheran representative in such an ecumenical situation may never have thought much about, or put much emphasis on,
his identification as a member of this particular denomination. It is
even possible that he had reservations about his allegiance to the
latter. Suddenly he now finds himself in a situation where everything
he says is interpreted as coming out of the Lutheran identification on
the basis of which he was asked to participate. Such social expectations have a way of becoming "self-fulfilling prophecies." To the
surprise of his former associates, if not himself, since typically such
processes are unreflected and half-conscious, our representative may
soon find himself speaking with the guttural self-assurance expected of
one sailing under this particular banner. After all, he was invited *qua*
Lutheran, he is expected to speak *qua* Lutheran, and whatever he says
is located within a frame of reference in which he is assumed to
represent the Lutheran point of view. No wonder, then, that his
Lutheran identity, previously but dimly perceived by him, becomes
increasingly enhanced the longer he is expected to perform in this role.
This sociological comedy of ideological role assignments can be easily
observed at ecumenical gatherings, especially those containing many
newcomers to this kind of situation. It is plausible to assume that this
vulgar social psychological mechanism is at work in most of the
situations where, to use the terminology of the ecumenical professionals, a "confessional heritage" is "rediscovered" in the "ecumenical

dialogue." In other words, a social psychological perspective may lead one to the suspicion that "invention" is a more accurate term than "rediscovery" to describe this process.

While such a social psychological approach, based on the commonly accepted premises of role theory, may shed considerable light on what goes on at many ecumenical meetings, it fails to explain the paradox with which we are concerned here. The failure is due to the presupposition that such meetings do, indeed, occur with sufficient frequency to make the process just described of significance to more than a small number of individuals. What is required here is a macro-sociological model of interpretation that will allow the micro-sociological perspective to be placed in proper context. It is the contention of this essay that such a macro-sociological model presents itself in a most useful way, if the denominations involved in the paradoxical situation are perceived as economic units which are engaging in competition within a free market.

Historical Factors

Before the model can be formulated a number of historical factors should be taken into consideration. These factors will also delimit from the beginning the boundaries within which the model can be applied. The boundaries are the main-line, middle-class denominations that Carl Mayer has called aptly the "central core" of American Protestantism; [4] although the denominations just to the "right" of this center, specifically, the Episcopalians and the Lutherans, are probably affected by these factors to almost the same degree. The most important historical factor to be taken into consideration is probably the fact that interdenominational cooperation in the United States began at least a decade before the influence of the ecumenical movement properly speaking was felt in American Protestantism. By "ecumenical movement properly speaking," I refer to that movement originating in Europe about the time of World War I which eventually led to the formation of the World Council of Churches. American interdenominational cooperation may have begun even earlier depending on just what degree of cooperation one regards as significant. In any case, it is probably accurate to say that the ecumenical movement in the more specific sense did not exert an important influence in the United States prior to the mid-1930s.[5] The 1920s, however, showed a remarkable growth of interdenominational cooperation in this country, both within and apart from the activities of the Federal Council of Churches which was founded in 1908.

The most significant result of this new cooperation was the development of "comity"; that is, the increasingly regulated way in which

Protestant denominations planned and operated their expansion programs in consultation with one another.[6] This process has been succinctly described by H. Paul Douglass: ". . . the recent unity movements that have taken place in the United States are to be described in general as the transition from competition to combination of churches, and from compromise to alliance, this implying equality and increasing cooperation." It should be noted that these words were written in 1934—three years before the Oxford conference that first envisaged the merging of the two principal ecumenical movements (Life and Work and Faith and Order) into an international agency.

If one speaks about ecumenicity in American Protestantism one ought, then, to distinguish two processes: 1) the process of increasing interdenominational cooperation based on largely practical, not to say pragmatic, considerations; and 2) the process by which the ecumenical movement originating in Europe, and imbued from the beginning with a much more theological rationale, came to exert an increasing influence in this country.[7] In view of the chronology of these two processes in the United States, it is hard to avoid the impression that the theological rationale emanating from the ecumenical movement proper has served as an *ex post facto* ideological legitimation of a process of cooperation with appreciably more mundane roots. This is not to deny the possibility that the two types of motives and self-interpretations may now frequently coincide in the minds of individuals engaged in the ecumenical enterprise in this country. Yet, if one compares the kinds of concerns that still predominate in local and regional councils of churches with the *pronunciamentos* emanating from the official spokesmen of ecumenicity in Geneva or New York, one will tend toward the view that the tension between practicality and ideology is still very much in evidence.

Where is one to look for the mundane roots of the process toward cooperation? It is not necessary to repeat here Robert Lee's detailed discussion of various social influences that has already been referred to. There are three factors, however, that ought to be particularly emphasized; factors that, in the opinion of this writer, are insufficiently stressed in Lee's work. These are: 1) the class specification of the population sociologically "available" for main-line Protestantism; 2) the effect of inflation on all the activities of religious organizations; and 3) the development of an increasingly autonomous denominational bureaucracy. A few words will be said about each of these factors, which together constitute the presuppositions for the model of interpretation.

Main-line Protestantism/ It has become almost a truism to say that the main-line Protestant denominations, omitting the special case of the Negro churches, have an increasingly homogeneous middle-class population.[8] The discussion of this phenomenon, however, has been

mainly concerned with the class character of the population constitut-
ing the present membership of these denominations. Equally important is an understanding of the class specificity of the *potential* membership. In other words, an understanding of the market for main-line
Protestantism. When denominational planners speak of "high potential" areas, they invariably refer to middle-class and most commonly to
suburban areas. This, of course, is perfectly rational, since it is in
these areas that likely candidates for church membership in these
denominations reside. As has been amply shown, however, suburbia is
inhabited by a population that is highly mobile, highly literate, and
highly selective in its patterns of consumption.[9] From the vantage
point of the denominational planner this means that the potential
subjects of his operations cannot be expected to have denominational
loyalties as a matter of course. Instead, they will have to be convinced
of the advisability of affiliating with his particular branch of Protestantism and that their criteria for affiliation are likely to be fairly
articulate. In a word, they will approach the matter with all the
sophistication of the higher-level consumer in an affluent economy.
What this means for the religious or pseudo-religious expectations that
go into church-joining in suburbia need not concern us here.[10] What it
means for the denominational organizations, however, is that they
confront a situation of intense competition for the allegiance of people
whose expectations are increasingly similar and increasingly shaped by
the consumption patterns of affluence. This factor alone, then, should
suggest that the activities of the denominational organizations will be
faced with problems not too dissimilar from those faced by organizations marketing more secular commodities.

Inflation/ The effect of inflation on the process of interdenominational cooperation is simple to understand. It has meant, of course,
an enormous rise in costs for every conceivable aspect of church
activity, from ministers' salaries to kneeling benches. But the most
relevant effect in terms of our problem is the rise in building costs. To
give some idea of the amounts of capital involved here, note that for
1959 a total of twenty-five religious bodies reported an expenditure of
$223,518,644 for new church buildings, while in 1960 only twenty-one
church bodies reported an expenditure for the same purpose which
totaled $941,603,638.[11] Since then the billion dollar mark has been
exceeded. The building of a conventional church edifice today costs
somewhere in the vicinity of $125,000,000, varying, of course, with the
functional requirements and architectural ambitions of the congregation in question. Under these circumstances, it is not difficult to see
that denominational planning is forced to become increasingly rational
in economic terms. Every move made by the denominational organization carries with it substantial economic risks. Cooperation, as expressed in a rational limitation of cutthroat competition, thus becomes

an economic necessity. As one speaker put it in the writer's hearing at a meeting of denominational executives called to consider a more cooperative planning process: "Gentlemen, you may as well face it—you have a multi-million dollar investment to protect."

Denominational bureaucracies/ The development of denominational bureaucracies that are increasingly autonomous *vis-à-vis* the so-called grass roots pressures is also related to certain economic facts. Paul Harrison, in his excellent study of the American Baptist Convention, has given us a vivid picture of the way in which such a bureaucracy operates.[12] I would argue that the impressive autonomy of this bureaucracy may be seen against the background of the astonishing investment capital controlled today by American denominations. This capital, operating from underneath the tax exemption umbrella of the United States Internal Revenue Code, is ever more frankly invested in speculative common stocks—as contrasted with a previous ecclesiastical tendency to invest in bonds and preferred stocks—accounting for an increasingly remarkable proportion of the income of the denominations in question.[13] The consequence of this trend—and it is probably unplanned—is to give the denominational bureaucracy an increasing independence *vis-à-vis* what ecclesiastical accounts refer to as "living sources," that is, the ongoing contributions of a frequently reluctant membership. In terms of our particular problem, this undoubtedly enables the bureaucracy to operate in an economically more rational manner, to engage in economically rational cooperation with their opposite numbers in other denominations. In connection with this, it is significant to note that ecumenical activities have in recent years been initiated by the denominational bureaucracies themselves as contrasted with the grass roots efforts of an earlier period. And, significantly, while the previous grass roots and local efforts toward cooperation have been typically the result of ecclesiastical indigence, the new "ecumenicity from above" is taking place in a situation of unequalled ecclesiastical affluence.[14]

In sum, it can be plausibly maintained that there are powerful social and economic factors pressuring American Protestant denominations toward an increasing rationalization of their activities. Simultaneously these factors enable the bureaucracies running these denominations to act in an increasingly rational manner. The model of interpretation now proposed is based on the presupposition of this rationalization.

Ecumenicity and Denominationalism

Ecumenicity in the American situation functions to rationalize competition. This competition, for a variety of well-known historical reasons, is given in the pattern of denominational pluralism. The individual denominations cannot count on special favors from the state, although they all benefit equally from certain political privileges such as the economic bonanza of the tax exemption laws. Therefore, they must compete with each other for the interest, allegiance, and financial support of their potential clientele. We are thus faced here with the classic picture of competition between a large number of units in a free market. The way in which this competition operated before the coming of ecumenical cooperation can, indeed, be described as falling in one of the fairly brutal categories of *laissez-faire* economics. This type of free enterprise can still be observed in certain areas as yet untouched by the new ecumenicity; these are commonly either geographical or sociological areas which are considerably removed from suburbia and its genteel modifications of robber-baron capitalism. For instance, the merciless competition still prevalent in large sectors of organized religion in the Negro community.

As has been suggested, such untrammelled competition becomes increasingly impractical and expensive for those denominations largely dependent on the middle-class, suburban market. Their bureaucracies are forced to rationalize their operations. In view of the fundamental economic pressures at work here, it should not surprise us that the methods of this rationalization bear close resemblance to those employed in the secular economy to make free enterprise a more civilized affair. Essentially, we have here the well-known process of cartelization, facilitated in the ecclesiastical case by the absence of a Sherman Act. This absence, incidentally, points to an interesting consequence of the separation of church and state. While the state continues to interfere in the secular economy in ways that often are economically irrational—although they may be perfectly rational in political or moral terms—the state is constitutionally unable to interfere in the inner affairs of the church. Thus the process of rationalization in the religious economy occurs free of political interference. To put this pointedly, the separation of church and state guarantees the dominance of economic over political factors in the shaping of church affairs. The point, however, cannot be pursued further here. Suffice it to repeat that the denominational bureaucracies find themselves in a situation in which cartelization is the logical course of conduct, and that they are free to follow this course both as a result of the absence of state controls, given in the constitution, and their increasing independence *vis-à-vis* their constituency; the latter produced by the inevitable entrenchment of bureaucratic forms of administration, but further reinforced by the fiscal factor referred to in connection with denominational investments.

Cartelization rationalizes competition by reducing the number of competing units by amalgamation and also by dividing up the market between the larger units that remain. This is precisely what has happened in the market under discussion; the number of competing units has been steadily reduced through ecclesiastical mergers. (See Lee, note 3, for an impressive list of mergers from 1906–1958.) Among the results of this process of amalgamation has been, of course, an increase in the size and the autonomy of the bureaucracy in charge of the new giant. This in turn accelerates the development of rationalization, one aspect of which may be further mergers. Here is a classic case of what Gunnar Myrdal has called the "cumulative effect." It is evident, however, that there is a point beyond which rationalization through mergers will not go, if only because of the vested interests of the bureaucracies in charge of its administration. In other words, the fears of denominational conservatives opposed to mergers that this trend will end in a gigantic "super-church" are probably unfounded. After all, the number of jobs available for bishops in such a religious monopoly would be rather circumscribed. Thus it would be asking a great deal of human nature to suppose that the bishops of now existing denominations will push very hard in this direction. The process being analyzed, therefore, is oligarchical rather than monopolistic in its tendency.

The large cartels now active in this market cooperate in a rational fashion. They base many of their actions on objective research, especially market research which is carried on constantly by the survey divisions of the church councils and of the denominations themselves. They engage in joint planning, and they have set up a large number of agencies for cooperation of specific tasks. They seek common positions vis-à-vis the state and other powerful institutions standing outside this regulated market system, the most significant of which is the Catholic Church. Most importantly, they parcel out the market in a rational fashion through the increasingly codified procedures of what was once called "comity," and now comes under a variety of largely obfuscating titles such as "planning," "evangelistic strategy," and most recently even "dialogue." The economic logic of all this is closely parallel to the one that forces the oligarchic corporations of the secular economy to "fix prices," which is but a nasty term of Washington lawyers for an irresistible process of rationalization.

So much for the way in which ecumenicity appears in the model of interpretation. What about denominationalism? Must it be called only a "countervailing movement," without interpreting it within our model? I contend that it is possible to go further and that, indeed, the model demonstrates its utility by virtue of this capacity.

As long as there are a large number of individual units competing in the market, products vary widely in character. As production is rationalized, the phenomenon of product standardization appears. This, however, poses its own problems in a consumer society, since some basis must be established on which the consumer can be persuaded to purchase brand A instead of brand B. In the ideology of contemporary capitalism, of course, this leads to "quality through competition." While one may liberally allow a certain margin of truth to this ideological assertion, the massive presence of advertising in our economy shows that, to say the least, it does not tell the whole truth. Typically brand A of a consumer product is set off against brand B by what economists know as marginal differentiation. And when it comes to typical consumer products today, this means largely functionally irrelevant embellishments and packaging of the product, but it also means the public image that is projected through advertising.

It has been pointed out that economically speaking, religion in our society is a typical consumer product. It is consumer patterns that determine its market process. It should not, therefore, be surprising if this religious economy bears further resemblance to the secular economic matrix within which it exists. American Protestant denominations have also undergone a process of intense product standardization, especially within the "central core." It is not the concern here to follow the history of this development, to delineate the profound doctrinal erosion that has occurred, or to argue that this process in its entirety can be understood in economic terms—very probably it cannot. The fact remains that considerable ideological acrobatics are needed today to convince a potential religious consumer in suburbia that he would get a substantially different product in a Presbyterian church, rather than in, say, a Congregational church in his area. Marginal differentiation between such churches takes many forms—in programming, in the selection of ministers' personalities, in the physical and aesthetic accoutrements of the "church plant"—all of which might aptly be subsumed under the phrase "functionally irrelevant embellishments and packaging."

An essential factor in marginal differentiation, however, is the plausible maintenance of a denominational "image" and its projection through publicity. I would argue that the new denominationalism—or "confessionalism" to use a more theologically reputable term—can be thus understood through the concept of marginal differentiation. In actual fact, all the denominations within this sector of society are marketing a highly standardized product; namely, the Protestant variety of what Will Herberg has called "American religion," and Martin Marty has described more sourly as "religion-in-general." [15] To admit this standardization, however, would be to declare economic bankruptcy, quite apart from what it would do to the theologically defined self-conception of the ecclesiastical functionaries. Denominationalism can thus be understood as highly functional in a situation where one wants to remain competitive in spite of product standardization. In terms of the immediate problem we would then say that the religious organizations must de-emphasize denominational rivalry for the sake of rationalizing the rules of the competitive game; but they must simultaneously re-emphasize denominational identity in order to remain in this game at all.

An interesting aspect of this need for a denominational ideology is the relationship of theology and theologians to the denominational bureaucracy. I would argue that theology has a legitimating function with respect to the process of marginal differentiation somewhat similar to the function already discussed with respect to ecumenicity. This problem, however, is beyond the scope of this argument and has been dealt with elsewhere by the writer.[16]

The model would, therefore, interpret ecumenicity and denominationalism as aspects of the same socio-economic process, thus resolving the paradox of the coexistence of ecumenicity and denominationalism. This is not the place to discuss the other phenomena of contemporary religion in the United States which might be illuminated by the application of the same model. A few comments should be added, however, concerning questions that might be raised about the immediate application.

Problems of Application

The most important question would concern the applicability of the model to the groups, largely fundamentalist, that have so far remained outside the scope of ecumenicity. I submit that the factor of class specificity can account for this phenomenon. The clientele of these religious groups is largely outside of the middle-class, suburban universe. Indeed, as Benton Johnson has cogently argued, part of the function of these groups can be understood through their indoctrination of their members with values that are conducive to social mobility into the middle-class universe.[17] As long, however, as such mobility remains the religious groups in question operate in an area of society that is still on the margin of the affluent consumer culture. In other words, these groups are dealing with a different sort of market, one that does not yet require the degree of rationalization that has been discussed above.

It can furthermore be maintained that as soon as such groups succeed in establishing themselves in the middle-class world, they become exposed to pressures pushing them in the direction of the denominations of the "central core." Specifically, these pressures are suburban consumer expectations and the economic and administrative measures that now become necessary to meet these expectations. A rational bureaucracy makes its appearance, and it is not long before it discovers its affinities with its counterparts in the denominations already on the scene. This bureaucratic transformation is an interesting

American variation on the familiar sociological theme of the development of sects into churches.[18] As far as the larger and less sectarian groups in this category are concerned, it can be plausibly maintained that they undergo the same pressures as they are drawn out of regional or ethnic isolation into the mainstream of American Protestantism. Present developments among Southern Baptists and Missouri Lutherans would be cases in point. The role of the "non-cooperative" groups in the Protestant religious scene in the United States thus is only seemingly "countervailing" in terms of our analysis of ecumenicity and denominationalism. If the factor of class is given its due weight, this role becomes understandable in the wider social system of American religion.

On the other hand, the market model is probably not suitable for the interpretation of intra-faith cooperation, compromise, and conflict. As the Protestant denominations, jointly and individually, relate themselves to the Catholic and Jewish participants in what Herberg called the "tripartite" American religious system, the logic operative here is likely to be more political than economic. As far as Protestant denominational strategy is concerned, Catholics and Jews are outside the market at which the strategy is aimed, except for marginal individuals who, for one reason or another, find their way into the Protestant camp. The major Protestant denominations do not actively seek to convert Catholics and Jews, thus they are not in direct competition for members and funds from the Catholic and Jewish faiths. There are, indeed, economic aspects to the relations between the three faith groups as, for instance, in the problem of sharing governmental largesse to educational and other institutions under religious auspices; but a political model of interpretation is more likely to account for the basic phenomena in this area. In addition, the model proposed here is not likely to shed much light on the ecumenical movement outside the United States where, in most cases, a pluralistic free market on United States lines does not exist; nor is it useful in explaining the international involvements of American Protestantism itself. This does not mean that economic factors are absent in these cases, but their investigation would have to proceed on different lines.

Conclusion

A few words need to be added concerning the sociologistic tenor of our model. A network of socio-economic pressures with which a rationally functioning religious bureaucracy must reckon has been pointed out. It hardly need be added that, in Robert Merton's sense, we are dealing here mainly with "latent functions." In other words, our analysis in no way questions the subjective sincerity of those actors in the situation who interpret their actions in theological terms that have nothing to do with the factors here described. It is also clear that economically irrational actions will play a part in the situation. The evidence at hand would lead to the conclusion, however, that such actions do not generally interfere with the overall imperatives of rationalization. Ecumenical circles in recent years have shown some interest in what they call "non-theological factors" affecting problems of Christian unity. This is very broad-minded of them. A sociological analysis of the matter will inevitably regard these factors as the prime motors in the phenomena under investigation; but such an analysis can reciprocate the broad-mindedness by conceding the possibility that "theological factors" may also play a part within the limits of what is rationally possible and may even upon occasion transcend these limits. In other words, sociological analysis of religious phenomena need not imply a sociologistic theory of history in which men are nothing but the instruments of socio-economic forces. As far as the immediate problem is concerned, I feel justified in concluding that, sociologically speaking, the relationship between *Oikoumene* and *Oikonomia* on the American Protestant scene is considerably more than an etymological one. Nor should this further evidence of the subjection of the spirit to the flesh "in this aeon" constitute an unusual shock for the Christian theologian.

NOTES

1. For instance, Charles Morrison, *The Unfinished Reformation* (New York: Harper & Bros., 1953), pp. 26 ff.

2. Almost any issue of the *Ecumenical Review* expresses this point of view. The same position, of course, is reflected in the pronouncements of the Amsterdam, Evanston, and New Delhi assemblies, and serves as the foundation of the theological work undertaken under the auspices of the World Council of Churches.

3. *The Social Sources of Church Unity* (New York: Abingdon Press, 1960), pp. 188 ff.

4. See my *Noise of Solemn Assemblies* (Garden City, N.Y.: Doubleday & Co., 1961), p. 50.

5. Clifton Olmstead, *History of Religion in the United States* (Englewood Cliffs, N.J.: Prentice-Hall Co., 1960), p. 536 ff.

6. Paul Douglass, *Church Unity Movements in the United States* (New York: Institute of Social and Religious Research, 1934).

7. I am indebted to my colleague Robert Paul for having first drawn my attention to this difference.

8. See note 4, pp. 72 ff., for a discussion of this phenomenon and for some of the substantiating evidence. For the forceful implications

of this point see Gibson Winter, *The Suburban Captivity of the Churches* (Garden City, N.Y.: Doubleday & Co., 1961), pp. 39 ff.

9. Cf., for instance, the best study so far of a North American suburb, John Seeley, *et al.*, *Crestwood Heights* (New York: Basic Books, 1956). For general discussions of the suburban way of life see William F. Whyte, *The Organization Man* (Garden City, N.Y.: Doubleday & Co., 1957); William Dobriner (ed.), *The Suburban Community* (New York: Putman & Sons, 1958), and Maurice Stein, *The Eclipse of Community* (Princeton, N.J.: Princeton University Press, 1960).

10. On this point see two reports recently undertaken in a New England suburb: Dennison Nash and Peter Berger, "Church Commitment in an American Suburb," *Archives de sociologie des religions*, vol. 13 (1962), pp. 105–20, and their "The Child, the Family, and the Religious Revival in Suburbia," *Journal for the Scientific Study of Religion* (Fall 1962), pp. 85–93.

11. *Yearbook of American Churches, 1960* (New York: National Council of the Churches of Christ, 1960), p. 276.

12. *Authority and Power in the Free Church Tradition* (Princeton, N.J.: Princeton University Press, 1959).

13. Francis Gibson, "The Investment Policies of Churches in America" (S.T.M. thesis, Hartford Seminary Foundation, 1962).

14. See, for instance, the efforts to achieve local inter-church cooperation in the face of economic disaster described by Arthur Vidich and Joseph Bensman in *Small Town in Mass Society* (Princeton, N.J.: Princeton University Press, 1958), pp. 247 ff. Cf. the sort of top-level bureaucratic activity triggered by the so-called Blake Proposal. I am indebted to Arthur Vidich for having drawn my attention to this discrepancy between "grass roots" and upper-echelon ecumenicity.

15. Will Herberg, *Protestant, Catholic, Jew* (Garden City, N.Y.: Doubleday & Co., 1955), pp. 85 ff.; Martin Marty, *The Shape of American Religion* (New York: Harper & Bros., 1958), pp. 31 ff.

16. "Religious Establishment and Theological Education," *Theology Today* (July 1962), pp. 178–191.

17. "Do Holiness Sects Socialize in Dominant Values?" *Social Forces* (May 1961), 39:4.

18. Cf. the extensive bibliographical references on this point in David Moberg, *The Church as a Social Institution* (Englewood Cliffs, N.J.: Prentice-Hall, 1962), pp. 100 ff.

QUESTIONS FOR DISCUSSION

1. What kind of organizational structure is being proposed for the ecumenical Protestant church of tomorrow?

2. How are theological conflicts generated out of conflicts that arise in carrying out the work of the church?

3. The question of authority has recently been raised in the Catholic Church. What are the issues at stake, and what are their implications for the organization of the church?

4. Do the teachings of seminaries that are under denominational control differ from those of seminaries that are not under denominational control?

5. Do churches, like many other organizations, show an oligarchical tendency over time; that is, does authority tend to become vested in the hands of fewer and fewer people?

ADDITIONAL READING

Cogley, John. "The Crisis," *Commonweal* (October 11, 1968), pp. 51 ff. An example of articles now appearing with considerable frequency, this one, by the renowned journalist-scholar, contends that something in the Catholic Church must give, and soon.

Harrison, Paul M. *Power and Authority in the Free Church Tradition, A Social Case Study of the American Baptist Convention.* Princeton, N.J.: Princeton University Press, 1959. One of the few published case studies of how religious organizations work. Drawing on historical and contemporary material, Harrison highlights the difficulty a modern denomination has in conducting its business according to Baptist principles of church government.

Lee, Robert. *The Social Sources of Church Unity.* New York: Abingdon Press, 1960. Lee attributes the movement for church unity in American Protestantism to a growing cultural uniformity in American life and to a reduction in social differences among denominations that are based on the class status of their members.

Wilson, Bryan. Chapters 8, 9, and 10 in *Religion in Secular Society.* London: Penguin (Pelican) paperback, 1969. Wilson emphasizes the role the clergy has played in the ecumenical movement and hypothesizes that churches seek union when they are weak rather than when they are strong.

Winter, Gibson. *Religious Identity.* New York: Macmillan, 1968. Based on a series of denominational studies, this book amply documents the increasing importance of denominational agencies in church affairs.

Chapter VI

The Religious Professional

Theologies, like other ideologies or systems of ideas and ideals, tend to be adhered to more closely by some than by others. Holy men, mendicants, traveling evangelists, religious autocrats, and so forth, are thus found throughout the history of man, even though most men most of the time can be described as religiously lukewarm. It was one of Max Weber's great contributions to point out that such religious "specialists" do not appear at random, however, nor, when they appear, do they randomly become one or another kind of specialist. Instead, the forces conducive to a particular type of theology, combined with the character of that theology, are likely to produce one of two distinctive styles of leadership. Otherworldly mysticism tends to give rise to individualistic elites, whereas innerworldly asceticism encourages a ministry oriented to a collectivity. The former is a specialist's personal path away from worldly concerns; the latter is a group's "representative," guiding them in their grappling with the world's ambiguities.

Though stated in purposely extreme form, Weber's general argument —that the Western world gave rise to the second kind of religion— does help in understanding the kind of leadership that predominates in America. Coming out of the Judeo-Christian, Western tradition, this leadership for the most part consists of specially trained categories of persons who enter into a "contract" with a religious "organization." The contract specifies what services will be provided lay clients in return for what salary. They are, in other words, "professionals" who conduct themselves in a style quite foreign to the Buddhist monk, the wandering holy man, or the keeper of the family shrine.

Despite the obvious differences among religious professionals, from rabbi to bishop, nun to seminary teacher, parish priest to missionary, another central fact about American religious leaders is their likelihood of having a bureaucratic location. Even in the instances of persons who begin as autonomous evangelists, the forces of organization

191

tend to overtake their endeavor; problems of planning, communication, continuity, and so on, almost always generate bureaucratic responses (see Harrison, Selection 13).

The professionalized, bureaucratically located religious leaders of the West are therefore more sharply distinguishable by occupation than are their counterparts in other parts of the world. Most American clergy, for example, are, occupationally speaking, clergy *only;* their chief identity, in their eyes and those of others, stems from their role in a religious organization. They undertake special training programs leading to certification and ordination for, promotion in, and "retirement" from, their profession.

But a sharply distinguishable occupation does not necessarily assure agreement on what that occupation should entail. Indeed, location in a bureaucracy—especially when that bureaucracy has diffuse goals, ostensibly open membership, and thus heterogeneous constituents— may increase the probability of conflict over the "proper role" for clergy to take. Such conflict, it is clear from the selection by Marshall Sklare, "Discontinuities and Conflicts: Problems in the Clergy Role" (Selection 16), can exist between the clergyman and various segments of a congregation, between seminary training and subsequent practice, even between an earlier tradition and present exigencies. This last source of conflict indicates something of the pressures that have turned "religious specialists" into professional bureaucrats; it provides an example of the shift from the rabbi as village spiritual and moral authority to the rabbi as organizational administrator and spokesman.

With or without conflicts, however, a clergyman represents, and is therefore expected to personify, a set of ideals. Most of his life is more public than most professionals' lives, so there is a sense in which his "front stage" behavior dominates his "back stage" behavior. He is "on," in other words, self-consciously performing with an eye to the performance's reception by the audience. Clearly the psychic burdens of such behavior can be immense, a situation that fairly cries out for comic relief. Charles Merrill Smith, a Methodist minister, must therefore have provided relief in his satirical *How to Become a Bishop Without Being Religious,* a portion of which, on "Selecting the Clerical Wife," is reprinted here (Selection 17). Written as advice to the young Protestant cleric who would make it to the top of his profession, Smith describes the difficulties in "image management" if, for example, one chooses an overly attractive wife. The method is spoof, of course, but the message is serious. Indeed, debate over the wisdom of clergy celibacy, currently a controversial subject in Roman Catholic circles, can be informed by this tongue-in-cheek discussion.

Wealth has characterized religious leaders only in some times and places. Vows of poverty and the expectation of later, otherworldly reward have instead been more the rule. Religious organizations may accumulate large sums of money, and the programs they underwrite —from overseas missions to bakeries to downtown temples—may involve large budgets. But rarely is the salary of the religious professional an item of major importance in the bookkeeping. Yet the demand for clergy is greater than the supply, a situation that in most occupations would have the effect of either raising salaries or increasing the number of recruits, neither of which apparently is happening in American religious professions. This economic puzzle is the starting point for William C. Bonifield's analysis, "The Minister in the Labor Market" (Selection 18). His data, of course, are restricted in time, denomination, and location, but they address a question of considerable theoretical importance, especially in a society where religious leadership is so professionalized and bureaucratized, thus presumably most vulnerable to market forces.

Religious leadership is as variegated as theology. The selections here treat only clergy, for example, and only some aspects of Jewish and Protestant clergy at that. Other aspects are touched on in other essays of this volume, so that the reader interested in clergy authority, for example, might turn to Chapter III (Roche, Selection 8), which describes lay challenges to Catholic hierarchic authority. Certainly, the essays by Johnson (Selection 20) on clergy party preference and Gurin, Veroff, and Feld (Selection 23) on the mental health "gatekeeping" function of clergy are appropriate further discussions of the religious professional. But it ought to be remembered that a comprehensive survey of the subject involves leaders other than clergy. Lay leaders, nuns, church administrators, cantors, and so forth, all constitute religious "professionals" to some degree. They all are instruments by which religious organizations try to influence society, and all, correlatively, change as society influences them. The three selections of this chapter illustrate those influences.

16

Marshall Sklare

Discontinuities and Conflicts:
Problems in the Clergy Role

It has already been pointed out that the Conservative functionary is crucial for the worship program. His importance in the educational and social activities has also been stressed. However, we have not as yet highlighted the fact that the rabbi—as the ranking professional on the synagogue staff—spearheads the *promotional* efforts of his congregation. The Conservative synagogue seeks to combat indifference to Jewish values. Also, it is in competition with other congregations and with extra-synagogual Jewish activities. As a consequence, the functionary must serve as a resource person delivering suggestions which are intended to place his institution ahead of its rivals. Since new features and attractions are important, he must read the bulletins published by other synagogues, discuss his problems with other rabbis, and solicit ideas from his lay people.

As the promoter of the congregation, it is required of the rabbi that he be active in non-congregational affairs. It is he who is chiefly responsible for relating the congregation to two larger structures: the Jewish community and the non-Jewish community. Consequently the successful rabbi is expected to be active in the affairs of both. In so doing he helps to reinforce the prestige of the congregation and thus makes membership in his particular synagogue desirable. Also, as is mainly characteristic in the smaller communities, he must seek to raise the status of his ethnic group in the eyes of the larger community.

Institutional maintenance requires that a certain level of integration within the congregation itself be achieved. This is difficult in the

Excerpted from Marshall Sklare, *Conservative Judaism* (Glencoe, Ill.: The Free Press, 1955), pp. 174–188. Reprinted by permission of the author. Marshall Sklare is a sociologist at Yeshiva University.

modern synagogue where congregants have *varied* interests and view-points. Because of such heterogeneity, the rabbi is required to serve as a figure to whom all can rally. If he exercises a measure of impartiality, he may succeed in integrating highly disparate forces around his person. It is therefore important that the Conservative rabbi, like his Reform colleague (and even the more traditional type of functionary who serves the modernized "neo-Orthodox" congregation), be a friendly person who is able to relate easily to others.

That the rabbi is a prime factor in achieving synagogual integration is further demonstrated when we realize that he seeks to establish for the congregant a special relationship with the institution—one which differs from that possessed by individuals who are numbered among the unaffiliated. The connection between the rabbi and the non-congregant tends to become essentially that of one "secondary group" member to another—the unaffiliated individual can hire the rabbi to render those services of a religious nature which he may require from time to time. Such relationships are contractual and are terminated upon performance of the ceremony. With the congregant, however, the bond is more primary, for the rabbi is *his* rabbi, and the functionary may attend family affairs and share in the congregant's joys and sorrows. Although the association between rabbi and congregant is in reality what may be termed "synthetic primaryship" (especially if we consider the turnover in congregational membership, as well as the constant stream of applications by functionaries for a change in their rabbinical posts), if adroitly handled it is capable of providing much comfort to the congregant and of integrating him closely into the institutional structure.

All of this is in contrast to the classical role of the rabbi—that of arbiter and expert in the history, doctrines and practices of the Jewish sacred system. However, notwithstanding the introduction of many new courses, much of the Seminary curriculum is still centered about the study of the Jewish legalistic tradition. Although Talmudic material is taught in a scientific manner, even such modernized studies cannot be of much practical use to the Conservative rabbi. The assumption for the concentration of courses on the sacred system is that individuals are interested in maximum observance—the rabbi should be able to indicate what constitutes this observance and to subsume novel situations under some traditional legal category. When circumstances compel change, individuals will consult with rabbinical authority to legitimate deviations. But Conservative Jewry—as an acculturated group—understandably does not take the steps which are required for the preservation of the integrity of the system. According to one rabbi, the fact that he is a specialist in Jewish law is of little interest to his congregants:

I receive practically no inquiries about ritual or legal problems. Only on one holiday do people ask me a few questions—that's Passover. A death in the family may also provoke a query or two about the proper observance of the rites for the departed. People do ask me questions, but generally this takes place at a dinner party and they start out this way: "By the way, Rabbi, there is something that I've been meaning to ask you." Then they recite ritualistic variation which they have observed or heard about, possibly from a parent or grandparent. Perhaps it is a Jewish adaptation of one or another East European peasant superstition. The question has no relevancy to the congregant's own religious observance but it is just a curiosity which he would like to have explained.

The functionaries tend to be "over-trained" in one area and under-prepared in others. It is true that the services in the Seminary synagogue serve as training for fulfilling the role of conductors of public worship, or *priests*. Training in homiletics is also given: students deliver addresses at the services and thus prepare themselves to serve as *preachers*. While both of these roles are outside of the work functions of the traditional rabbi, a compromise has been effected and whether by formal or informal means, some training is being given in these two important areas. However, Conservative spiritual leaders must perform many other roles in addition to their duties as preacher-priest and rabbi, and while the aspirants may be given a brief course in "practical rabbinics," they are relatively unprepared for these further roles. First, they serve as *clerics*—as an arm of the state which has empowered them to perform certain rituals and requires them to record these ceremonies. While this role may not call for any preparation, many rabbis feel that in their capacity as *rectors*, or administrators, they require specialized training. Since they give counsel, guidance, and assistance to individuals in meeting the crises of life, the rabbis function as *pastors*, and in this role lack of orientation is felt to be even more serious. Also of significance is the fact that although they head their own families, the functionaries are in a sense members of many families. Assuming the headship of congregations, in a psychological sense they serve as *fathers*. Lastly, since the spiritual leaders are personages of some consequence in their communities and are given membership on various boards, semi-public bodies, and agencies in the field of social welfare, they act as *parsons*.

It will be helpful if these developments are placed in historical perspective. Traditionally, the Jewish functionary has served as a "scholar-saint" in a sacred society. He has been granted the authority to interpret, and ultimately to administer, a well-esteemed and highly intricate religious code. In the network of power relations, his place as a religious specialist who had to be reckoned with in the decision-

making process was recognized. He was able to control some of the
conditions relative to his role and function. But in the present-day
Jewish community, as a result of the new system of shared values
which has served as the background for our investigation, there is a
radical readjustment in the role of the religious specialist. The crux of
the change is the decay of the "rabbi" role. It is being relegated to an
inferior position, and the roles of preacher, pastor, rector, and priest
are coming to occupy the resulting void.

These changes modify the very "face" of the profession. The sanction of the rabbi is no longer required for the correct practice of
Judaism. The authority previously possessed by the religious specialist has for all practical purposes been transferred to the laity. The
laity have always influenced what shall—and shall not—constitute
Jewish law. Until the modern period, however, social change was
always gradual, and revisions were arrived at in consultation with
rabbinic authority. Thus the influence of the laity was obscured.

The Jewish spiritual leader has had comparatively little preparation
which would serve to reconcile him to the transfer of authority. Since
the process has been so sudden, it poses far-reaching problems for the
religious specialist. It not only forces him to rearrange somewhat the
rank order of his roles as well as to encompass some which traditionally do not belong to him, but actually he must change his self-image.
Also, the skills learned by the aspirant at his rabbinical school now
require more than the kind of supplementation which can be gained
through the serving of a brief internship as in other professions.
Rather, they tend to be almost completely obsolete.

For his former authority, the functionary can try to substitute the
force of personality; he may also compensate by fulfilling his varied
roles with thoroughness and skill. But even if he is a highly successful
spiritual leader, the rabbinical role comes to occupy for the Jewish
religious specialist a position rather akin to its place in the role
constellation of the Protestant minister. It is true that the importance
accorded to the functionary because of his role as preacher, pastor,
rector, and parson may serve to reinforce professional status and to
improve damaged self-esteem. But it can never fully compensate for
the deprivation felt by those who come from an East European background and who thus may have internalized some of the traditional
attitudes with respect to their roles. Having no alternative, the Conservative functionaries have *had* to accede to these changes. However,
if we review the large amount of material written or spoken by rabbis
primarily for circulation among their colleagues, it becomes apparent
from the content that what is involved essentially is a quest for
legitimation on the part of those who are failing to exercise the
traditional rabbinical role.

Significantly, congregants are unaware of this whole problem—as laymen they are hardly in a position to appreciate the difficulties encountered by their spiritual leaders in the readjustment process. They, of course, lack any of the role conflicts suffered by the functionaries. Being relatively ignorant of problems in the area of systematic theology, they cannot appreciate the intellectual dilemmas encountered by those whose profession entails the manipulation of such categories.

· · ·

One of the important factors influencing the adjustment of the novice to his future professional role is the nature of his training. In many professional schools the teachers are not practitioners, or even ex-practitioners. Because of their isolation, they are not subject to the demands made upon those who are "out in the field." The curriculum which they fashion may not always stress practical studies, or it may not even include a consideration of the latest methods. In most cases the proclivities of the schoolmen—in whatever direction they may be—are moderated by the strong influences exercised by the practitioners on the professional school. Practitioners are usually well represented on evaluation committees, boards of trustees, and other institutional policy-making bodies. This occurs because they generally have behind them strong professional associations and they can also claim to represent the public interest. Successful alumni are in a position to provide sizeable endowments or to influence grant-giving organizations. Even though the schoolmen, tending to constitute themselves into centers of semiautonomy, might not be overly concerned with the future adjustment of the aspirant (they may be more interested in inculcating pure rather than applied knowledge), the practitioner exercises his influence to keep the scales in balance.

In regard to the Seminary, this basic process has been more or less absent. The interaction between student and teacher (and hence between alumnus and teacher) has differed from that which is found in non-Jewish theological schools, not to speak of the average type of professional training institution. Seminary students and alumni tend to *defer* to their mentors to an unusual degree. In this instance, practitioners are very hesitant about interfering with schoolmen. How has this come about? Why the deviation from general patterns?

Attitudes in this area can be traced back to age-old Jewish culture patterns. According to the traditional system, the association between master and pupil has quality of *sacredness* about it. The student is highly dependent upon his mentor, for it is the teacher who raises him from the dishonor of ignorance and makes him a knowledgable member of society. In the final analysis the association between teacher and student bears a strong resemblance to the parent-child relationship. All of this of course derives from the high value placed upon learning. While most Jews have by now moderated such attitudes or have channelized them into secular fields, as might be expected, rabbinical aspirants have tended to retain the traditional viewpoint longer than others.

The teachers whom the Conservative rabbinical student encountered at the Seminary not only approached Jewish subjects in conformity with the standards of higher learning, but their technical mastery of the corpus of Jewish law and literature was equal or superior to the level found in the *yeshiva*. Questions to which former Orthodox teachers had no satisfactory answers hardly puzzled these instructors. In relating what Ginzberg's courses meant to him as a student who had received his preliminary schooling in institutions of the traditional kind, Goldman had this to say:

> . . . he has given the lie to the cry of legalism, and if he has not silenced the detractors of Pharisaic Judaism . . . he has certainly caused them to reel. With . . . an abundance of erudition he has demonstrated once and for all that the law had not been static but evolving . . . and that differences of opinion among the Rabbis were not formalistic, a kind of show of skill in pedantry, but concerned living issues. Employing by way of illustration the disagreements between the Hillelites and Shammaites, the matrix of nearly all Talmudic controversy, he consigns to oblivion . . . an infinite number of conjectures . . . regarding these schools. It is strange that men should have for generations repeated their words and debated their meaning, without wondering why it was that these two schools should have been so persistently . . . contradictory of each other. No one thought of inquiring into the motives and factors that had divided them. It was left to Professor Ginzberg to enlighten us. The Hillelites and the Shammaites, he revealed, were not recluse pedants engaged in a battle of words but the representatives of different economic and social strata clashing over the interests of their respective groups. What a revelation that was. . . .[1]

Under these conditions the fledgling rabbi has tended to transfer adoration—which normatively he was required to give to the learned class but which he could no longer accord to Orthodox instructors—to the Seminary teachers. In a relatively secularized atmosphere, the student attempted to recreate a relationship more appropriate to the sacred environment from which he sprang, and from which he had become alienated both on philosophical grounds as well as because of his aspirations to serve a *middle class* Conservative congregation instead of a more humble Orthodox synagogue.

The existence of such deference, being inappropriate in a secular order, has had ramified consequences. Since the practitioner is hesitant about demanding a revision of the curriculum and thus is actually best prepared for a role which becomes only a minor professional function, much of his activity is consequently improvised and learned while "on the job." Those who are somewhat rigid or who lack imagination fail to find much satisfaction in their work situation. There exists some rather generalized resentment as a result of the Seminary's failure to train for all of the roles which are exercised and hence to truly prepare the novice for the adjustment he will be required to make.

Given his Orthodox background, however, the practitioner may wish to perpetuate the fiction that he is actually exercising the rabbinical role to some degree. He may do so when in the company of his colleagues. Since attendance at rabbinical conventions is confined to functionaries, long and heated debates may be held there on various problems of Talmudic law. In addition the rabbi can develop support for the Seminary and strive to make it a "bulwark of Torah"—that is, help solidify its financial structure so that the institution can withstand external pressures and carry out a type of program which he would not attempt in his local synagogue. By strengthening the Seminary, the practitioner creates a center of rabbinical learning—one where the older values can be conserved in spite of the impact of the environment. While the rabbi cannot but feel somewhat alienated from the local Conservative synagogue (it is after all the province of the layman), the Seminary can give him a sense of expansiveness, *for here a type of "rabbinical culture" is being preserved safe from the influence of the uninitiated.*

NOTE ——

1. Solomon Goldman, "The Portrait of a Teacher," in *Louis Ginzberg: Jubilee Volume of the Occasion of His Seventieth Birthday* (New York: American Academy for Jewish Research, 1945), pp. 9–10.

17

Charles Merrill Smith

Selecting the Clerical Wife

The most important one piece of equipment the aspiring clergyman will acquire is a wife. So vital is the wife to the success of the minister that the care he should exercise in selecting her cannot be overstressed.

Other authorities have shown how the wrong kind of wife can hamper and inhibit an otherwise promising executive career. The harm that the worst imaginable executive wife can do to her husband's career, however, is but a negligible annoyance compared to the shattering effect an unsuitable parsonage spouse has on her consort's labors in the Lord's vineyard.

It may be that you are already married. Clergymen, for some reason which needs more research, have an unfortunate tendency to marry quite young. And when a man marries young, he has almost always married for the wrong reasons so far as his future professional success is concerned.

If you find yourself in the difficult position of beginning your ministry equipped with a wife you married because you fancied you were in love, or because you found her charming, or because you were sexually attracted to her, or for any other irrelevant reason, you are up against what will probably turn out to be the most baffling problem of your professional life. Barring the unlikely possibility that by chance and blind luck you picked the right type for the parsonage (which would be the equivalent of breaking the bank at Monte Carlo or filling an inside straight) about all you can do now is to institute a program of education designed to bring her up to minimum standards of performance (which you should begin by calling her attention to this chapter).

However, you should be cautioned against excessive optimism as to the probable results. Observation of such educational efforts have been depressing, the woman who marries a minister without understanding the nature of the demands his profession places on her usually proving quite intractible when it is suggested, even with considerable tact, that she make over her personality to the satisfaction of her husband's present and anticipated congregations.

However, we will assume that we have caught you in time, that you are reading this while still a bachelor and without any unbreakable alliances entangling you, that you are legally and morally in a position to select a wife in accordance with the principles and the wisdom here offered.

You must begin by fixing in your mind the fact that your chosen work has already determined the qualities you will look for in a wife. She must be selected to fit these specifications.

Now if you have been corrupted by the silly ideals of romantic love poured over us in a sticky and seemingly inexhaustible cascade by the movies, television and the popular women's magazines, you may at first recoil from this suggestion. But upon mature and calm reflection, you will see how very right is this principle.

You will not deny, surely, that any reasonably healthy female is capable of performing all the functions of a wife. She will be able to cook, keep house and bear children. Further, if romantic illusions are necessary to your emotional well-being, you can check with any psychologist and be assured that these depend not on the loved but on the lover. Or to put it simply, it's all in *your* head. Therefore, it places no exceptional psychological demands upon you to invest any girl with the aura of romance.

It should be clear to you by now that the proper sequence of events is to select a girl who meets the predetermined specifications and then fall in love with her, rather than allow your romantic fancy to light upon just any young female who happens to appeal to you for irrelevant reasons (some of which were mentioned earlier), and then have to make the best of it if she turns out to be—as she almost surely will —poorly fitted for the role she is expected to assume.

The Reasons Why You Must Marry

If by now you are contemplating the advantages of clerical celibacy (which would not be an unreasonable reaction considering the problems involved in your selection) dismiss such thoughts at once. Protestant Christians expect their clergy to marry. The folklore of the trade holds that it is necessary for a minister to marry in order to set an example of Christian family life.

You will want to pretend that this is true, just as you will find it expedient to pretend that you dwell in a state of marital bliss the calm waters of which are never rippled by a cross word, let alone a quarrel. The nervous strain involved in such pretensions is of awesome proportions, and is known to have pushed parsonage wives into emotional breakdowns and turned parsonage children into church-hating delinquents. However, all good things in this life are bought at a price.

The real reasons why you should marry are, of course, not at all related to the folklore.

First, a clergyman who remains unmarried for more than a year after graduation from seminary is suspected of being abnormal, immoral or chicken.

Second, there will be those who will speculate that he has taken St. Paul on marriage too seriously and has made a secret vow of celibacy. So far as your parishioners are concerned, you may be as celibate as a Cistercian monk, but they will insist that you practice it within the married state.

Third, somewhat more than half of your congregation will be women, and all women—single, married or widowed (including grass widows)—resent a male eligible for marriage who chooses to remain unwed.

Fourth—and here is the overriding argument in the mind of the congregation—since the church owns a parsonage and already has arrived at a salary figure below which it cannot go and maintain its conviction, however illusory, that it is a humane institution, it is only sensible to get two employees for the price of one. Therefore, it boils down to a business proposition. It would be damaging and vulgar to admit to this, however, so the tradition and the folklore were manufactured to mask it.

Actually it is very good business from the church's point of view. Most girls are piano players of sorts, and anyone can learn to operate a typewriter or mimeograph. Add to these accomplishments the intellectually untaxing duties of Sunday School teaching, choir singing, ladies' aid work and a miscellany of other small parish chores all of which your wife will be expected in your first small churches to perform (it's part of the tradition) and you have a job analysis which, were it filled by a salaried employee, would require no small addition to the annual budget. Hence the tradition of a married clergy.

Let us assume that you are now convinced that you have no choice but to marry—and not because, as St. Paul so delicately put it, your only alternative is to burn. The exhausting life of the parish ministry and cold showers eliminate or greatly minimize this problem. The frightening alternative to marriage for you is the unappetizing prospect of a career in back-country or run-down city parishes.

To be sure Phillips Brooks and a few others made it big in the ministry without taking unto themselves wives. But they were the rarest of exceptions. If you want to be a preacher and a bachelor, be prepared for a dismal future and renounce now the hope for status, prestige, emolument, luxury and all of the spiritual joys which accompany a plush suburban pastorate. The author does not question the preacher's right to take a vow of chastity, but he'd better darn well understand that a vow of poverty goes along with it. However, it is unlikely that anyone who has read this far is uncommitted to the ideal of advancement in his chosen profession. So let us proceed to the rules for selecting the suitable clerical wife.

We are immediately struck by the realization that it is far easier to describe what the suitable wife for the ambitious clergyman is not than to delineate the precise qualities and characteristics which make her suitable.

The Stylish, Sexy and Other Types of Girls to Avoid

Since the one thing the congregation will notice first and most often about her is her appearance, special attention must be paid to this facet of her personality. To cover the rule in a sentence, she must not be beautiful, stylish or sexy.

This does not mean that she should be homely and frumpy. The smallest rural circuit will appreciate a presentable preacher's wife. And when pulpit committees from larger churches come looking you over, they will take a good look at her, too. More than one clerical career has been nipped in the bud when a committee thought they had their man but, finding that taking him meant taking a shabby-looking wife too, decided to look elsewhere.

Nor does this rule prohibit you from marrying a real stunner. Any woman, even if she won the Miss America contest in a walk and brings on attacks of pop-eyes and shortness of breath among the males present when she strolls through a hotel lobby, can learn to tone down these assets to a level acceptable to most congregations. She can go easy on the make-up, wear serviceable but not overly stylish dresses and sensible shoes, and go to a hairdresser of indifferent skill. This will do wonders, in reverse, for her appearance without rendering her in any way unattractive.

If she asks why she must submit to this sort of thing, remind her that the women of the congregation actually run the church, either by getting a stranglehold on the key committees or by telling their husbands how to run it, or both. So a preacher really has to please the women if he expects to keep a pulpit, and give the distinct impression that he knows how to please the women if he expects to get a better one.

There is no possibility of pleasing the ladies if he flaunts a knockout of a wife, for she is a constant threat to their peace of mind, and he will have nothing but trouble. If she is so lovely as to make the ladies of the church feel homely, and so stylish as to make them feel dowdy, his prospects for a shining career in the church, which may be otherwise quite bright, are dimmed by several thousand candlepower. The ladies simply will not put up with such a woman in the parsonage.

And for a clergyman to marry a woman who possesses an abundance of sex appeal is absolutely fatal to his career. The men of the congregation will appreciate her, of course, which is the first reason that their wives won't.

Remember, too, that your image depends in part on the inability of the congregation to imagine you engaging in sexual intercourse. That you have children, and that practically nobody nowadays believes the stork brings babies might be thought to destroy this part of the image. But it is not as serious as you might suppose, although there is something to be said for the childless clergyman (including the economic facts of parsonage life).

But children in the parsonage do not confuse overmuch the image of the preacher as a member of a third sex. If they think about it at all, the congregation will imagine that the accouchements were accomplished through immaculate conception or parthenogenesis or artificial insemination. At the very worst they should be able to believe that their pastor was only fulfilling his social responsibility of fathering children and that he really didn't enjoy the procedure essential to this end very much. It is not easy to believe this, of course, if the pastor's wife has a high-voltage look about her.

From your own point of view, an overly attractive wife can be a millstone around the neck of progress in your profession. She will be a constant distraction to you, and you will be tempted to spend time with her much better invested in getting on with your career.

Such an eminent authority on executive success as Vance Packard has pointed out that in the world of big business the man who is entirely happy with his home life is not a good bet for heavy responsibility. One way to spot a real comer in the corporation is to find the fellow who is a bit discontented with his marriage.

As a pastor you should never even entertain the thought that you are discontented with your marriage. The same end can be achieved by refusing to become too much absorbed in it. A good, plain-looking wife whom you like and about whom you can think with affection but without passion is an inestimable aid in directing your primary devotion to your church and its duties. If it is no hardship to stay away from home, you will not have to fight frequent spiritual battles over the choice between one more pastoral call or that important committee meeting and an evening at home. Any pro will tell you it is that extra effort, that last push which wins the game. So if getting home to the wife is not a prospect which is irresistibly attractive, then no great sacrifice is entailed in absenting yourself in order to get in a few more licks on the job.

It will not occur to the members of your flock that you are working hard and putting in long hours because you would just as soon work as to hang around the house. They will conclude that you are driven by devotion to your calling and an acute sense of responsibility toward the welfare of your church. There is no need to rectify their thinking on this matter, of course, and it is well if you think along the same lines.

Perhaps the best possible approach to the problem of clerical mate selection is to imagine that you are planning to employ an assistant pastor and are scouting the prospects. This will focus your attention on the genuine issues at stake and compensate for the normal male irrelevancies which becloud the true values we should seek. Never forget that you are a clergyman first and a man second.

The Advantages of Marrying a Girl Who Wants to Marry a Minister

Another excellent rule to follow as you make your selection is "look for a girl who is looking for you." By this we mean that you can hardly go wrong if you choose a young lady who has set out to marry a preacher.

Be assured that there exists at any given moment a fair number of nubile females who actually have marriage to a clergyman as their goal in life. The advantages, for you, of an alliance with a young lady in this category cannot be dismissed lightly and should be sufficient to stimulate you to a diligent search for her.

For one thing, she will be likely to understand what she is getting into better than a girl who would find a registered pharmacist as acceptable to her as a clergyman. Further, it can be asserted that she will really enjoy the role of minister's wife, and will not find it tedious, boring and artificial as many girls do. She will accept without complaint the economic restrictions imposed on her by your profession, and won't swear at the good matrons of the Women's Society even in private.

Also, psychologists who have done research on the subject report that girls who want to marry preachers generally have a low sex drive and, convinced by the pious Protestant image of the clergy, believe that an ordained husband will be modest in the carnal demands he makes of her. (It is inevitable, of course, that it won't always work out this way for the girl since a few lusty characters do manage to find their way into the ministry, but the odds are very probably in her favor.) You can readily see that if you choose such a girl you will be gaining a dividend of time and energy in amounts nearly beyond calculation which can be applied to your professional duties. It gives you an advantage over your clerical competitors whose marital situation is less fortunate, which seems almost unfair.

The Tremendous Advantage
of Marrying a Girl
Who Has Money

The author hesitated long before including the following final word of counsel, knowing that he risks misunderstanding and that to some it will seem indelicate. However, be that as it may, he decided to run these risks because of the joy it may bring to those who heed it. The counsel is this: When choosing a wife, make every effort to locate one who has some money of her own.

It is not so difficult as you might think to bring off. The population has a glut of marriageable females and some of them have already, or will in time, come into an inheritance. Why should not you, too, the Lord's faithful and self-sacrificing servant, share in this bonanza?

You will be gratified, should you carry out this counsel, to discover how even a few hundred extra a year will palliate the hardships, the meager income of your early pastorates. And even in your later and better-salaried days, your wife's remittance will mean the difference between relaxing in comfort in an air-conditioned hotel, and dining in the better restaurants or sweating it out in some flea-bag while you subsist on hamburgers and beans during the frequent conferences and conventions you will be expected to attend. And if you are careful enough or fortunate enough to marry a girl who is really loaded, you will take trips to the Holy Land and vacation in Florida while your ministerial brethren who are forced to live on their own income will curse their grocery bills and envy you.

And if you consider this suggestion to be crass and revolting materialism, keep in mind the fact that your larger income means a larger tithe (10 per cent of income after taxes) which you can devote to the Lord's work. This thought should be sufficient to tranquillize any fears that you are succumbing to the lures of this present world.

If you can manage to marry a bit of money, the esteem in which your congregation will hold you is bound to be quite high. The one thing all Americans respect without qualification is money. And the classic

Protestant ethic holds that when a man is blessed with material rewards it is a sign that he has found favor in the eyes of Jehovah. Since you are theologically sophisticated, you may have your doubts about the validity of such an ethic, but your congregation won't.

Marriage is always fraught with uncertainties and incalculables. No one can ever be certain, in advance, that a marriage will work out along the lines planned and hoped for. Everyone should enter it rationally, realistically, and only after the suitability of the intended partner has been scrutinized as carefully as possible. And what everyone should do (but not very many do do, or the divorce rate in our country would be much lower than it is) the clergyman must do if he has expectations of advancement in his profession as well as a felicitous atmosphere in his home.

With the counsel here given, you will be able to reduce the hazards in this extremely hazardous enterprise, and choose a mate who not only will grace your parsonage but be a co-worker in and an ornament to your holy calling.

18

William C. Bonifield

The Minister in the
Labor Market

There is a continuing shortage of qualified clergy to staff the churches of this country,[1] yet the salary and benefits paid to clergymen have declined relative to other comparable occupations.[2] This statement is paradoxical to say the least. According to economic theory, a shortage of labor should cause the wage to rise in order to ration out the available supply among the buyers and to attract new supplies into the market. For example, if engineers are scarce, beginning salaries for engineering graduates and salaries paid to experienced engineers rise, firms hire fewer engineers, and more students enter engineering schools.

However, in the face of a persistent shortage of ministers, the income received by ministers (including housing allowances and other ministerial perquisites) has fallen relative to that of other professionals. While this statement is true for ministers of all denominations to some extent, the nature and severity of the shortage varies from one denomination to another. The United Presbyterian minister receives the highest income among the Protestant clergy while he is also in more plentiful supply (relative to the demand for his services) than are his brethren in other denominations. Methodist ministers earn more than American Baptists but much less than the United Presbyterian clergy. The ministerial labor markets of these three denominations are examined here in an attempt to shed some light on the puzzle mentioned above, for example, the relative decline in clergy income in the face of increasing demand for ministers.[3]

The data for this article are taken from two principal sources. The

This is an original essay prepared especially for the present volume, by permission of the author. William C. Bonifield is an economist at Wabash College.

information furnished by the ministers is part of a larger survey conducted by the Bureau of Research and Survey, The National Council of Churches of Christ in the United States in 1964. It mailed questionnaires to 8,492 ministers of 15 denominations drawn on a random basis by the respective denomination executive secretaries. Ministers returned 5,623 completed documents (66 percent). The former director of the Bureau of Research and Survey, Dr. Ross P. Scherer, kindly permitted the author to use the data gathered from ministers in the American Baptist Convention, the Methodist Church, and the United Presbyterian Church who were serving churches in Illinois, Indiana, Michigan, Minnesota, and Wisconsin at the time of the survey. This sample contained 55 Baptist ministers, 117 Methodists, and 121 Presbyterian clergy.

The information supplied by lay church officers was gathered by the author in 1966 with a sample drawn to approximate the sample used by the Bureau of Research and Survey. A ten percent random sample of the local American Baptist and United Presbyterian churches and a five percent random sample of the Methodist churches in the above five-state geographical area were drawn. Three hundred eighty-seven (387) questionnaires were mailed, and forty percent of the laymen returned completed documents (81 Presbyterians, 45 Methodists, and 30 Baptists).

Though this return rate was smaller than the 66 percent response rate of the ministers, the respective denominations responded in the same order, that is, the Presbyterians returned the largest proportion, the Baptists returned the second largest while the Methodists were least responsive in completing and returning the questionnaires.

The comparison of data taken from these two surveys is intended to answer some of the typical questions that arise when a labor market disequilibrium exists without an apparent movement of wages to eliminate it. There are a number of possible explanations for the lack of response by the wage to the continuing shortage of ministers. The possibilities include structural defects in the labor markets, irrational behavior by participants in the markets, as well as unique characteristics found in the markets themselves. If the markets in which ministerial labor is traded are imperfect, knowledge of the shortage, competitiveness of the going wage, and the availability of supply may not be transmitted to the buyers seeking ministers. In addition, an imperfect market may prevent higher wage offers from being communicated to those ministers who would relocate. If, on the other hand, the market functions relatively well, the reason for the lack of wage response to the shortage may be the willingness of buyers to accept a lower quality minister, rather than compete for one through the offer of higher wages. In addition to these possible explanations which may apply to any market, there may be certain unique characteristics operating in the *ministerial* labor markets which help to explain the persistent disequilibrium. An attempt to assess the employer's and employee's perceptions of the adequacy of ministerial income seems to be a logical beginning.

I

When ministers and laymen were asked to appraise the adequacy of ministerial income according to selected criteria, striking agreement was found (see Table 1). The clergy and laymen in each denomination were asked to select one response from among the following five choices: (1) much too low, (2) a little too low, (3) just right, (4) a little too high, (5) much too high, to describe their opinion of the relationship between ministerial income and each of the following five standards of comparison: (1) his personal and family needs, (2) the work required of him, (3) the income paid to other comparably educated professionals, (4) his fellow clergy, (5) the living level of his congregation.

TABLE 1 PROPORTION OF MINISTERS AND LAYMEN VIEWING CLERGY COMPENSATION AS UNSATISFACTORY*

	American Baptist		Methodist		United Presbyterian	
	Minis- ters	Lay- men	Minis- ters	Lay- men	Minis- ters	Lay- men
Compared with:	%		%		%	
Personal and family needs	67	57	67	63	68	53
Work required	63	62	44	45	52	49
Other comparably educated professionals	84	74	83	83	84	80
Other ministers	46	48	36	35	49	31
Living level of the congregation	43	43	51	49	52	38

* Those who answered that ministerial compensation was either much too low or a little too low when compared with the above criteria.

It seemed likely that one reason for the low level of ministerial income might be the lack of knowledge on the part of the laymen as to how low it really is when compared with certain criteria. However, the data suggest that this is not true, especially of the Baptist and Methodist laymen. The responses of the laymen and ministers in those two denominations are in such close agreement that there are fewer than five chances in one hundred that it is simply coincidental. When the answers given by Presbyterian laymen and ministers are compared, it is apparent that though they are not in as close agreement as are those in the other denominations, even they concur regarding the adequacy of ministerial wages when compared with the work required of them and with the income of other professionals.

The results of these comparisons, then, only add to the paradox. The Methodist and Baptist ministers who receive substantially smaller incomes than Presbyterians (see Table 2) have laities who acknowledge the inadequacy of their income, while Presbyterian laymen correctly consider their ministers more adequately compensated. Inaccurate knowledge, thus, is not an answer to the puzzle.

TABLE 2 MONEY INCOME OF SELECTED FULL-TIME MALE WORKERS AGED 14 AND OVER COMPARED WITH PROTESTANT CLERGY IN 3 DENOMINATIONS, 1963

Occupation of Worker	Median Income
Self-employed medical-health	$12,678
Other self-employed professionals	10,932
Engineers, technical	9,512
Professional social workers *	8,820
College professors *	8,163
Salaried managers and officials	8,115
Foremen	7,038
Elementary and secondary teachers	6,950
United Presbyterian ministers †	6,905
Salesworkers	6,537
Craftsmen	6,173
Methodist ministers †	5,949
Clerical	5,864
Male full-time worker average	5,663
American Baptist ministers †	5,590
Operatives and kindred	5,543

SOURCES: All statistics except for professional social workers, college professors, and Protestant clergy are from U.S. Department of Commerce, Bureau of the Census, *Income of Families and Persons in the United States: 1963,* Current Population Reports, Series P-60, No. 43, September 29, 1964, Table 25, page 44.

* Statistics on professional social worker and college professor incomes are taken from Ross P. Scherer, "Income and Business Costs of the Protestant Clergy in 1963," *Information Service,* Bureau of Research and Survey, National Council of Churches, New York, December 5, 1964.

† Statistics on Protestant clergy are computed from data supplied in mimeographed tables accompanying a paper presented to the American Sociological Association in Chicago on September 2, 1965 by Dr. Ross P. Scherer entitled *The White Protestant Denominations: Some Central Tendencies and Variations in Their Clergy.* The income figures include housing allowance, auto allowance as well as cash salary.

Another possible explanation of the lack of wage response to an excess demand for ministers may be the lack of agreement between ministers and laymen as to the importance of various factors in the wage determination process.

If laymen consider certain duties, functions, or people to be important in the determination of ministerial compensation, the ministers might receive lower wages if they rank these duties, functions or people in different orders of importance.

When the agreement between ministers and laymen with respect to the relative importance of fourteen selected factors [4] was tested, ministers and laymen of the same denomination ranked the factors in substantially the same order. The ministers were asked to rank each factor as (1) very important, (2) somewhat important, or (3) not important to the actual determination of their salary. The laymen were asked to rank the same fourteen factors in a similar way. The ministers' and laymen's rankings were then compared first by taking the proportions which responded very important and computing Spearman rank correlation coefficients. The coefficients are significant at the 99 percent level of confidence in each denomination. Therefore there is less than one chance in one hundred that the close agreement between the rankings by the laymen and ministers is accidental. Next, the proportions of laymen and ministers which answered either very important or somewhat important were compared. This comparison yielded Spearman coefficients which were still significant at the 99 percent level. The ministers and laymen of each denomination are in basic agreement, therefore, as to the actual importance of selected factors in the determination of the minister's salary.

Another indication of the functioning of a market is the degree of agreement between employer and employee with regard to the location of the power to raise ministerial income. If there is agreement between ministers and laymen in a denomination as to who is influential in changing ministerial wages,[5] there would be little likelihood that the ministers' performance of tasks and duties which satisfy the wrong party (that is, wrong only in the sense that he cannot influence the level of wages paid to the minister) is the reason for the lack of wage improvement. For example, if the ministers believe denomination officials are the ones who influence salary levels while laymen believe laymen influence the salary, the minister may receive lower income if he performs duties which the denomination official considers important, but which laymen consider unimportant. Of course, agreement between ministers and laymen as to the locus of salary-determining influence is insufficient to guarantee harmony of performance. Ministers may know where the power resides and still engage in activities which displease the influential parties.

In order to find out if laymen and ministers rank the influence of selected persons in ministerial salary determination similarly, each sample was asked to select the three groups of people most influential in changing ministerial income. The ministers and laymen ranked their choices from one to three, but the comparison was made by ranking the two groups on the basis of one vote for each person regardless of its being a first, second or third place vote.

These comparisons between laymen and ministers indicate that the two groups generally agree as to the sources of influence on ministerial income, though United Presbyterians tend to be less agreed than Methodists or Baptists. When the respective rankings are compared, for example, the agreements between the Methodists and between the Baptists could have arisen by chance only five times out of one hundred. All groups, however, laymen and ministers alike, did recognize that laymen are the most influential in the determination of ministerial wages.

When the salary paid by congregations in our sample was compared with selected variables such as size of community, size of congregation, and level of congregation income, we found the relationships which would be expected. The size of the community does not seem to have a consistent effect on ministerial income. However, the size of the congregation served by the minister does affect the amount of income received by the minister. If he serves a larger congregation, he receives more money. Further, the income of the lay officer who completed the questionnaire was compared with his minister's income. Ministers tend to receive higher incomes in those churches where lay officers (and presumably the congregation) have higher incomes.

The results of the preceding analyses of the data do not reveal unusual malfunctioning labor markets. The information possessed by employers and employees is about as complete as that in other professional labor markets. In fact, the market which seems to be functioning most satisfactorily in terms of the wage response to the shortage, the Presbyterian market, is the market in which the employers and employees are in least agreement as to the condition of the employees. In general though, the employers seem to know how poorly the minister is paid. The employees recognize the duties that are important to their employers, and also where the salary raising power lies. The lack of wage response to the persistent shortage of ministers must be attributable, therefore, to other factors inherent in the operation of the labor markets. It is to these characteristics that we now turn.

II

The ministers in some denominations are receiving incomes which are rising faster than others, and the shortage of ministers is not as severe in some denominations. Since the Presbyterian minister is not only better paid but also in more plentiful supply relative to the demand than are ministers in the other two denominations, the explanation of the puzzle should reflect this difference.

One very important reason for the favorable position of the Presbyterian minister would seem to be the low cost information about alternatives which is available to suppliers and demanders of ministerial labor. The Presbyterian Church maintains a central placement bureau in which the dossiers of all Presbyterian ministers as well as those of other ministers seeking Presbyterian churches are kept on file. The dossiers are classified according to the expressed willingness of the ministers to relocate. Each dossier is cross-catalogued according to various characteristics of the minister. Churches which are seeking ministers are encouraged to request dossiers by characteristics, that is, a church may seek all those dossiers completed by ministers under forty years old, married, seeking a Midwestern church, and willing to relocate at a $7,500 salary.[6] Ministers and churches are thus able to investigate alternative opportunities more intensively because of the low cost information, but this intensive search also excludes from the market buyers who are unable (or unwilling) to pay the going wage.[7] Moreover, the availability of low cost information enables buyers and sellers who do not make intensive searches themselves to benefit from others' knowledge of the market through the operation of economies of scale.[8] Information in the Methodist and Baptist markets is more expensive, and hence participants conduct less thorough searches. The smaller searches inhibit the communication of information concerning alternative opportunities and compensation.

It is interesting to note that other denominations are beginning to recognize the need for a central placement agency to provide low cost information. The Church of England's labor market was studied recently and a major recommendation was to establish a central agency to bring together the demand and supply of clergy.[9] The Episcopal Diocese of New York has also recognized the need for a better placement system. Reverend Richard Gary was commissioned to draw up a plan to reorganize the ministerial placement operation of the diocese. He called the present procedures "pure vintage pieces" that utilize little more than "discreet" inquiries or knowledge of "who was whose house guest last summer."[10]

Wages are further insulated from market pressure by the practice of filling pulpits with non-ordained supply. Utilization of non-ordained substitutes is quite common in the Methodist labor market. Each bishop is charged with filling all pulpits in his conference. He, therefore, uses non-ordained supply whenever he has an insufficient number of ministers. The filling of pulpits with non-ordained personnel is not as common in the Presbyterian market as it is in the Methodist and Baptist denominations, so Presbyterian ministers experience less competition from lower priced substitutes than do the others.

It should be noted that these two reasons apply primarily to situations in which ministers are moving from one position to another.

Presbyterian ministers and churches have at their disposal a more
efficient market in which to conduct their respective searches, and they
have fewer non-ordained substitutes available to insulate churches
from paying higher wages to attract a new minister. The minister who
is not mobile, and the church which is not on the market for a new
minister are not subject to as much pressure on ministers' wages,
however. Since the minister and lay officials of the local church
negotiate the annual salary changes in relative isolation from the
market, therefore, if the minister is unfortunate enough to serve a
church in which there are few laymen who are concerned with his
economic welfare, he may have to risk being considered "undedicated"
and bring up the subject of his compensation or else simply endure his
poverty. Why, in this situation, would laymen put such low money
value on their clergy?

III

The persistence of low wages for clergymen
seems to be attributable to the reluctance of laymen to consider the
minister as a productive input in society. The congregations of many
churches determine the minister's salary after all other expenses have
been budgeted. The guide most often mentioned in salary determination was the previous minister's salary. Laymen do not encourage
their minister to bring up the subject of his compensation.[11]
The prevalent attitude toward ministerial compensation seems to be
one in which the pay is fixed by a congregational committee, and the
quality of the minister sought is adjusted to this fixed price. The
quality seems to be so adjustable that if the congregation is unable to
attract a full-time minister at the set price, it does without one rather
than increase its offering price. This is true in many instances even
though the church is not restricted by revenue raising limits. The
notion that a minister might be attracted to a church at a $7,000 salary
when he is not at $6,000 is ignored by many lay leaders.
Many congregations discover, after being unsuccessful in their attempt to hire a full-time minister, that the filling of their pulpits on
Sunday by a seminary student or a retired minister is *almost* as
satisfactory. The satisfaction is incomplete because the members of
other churches continue to inquire about the progress of their search.
If it were not for the embarrassment of belonging to a minister-less
church, many church members would willingly forego the luxury of a
seven-day minister and spend the savings on other more "tangible"
evidence of their commitment, such as a new sanctuary.
The demand for the services of a minister is something that is hard
to describe. Parishioners want a minister who is an interesting

preacher. They want him to be a devout man of God, but they do not want him to do those things which will make them feel uncomfortable. Most church members have little need of a minister beyond the Sunday service. He may counsel them in time of need, and he is called upon to marry and bury church members, but these are not time-consuming or widely visible functions. Therefore the demand for a minister arises largely because a preacher is needed, and even this demand is felt by only the fraction of the members who attend Sunday services regularly.

Some ministers seek to serve those who experience a stronger demand for their services, the poor and the oppressed. When the minister of a local church begins to concern himself with the unchurched, his congregation may wonder why someone who is employed and paid by them should be providing services to others. Even though the congregation may make few demands on the time of its minister, it typically wants his time to be at their disposal. Therefore a minister may find his employers happier with him if he is idle and available rather than occupied with non-members' needs.

The insensitivity of laymen to the competition from other demanders of ministers is fostered by the way in which ministerial services are distributed to the users. The provision of services by ministers without charge in an atmosphere wherein he is compensated through free will offerings does not permit a market evaluation of his services. It was pointed out by Richard Musgrave [12] that people who consume public goods are tempted to underestimate the value of their consumption when it is time to pay for them. Since it is the nature of public goods that no one can be excluded from their consumption, that is, they are provided to all who wish to consume them, users receive the same amount regardless of the size of their contribution. The minister provides as much service to his congregation as it desires, but he is compensated without regard to the value of most of his services.

When the topic of ministerial income comes up for consideration by the congregation, then, some may underestimate the value of that part of the services which they consumed because they know the amount provided by the minister will be the same whether they pay or not. In addition, others may be unable to accurately assess the value of the benefits because of their nature.[13] A third group of laymen may simply place a very low value on the services of its minister. All three groups exert downward pressure on ministerial income.

Others in the congregation are certain to exert an upward influence on the wage because of their concern for the minister's well-being and/or because of their high evaluation of the benefits provided by the minister. However, this group is unlikely to constitute a majority of the congregation, hence the churches in which the minister is well compensated (as compared with other comparably educated professionals) will most likely be those in which the minority which is concerned with paying a higher wage also controls a large proportion of church income.

Even though each denomination has a number of small (primarily rural) churches which have revenue raising limits that prevent them from paying adequate ministerial income, they do not comprise the main retarding factor in clergy income. Instead, the attitude of laymen is one of unwillingness to recognize the minister as a productive input which has to be attracted into a particular usage by a combination of benefits, not the least of which is compensation. Though ministers are professionals, they are not immune to the pressures and forces of the world. Other professionals such as physicians, attorneys, and teachers pursue their professions with little regard (outwardly at least) to the material rewards, but because of the operation of the respective labor markets their services command higher returns when they are relatively scarce.

It seems inevitable that the continuation of the 1956–1963 trend in seminary enrollments and church formation[14] will create sufficient pressure to raise ministerial income relative to the rest of the income distribution. However, it will take a long time due to the willingness of laymen to allow the quality of the minister to deteriorate to extremely low levels before attempting to attract new ministers with higher compensation. The duration of the period during which the shortage can persist without a wage response is lengthened by the substitution of less qualified personnel. These substitutes have smaller investments in their education and hence can afford to work for less. This solves the immediate problem faced by the church and prevents the pressure from bidding up the ministerial wage rate, but it is not a permanent solution so long as denominations continue to require a theological degree for ordination. The decline in seminary enrollments is a definite indication that the long-run supply of ministers is responsive to the conditions present in the ministry; prospective ministers are not being attracted into seminaries in sufficient numbers to satisfy the demand for their services.

As young people observe the minister in the community, they may receive the impression that he is one of the community decision makers, but they also hear of the low pay in the ministry and perhaps see evidence of it as well. The decisions made by prospective ministers are not dissimilar to those made by prospective lawyers, doctors, and teachers.[15] It seems fairly clear that a large part of the reason for the teacher shortage today is the low pay experienced by members of the teaching profession during the forties and fifties; perhaps the ministry needs a spiritual *Sputnik* to increase its influence, affluence, and consequently its supply.

NOTES ————————————————————————————————————

1. In addition to numerous complaints by denomination officials concerning their inability to adequately staff local churches, the federal government describes the Protestant clergy as a profession in persistent shortage since the second world war. This description by the federal government is contained in the *Occupational Outlook Handbook* of 1966.

2. Clergy income has fallen from the third decile from the top of the income distribution of the professions in 1939 to near the bottom of the same distribution at the present time. These data are from Herman P. Miller, *Income of the American People* (New York: John Wiley and Sons, 1955), p. 56, and U.S. Department of Commerce, *1960 Census Subject Reports*, PC (2) 7A (Washington, D.C.: Government Printing Office, 1962), p. 232.

3. These denominations were selected as being representative of the three principal forms of ministerial labor market. The American Baptists use a congregational labor market in which each church and minister is autonomous. The Methodists are placed by a denomination official in an episcopal type of labor market. The United Presbyterian ministers and churches consummate their own employment pact, which is then ratified by a denominational group called a presbytery.

4. The thirteen factors tested were: size of church membership, size of church budget, rate of congregational growth, economic conditions in the community, key laymen in the local church, clergyman's education, length of service, all-around pastoral competence, size of family, participation in community activities, skill in personal relations, dedication to his calling, and his reputation among other clergy.

5. The list of people who might influence clergy compensation includes: national denominational leaders, state denominational leaders, local denominational leaders, individual pastors in local churches, key laymen, key lay women, and an interdenominational council of churches.

6. The first sorting of the dossiers is done on the characteristic of "salary sought."

7. George J. Stigler, "Information in the Labor Market," *Journal of Political Economy*, Vol. LXX, No. 5, Part 2, Supplement (October, 1962), p. 104.

8. *Ibid.*

9. Leslie Paul, *The Deployment and Payment of the Clergy* (Westminster, Eng.: Church Information Office for the Central Advisory Council for the Ministry, 1964), pp. 108–109. Though the problems in the Anglican Church differ from the problems in American churches in many respects, the inability of vacant churches to attract ministers is attributed by Paul to the lack of information re "unspectacular Parish priests," who would be hired if the churches only knew of their existence.

10. George Dugan, "Episcopal Calling of Clergy Criticized," *New York Times*, April 21, 1969.

11. When lay officers in the sample were asked if they "would encourage their minister to bring up the subject of his compensation, *if he felt it was too low*," only 69 percent of the Presbyterians, 56 percent of the Methodists, and 53 percent of the Baptists responded with an unqualified yes.

12. Richard A. Musgrave, *The Theory of Public Finance* (New York: McGraw-Hill Book Company, Inc., 1959), p. 134.

13. Most of the minister's services are provided through personal and private contacts so that his sermons tend to be the only relatively public criterion of his quality.

14. The enrollment in seminaries affiliated with the American Association of Theological Schools (enrolling 95 percent of the post AB theological students in the country) declined from 19,995 in 1956 to 19,860 in 1963 as stated in the *Report* issued by the A.A.T.S. in November, 1963. During this same period of time, churches increased from 281,687 to 292,233 according to Benson Y. Landis (ed.), *Yearbook of the American Churches*, National Council of Churches, 1965, p. 276.

15. Eli Ginsberg, Sol W. Ginsburg, Sidney Axelrad, John L. Herma, *Occupational Choice: An Approach to a General Theory* (New York: Columbia University Press, 1951), p. 14.

QUESTIONS FOR DISCUSSION

1. Can the "religious cultures" of Jews, Catholics, and Protestants (as depicted, for example, in Parenti, Selection 19) be traced to differences characteristic of their clergy?

2. What are some techniques by which clergy deflect or minimize the amount of conflict that could arise from the differing expectations held of them?

3. What is the relationship between religious professionals' authority and salary on the one hand and the way they conduct their jobs on the other? In other words, how do changes in one bring about changes in the other?

4. Probably more is known about the professional training of doctors, teachers, lawyers, and athletes than is known about clergy. What are strategic questions that research in this area should ask?

ADDITIONAL READING

Berger, Peter L. "Charisma and Religious Innovation: The Social Location of Israelite Prophecy," *American Sociological Review*, 28 (December 1963), 940–950. A specification of Weber's discussion of the source or location of prophecy, this essay provides a clearer portrait of "professional" vs. "nonprofessional" challenges to the religious status quo.

Fichter, Joseph H., S.J. *Religion as an Occupation: A Study in the Sociology of Professions.* Notre Dame, Ind: University of Notre Dame Press, 1966 (paperback). This is a compilation of many studies of various religious professionals, their recruitment, training, life styles, problems, and so forth.

Gustafson, James M. "The Clergy in the United States," *Daedalus,* 92 (Fall 1963), 724–744. Summarizing much of the "role conflict" material about clergy, Gustafson provides a good social structural analysis of the occupation.

Weber, Max. *The Sociology of Religion,* especially Chapters 4 and 5. Translated by Ephraim Fischoff. Boston: Beacon Press, 1963. Laying out his distinction between exemplary and ethical prophecy, Weber here discusses the differential tendency of these two religious styles to produce priests or other "functionaries" of religious organizations.

Whitley, Oliver R. *Religious Behavior,* especially Chapter 7. Englewood Cliffs, N.J.: Prentice-Hall, 1964. Whitley analyzes the clergy role in dramaturgical terms as involving presentation on a stage before an audience.

Part Three

Religion's
Involvement
in American
Society

Chapter VII

The Church
and
Public Affairs

Politicians have long been aware that the American voter's political behavior is influenced by his religious affiliation. Many social scientists once had their doubts, but survey data collected over the past several decades have made it clear that the politicians are right. The relationships between religion and political preference are clear-cut and have been remarkably stable over time. Roman Catholics are more likely than Protestants to vote for Democratic candidates for public office and to favor measures to improve the financial well-being of the working class. White Protestants are the most Republican of all the major religious groups. Jews, on the other hand, are more likely than Catholics to vote Democratic, and they are more likely than any other major religious group to take a liberal stand on a wide variety of public issues ranging from welfare measures and civil rights to international relations. Some have argued that the relation between religion and political preference really reflects a more basic relationship between socioeconomic status and political preference. For example, it has been held that Catholics are more likely than Protestants to be Democrats not because they are Catholics but because they tend to be members of the working class. But surveys show this argument to be false. Religious affiliation affects voting and political attitudes independently of socioeconomic status. Working-class Protestants are more likely to be Republican than working-class Catholics, and Jewish doctors and lawyers are more likely to be politically liberal than Protestant doctors and lawyers.

It seems clear, therefore, that religious groups are distinguished from one another not only by theology, moral precepts, and modes of worship but by political values as well. But where do these political values come from? Michael Parenti (Selection 19, "Political Values

225

and Religious Cultures: Jews, Catholics and Protestants") argues that
they are derived from underlying religious beliefs, for example, beliefs concerning man's nature and his relation to the temporal world.
Parenti discerns a similarity of religious outlook between Catholicism and Protestant fundamentalism on the one hand and Judaism and
Protestant modernism or liberalism on the other. Both Catholicism
and fundamentalism stress individual salvation and look with
skepticism on serious efforts to improve man's worldly condition.
They tend to accept and even to defend the traditional structure
of society. This tendency leads them to adopt a conservative or reactionary political posture. Theological liberalism, on the other
hand, has little to say about the afterlife but a great deal to say
about the importance of humanizing the conditions of this life. It
is therefore likely to lead to political liberalism. Parenti's thesis is
given empirical support in Benton Johnson's paper on the political
preference of Protestant ministers (Selection 20). Like Parenti, he
considers the liberal-fundamentalist distinction to reflect the most
deep-seated theological differences in contemporary American religion.
Using a statewide sample of Methodist and Baptist ministers, Johnson
shows a strong relationship between theological and political liberalism on the one hand and theological fundamentalism and political
conservatism on the other.

There are many, however, who are not convinced that religious
beliefs are the major source of the political orientations of religious
groups. The political preference of Catholics, for example, varies
markedly from country to country. Catholic preference for left-of-
center parties is confined for the most part to countries in which
Catholics have historically been a minority group. There are some who
believe that Jewish liberalism developed during the nineteenth century
struggles for Jewish emancipation and that it has few clear roots in
traditional Jewish religious teachings. And if it is true that the main
body of American Protestants inclines toward Republicanism, there
is also strong evidence that in the early days of the United States many
Protestant groups were identified with the political left. Much research remains to be done before we will have a general understanding of how the political values of religious groups are shaped.

What impact have religious groups had on the making of law and
public policy in the United States? Although the American churches
have generally avoided open alliances with political parties or secular
interest groups, they have played major roles in several campaigns
to influence legislation and public opinion. The temperance movement, which was almost exclusively a campaign of the Protestant
churches, is the most dramatic example of church involvement in politics in all of American history. Like many such movements, its earliest
efforts were mainly educational. Only later, after large numbers of

churchmen had been persuaded that drinking was evil, did the movement undertake direct action against the liquor traffic. As the movement gained support, its aims became more radical and more political in character. A similar development has taken place in the churches' recent campaign for equal rights for Negroes. Until only a few years ago this campaign consisted chiefly in rather abstract moral pronouncements on the part of leading churchmen. But as Henry Clark's article (Selection 21) documents, by the mid 1960s many churchmen felt that the time for direct action had arrived. They helped organize the famous March on Washington, assisted civil rights workers in Mississippi, and helped secure passage of the Civil Rights Act of 1964. Since that time many denominational agencies and individual clergymen have become involved in a wide variety of more radical projects to aid black Americans and other oppressed groups. And yet, as Clark's article suggests, many ordinary churchmen remain unconvinced of the need for further social change. Decades of moral pronouncements had persuaded them to accept civil rights legislation, but only a few seem prepared to support direct action of a more radical character. The great mass of white church people are not yet willing to give justice for black people the kind of enthusiastic support their fathers once gave prohibition. But many radical church leaders feel the demands of justice are too urgent to put off any longer. They are willing to take direct action even if they have to go it alone, even if their action provokes opposition from church members, dries up financial contributions, and drives many into the less disturbing atmosphere of conservative denominations and parishes. They are not willing to wait the years it may take to convince white churchmen that more change is needed. Yet there are many who feel that basic social changes cannot be made without the support of a major portion of those who make up the membership of the Christian churches of the country. It remains very much an open question what part, on balance, the churches will play in American politics during the remainder of this century.

19

Michael Parenti

*Political Values and
Religious Cultures:
Jews, Catholics and Protestants*

The literature on pressure groups and voting behavior demonstrates that American politics are, for the most part,
"rational." That is to say: group attitudes and actions are generally
directed toward promoting some kind of substantive measure which
the group deems beneficial to its interests. Thus we can observe
party-class voting correlations, union support of the closed shop, business opposition to certain state regulations, rural opposition to reap-
portionment, Negro support of civil rights, Catholic support of parochial school aid, etc. The objective position an individual or group
occupies in the social structure, and the material conditions operating
therein, determine much about individual or group perceptions and
evaluations of life, including political life.

Corresponding to the above definition of "rational," *"irrational"*
political behavior would be that kind of action or attitude which is
intended to minimize rather than maximize socio-economic self-interest (for instance, unions opposing the closed shop and Negroes supporting an inferior status for themselves). Are there such instances of
political behavior, and if so, how might they be explained?

In the Wilson and Banfield study [1] of twenty referenda elections for
bond issues to pay for public services such as hospitals, schools and
parks, it was found that the groups which because of their income

From Michael Parenti, "Political Values and Religious Cultures: Jews,
Catholics and Protestants," *Journal for the Scientific Study of Religion,* **7**
(Fall 1967), 259–269, by permission of the author and publisher. This is a
revised version of a paper presented at the annual meeting of the Society
for the Scientific Study of Religion, New York, October 29, 1965; Benjamin
Nelson, program chairman. Michael Parenti is a political scientist at the
University of Illinois.

level would pay little or nothing at all and yet benefit most from the services were also the groups which were most opposed to such services. These were the Poles, Czechs, Italians, Irish and other Catholic ethnic groups. Conversely, upper-income white Protestants and Jews, the very groups that would be paying the costs while benefitting least, were the strongest supporters of the proposed expenditures. (The only group acting according to rational self-interest was the low-income Negroes, who were supporters of public services.) The correlations were too compelling to assume that the voters of all groups were acting out of ignorance of their actual material interests; such ignorance would have produced more random results. It might be that upper-income groups place less value on the dollar or are better schooled civically, but these appear to be, at best, only partial explanations. More likely, the authors conclude, the WASP and Jewish sub-cultures tend "to be more public-regarding and less private- (self or family) regarding" than are the Catholic ethnic sub-cultural groups.[2]

While no delineation of these cultural ingredients was attempted by Wilson and Banfield, their findings do lead us directly to Max Weber's consideration of culture as a force operating independently of the objective or material factors, an understanding Weber submitted not to confound but to complement the usually recognized materialist interpretations of causality.[3] According to Weber, different social groups possess some kind of "style of life" and operate under the influence of distinct, albeit sometimes implicit, moral ideas, among which are those associated (or originally associated) with religion. These ideas or values, while frequently a response to material conditions, are also often the product of other ideas which persist in the face of drastically changing material conditions.[4] Ideas, for Weber, are also an expression of human aspirations and longings that seem to transcend a particular material environment, frequently in response to some deep-seated spiritual challenge.[5] Religious belief systems possess both the inspirational and the durable traditional qualities and through much of history have played a key role in the determination of moral and normative codes. While not all religions afford guidance on the many particulars of secular life (some are relatively indifferent to certain economic and political questions), the belief systems of all do provide principles and assumptions that shape many of the basic orientations toward worldly activity.

Herein, I shall attempt to trace the religio-political value derivatives of the major American denominations. Despite the allegedly growing "Americanization," "homogenization" and secularization of religions in this society,[6] there exist significant differences in the ideational content of sectarian systems, especially in regard to beliefs about man's nature, his redemption and his commitments to the temporal world. These beliefs may produce, or help explain, political orientations that cannot

readily be explained as manifestations of rational material self-interest.

The following discussion is to be considered suggestive rather than
exhaustive in its scope. At no time is it being contended that socio-economic interests are of no importance for the shaping of group political
attitudes. Nor is it to be assumed that there may not be normative
persuasions other than those of a religious origin that lead to responses counter to rational self-interest (*e.g.*, some of those propa-
gated in the name of "patriotism"). Our concern here, however, is
with certain of the key components of religious sub-cultures.

Jewish Liberalism

One of the more striking examples of the influ-
ence of religious sub-culture is to be found in American Jewry. By
most objective measures of class level, Jews occupy as high a status as
the more well-to-do white Protestants. Yet support of civil rights and
civil liberties, and, more significantly, support of welfare expenditures
and reforms on behalf of lower strata groups (along with an addiction
to the Democratic Party) remain characteristic of Jewish political
behavior.[7]

It may be that Jews, despite high income and occupational status,
still suffer many of the social disabilities of an "underdog" group, as
evidenced by the exclusionist practices of an unofficial but quite prevalent upper-class anti-semitism.[8] Nor is this underdog sensitivity weakened by a history of ruthless oppression. Thus, it might be said that
Jewish liberalism is a reaction to the marginality that challenges a
seemingly solid economic position.

Without denying what was affirmed at the onset, *viz.*, the importance
of the group's position in the social system in determining its perspectives, we might still wonder whether such explanations take all factors
into account. First, it might be noted that Catholic ethnic groups such
as the Irish, Italians, and Poles have had somewhat comparable centuries of hardship behind them. Starvation, oppression, and harsh military occupation is the history of Ireland, Poland and Southern Italy.
Similarly, the discrimination and exploitation accorded the Catholic
newcomers in America were at least as severe as anything the Jewish
immigrants encountered. Yet among the Catholic groups we find few
traces of that liberal reform-mindedness which seems a substantial
sentiment in the Jewish community.[9]

If oppression and marginality have been, then, the common lot of
many, it may be said that the various groups have defined and reacted
to such historical experiences in accordance with their respective value
systems. Is there anything in the Judaic view of life that might help

explain Jewish liberalism? Fuchs and others have observed several distinct themes:[10]

(1) The usual tension between faith and intellect does not grip Judaism. If anything, the spiritual leader in the Jewish community was traditionally not one who cultivated an inner-worldly asceticism or other-worldly spirituality, but one who was expert in the interpretation and application of the law. The synagogue was also the *shul*, a place of study as well as a place of worship. Given this intimate connection between learning and religion, "the religious virtuoso was not the saint but the scholar."[11] Historically, for Jews, the intellectual has not been an object of scorn, but a man to be esteemed and entrusted with the responsibilities of leadership and power.[12]

(2) In modern times, Judaism has been less an other-worldly theology and formulated creed than a system of practices, observances and moral commitments. An important component of the morality of Judaism is the continuing obligation to live with some dedication to social betterment and justice. Prayer and personal piety alone do not make one a Jew. Redemption is to be found in the worldly enactment of God's love and charity as evidenced by one's efforts on behalf of his fellow men and his community: one must be "a Jew for the world." Closely associated with the idea of social justice is the belief that the Jews, as the chosen people, serve a distinct missionary purpose in the world. Exile is not seen as the punishment of a wrathful Yahweh, but as fulfillment of the divine purpose: they are to serve God by working for social righteousness wherever Jews be found. "Our secret weapon as a people," David Ben-Gurion instructs, "is our moral, intellectual and spiritual superiority which we inherited from the Bible."[13]

(3) Whatever may be said of orthodox Old Testament strictures, Judaism does not, like traditional Christianity, teach ascetic renunciation as the prime means to personal salvation. A high value is placed on life in this world. Bodily appetites are understood to be natural and acceptable rather than sinful, and one does not face the world in a chronic state of antagonistic, guilt-ridden self-denial. Liberal reforms designed to maximize man's well-being and happiness on earth are part of a noble quest untainted by a fear of worldliness, sin, or loss of salvation. Life is reaffirmed rather than renounced.

Even if we were to grant Nathan Glazer's contention that contemporary Jewish liberalism derives more from nineteenth century liberalism and socialism than from the Judaic religious tradition,[14] we might still wonder why Jews of that day responded to and initiated such political traditions rather than electing any one of several other alternatives open to them. Jewish liberalism today may be an example of how the value commitments of a religion persist as an "idea of life" well after the specific theological underpinnings are discarded. This is what Weber meant when he spoke of the "ghost of dead religious beliefs." To the extent that Jews today are concerned with questions like "What examples of Jewish life shall we present to the world?" and "What are the special ethical demands made upon a man who calls himself a Jew?" they are still involved in a distinct ethno-religious tradition.

Catholic Conservatism

In contrast to Jewish political behavior, the Catholic tradition in America could hardly be characterized as liberal-reformist. Democratic party affiliations among Catholic voters reflect their urban working class background and status interests (viz., the status attractions of Democratic Catholic candidates for high office), rather than any commitment to liberalism. And their loyalty to the Democratic party, especially in the postwar years, has been markedly less stable than that of Jews and Negroes.[15]

The special popularity enjoyed by Father Coughlin and Senator Joseph McCarthy and the lukewarm response to civil rights among the Catholic lay public, along with somewhat conservative attitudes toward civil liberties, censorship and Communism, place American Catholics decidedly further from the liberal side of the political spectrum than might be supposed, were judgments made solely on the basis of voting returns.[16] Among lower middle-class Catholics there is growing evidence of an ultra-conservatism at least as virulent as any found among middle-class urban Protestants, and certainly of a kind alien to middle-class Jews. One Catholic writer suggests that the conservatism of William Buckley is probably preferred to the liberalism of *Commonweal* by most of the rank and file faithful "and the less articulate of the clergy." [17]

An explanation may be found in the fact that the American Catholic belief system contrasts sharply with the Judaic orientation on each of the major value areas previously discussed.

(1) There is a wealth of evidence, most of it from the pens of devout Catholics, suggesting the existence of a strong anti-intellectual strain in the Catholic constituency. A religious system which stresses the unchanging truth and purity of its sacred dogma and lay obedience to hierarchical teachings is prone to view the secular and sometimes irreverent scholarship of the modern age with something less than unmitigated enthusiasm. "[In the minds of many Catholics] . . . 'Science' is irretrievably allied with 'atheism,'" observes one Catholic sociologist, "and to ask why we have so few Catholic scientists of note is equivalent to asking why we have so few Catholic atheists." [18]

This "censorship mentality" has been a long-standing trait of Catholic America. In his study of nineteenth century Irish immigrants in

Boston, Handlin notes that books and public schools were considered instruments of heresy, licentiousness, and secularity.[19] The heroic Catholic effort in parochial education can be seen not as any commitment to worldly intellectuality, but rather as a protection against it.

The effects of this education tell us something about Catholic value orientations: Lenski finds, after controlling for income level and family party affiliation, that parochially educated Catholics rank obedience ahead of intellectual autonomy and tend to be more doctrinally orthodox and politically conservative than publicly educated Catholics.[20] A survey of midwestern Catholic students yielded the following results: only 53 per cent agreed that "love of neighbor is more important than fasting on Friday." Only 55 per cent thought that "the heart of the race question is moral and religious." Fifty-eight per cent declared that they would not "share our food with people of Communist countries if their need is great." And in choosing between "a comfortable life" and "a job which enabled you to do good to others," 77 per cent voted for personal comfort.[21]

(2) Catholicism is essentially a theology of personal salvation. Good works are acts of personal faith directed toward the propagation of spiritual rather than earthly values. Catholic concern for the poor traditionally has confined itself to charity work and rarely includes reformist attacks upon the abuses of the existing social system. The American hierarchy has issued statements reaffirming the necessity for individual responsibility in social and economic life and less reliance on the "inordinate demand" for benefits that arise from the pressures of organized social action.[22] It is felt that by relying on temporal rather than spiritual agencies, liberals propagate worldly values and obscure the far greater task of saving one's eternal soul.[23]

(3) "One often has the impression," observes a noted French Dominican, "that American Catholics are more Puritan than anybody else and that they are very close to setting themselves up as the Champions of Puritanism."[24] (The same writer conjectures that it was this Puritan mentality of "either virtue or the reign of terror" that made Catholics so responsive to McCarthyism.) The Catholic Church, while not as ascetic as many Protestant fundamentalist sects (dancing, drinking, and gambling in moderation are not sinful), contains within it a strong antagonism toward the erotic and pleasurable components of life. The orientation is "puritanical" insofar as it emphasizes the inherent propensity for sin in man's nature, the dangers of fleshly temptation, the proximity of hell, and the pitfalls of "too much freedom." Evil is willed and individually, rather than socially, caused. Viewed from this perspective, liberalism frequently appears as an invitation to self-indulgence, license and concupiscence. What are, for the liberal, social problems calling for social solutions (e.g., juvenile delinquency and crime) are, for many Catholics, problems of discipline, authority, and

personal rectitude.[25] Lacking true religious commitment, and suffering under the illusion that man is perfectible without divine intervention, the liberal coddles the evil-doers while encouraging moral irresponsibility. He strives too hard for happiness in this world because he does not believe in the happiness of the next.

In conclusion, it might be observed that much of American Catholic socio-political conservatism might be ascribed to the peasant ethnic cultures of the various Catholic groups rather than to religious belief systems *per se*.

Yet, lest undue reliance be placed on the secular antecedents of immigrant life, it should be remembered that the Old World peasant values themselves emanated from, and were heavily influenced by, Catholicism. This is certainly true of the group that has shaped and dominated the American Church—the Irish Catholics.[26] Finally, it should be kept in mind that whatever the peculiarities of Jansenist-Irish or Italian and Polish peasant conservative influences, the Catholic belief orientations described above are not exclusively American. It need only be noted that liberal English Catholics have observed in English Catholicism the same elements of insularity, "censorship mentality" and want of liberal social commitment.[27]

Protestant Fundamentalism and Modernism

The particulars of historical origin, name and ecclesiology that distinguish the many Protestant churches are less crucial for the purposes of this analysis than the differences between fundamentalists and modernists which, even while separating one sect from another, also tend to cut across denominational lines.[28] One should take exception to the presumption that every theological conservative is a political conservative, but one cannot deny the existence in Protestantism of a congruence between religious belief and political orientation.

What is especially interesting is the striking resemblance in underlying belief orientations between fundamentalist Protestantism and Catholicism on the one hand, and liberal Protestantism and Judaism on the other. Most sects of a predominantly fundamentalist hue eschew hierarchical control, priest administered sacramental grace, and elaborate liturgy and canon doctrine; there does exist, however, a distrust of intellectuality, a strong faith in sacred dogma, an other-worldly emphasis on salvation, and an ascetic rejection of secularity, of the kind represented in Catholicism. For the fundamentalist, the Bible is the unchallengeable source of Christian faith and the font of all sacred wisdom. The truth is final, fixed and revealed, something to be learned and obeyed; the intellectual search, therefore, can only lead one astray. As with many Catholics, the fundamentalists often consider secular intellectuality to be a potential threat to faith; at best, it is a form of excessive worldliness, and at worst, an open invitation to heresy.[29]

For the fundamentalist, it is God alone who rewards and punishes and who will deliver final judgment at the Second Coming. Man is guilty of hubris in thinking that he can solve the world's ills through secular effort. One's real task is to attend to personal faith and piety and wait for the day when God will decide that righteousness shall prevail in His universe. The fundamentalist ethos has little concern for social, racial, and international justice, for it "denies the existence of this world and its woes" and substitutes a "putative society in the Kingdom of God," wherein the underprivileged, by virtue of their piety and special religious endowment, will be the elite.[30]

Rejection of worldliness, however, means neither withdrawal from the world, nor protest against the established structure of society. Thrift and industriousness which foster steadiness in work and individual achievement are, as in Calvin's day, traits of the good Christian.[31] The faithful must believe in the avoidance of worldly pleasures, amusements and esthetic frivolities and must be, in Weber's phrase, devoted to "the destruction of spontaneous, impulsive enjoyment." [32]

There is substantial evidence to support the proposition that fundamentalism may lead to certain kinds of conservative political derivatives. One only has to note, as have Liston Pope and others, the affinity between the values of ascetic Protestantism and the ideals and interests of the business community, or the nature of fundamentalist political attacks upon the liberal National Council of Churches, or the response of fundamentalist populations to right-wing candidates (especially discernible during the 1964 elections), or the prominence of fundamentalist preachers in those movements preoccupied both with the "devil influence" of Communism and with apocalyptic anticipations of an East-West conflagration—a kind of political rendition of the Last Judgment.[33]

Theologically liberal Protestantism, in contrast to fundamentalism, does not place exclusive reliance on the Bible as the source of spiritual guidance and faith; rather it entertains the proposition that the Scriptures contain historical errors and occasional ethical contradictions and aberrations which are open to the challenge of modern scholarship and the human intellect. Emphasis is on God's immanence in Nature and the present world. Like the Jews, and in contrast to Catholics and fundamentalists, modernist Protestants have largely discarded the ideas of hell and devil. Personal sin is not the cause of all the world's ills; rather, attention should be focused on social, economic and political forces.[34] The Christian ethic, then, must be applied not only to private conduct but to the public sphere as well. Redemption is achieved by participation in the kind of social commitment that will lead to the Christianizing of the economic, political and social order, the true fulfillment of the Church's mission in this world. With its antecedents in the Social Gospel movement of the early part of this century, liberal Protestantism represents a decisive gravitation away from the theistic and traditional elements of Christianity and toward the humanistic and reformist.[35]

The political effects of this kind of belief orientation are perhaps most visible in the "irrational" positions held by articulate elements of the mainstream Protestant ministry and by organizations like the National Council of Churches on such issues as race relations, international affairs, and social welfare—especially when these positions are compared to those assumed by fundamentalist groups.[36] Rational responses to material self-interest, however, are still evident among the faithful rank and file. Thus, Benton Johnson finds that parishioners among the liberal denominations tend, in accordance with their higher socio-economic status, to be more Republican than are fundamentalist believers,[37] and most studies support the impression that modernist Protestant clergy are usually more liberal than their followers. Nevertheless, the influence of the church's orientation on the political predispositions of the faithful is not to be discounted. Johnson also discovers that upper-income mainstream Protestants who attend church frequently are less Republican than those who seldom attend. The converse holds true for fundamentalists. When comparing frequent attenders of all denominations, it was found that fundamentalists are more Republican than those attending the modernist Protestant churches, even when occupational class is controlled.

Conclusion

This investigation has not focused on those political issues usually identified in the public mind with denominational controversies (e.g., divorce laws, sabbath observances, parochial school aid, etc.), but rather on the less readily observable political derivatives of religious belief systems—specifically liberal-conservative orientations.

The differences in ecclesiology and social origin that usually distinguish sect from church are less pertinent to an understanding of religiously based political valuations than are the similarities and disparities among the belief systems of the major faiths. Thus, the Roman church and the Protestant sects, while polar extremes on the church-sect spectrum, bear a striking resemblance to each other in certain crucial underlying beliefs. By the same token, the semblances that Episcopalianism bears to Catholicism in liturgy, rites, services, conditions for membership and church organization should not hide from view the differences in religious and political belief.

The key components of belief that seem best to distinguish the politically conservative from the liberal may be summarized as follows:

(a) The extent to which divine teaching is considered fixed, final and unchallengeable, as opposed to being susceptible to rational investigation and modification, and consequently, the extent to which intellectualism, and many of the values associated with it, are opposed or welcomed.

(b) The extent to which the drama of redemption and atonement is defined as a personal battle one wages for one's soul for the sake of eternal salvation, rather than as a moral commitment to a this-worldly social betterment of mankind.

(c) The extent to which sin and evil are defined as inherent in man's nature (*e.g.*, original sin) and inevitable in his behavior (*e.g.*, concupiscence), rather than as social effects of widespread environmental causes.

(d) The extent to which human well-being and natural pleasures are manifestations of a "lower," corrupting realm of nature, something to be repressed as the contamination of the spiritual, rather than responsibly cultivated as the fulfillment of God's beneficence.

We return to Weber's view that the cultural (or subcultural) ethic is rarely exclusively a response to "objective" factors shaped by the productive forces. An individual or group might give any one of a variety of ideational constructions to any particular material condition before reacting to it; therefore, the question is not *whether* a people are responding to their material conditions, but rather, *why* they are responding in this way rather than in some other way. The evidence offered herein suggests that certain political predispositions which ordinarily might be defined as "irrational" as measured against narrowly defined rational material self-interest might better be understood as reflections of subcultural religious matrices. Despite the alleged secularistic dilution of religious devotion, the beliefs held regarding man's nature, his redemption and his commitments to this and the next world compose a crucial component of that ideational environment which defines responses toward political conditions.

NOTes

1. James Q. Wilson and Edward C. Banfield, "Public Regardingness as a Value Premise in Voting Behavior," *American Political Science Review*, 58 (1964), 876–887. These elections were held in seven major cities between 1956 and 1963.

2. *Ibid.*, 882–885. Wilson's study of the Democratic reform movement in New York shows a similar division between liberal-activist-reformist Jews and WASPs on the one hand, and conservative, non-ideological, politically traditional Irish and Italian Democrats on the other. See James Q. Wilson, *The Amateur Democrat* (Chicago: University of Chicago Press, 1962).

3. Weber's best known and probably most pertinent work on this question is *The Protestant Ethic and the Spirit of Capitalism* (New York: Charles Scribner's Sons, 1958).

4. For application of this proposition to the American scene, see Seymour Martin Lipset, *The First New Nation* (New York: Basic Books, 1963), especially the sections entitled "The Unchanging American Values and Their Connection with American Character" and "The Inadequacy of a Materialistic Interpretation of Change," pp. 110–129.

5. See Reinhard Bendix's discussion of these points in *Max Weber, an Intellectual Portrait* (Garden City, N.Y.: Doubleday, 1962), pp. 59 ff. For a broader statement on the transcendent quest, see Benjamin Nelson, "The Future of Illusions," in Contemporary Civilization Staff, Columbia University (eds.), *Man in Contemporary Society* (New York: Columbia University Press, 1956), II, 958–976. I wish to acknowledge a personal debt to my former colleague, Nelson, for much of my own interest in, and understanding of, Weber's work.

6. Representation of this homogenization theme may be found in Will Herberg, *Protestant-Catholic-Jew* (Garden City, N.Y.: Doubleday, rev. ed. 1960); Martin E. Marty, *Varieties of Unbelief* (New York: Holt, Rinehart & Winston, 1964). For a discussion of the theological and material factors that foster denominational consensus in America, see Talcott Parsons, "The Cultural Background of American Religious Organization," in Harlan Cleveland & Harold D. Lasswell, *Ethics and Bigness, Scientific, Academic, Religious, Political and Military* (New York: Harper & Brothers, 1962), pp. 141–167.

7. The Allinsmiths find that while Jews are like Presbyterians and Congregationalists in their professional and white collar SES level, their opinions on policies affecting job security are like those of the Baptist and Catholic urban workers. Wesley and Beverly Allinsmith, "Religious Affiliation and Politico-Economic Attitude," *Public Opinion Quarterly*, XII (1948), 377–389. See also Lawrence Fuchs, *The Political Behavior of the American Jews* (Glencoe, Ill.: The Free Press, 1956).

8. Cf. E. Digby Baltzell, *The Protestant Establishment, Aristocracy and Caste in America* (New York: Random House, 1964). On the distinction between the Jews' high economic status and their social "subordination," see W. Lloyd Warner and Leo Srole, *The Social System of American Ethnic Groups* (New Haven: Yale University Press, 1945), p. 96.

9. See Allinsmith, *op. cit.;* also Milton Himmelfarb, "The Jew: Subject or Object?" *Commentary*, XL (1965), 54–57.

10. Fuchs, *op. cit.*, pp. 171–203; also Himmelfarb, *op. cit.;* Werner J. Cahnman, "The Cultural Consciousness of Jewish Youth," *Jewish Social Studies*, XIV (1952), 198–199; Israel S. Chipin, "Judaism and Social Welfare," in Louis Finkelstein, *The Jews, Their History, Culture and Religion* (New York: Harper & Brothers, 1949), Vol. I, Chapter 16.

11. Marshall Sklare, *Conservative Judaism: An American Religious Movement* (Glencoe, Ill.: The Free Press, 1955).

12. The Israeli "Knesset is as packed with historians and economists as our Congress is studded with lawyers." Fuchs, *op. cit.*, p. 180 fn.

13. Quoted in the *New York Times*, May 26, 1965, "Ben-Gurion Urges Jewish Renewal." See also Oscar Handlin, "Judaism in the United States," in James Ward Smith and A. Leland Jamison, *The Shaping of American Religion* (Princeton, N.J.: Princeton University Press, 1961), pp. 122–161.

14. Nathan Glazer, *American Judaism* (Chicago: University of Chicago Press, 1957), Chapter 8.

15. Catholic attachments to the Democratic party have been evident at all income levels. However, unlike the Jews, Democratic affiliation decreases as income rises. See P. F. Lazarsfeld *et al.*, *The Peoples Choice* (New York: Duell, Sloan and Pearce, 1944). See Angus Campbell *et al.*, *The American Voter* (New York: John Wiley & Sons, 1960), pp. 301–306. The Catholic vote in 1956 actually went Republican despite the low Catholic SES level. The appearance of John Kennedy brought this group's vote back into the Democratic column in 1960.

16. Cf. Gary Wade Marx, *The Social Basis of the Support of a Depression Era Extremist: Father Coughlin* (Berkeley, Calif.: Survey Research Center, University of California, 1962); Alan F. Westin, "The John Birch Society," in Daniel Bell (ed.), *The Radical Right* (Garden City, N.Y.: Doubleday, 1964), pp. 239–268; Seymour Martin Lipset, "Three Decades of the Radical Right: Coughlinites, McCarthyites and Birchers," *ibid.*, pp. 344–373.

17. Henry J. Browne, "Catholicism," in Smith and Jamison, *op. cit.*, p. 107; Lipset, *op. cit.*, p. 431, shows that the John Birch Society appeals somewhat more to Catholics than to Protestants among well-to-do Republicans; Robert D. Cross concludes that the Church's liberal element has long been "conscious that the majority of Catholics in America were indifferent if not actually hostile to their program . . ." *The Emergence of Liberal Catholicism in America* (Cambridge, Mass.: Harvard University Press, 1958), p. 50.

18. Thomas F. O'Dea, *American Catholic Dilemma* (New York: New American Library, 1962), p. 23; see also John Tracy Ellis, "The American Catholic and the Intellectual Life," *Thought*, XXX (Autumn, 1955). For a discussion of the hostility of Catholic culture toward Catholic intellectuals see Daniel P. Moynihan, "The Irish," in N. Glazer and D. Moynihan, *Beyond the Melting Pot* (Boston: M.I.T. Press, 1963), pp. 276–286.

19. Oscar Handlin, *Boston's Immigrants* (Cambridge, Mass.: Belknap Press, 1959), pp. 130–144.

20. Gerhard Lenski, *The Religious Factor* (Garden City, N.Y.: Doubleday, 1963, rev. ed.), pp. 268–270.

21. Cited in Emmet John Hughes, "God, Man and Holy Cross," *Newsweek*, May 3, 1965, p. 21.

22. Quoted in Roger A. Freeman, "Big Government and the Moral Order," *The Catholic World*, May, 1962, p. 88.

23. William A. Osborne, "The Catholic Church and the Desegregation Process" (a paper presented at the 1965 Conference of the Society for the Scientific Study of Religion), notes the dysfunctional effects of such a theology with respect to the civil rights struggle.

24. Rev. R. L. Bruckberger, O.P., "The American Catholics as a Minority," in Thomas T. McAvoy (ed.), *Roman Catholicism and the American Way of Life* (Notre Dame, Ind.: University of Notre Dame Press, 1960), pp. 46–47.

25. See Leo Pfeffer, "Changing Relationships Among Religious Groups," *The Journal of Intergroup Relations* (1960), 81–93, for a brief comparison of the Jewish, Protestant and Catholic views.

26. The peculiarly Jansenist qualities of American Catholicism are ascribed by most informed observers less to the influence of American Protestantism and more to the overbearing impact of the Irish. See Moynihan, *op. cit.;* Rev. James Shannon, "The Irish Catholic Immigration," in McAvoy, *op. cit.,* pp. 204–210.

27. See the essays by a group of English Catholics in Michael de la Bedoyère (ed.), *Objections to Roman Catholicism* (Philadelphia: J. B. Lippincott, 1965).

28. See A. Leland Jamison, "Religions on the Christian Perimeter," in Smith and Jamison, *op. cit.,* pp. 182 ff., for a discussion of the historical background of the liberal-orthodox controversy. Also Winthrop S. Hudson, *American Protestantism* (Chicago: University of Chicago Press, 1961), pp. 143 ff.

29. Browne observes, "It is probably not so well known what a large percentage of Catholics—and Southern Protestants—the Federal Bureau of Investigation is glad to have as employees in work that requires a certain high moral stability." Browne, *op. cit.,* p. 117.

30. Quoted from Walter Goldschmidt, "Class Denominationalism in Rural California Churches," *American Journal of Sociology,* IX (1944), 354. See also René de Visme Williamson, "Conservatism and Liberalism in American Protestantism," *The Annals of the American Academy of Political and Social Science,* 344 (Nov., 1962), 76–84.

31. Cf. Charles C. Cole, Jr., *The Social Ideas of the Northern Evangelists* (New York: Columbia University Press, 1954); also Liston Pope, *Millhands and Preachers* (New Haven: Yale University Press, 1942).

32. See Benton Johnson, "Do Holiness Sects Socialize in Dominant Values?" *Social Forces,* XXXIX (1961), 309–316.

33. Pope, *op. cit.;* Cole, *op. cit;* Williamson, *op. cit.;* David Danzig, "The Radical Right and the Rise of the Fundamentalist Minority," *Commentary,* XXXIII (April, 1962), 291–298; and Danzig's "Conservatism after Goldwater," *Commentary,* XXX (March, 1965), 31–37. Several of the essays in Bell, *op. cit.,* also draw the link between fundamentalism and ultra-conservatism. Also, Richard Dudman, *Men of the Radical Right* (New York: Pyramid Books, 1962).

34. Cf. John Dillenberger and Claude Welch, *Protestant Christianity* (New York: Charles Scribner's Sons, 1954), pp. 217–223. Also Jamison, *op. cit.;* Hudson, *op. cit.;* and Williamson, *op. cit.*

35. Cf. Walter Rauschenbush, *Christianizing the Social Order* (New York: Macmillan, 1912).

36. Cf. Murray S. Stedman, Jr., *Religion and Politics in America* (New York: Harcourt, Brace & World, 1964), *passim;* Benton Johnson, "Ascetic Protestantism and Political Preference," *Public Opinion Quarterly,* XXVI (1962), 39–40; also Pope, *op. cit.,* p. 164; James Otis Smith and Gideon Sjoberg, "Origins and Career Patterns of Leading Protestant Clergymen," *Social Forces,* XXXIX (1961), 290–296, find that the reasons given for choosing the ministry as an occupation reflect significant denominational orientations. Thus, Episcopalian clergy tend to cite and desire to perform "service," while the fundamentalist Baptists more often speak of "God's calling."

37. Johnson, "Ascetic Protestantism and Political Preference," *op. cit.* Republicanism is treated as an indicator of conservatism.

20

Benton Johnson

Theology and Party Preference Among Protestant Clergymen

It has been common in social science circles to discount the influence of religion on the political outlook of persons affiliated with Protestant churches. Early voting studies did show a significant correlation between Protestantism and Republican preference,[1] but subsequent analysis of this finding suggested that the relationship was in reality the product of socioeconomic factors.[2]

Recently, however, the author advanced the proposition that the observed relationship between Republicanism and Protestantism might be due in part to the independent influence of religious factors. If Max Weber was right about the affinity between the social outlook of "ascetic" Protestantism and the values of industrial capitalism, then we may suppose that individuals who adhere strongly to traditional Protestant theologies are inclined to support political movements that emphasize individualism, limited government, and private enterprise. In the United States this means that they would be likely to espouse what would now be called a conservative political outlook, an outlook very likely to be translated into Republican party voting.[3] Consequently, the author hypothesized that among theologically conservative or fundamentalist Protestants religious involvement would be positively associated with a tendency to prefer the Republican party and to vote for Republican candidates for public office.

From Benton Johnson, "Theology and Party Preference Among Protestant Clergymen," *American Sociological Review*, **31** (April 1966), 200–208, by permission of the author and the American Sociological Association. Revised version of a paper presented to the annual meeting of the Western Political Science Association, San Diego, California, March 1963. The data were gathered and analyzed with the aid of funds granted under National Institute of Mental Health Research Grant M-4309. Benton Johnson is a sociologist at the University of Oregon.

242

Not all American Protestants are theologically conservative, however. Like American political ideology and the American party system itself, Protestantism has for several generations been divided into two major theological camps which cross-cut denominational lines. The fundamentalist, or conservative, camp claims to maintain theological continuity with the Protestant past. Its spokesmen have strongly defended the supernatural foundations of historic Christianity. The liberal, or modernist, camp has deviated in a number of significant respects from the positions of historic Protestant theology. For our purposes it is especially significant that theological liberalism provided much of the impetus to the social gospel movement, a movement that produced a profound reorientation toward social and economic questions among many Protestants. The leaders of this movement advocated reforms urged by political liberals and progressives. For this reason we also hypothesized that among theologically liberal Protestants religious involvement would be positively associated with a tendency to prefer the Democratic party and to vote for Democratic candidates for public office.

The author investigated these hypotheses by means of cross-section surveys of urban voting-age males in two widely separated American communities. When denominational lines were ignored and Protestant congregations were classified as theologically liberal or conservative on the basis of the stated views of their pastors, both sets of data revealed that frequency of attendance at theologically conservative churches was directly associated with Republican party preference and Republican voting.[4] But frequency of attendance at theologically liberal churches was inversely associated with Republican party preference and Republican voting. Moreover, when frequent church attenders were compared, those who attended conservative churches were more likely to report that they preferred the Republican party than were those who attended liberal churches. Finally, these relationships all persisted when a control for occupational class was introduced.[5]

These two independent sets of findings go a long way toward dispelling the notion that, among Protestants, political preference is simply a consequence of the socioeconomic status of the laity. But the findings also leave a number of questions unanswered. This paper will explore one of these questions.

Although our previous research gives us no basis for asserting just how the observed relationships between theology and political outlook have been brought about, it has been our contention all along that they are in large measure the result of the preaching and the teaching of the clergy.[6] An important first step in investigating this proposition is to determine whether the relationships which we found among the laity are also present among the clergy. If they are not, then we will have to search for their source outside ministerial circles and perhaps outside the ecclesiastical structure itself. If, however, we do find them among the clergy we will be justified in designing studies to test our assertion that what we have found among the laity can be attributed to the influence of the clergy.

The purpose of this paper is to test the hypothesis that among ascetic Protestant clergymen theological conservatism is positively associated with Republican party preference and that theological liberalism is positively associated with Democratic party preference. In so doing it will also be possible to clarify a number of related issues which our previous studies could not resolve.

Procedures

Data to test our hypotheses were obtained from responses to questionnaires mailed in the spring and summer of 1962 to the Baptist and Methodist pastors of the state of Oregon. These two denominations were chosen because they are the two most numerous Protestant denominational families in the United States as well as in Oregon and because they are known to include pastors of both liberal and conservative theological views. Only those Methodist pastors officially connected with the Methodist Church were sent questionnaires.[7] The various all-Negro Methodist bodies, as well as the Free Methodists and the Wesleyan Methodists, were not included. Five Baptist bodies were surveyed. In addition to the American Baptists, pastors affiliated with the Conservative, Southern, North American, and Baptist General Conference bodies were sent questionnaires.[8] All questionnaire items referred to in this paper were worded identically for both Baptists and Methodists.

Eighty-two per cent of the Methodist pastors and seventy-one per cent of the Baptist pastors returned their questionnaires. Although such a rate of return of mailed questionnaires is considered very good, it is possible that those who did not return their questionnaires have characteristics that render our returns a biased sample of the population they are supposed to represent. Unfortunately, the necessity of guaranteeing anonymity precluded the inclusion of direct identifying information on the questionnaire. It is possible, however, to make certain rough checks on the representativeness of the sample. It is well known that those who attend Baptist churches are less likely to be of high socioeconomic status than those who attend Methodist churches. All the pastors were presented a list of three classes, viz., working class, middle class, and upper-middle class. They were asked to check the class to which they believed most members of their church belonged. Although this procedure is not very reliable, it seemed the best method by which comparable data on socioeconomic composition of congregations could be obtained under the circumstances. Because of the small number of cases in the upper-middle class category these have been combined with the middle-class category.

Table 1 reveals that 67 per cent of Baptist respondents but only 28

TABLE 1 PER CENT OF BAPTIST AND METHODIST PASTORS REPORTING THEIR CONGREGATIONS PREDOMINANTLY WORKING CLASS

Baptist	67	(N = 179)
Methodist	28	(N = 141)

per cent of Methodist respondents report that their congregations are predominantly working class.[9] It is also well known that working-class congregations are more likely to have pastors who are theologically conservative or fundamentalist than are middle-class congregations. Table 2 shows that this pattern holds true among the pastors who

TABLE 2 PER CENT OF CONGREGATIONS, BY MODAL CLASS LEVEL OF THEIR MEMBERS, SERVED BY PASTORS OF LIBERAL, CONSERVATIVE, AND NEO-ORTHODOX THEOLOGICAL VIEWS

	Liberal	Conservative	Neo-Orthodox	Total
Middle-class Congregations	39	48	13	100 (N = 141)
Working-class Congregations	10	83	7	100 (N = 147)

returned their questionnaires. All the respondents were asked to place themselves in one of four theological categories, viz., liberal, neo-orthodox, conservative, and fundamentalist. Eighty-three per cent of the pastors ministering to predominantly working-class congregations report themselves theologically conservative or fundamentalist, but only 48 per cent of pastors ministering to middle-class congregations.[10] These findings increase our confidence that the data are actually representative of the Baptist and Methodist pastors of Oregon.

Theology and Party Preference

A preliminary inspection of the theological positions, as reported by the two sets of pastors, reveals that Baptists are far more likely than Methodists to report themselves as theologically conservative. Not a single Baptist respondent listed himself as a theological liberal.[11] Only three listed themselves as neo-orthodox. Ninety-eight per cent of the Baptists placed themselves within the conservative or the fundamentalist categories. Among the Methodists,

59 per cent listed themselves as liberal. The remaining 41 per cent split almost evenly between the neo-orthodox and conservative categories. These results are summarized in Table 3. In short, the Baptists

TABLE 3 Per Cent of Baptist and Methodist Pastors in Each Major Theological Category

	Liberal	Neo-Orthodox	Conservative	Total
Baptist Pastors	—	2	98	100 (N = 173)
Methodist Pastors	59	20	21	100 (N = 119)

are overwhelmingly, almost unanimously, conservative. A majority of the Methodists are liberal, but two strong minority positions are also represented among them.

All the pastors were asked the following question: "In elections held over the past five years, which party have you tended to favor?" When, as in our earlier studies, denominational lines are ignored and respondents are classified on the basis of theology, the familiar tendency emerges very clearly for the theological conservatives to be far more likely than the theological liberals to favor the Republican party. This tendency is shown in Table 4. Eighty per cent of theological

TABLE 4 Political Preference of Liberal, Neo-Orthodox, and Conservative Pastors (in per cent)

	Liberals	Neo-Orthodox	Conservatives
Republican	43	33	80
Democratic	41	41	7
Both equally	16	26	13
Total	100	100	100
	(N = 69)	(N = 27)	(N = 188)

conservatives have preferred the Republican party during the preceding five years. On the other hand, only 43 per cent of the theological liberals have done so. Moreover, liberals are far more likely than conservatives to prefer the Democratic party. Not only, then, does this table support our hypothesis, but the degree of association between theology and party preference appears to be considerably greater among them than among the laymen investigated in our previous studies.

Table 4 also reveals that the political preference of neo-orthodox pastors resembles that of the liberals much more closely than it does the political preference of the conservatives. Neo-orthodox respondents are, in fact, somewhat less likely than liberals to express a Republican preference, although they are equally likely to express a Democratic preference. In our previous studies we were not able to treat neo-orthodoxy as a separate category because of the small number of neo-orthodox respondents. Instead we classified them together with the theological liberals. We did this because the major neo-orthodox spokesmen in the United States, of whom Reinhold Niebuhr is the most prominent, have been strongly identified with left-wing principles on public issues.[12] Nevertheless, an argument could easily have been made for the classification of the neo-orthodox with the theological conservatives. Neo-orthodoxy arose a generation ago as a reaction against the liberal assertion of the goodness and perfectability of man within modern society and the grounding of Christian thought in the methods and findings of modern science and in the philosophy of secular humanism. While not rejecting science or social reformism as valid postures in the modern world, neo-orthodoxy has insisted that theology is an autonomous discipline based on revelation and it has revived the historic Christian skepticism concerning the ultimate perfectability of human society. Some old-line theological liberals have in fact expressed concern that neo-orthodoxy is leading to a lack of interest in vital public issues.[13]

The present findings regarding the party preference of neo-orthodox pastors suggest, however, that our previous classification of them with the liberals was correct. Neo-orthodox and liberal respondents will be combined into a single category in the remaining tables of this paper.

Although there has been a good deal of speculation concerning the influence Protestant laymen exert on the social and political expressions of pastors, this matter has never been systematically investigated.[14] There are good reasons for believing that the modern Protestant minister is more susceptible to pressure from the laity than clergymen have been traditionally. From its very beginning, Protestantism denied its ministers the kinds of ultimate spiritual sanction which the Roman Catholic clergy have at their disposal. In later years religious pluralism and voluntarism have further eroded the formal prerogatives of the clergy in relation to the laity. Moreover, most American Protestant denominations permit parishes to select their pastor and many permit them to terminate his employment. The pastor's salary is often dependent on the voluntary contributions of the members of his congregation, and he must usually refer proposals for developing new church programs or using church funds and facilities to an official board composed of laymen.

It is plausible to argue that the association between theology and political outlook among the clergy may in fact be due to the influence of the laity. Since Protestant congregations tend to be relatively homogeneous with regard to the socioeconomic status of their members, and since socioeconomic status is known to be a major factor in political party preference, it can be argued that pastors may be influenced in their party preference by the class-based preference of the majority of their members.

Table 5 permits us to test the hypothesis that the modal class level of

TABLE 5 Political Preference of Liberal, Neo-Orthodox, and Conservative Pastors with Modal Class Level of Their Members Controlled
(in per cent)

	Liberal and Neo-Orthodox		Conservative	
	Working-Class Congregations	Middle-Class Congregations	Working-Class Congregations	Middle-Class Congregations
Republican	33	43	78	84
Democratic	50	37	7	7
Both equally	17	20	15	9
Total	$\overline{100}$	$\overline{100}$	$\overline{100}$	$\overline{100}$
	(N = 24)	(N = 72)	(N = 121)	(N = 67)

the congregation accounts for the relationship between the theology and party preference of pastors. As in Tables 1 and 2, a simple working-class, middle-class breakdown has been used, based on the reports of the pastors themselves. Table 5 shows that there is indeed some relationship between modal class level of the pastor's congregation and his own political preference. Regardless of theological category, pastors whose church is predominantly middle class are more likely to prefer the Republican party than are pastors whose church is predominantly working class. And although the class level of the congregation does not seem to affect the inclination of theologically conservative pastors toward the Democratic party, among liberals and neo-orthodox, social class does make some difference. But the most striking pattern revealed by the table is the persistence of the strong relationship between theology and party preference. Eighty-four per cent of the conservative pastors of middle-class churches prefer the Republican party, whereas only 43 per cent of the liberal and neo-orthodox pastors of middle-class churches do so. An even larger percentage difference emerges when working-class pastors of different theological persuasions are compared. A similar pattern holds for Democratic party preference. Laymen may influence their pastors in many important ways, but this table gives us only minimal grounds for concluding that the political preference of pastors is affected by the modal class level of their present parishioners.

Although it is well known that the distinction between theological liberalism and theological conservatism cuts across denominational lines, our previous studies did not enable us to determine whether denomination affects the observed relationship between theology and political preference. Controls for denominational affiliation were not feasible in these studies because of the great number of denominations represented among our respondents and because controls necessary to test the basic hypotheses substantially reduced the number of cases in each category.

Table 6 permits us to assess the relationship of both theology and

TABLE 6 POLITICAL PREFERENCE OF LIBERAL, NEO-ORTHODOX, AND CONSERVATIVE PASTORS WITH DENOMINATION CONTROLLED

(in per cent)

	Republican	Democratic	Both Equally	Total	N
Liberal and Neo-Orthodox:					
Methodist	39	42	19	100	93
Baptist	—	—	—	—	3
Conservative:					
Methodist	63	4	33	100	24
Conservative Baptist	90	3	7	100	99
American Baptist	74	17	9	100	23
Southern Baptist	65	16	19	100	31
North American and General Conference Baptist	85	0	15	100	13

denomination to political preference. It does not permit a complete assessment, however, because of the lack of sufficient liberal and neo-orthodox respondents among the Baptist clergy. We cannot, therefore, examine the relationship between denomination and political preference among liberal and neo-orthodox pastors. And only in the case of the Methodists can we examine the relationship between theology and political preference when denomination is held constant.

The table shows that among Methodist pastors there is still a marked difference in the political preference of conservatives on the one hand and liberals and neo-orthodox on the other. Sixty-three per cent of the former but only 39 per cent of the latter report a Republican choice. Four per cent of the conservatives but 42 per cent of the liberals and neo-orthodox prefer the Democratic party. Although a lower proportion of Methodist conservatives than of Baptist conservatives make a Republican choice, the political preference of the Methodist conservatives is still sharply differentiated from that of their liberal and neo-orthodox co-religionists.

Turning to denominational differences among the theological conservatives, we may rule out the influence of Baptist affiliation *per se* on the political preference of our respondents. Although the Conservative, American, and two small ethnic Baptist bodies report a higher proportion of Republican choices than do the Methodist conservatives, a fifth, the Southern Baptists, do not. It is significant that the first four Baptist bodies are all overwhelmingly conservative in theology— at least in Oregon—and all of them are denominations whose major centers of strength have been in the north and west, where the political tradition of ascetic Protestantism has been Republican. In Oregon, and perhaps in many other areas as well, the leadership of these bodies continues to be wedded to the Republican party.[15] These pastors share a Republican heritage that is continually reinforced by their interactions with colleagues. But theological conservatives who are Methodists and Southern Baptists face a different situation. Even though the great majority of Southern Baptist pastors are probably theologically conservative, Southern Baptist strength is greatest in the south, which has traditionally been a Democratic region. Methodist conservatives, once in the majority, now find themselves a dwindling minority in a church increasingly dominated by pastors of liberal theological and political views.[16] The relatively low proportion of Republicans among Southern Baptist and conservative Methodist respondents may reflect the fact that these pastors have been subjected to Democratic political influences in their early years or in their interactions with colleagues. These considerations lead us to offer the proposition that denominational variations in the strength of the association between a theological position and its appropriate political expression are dependent on variations in the likelihood that pastors who hold that position have been subjected to influences that might forestall their making an appropriate choice. It might, for example, be predicted that the proportion of theological liberals making a Democratic choice will be greater among Congregationalists than among American Baptists, since presumably liberals are relatively more numerous in the former denomination than in the latter.

Although Table 6 gives us no way of knowing whether the proportion of liberal and neo-orthodox Methodist respondents reporting a Democratic choice is to be considered high or low in relation to other denominations, the proposition set forth above would lead us to expect somewhat more than 42 per cent of these pastors to prefer the Democratic party. After all, 63 per cent of their conservative colleagues, who are a distinct minority within Oregon Methodism, make an appropriate party choice. A possible resolution of this anomaly is suggested by the fact that a strong Democratic party has existed in Oregon only since World War II. For many years both liberal and conservative voters in the state normally chose from among Republican candidates for public office. Moreover, it has only been since the New Deal that the Democratic party has acquired its present image as the party of liberalism. We are suggesting that a generational factor accounts for a large part of the failure of many liberal and neo-orthodox respondents to make a Democratic party choice. Those whose political socialization took place prior to World War II may find it harder to identify with Democrats than those who reached maturity during the war years or later.

To test this interpretation, the liberal and non-orthodox pastors were divided into two age categories, those 45 and younger, and those 46 and older.[17] Table 7 shows the political preference of liberal and neo-

TABLE 7 POLITICAL PREFERENCE OF LIBERAL AND NEO-ORTHODOX METHODIST PASTORS, WITH AGE CONTROLLED

	45 and Under	46 and Over
Republican	29	53
Democratic	51	29
Both equally	20	18
Total	$\overline{100}$	$\overline{100}$
	(N = 55)	(N = 38)

orthodox respondents by age group. This table reveals that younger liberal and neo-orthodox pastors are considerably more likely than their older colleagues to prefer the Democratic party. Fifty-one per cent of the younger age group but only 29 per cent of the older age group make a Democratic choice. Similarly, the younger group is much less likely than the older group to report a Republican choice. Although only a bare majority of the younger liberals and neo-orthodox make a Democratic choice, Table 7 does support the contention that a generational factor, at least in old Republican areas such as Oregon, is responsible for the failure of many liberals and neo-orthodox to make an ideationally appropriate party choice.[18] If our interpretation is correct, then the proportion of liberal and neo-orthodox pastors who are Democrats should increase steadily over the next few years in Oregon Methodism.[19]

Conclusions

The findings of the present study, together with the findings of the two previous studies of laymen, make it increasingly evident that there is an important relationship between theology and political party preference among the "ascetic" branches of Protestantism in the United States. Among laymen this relationship has withstood controls for socioeconomic status and among pastors it has withstood controls for the modal class position of parishioners and, in the case of Methodists, for denominational affiliation. We believe the findings of the present study justify an investigation of the hypothesis that the political preferences of Protestant laymen are shaped in part by clergymen and perhaps by other ecclesiastical influences as well. Moreover, the strong bearing that the liberal-conservative distinction seems to have on political outlook suggests that this distinction may also help account for differences in the attitude and behavior of pastors and laymen outside the political realm.

This study has also provided us with insight into the manner in which the denominational milieu may affect the relationship between theology and political preference. Our data suggest that traditional denominational differences are less important in shaping political preference than are the proportions of liberals and conservatives within a denomination and the prevailing political characteristics of the region in which it has its major strength. This proposition also merits investigation.

There is, beyond these research questions, the basic issue of the source of the relationship between Protestant theology and political orientation. We do not really know the extent to which theological considerations have played an active part in initiating or supporting the relationships we have found. Religious values may be only one of several sources of the political identity of a religious group. Comparative studies of groups sharing similar theological positions both in this country and abroad should help clarify this issue, as should studies of shifts that occur from time to time in the political alignment of religious bodies.

NOTES

1. See, for example, Paul Lazarsfeld, Bernard Berelson, and Hazel Gaudet, *The People's Choice,* New York: Columbia University Press, 1948, p. 22 ff.

2. This position is based largely on the work of the Allinsmiths. See Wesley and Beverly Allinsmith, "Religious Affiliation and Politico-Economic Attitude," *Public Opinion Quarterly,* 12 (Fall, 1948), pp. 377–389.

3. Benton Johnson, "Ascetic Protestantism and Political Preference," *Public Opinion Quarterly,* 26 (Spring, 1962), pp. 35–46; *ibid.,* "Ascetic Protestantism and Political Preference in the Deep South," *American Journal of Sociology,* 69 (January, 1964), pp. 359–366.

4. Lipset's recently published review of the historical literature on religion and politics in the United States suggests strongly that northern and western Protestantism has provided the Republican party with much of its voting strength for over 100 years. See Seymour Martin Lipset, "Religion and Politics in the American Past and Present," in Robert Lee and Martin E. Marty (eds.), *Religion and Social Conflict,* New York: Oxford University Press, 1964, pp. 69–126.

5. Johnson, "Ascetic Protestantism and Political Preference," *loc. cit.,*

p. 44, Table 5; Johnson, "Ascetic Protestantism and Political Preference in the Deep South," *loc. cit.,* p. 363, Table 3.

6. Johnson, "Ascetic Protestantism and Political Preference," *loc. cit.,* pp. 37–39.

7. Questionnaires were sent to all ministers, excluding bishops and district superintendents, who held an appointment in the Oregon Annual Conference as of May, 1962. Questionnaires were also sent to those members of the Idaho Annual Conference holding appointments in the state of Oregon. The Idaho Conference includes several counties in extreme eastern Oregon. The author is indebted to Rev. Robert Kingsbury, Director of the Wesley Foundation of the University of Oregon, for making mailing lists available.

8. These denominations represent the major mainline Baptist bodies in the state. The American Baptist Convention, known prior to 1950 as the Northern Baptist Convention, has traditionally been the largest Baptist group outside the South. The Conservative Baptist Association of America, organized in 1947 by conservative and fundamentalist elements within the Northern Baptist Convention, currently has more affiliates in Oregon than does any other single Baptist body. The presence of Southern Baptists in the Pacific Northwest is largely the result of missionary activity on the part of the Southern Baptist Convention since the 1930's. The North American and the Baptist General Conference bodies are small denominations of descendants of European immigrants converted in Europe during the 19th century by American Baptist missionaries. The author is greatly indebted to Rev. Albert W. Wardin, Jr., Portland, Oregon, for making available his mailing lists of Baptist pastors. Without Mr. Wardin's encouragement and endorsement this study would not have been possible.

9. In this table and the tables to follow all respondents who failed to check one of the major response categories were excluded from analysis.

10. Six per cent of the Baptist and 18 per cent of the Methodist respondents are excluded from analysis because their theological responses were unclassifiable. In all the tables the fundamentalist and the conservative response categories have been combined into one theological category labeled conservative. There are negligible differences in the political tendencies of fundamentalist and conservative respondents.

11. This should not surprise anyone acquainted with Oregon Baptist history. The strongly fundamentalist preamble to the constitution of the Oregon Baptist State Convention (American Baptist affiliate), adopted in the 1920's as a protest against liberalism among Northern Baptists elsewhere, remains unaltered to this day. Moreover, the controversy that led to the defection of the Conservative Baptists in Oregon in 1947 did not center about theology, since both factions claimed to be conservative. The controversy concerned whether it is appropriate for conservatives to support a national denomination that tolerates or encourages liberalism.

12. A recent thorough discussion of the development of neo-orthodox social thought to World War II and beyond is contained in Donald B. Meyer, *The Protestant Search for Political Realism, 1919–*

1941, Berkeley and Los Angeles: University of California Press, 1960. See specifically chapters 13–16. Neo-orthodox spokesmen and social gospel-minded liberals differed among themselves in their reasons for leftward leanings and on the specific policies they espoused, but most of them shared a strong antipathy for traditional Republicanism and for laissez-faire capitalism.

13. J. Milton Yinger, *Religion, Society and the Individual*, New York: Macmillan, 1957, pp. 276–277.

14. See David O. Moberg, *The Church as a Social Institution*, Englewood Cliffs, N.J.: Prentice-Hall, 1962), pp. 502–503.

15. There is, however, an influential liberal and neo-orthodox minority within the American Baptist Convention. This group is strongest in the eastern states.

16. That conservatives are a dwindling minority is suggested by the fact that whereas 33 per cent of our Methodist respondents aged 46 or older (N = 57) consider themselves conservatives, only nine per cent of those 45 or younger (N = 60) are conservatives.

17. In order to rule out the possibility that aging itself or a generational factor affecting all our respondents alike is responsible for the results in Table 7, the political preference of older and younger conservatives should have been incorporated into the table. Unfortunately, however, no age question was included in the Baptist questionnaire, and there were too few Methodist conservatives in the younger age categories to permit a generational comparison to be made. Fifty-three per cent of the older Methodist conservatives (N = 19) reported a Republican preference, a percentage that is somewhat lower than the figure for the Methodist conservatives as a whole.

18. Our data also contain evidence that much of the Republicanism among our pastors reflects a liberal rather than a conservative political outlook. The data also show that Democratic preference almost never reflects a conservative political outlook. All the pastors were asked to report whether their political philosophy was liberal or conservative. When political philosophy was used as the criterion of political preference the relationship between theology and its appropriate political expression was equally strong among both theological groups. Eighty-three per cent of the Methodist conservatives reported a conservative political philosophy, and 82 per cent of the Methodist liberals and neo-orthodox reported a liberal political philosophy. Now 73 per cent of the political conservatives (N = 40) made a Republican choice, but only 50 per cent of the political liberals (N = 94) made a Democratic choice. Ninety-six per cent of those reporting a Democratic party preference (N = 49) considered themselves to be political liberals, but only 54 per cent of those reporting a Republican choice (N = 54) considered themselves to be political conservatives.

19. The proportion of theologically conservative pastors in the south who prefer the Republican party should also increase during the next few years. With the present identification of the national Democratic party with liberalism and with the emergence of effective local and state Republican parties in the south, an increasing number of theological conservatives should gravitate toward Republicanism.

21

Henry Clark

The National Council of Churches' Commission on Religion and Race: A Case Study of Religion in Social Change

Before the 1960s, American religious groups had been active in the area of race relations mainly through pronounce-ments. As early as 1920 the social creed of the Federal Council of Churches included support for adequate and equal opportunities for Negroes, and by 1946 the Federal Council was advocating "an inte-grated church in an integrated society." After World War II, the frequency and the urgency of rather generalized and abstract anti-segregation statements increased, and with the Supreme Court decision of 1954, a new specificity became evident. As Robert Spike remarks in *The Freedom Revolution and the Churches*, religious institutions have had a fairly clean record insofar as officially declared policy is con-cerned. They usually *said* the right thing.

But implementation was another matter, and apart from action by individuals, by local groups (particularly in the area of housing dis-crimination), and by special "gadfly" agencies (such as the Episcopal Society for Cultural and Racial Unity or the Catholic Council for Interracial Justice), the churches did little but make pronouncements prior to the early 1960s.

The Chicago Conference on Religion and Race, held in January 1963,

---

This is an original essay prepared especially for this volume, reprinted by permission of the author. Henry Clark is in the Department of Religion at Duke University.

is an important milestone in the development of the church's role in social change. Instead of making general statements, or affirmations of support of policies already laid down by government, participants in this interfaith conference called for very specific action by churches as institutions: the abolishment of discrimination in religiously sponsored educational institutions, in the employment and promotion policies of denominational agencies, and in worship services and membership policies; a review of all investment holdings and of the practices of contractors with whom the churches had dealings, and so forth. Religious groups were even enjoined to refuse free land offered by suburban housing developers unless a nondiscriminatory policy was to be followed in accepting tenants and buyers in the development where the free land was being offered. And of course the Chicago Conference called for all kinds of involvement in social action at the community, state, and national levels. Following the Chicago Conference, a follow-up commission was created, and a "target cities" program was undertaken to mobilize action on behalf of racial justice in a number of large metropolitan areas.

But the decisive step forward was taken in June 1963 with the formation of the National Council of Churches' Commission on Religion and Race (CORR). Its first major project was mobilization of church constituencies for the March on Washington in August of that year. By recruiting more than twenty-five thousand white churchmen from member churches for this controversial venture, CORR played the key role in a dramatic event which certified the commitment of organized religion in this country to the civil rights struggle. It is easy to forget, in retrospect, how afraid many observers were of the March on Washington: all kinds of dire predictions of violence were made, and innumerable behind-the-scenes efforts were made to dissuade its planners from carrying through with their ideas. That church groups would give wholehearted support to such a risky endeavor was proof that they had finally realized the inadequacy of always playing it safe. As a matter of fact, many Negro leaders were downright alarmed by the extent of church participation—they feared that the whole thing was going to be turned into a nice little church tea party!

After the Washington March, CORR mounted a very sophisticated lobbying campaign on behalf of civil rights legislation. Commission strategists rightly calculated that the legislation would pass or fail according to the votes of congressmen from the Midwest and the Rocky Mountain states. They knew that Southern legislators would be making all kinds of promises to support bills in agriculture or mining or flood control or anything else of vital interest to Midwestern legislators in exchange for opposition to the civil rights bill, so they tried to insure that churchmen in these same areas would let it be known that they had a moral stake in passage of civil rights legislation. A major conference was held in Lincoln, Nebraska, in early September 1963. Present here were congressmen, experienced lobbyists (such as Clarence Mitchell of the Washington bureau of the NAACP and Victor Reuther of the AFL-CIO), theologians, and several hundred church leaders from Midwestern and Rocky Mountain states. Follow-up conferences at the state and local level brought the religious, political, and strategic arguments presented in Lincoln to rank-and-file churchmen in twelve states.

During the following winter in Washington, church lobbyists brought a steady stream of churchmen from all over the country to see their senators and representatives. They kept a close eye on additions to or deletions from the proposed legislation in committee hearings. And they sustained the proponents of the legislation by giving them eagerly sought moral support. One of the CORR staff members who worked rather closely with Senator Humphrey declared that the Senator once said to him, "You know, this is such a hard fight, such a discouraging fight, and it takes so much out of you personally, that I really need the pastoral help of you preachers." Evidently Humphrey would occasionally seek out some of the religious leaders and say, "Come on, tell me one more time that this thing is *right*. I'm about to give out; restore my flagging zeal!"

CORR-sponsored church action in Mississippi during the summer of 1964 can be thought of in three categories: orientation training of civil rights workers and students enlisted for the summer; the "ministry of reconciliation" performed by clergymen who sought to mediate between opposing forces in the state, and legal assistance. The first and last of these categories are, I think, self-explanatory; we need say nothing further about them until we evaluate their effectiveness. The ministry of reconciliation perhaps requires a word of explanation:

> Roughly 235 churchmen (ministers, rabbis, adult laymen) with one to two weeks to serve worked on already established NCC voter registration projects. Sixty-one ministers and rabbis served as minister-counselors. Their function varied widely. The number of men available for these crucial ministries increased appreciably following the renewed appeal to denominational leaders at the end of June. All served from two to four weeks, a few for the entire summer. They were asked to make themselves available to the projects in the most meaningful way possible. Different men at different times found themselves involved in chauffeuring, teaching, counselling, "spreading oil on troubled waters" in a project, visiting people in jail, going to jail, interceding with white members of communities where projects were located, talking theology, listening, building community centers, playing with children, participating in Freedom Days, getting vilified, getting beaten. In the midst of the problem of pinpointing exactly what a minister-counselor did or should do, the key fact was that in nearly every

major crisis that erupted on any of the 27 projects during the
summer, a representative of the church was there, either to be of
some service, though most of the volunteers were remarkably
equipped internally to deal with crises, or to call upon additional
resources, legal and otherwise, that the NCC office in Jackson could
provide. While many minister-counselors had opportunities, as
time and circumstance permitted, to speak with white Mississip-
pians, there were eight people whose specific assignment was to
carry on ministries of listening, talking and reconciliation with
white members of communities where there were projects.[1]

Analysis

A useful framework for analysis of the activities
of CORR is provided by Hans Spiegel's notion of the four types of
social action intervention. In "first party intervention," the agent in
question (for our purposes, the churches) initiates and carries the
main burden of efforts which directly challenge the status quo; in
"second party intervention," one participates "as a supportive joiner
rather than the prime mover"; "third party invertention" is mediation
between opposing camps; "fourth party intervention" consists of an
attempt to contribute to change indirectly by "changing the climate of
opinion" in a situation where resistance is already evident or is anticipated.[2]

If we classify the activities of churches discussed here according to
Spiegel's categories, one explanation of the dramatic difference between the apparent impact of these activities before 1963 and since
that date is immediately apparent: almost everything done by church
agencies with broad support and ample financial backing before 1963
was fourth party intervention; much of what has been done since then,
including almost all of the work done by CORR, has been first, second,
or third party intervention.

That is not to say that all of the pronouncements and manifestoes
and policy statements poured out by religious organizations during the
1950s and early 1960s were a total loss. It is to say, however, that the
effect of these pronouncements (if one grants that they indeed had
some effect) was latent rather than immediately manifest. It is to
suggest, moreover, that the effect of this type of action is much more
difficult to perceive and measure than is the effect of other types of
intervention. And it is to suggest, furthermore, that the effect of fourth
party intervention is apt to remain latent until other forms of social
action test and exploit the changed community atmosphere supposedly
produced by the more indirect form of action. I would argue that the
apparent ineffectiveness of church pronouncements in the area of race
prior to 1963 is a perfect illustration of the futility of assuming that the

norms and role-definitions of various social systems and reference groups in a society will automatically change just because a new interpretation of values has been made at the cultural level. Unless the new values are made function-specific and situation-specific by those who speak with some kind of legitimate authority in lower order social systems and reference groups, change will be very, very slow in coming.

The ministry of reconciliation carried out by scores of clergymen in Mississippi during the summer of 1964 is the epitome of third party intervention. Also in this category would be the attempts on the part of churchmen to restrain violence, whether by angry whites in a previously restricted residential area outside Chicago, by angry Negro youth in Harlem or Rochester, or by the state troopers of Alabama. (The Methodist bishop in Alabama is given some credit for persuading Governor Wallace to guarantee protection to the Selma marchers after the horror of the first Sunday evening's brutality there.)

Still within the realm of third party intervention, though one step shy of reconciliation, is the communication function served by church leaders in many tense situations. Sometimes the bridge had to be built between civil rights groups and Mississippi politicians; sometimes between rights workers and Federal agents; sometimes between the local power structure and Federal representatives; sometimes, even, between different civil rights groups themselves! Staff members of the religious agencies were often the only persons present on the scene whom all parties could trust, and the liaison work performed in situations of this kind was occasionally quite significant.

Under the heading of second party intervention would come religious participation in the planning and execution of the marches on Washington and Montgomery, the training and orientation of students bound for Mississippi in the summer of 1964, help with the various citizenship training and education projects carried out in Mississippi, and the furnishing of bail and legal assistance to the Mississippi volunteers. It should be recorded, incidentally, that the first two-week orientation session for Mississippi-bound students was vitally important for other reasons as well: it was the time in which *policy* for the summer's operation was thought out in detail for the first time. Until the orientation program actually began, the Mississippi project was little more than an idea; for its originators had had no opportunity to make detailed plans.[3]

The most prominent example of first party intervention by churchmen, of course, is the intensive campaign waged by religious organizations in support of the 1964 Civil Rights Act. As I intend to assert in a moment, when I discuss the effectiveness of some of the actions mentioned, this campaign is in a class by itself. Other examples of first party intervention, though, are the efforts to mobilize the ghetto community in large Northern urban centers, notably Rochester, and denominational crackdowns on discrimination in their own educational institutions, building operations, employment patterns, and investment activities. Although little effective power is evident, one would have to classify testimony before the platform committees at political conventions as first party intervention, since something more than a general change in climate of opinion was being sought.

Effectiveness

The optimism of the typical church leader about the effectiveness of fourth party intervention by religious organizations is well expressed in the following words of a seminary professor:

> Once the pressure of contemporary events has forced the problem of race to public attention, the view which has been officially formulated and vigorously inculcated by the churches becomes the framework in which the problem is viewed and solutions sought. The guilty conscience of America about segregation, the basis for our international vulnerability on the issue, is in no small measure due to the teaching of the churches at home and abroad.[4]

It would be extremely difficult to prove this assertion—or to disprove it. Confirmation would have to rest on an appeal to something of an argument from silence; that is, an inference from the silence (or even the passive support) of the vast majority of American churchmen during 1963–1964 that all of those official church pronouncements condemning racial injustice were not altogether empty. There was, of course, a great deal of grumbling about the Negro revolution among white parishioners; there was even a considerable amount of organized opposition to it and to efforts on the part of church leaders to support it. Yet most of those who grumbled were unwilling to join with the angry conservatives in their congregation or in their denomination who wanted to put genuine pressure on church leaders to dissuade them from participation in the movement. They might complain that things were being pushed too fast, they might even reduce their pledges as an act of silent, passive aggression. But they were ashamed to fight openly against the prophets in their ranks. They were on the defensive, for the accumulated weight of years of pronouncements and resolutions had convinced them that segregation was indeed morally wrong. When political leaders, union executives, and businessmen all began to proclaim that remedial action was necessary, they remembered that their churches had been saying this for a long time, too— and when they heard their pastors say it once again, with urgency, they had to nod assent, or at least muffle their dissent. And of course many churchmen responded much more positively than this: they signed open housing covenants, they wrote letters to their congressmen, they sought new Negro employees, and they even took pride in the realization that they were doing what was right.

But the shortcomings of church pronouncements on the deeper issues of good will and brotherhood are all too apparent. When some other agent enters the field and appeals to a sacred cultural value, interpreting it in such a way that conservative norms and rules are approved in concrete situations, behavior may be reactionary rather than progressive. In California, the proponents of Proposition 14 appealed to the value of "freedom" in urging citizens of the state to repeal the state's fair housing law, and they won a smashing 2-to-1 victory. We may be certain that thousands of the supporters of that proposition were churchmen who would of course affirm their belief in good will and brotherhood, but who had either ignored attacks on Proposition 14 in particular and on housing discrimination in general by church leaders or had not been taught to perceive the connection between the abstract values they affirmed and their normative role-obligations as landlords, potential sellers of property, and neighbors.

An evaluation of third party intervention by the churches again gives us an ambiguous verdict. The reconciling work done by clergymen in Mississippi doubtless strengthened the convictions of many moderates, and there is good reason to believe that the appeals for reason, law, and order which were uttered by leading citizens in McComb, Mississippi, in the fall of 1964 were a direct result of some of the intensive work done by clergymen there during the summer. Yet the limits of penetration of this ministry of reconciliation are also apparent in McComb—for it was in this area that virtually all Negro churches, including many which had no connection with the movement whatsoever, were destroyed by bombings and fire. Perhaps what is best illustrated in McComb is Simmel's theory about the tendency of social conflict to establish and maintain the identity and boundary lines of societies and groups. The die-hard resisters drew more tightly together with strengthened determination to act against integration; the moderates closed ranks with determination of their own to speak out against oppression and mob rule.

As for second party intervention, it is best illustrated in the orientation program for Mississippi Summer volunteers. Without this training—which included practical tips about how to avoid pointless antagonizing of Southern whites as well as more lofty theoretical instruction in the philosophy of nonviolence—the murder of Chaney, Goodman, and Schwerner might not have been an isolated phenomenon. The provision of bail money and legal counsel for all volunteers is another solid achievement, and the Selma March was undoubtedly a factor in the passage of the 1965 voting rights bill. Yet the very need for the Selma March is striking proof of the inability of second party intervention by religious organizations to make successful a social action project with too many cards already stacked against it. The attempts to register voters in Mississippi during the summer of 1964 were miserable failures, for existing conditions and laws simply did not permit success.

CORR-led church participation in the campaign for civil rights legislation is the best example of first party intervention discernible in recent years, for even though it cannot be maintained that the churches were the originators of the 1964 bill, it can be asserted that they ran an independent lobbying operation of enormous scope and magnitude. Once again, no truly scientific evidence is available to show that the church's role in getting this legislation passed was in fact decisive; nevertheless, most observers, from columnists such as James Reston to politicians such as Richard Russell, regarded the pressure supplied by preachers and priests as the influence which made passage of the bill inevitable. One Western senator complained to a conservative constituent that he did not really want to vote for the bill, but he had to because, as he said, "I've got all these preachers on my back." Senator Russell is reported to have blamed defeat of his efforts to block the bill on the fact that "all these damned preachers got the idea it was a moral issue." Some analysts are also of the opinion that church pressure was crucial in seeing to it that the bill was not watered down in committee. There was one point in the hearings when the administration was about ready to accept a compromise measure worked out between Justice Department officials and conservatives in the House. Church pressure was so influential in destroying this compromise that former Attorney General Nicholas Katzenbach was furious with religious lobbyists. One member of the CORR staff says that he will never forget the day he walked into Katzenbach's office and was greeted by enraged charges to the effect that "You damned preachers, you've messed it all up. We had a deal that would go through, and you wrecked it. To hell with your idealism!" [5]

An example of first party intervention which has, up to the present time, failed is the effort of religious groups to establish a combine of investors which could influence corporation policies in employment by shifting investments away from companies practicing discrimination. Preliminary attempts to recruit participants among universities, religious organizations, and other putatively liberal institutions with substantial financial holdings have come to naught, and it remains a real question whether intervention of this kind can be effectively carried out.

Internal Effects

Assessment of the external effects of religion's role in social change is only one side of the coin; the other, which we shall now investigate, is the impact of social action intervention upon the internal structure and processes of "Establishment" religious organizations. The impact of involvement upon mainline white denominations may be summed up as follows: (1) A significant minority of members in various sections of the country have expressed their disapproval of this involvement by withdrawing their support or by attacking the denominational or ecumenical agencies implementing religious involvement; (2) denominational and ecumenical officials have responded to these defections or attacks by seeking to interpret their work in a more favorable light and by seeking to "clear themselves" of damaging charges made by the opposition; (3) a whole battery of new special agencies, task forces, and institutional structures have been brought into existence; and (4) a new theological understanding of the relationship between the world and the church is being forged in the heat of the revolutionary fires.

No one is as yet able (or no one is willing) to say precisely how serious withdrawals of support have been. One can document this point only by the illustrative method, pointing to the split in a large Presbyterian congregation in Memphis, to an estimated 50 per cent cut in pledges in a wealthy Episcopal diocese in southern California, or to stories of individual transfers of membership or reductions of pledges in Northern suburbs. The two most important cases of destructive impact are probably the attack upon the tax-exempt status of the National Council of Churches and the withdrawal from the NCC (and, in some cases, from the mother denomination) of several Protestant bodies or local parishes. The former threat did not materialize, because NCC lawyers were able to demonstrate to the satisfaction of the Internal Revenue Service investigators that activities of the Commission on Religion and Race were not in violation of existing statutes— but the very attempt to strip away the ecumenical body's privileged tax position indicates how seriously its activities were taken by opponents of integration. The withdrawal from the NCC and mother denominations has reached serious proportions in several parts of the South, especially within the Methodist Church and the Southern branch of the Presbyterian Church. CORR staff members declare that the animus is so bad in some localities that mere contact with local white churchmen is rendered impossible if it is learned that visiting clergymen have anything to do with the NCC or an offending parent denomination. A third development with ominous potential is the establishing (or the strengthening) of gadfly agencies within denominations whose purpose it is to oppose civil rights goals and undermine those who work for such goals.

Efforts on the part of Establishment denominations to adjust to these threats are interesting. They frequently endeavor to calm the fears of their constituents by stressing the positive side of their affiliation with the NCC, as in an article in *Presbyterian Survey* which has been given wide distribution as a reprinted pamphlet. Making no mention whatsoever of the race issue, this article on "What Our Church Does in the N.C.C." assures its readers that the NCC is not a Communist-front organization and that denominational leaders are in unanimous agreement in asserting "that the church's work attains greater and more effective scope through the denomination's participation in the NCC." Occasionally, however, the denomination accepts the charge leveled against it as a compliment, and brings action against its attackers for violating officially stated denominational policy. This latter course of action was taken in the Methodist Church, where Mississippi churches which had refused admission to integrated groups were accused of betrayal of Methodism. That a formal case of this kind could even be instituted within Methodism is evidence of a new determination on the part of liberal forces within the denomination to make an issue of racial discrimination and fight it through to a decisive conclusion, because a very significant reduction in denominational funds can be expected if Alabama and Mississippi Methodist churches leave the denomination, or are forced out, in large numbers.

The salience of the NCC Commission on Religion and Race in this discussion is testimony to the importance of the third aspect of the internal impact of religious involvement in the movement: that is, the creation of new special agencies whose express purpose it is to take risks in fighting for racial justice. Before 1960, these new agencies were usually established outside the really powerful structures of a denomination; they were "gadfly" agencies which were merely tolerated by the denomination as a whole because a few liberal leaders felt that these special outfits could help to prick the conscience of the larger body. The Episcopal Society for Racial and Cultural Unity is an outstanding example of this kind of agency. Now, though, a high priority for racial justice has been established: The denominational or ecumenical task forces which sweep down upon "target cities" serve to galvanize the established leaders of that city into action. Thus a good deal of denominational activity, and a good deal of interfaith conversation and joint planning, take place on the local level as a result of operations at the national level.

There is, finally, the theological impact of involvement, and it is quite conceivable that this might prove to be, in the long run, the one most important effect, external or internal, of religion's role in the

social change going on all about us just now. Robert Spike sums up
the theological impact of the freedom revolution by saying that it has
proven the bankruptcy of propositional theology; that is to say, it has
shown that ethical action is an essential part, not just of the implementation of religious faith, but of the *understanding* of that faith. It has
shown, he says, that "There must be a deed before there can be a
doctrine that makes any sense. Commitment is not a decision to do
something about a belief; it is the belief that comes from having acted
obediently" to God.[6] The freedom movement has reinforced the theology of secularity in a decisive way, and a whole generation of Protestant students has a radically new understanding of the meaning of
Christian faith because of the movement and the participation of
churchmen in it.

NOTES

1. The sentences are taken from an unpublished "Summary Report
of the Commission on Religion and Race, June 5, 1964–December 3,
1964" presented at the meeting of the General Board of the National
Council of Churches in December 1964.

2. Hans J. Spiegel, "Intervention, Anyone?" *Interracial News
Service*, XXXII, 1 (January–February 1961), 1–2.

3. Interview with the Rev. Bruce Hanson, CORR staff, February 16,
1965.

4. Charles McCoy, "The Churches and Protest Movements for Racial
Justice," in Martin Marty and Robert Lee (eds.), *Religion and Social
Conflict* (New York: Oxford University Press, 1964), p. 43.

5. All of the material presented in this paragraph is drawn from
the interview with Mr. Hanson.

6. Robert W. Spike, *The Freedom Revolution and the Churches* (New
York: Association Press, 1965), p. 83.

QUESTIONS FOR DISCUSSION

1. What influence do the laity's political opinions have on the political
opinions of the clergy—and vice versa?

2. What are the prospects for a formal political alliance between Protestant
fundamentalists and conservative Catholics?

3. How can the churches be deeply divided on political questions and yet
subscribe to the common "civil religion" that Cherry describes in Selection 25?

4. What effect do the political values of the clergy have on a denomination's
ability to attract new members and hold on to old members?

ADDITIONAL READING

Glock, Charles Y., and Rodney Stark. Chapters 9, 10, and 11 in *Religion and Society in Tension*. Chicago: Rand McNally, 1965. Glock and Stark argue that religious commitment and involvement in radical politics are mutually incompatible, and they present data from several countries, including the United States, to support their argument.

Gusfield, Joseph R. *Symbolic Crusade: Status Politics and the American Temperance Movement*. Urbana, Ill.: University of Illinois Press, 1963. Gusfield interprets the American temperance movement as an attempt by the evangelical Protestant community first to gain public recognition and respect and later to protect its cultural dominance and prestige from the challenge of immigrant groups of alien culture and religion.

Hadden, Jeffrey. *The Gathering Storm in the Churches*. Garden City, N.Y.: Doubleday, 1969. Using recent survey data Hadden documents the existence of sharp differences of opinion among both clergy and laity about theological questions, civil rights, and other public issues. He argues that the Protestant churches are in the midst of a deepening crisis over the very nature of the Christian faith.

Lazarsfeld, Paul F., Bernard Berelson, and Hazel Gaudet. *The People's Choice*. New York: Columbia University Press, 1968 (originally published in 1944). An early classic empirical study of the factors affecting the way people vote. The effect of religious affiliation is clearly documented.

Lipset, Seymour Martin. "Religion and Politics in the American Past and Present," in Robert Lee and Martin E. Marty (eds.), *Religion and Social Conflict*. New York: Oxford University Press, 1964. Using both historical and recent survey data, Lipset traces the development of the political values of the major American religious groups.

Marx, Gary T. "Religion: Opiate or Inspiration of Civil Rights Militancy Among Negroes?" *American Sociological Review*, 32 (February 1967), 64–72. Despite the fact that Negro ministers have been prominent in the civil rights movement, Marx's survey data show that among black laymen religious involvement is negatively, not positively, related to sympathy with the struggle for civil rights.

Miller, William Lee. "American Religion and American Political Attitudes," in James Ward Smith and A. Leland Jamison (eds.), *Religious Perspectives in American Culture*. Princeton, N.J.: Princeton University Press, 1961. Miller argues that certain distinctive traits of American political life have their roots in the Protestant tendency to define political issues in moral terms.

Chapter VIII

The Integrative Role of Churches

Émile Durkheim's *Elementary Forms of Religious Life* (originally published in French in 1912) must be given credit for making explicit the role religion may play in social integration. Though previous scholars considered the question, it was not until Durkheim tried to show how religion underlay moral unity (or "collective conscience") among the Arunta, a primitive people in Australia, that this central sociological issue was critically posed. The issue is not without ambiguities, however, especially when posed in the context of modern industrialized societies. For social integration may be analyzed at least at two levels—the collective and the individual. That is, by moral unity one might have in mind value homogeneity or one might mean the absence of disruption by individual "deviants." In the religious context, then, the *collective* interpretation refers to the presence of religious leadership, rituals, norms, and organizations which "force" onto a society its value commonality, thus unifying it. By contrast, the *individual* interpretation refers to religion's role in preventing disruptive behavior by providing persons with ways to respond to otherwise sundering experiences.

This chapter's initial selection, Walter Lippmann's "The Breakdown of Religious Authority" (Selection 22), indicates how the church, even if it once had unifying power through its establishment as an *only* church, certainly enjoys no such position in the current scene. Quite clearly, as Lippmann says, the rules of law, even of art, which once the church helped define and administer are now defined and administered elsewhere. Churches are not totally uninvolved in societal integration, however, as the next two selections indicate. By shifting analysis to the individual level, one observes churches' intimate involvement in the integration process—by providing guidance at times of emotional distress (in the research presented by Gerald Gurin, Joseph Veroff, and Sheila Feld, Selection 23), or by providing a community of friendship (in the research by Rodney Stark and Charles Y. Glock, Selection 24). In either case, it might be said, at this intimate, personal level, churches may "bind" individuals into the society and thus contribute to its integration by contributing to theirs. The first of these two readings has the advantage of dealing with a cross-section of American adults, not simply church members or "believers" of one or another tradition. Thus, the evidence is perhaps doubly surprising in showing how frequently persons who seek help with "personal problems" consult clergy. Clergy, in fact, outrank by considerable measure the next most used source of help, physicians, though not for all kinds of problems, it is true.

If the piece by Gurin and his associates indicates widespread use of the church for personal help, the selection by Stark and Glock shows how different are American denominations in this respect. In some, a majority of members are closely bound together by ties of friendship and organizational involvement, whereas in others, members constitute not so much communities as "audiences." Information on help-seeking is not included in this last selection, of course, but the reader can readily speculate about appropriate lines of further research.

As should be clear by now, the mosaic, pluralistic nature of American churches is enough to ensure their loss of authority or power. What witting influence churches may have in altering the course of society is small indeed. But as we saw in Chapter VII—that their *unwitting* political impact may be sizeable—so also we observe in the present chapter that the unintended aim of social integration may be nevertheless served by churches as they go about their ostensibly unrelated tasks.

22

Walter Lippmann

The Breakdown of
Religious Authority

1. God's Government

The dissolution of the ancestral order is still under way, and much of our current controversy is between those who hope to stay the dissolution and those who would like to hasten it. The prime fact about modernity, as it presents itself to us, is that it not merely denies the central ideas of our forefathers but dissolves the disposition to believe in them. The ancestral tradition still lives in many corners of the world. But it no longer represents for us, as it did for Dante and for St. Thomas Aquinas seven hundred years ago, the triumphant wisdom of the age. A child born in a modern city may still learn to use the images of the theological drama, but more or less consciously he is made to feel that in using them he is not speaking of things that are literally and exactly true.

Its dogma, as Mr. Santayana once said, is insensibly understood to be nothing but myth, its miracles nothing but legend, its sacraments mere symbols, its bible pure literature, its liturgy just poetry, its hierarchy an administrative convenience, its ethics an historical accident, and its whole function simply to lend a warm mystical aureole to human culture and ignorance. The modern man does not take his religion as a real account of the constitution, the government, the history, and the actual destiny of the universe. With rare exceptions his ancestors did. They believed that all their activities on this earth had a sequel in other activities hereafter, and that they themselves in their own persons would be alive through all the stretches of infinite time to experience this fulfillment. The sense of actuality has gone out of this tremendous conception of life; only the echoes of it persist, and in our memories they create a world apart from the world in which we do our work, a noble world perhaps in which it is refreshing to dwell now and then, and in anxiety to take refuge. But the spaces between the stars are so great; the earth is now so small a planet in the skies; man is so close, as St. Francis said, to his brother the ass, that in the daylight he does not believe that a great cosmic story is being unfolded of which his every thought and act is a significant part. The universe may have a conscious purpose, but he does not believe he knows just what it is; humanity may be acting out a divine drama, but he is not certain that he knows the plot.

There has gone out of modern life a working conviction that we are living under the dominion of one supreme ideal, the attainment of eternal happiness by obedience to God's will on earth. This conviction found its most perfect expression in the period which begins with St. Augustine's *City of God* and culminates in the *Divine Comedy* of Dante. But the underlying intuitions are to be found in nearly all popular religion; they are the creature's feeling of dependence upon his creator, a sense that his destiny is fixed by being greater than himself. At the bottom of it there is a conviction that the universe is governed by superhuman persons, that the daily visible life of the world is constitutionally subject to the laws and the will of an invisible government. What the thinkers of the Middle Ages did was to work out in elaborate detail and in grandiose style the constitutional system under which supernatural government operates. It is not fanciful, and I hope not irreverent, to suggest that the great debates about the nature of the Trinity and the Godhead were attempts to work out a theory of divine sovereignty; that the debates about election and predestination and grace are attempts to work out a theory of citizenship in a divine society. The essential idea which dominates the whole speculation is man's relation to a heavenly king.

As this idea was finally worked out by the legists and canonists and scholastics

> every ordering of a human community must appear as a component part of that ordering of the world which exists because God exists, and every earthly group must appear as an organic member of that *Civitas Dei*, that God-State, which comprehends the heavens and the earth. Then, on the other hand, the eternal and other-worldly aim and object of every individual man must, in a directer or an indirecter fashion, determine the aim and object of every group into which he enters.
>
> But as there must, of necessity, be connection between the various groups, and as all of them must be connected with the divinely ordered Universe, we come by the further notion of a

divinely instituted Harmony which pervades the Universal Whole
and every part thereof. To every Being is assigned its place in that
whole, and to every link between Beings corresponds a divine
decree. . . .

There is no need to suppose that everyone in the Middle Ages
understood the theory, as Gierke describes it here, in all its architectural grandeur. Nevertheless, the theory is implicit in the feeling of
simple men. It is the logical elaboration of the fundamental belief that
the God who governs the world is no mere abstraction made up of hazy
nouns and a vague adoration, but that, as Henry Adams says, he is the
feudal seigneur to whom Roland, when he was dying, could proffer "his
right-hand glove" as a last act of homage, such as he might have made
to Charlemagne, and could pray:

> O God the Father who has never lied,
> Who raised up Saint Lazarus from death,
> And Daniel from the lions saved,
> Save my soul from all the perils
> For the sins that in my life I did!

2. The Doctrine of the Keys

The theory of divine government has always pre-
sented some difficulties to human reason, as we can see even in St.
Augustine, who never clearly made up his mind whether the City of
God was the actual church presided over by the Bishop of Rome or
whether it was an ideal and invisible congregation of the saved. But
we may be sure that to plainer minds it was necessary to believe that
God governs mankind through the agency of the visible church. The
unsophisticated man may not be realistic, but he is literal; he would be
quite incapable, we may be sure, of understanding what St. Thomas
meant when he asked "why should not the same sacred letter . . .
contain several senses founded on the literal?" He would accept all
the senses but he would accept them all literally. And taking them
literally he would have to believe that if God governs the world, he
governs it, not in some obscure meaning of the term, but that he
actually governs it, as a king who is mightier than Charlemagne, but
not essentially unlike Charlemagne.

The disposition to believe in the rule of God depended, therefore,
upon the capacity to believe in a visible church upon earth which holds
its commission from God. In some form or another all simple people
look to a priestly caste who make visible the divine power. Without
some such actualization the human imagination falters and becomes
vagrant. The Catholic Church by its splendor and its power and its
universality during the Middle Ages must have made easily credible the

conception of God the Ruler. It was a government exercising jurisdiction over the known world, powerful enough to depose princes, and at its head was the Pope who could prove by the evidence of scripture that he was the successor to Peter and was the Vice-regent of God. To ask whether this grandiose claim was in fact true is, from the point of view of this argument, to miss the point. It was believed to be true in the Middle Ages. Because it was believed, the Church flourished. Because the Church flourished, it was ever so much easier to be certain that the claim was true. When men said that God ruled the world, they had evidence as convincing as we have when we say that the President is head of the United States Government; they were convinced because they came into daily contact with God's appointees administering God's laws.

It is this concrete sense of divine government which modern men have lost, and it may well be that this is where the Reformation has exercised its most revolutionary effect. What Luther did was to destroy the pretensions not only of the Roman Catholic Church, but of any church and of any priestly class to administer God's government on earth. The Protestant reformers may not have intended to destroy as deeply as they did; the theocracies established by Calvin and Knox imply as much. But, nevertheless, when Luther succeeded in defying the Holy See by rejecting its claim that it was the exclusive agent of God, he made it impossible for any other church to set up the same claim and sustain it for any length of time.

> Now Christ says that not alone in the Church is there forgiveness of sins, but that where two or three are gathered together in His name, they shall have the right and the liberty to proclaim and promise to each other comfort and the forgiveness of sins. . . . We are not only kings and the freest of all men, but also priests forever, a dignity far higher than kingship, because by that priesthood we are worthy to appear before God, to pray for others, and to teach one another mutually the things which are of God.

This denial of the special function of the priesthood did not, of course, originate with Luther. Its historical antecedents go back to the primitive Christians; there is quotable authority for it in St. Augustine. It was anticipated by Wyclif and Huss and by many of the mystics of the Middle Ages. But Luther, possibly because the times were ripe for it, translated the denial of the authority of the priesthood into a political revolution which divided Christendom. When the Reformation was an accomplished fact, men looked out upon the world and no longer saw a single Catholic Apostolic Church as the visible embodiment of God's government. A large part of mankind, and that an economically and politically powerful part, no longer believed that Christ gave to Simon Peter and his successors at the Roman See the Keys of the Kingdom of Heaven with the promise that "whatsoever thou shalt bind on earth shall be bound in heaven: and whatsoever thou shalt loose on earth shall be loosed in heaven."

3. The Logic of Toleration

As a result of the great religious wars the governing classes were forced to realize that unless they consented to the policy of toleration they would be ruined. There is no reason to suppose that except among a few idealists toleration has ever been much admired as a principle. It was originally, and in large measure it still is, nothing but a practical necessity. For in its interior life no church can wholly admit that its rivals may provide an equally good vehicle of salvation.

Martin Luther certainly had none of the modern notion that one church is about as good as the next. To be sure he appealed to the right of private judgment, but he made it plain nevertheless that in his opinion "pagans or Turks or Jews or fake Christians" would "remain under eternal wrath and an everlasting damnation." John Calvin let it be known in no uncertain tone that he did not wish any new sects in Geneva. Milton, writing his beautiful essay on liberty, drew the line at Papists. And in our own day the *Catholic Encyclopedia* says in the course of an eloquent argument for practical civic toleration that "as the true God can tolerate no strange gods, the true Church of Christ can tolerate no strange churches beside herself, or, what amounts to the same, she can recognize none as theoretically justified." This is the ancient dogma that outside the church there is no salvation—*extra ecclesiam nulla salus*. Like many another dogma of the Roman church, it is not even in theory absolutely unbending. Thus it appears from the allocution of Pope Pius IX, *Singulari quadam* (1854), that "those who are ignorant of the true religion, if their ignorance is invincible (which means, if they have never had a chance to know the true religion) are not, in this matter, guilty of any fault in the sight of God."

As a consequence of the modern theory of religious freedom the churches find themselves in an anomalous position. Inwardly, to their communicants, they continue to assert that they possess the only complete version of the truth. But outwardly, in their civic relations with other churches and with the civil power, they preach and practice toleration. The separation of church and state involves more than a mere logical difficulty for the churchman. It involves a deep psychological difficulty for the members of the congregation. As communicants they are expected to believe without reservation that their church is the only true means of salvation; otherwise the multitude of separate sects would be meaningless. But as citizens they are expected to maintain a neutral indifference to the claims of all the sects, and to resist encroachments by any one sect upon the religious practices of the others. This is the best compromise which human wisdom has as yet devised, but it has one inevitable consequence which the superficial advocates of toleration often overlook. It is difficult to remain warmly convinced that the authority of any one sect is divine, when as a matter of daily experience all sects have to be treated alike.

The human soul is not so divided in compartments that a man can be indifferent in one part of his soul and firmly believing in another. The existence of rival sects, the visible demonstration that none has a monopoly, the habit of neutrality, cannot but dispose men against an unquestioning acceptance of the authority of one sect. So many faiths, so many loyalties, are offered to the modern man that at last none seems to him wholly inevitable and fixed in the order of the universe. The existence of many churches in one community weakens the foundation of all of them. And that is why every church in the heyday of its power proclaims itself to be catholic and intolerant.

But when there are many churches in the same community, none can make wholly good the claim that it is catholic. None has that power to discipline the individual which a universal church exercises. For, as Dr. Figgis puts it, when many churches are tolerated, "excommunication has ceased to be tyrannical by becoming futile."

4. A Working Compromise

If the rival churches were not compelled to tolerate each other, they could not, consistently with their own teaching, accept the prevailing theory of the public school. Under that theory the schools are silent about matters of faith, and teachers are supposed to be neutral on the issues of history and science which bear upon religion. The churches permit this because they cannot agree on the dogma they would wish to have taught. The Catholics would rather have no dogma in the schools than Protestant dogma; the fundamentalists would rather have none than have modernist. This situation is held to be a good one. But that is only because all the alternatives are so much worse. No church can sincerely subscribe to the theory that questions of faith do not enter into the education of children.

Wherever churches are rich enough to establish their own schools, or powerful enough to control the public school, they make short work of the "godless" school. Either they establish religious schools of their own, as the Catholics and Lutherans have done, or they impose their views on the public schools as the fundamentalists have done wherever they have the necessary voting strength. The last fight of Mr. Bryan's life was made on behalf of the theory that if a majority of voters in Tennessee were fundamentalists then they had the right to make public education in Tennessee fundamentalist too. One of the standing grievances of the Catholic Church in America is that Catholics are taxed to support schools to which they cannot conscientiously send their children.

As a matter of fact non-sectarianism is a useful political phrase rather than an accurate description of what goes on in the schools. If there is teaching of science, that teaching is by implication almost always agnostic. The fundamentalists point this out, and they are quite right. The teaching of history, under a so-called non-sectarian policy, is usually, in this country, a rather diluted Protestant version of history. The Catholics are quite right when they point this out. Occasionally, it may be, a teacher of science appears who has managed to assimilate his science to his theology; now and then a Catholic history teacher will depart from the standard textbooks to give the Catholic version of disputed events during the last few hundred years. But the chief effect of the non-sectarian policy is to weaken sectarian attachment, to wean the child from the faith of his fathers by making him feel that patriotism somehow demands that he shall not press his convictions too far, that commonsense and good fellowship mean that he must not be too absolute. The leaders of the churches are aware of this peril. Every once in a while they make an effort to combat it. Committees composed of parsons, priests, and rabbis appear before the school boards and petition that a non-sectarian God be worshipped and the non-controversial passages of the Bible be read. They always agree that the present godless system of education diminishes the sanctions of morality and the attendance at their respective churches. But they disagree when they try to agree on the nature of a neutral God, and they have been known to dispute fiercely about a non-controversial text of the Ten Commandments. So, if the sects are evenly balanced, the practical sense of the community turns in the end against the reform.

5. The Effect of Patriotism

Modern governments are not merely neutral as between rival churches. They draw to themselves much of the loyalty which once was given to the churches. In fact it has been said with some truth that patriotism has many of the characteristics of an authoritative religion. Certainly it is true that during the last few hundred years there has been transferred to government a considerable part of the devotion which once sustained the churches.

In the older world the priest was a divinely commissioned agent and the prince a divinely tolerated power. But by the Sixteenth Century Melanchthon, a friend of Luther's, had denied that the church could make laws binding the conscience. Only the prince, he said, could do that. Out of this view developed the much misunderstood but essentially modern doctrine of the divine right of kings. In its original historic setting this doctrine was a way of asserting that the civil authority, embodied in the king, derived its power not from the Pope, as God's viceroy on earth, but by direct appointment from God himself. The divine right of kings was a declaration of independence as against the authority of the church. This heresy was challenged not only by the Pope, but by the Presbyterians as well. And it was to combat the Presbyterian preachers who insisted on trying to dictate to the government that King James I wrote his *True Law of Free Monarchy,* asserting the whole doctrine of the Divine Right of Kings.

In the Religious Peace of Augsburg an even more destructive blow was struck at the ancient claim of the church that it is a universal power. It was agreed that the citizen of a state must adopt the religion of his king. *Cuius regio ejus religio.* This was not religious liberty as we understand it, but it was a supreme assertion of the civil power. Where once the church had administered religion for the multitude, and had exercised the right to depose an heretical king, it now became the prerogative of the king to determine the religious duties of his subjects. The way was open for the modern absolute state, a conception which would have been entirely incomprehensible to men who lived in the ages of faith.

We must here avoid using words ambiguously. When I speak of the absolute state, I do not refer to the constitutional arrangement of powers within the state. It is of no importance in this connection whether the absolute power of the state is exercised by a king, a landed aristocracy, bankers and manufacturers, professional politicians, soldiers, or a random majority of voters. It does not matter whether the right to govern is hereditary or obtained with the consent of the governed. A state is absolute in the sense which I have in mind when it claims the right to a monopoly of all the force within the community, to make war, to make peace, to conscript life, to tax, to establish and disestablish property, to define crime, to punish disobedience, to control education, to supervise the family, to regulate personal habits, and to censor opinions. The modern state claims all these powers, and in the matter of theory there is no real difference in the size of the claim between communists, fascists, and democrats. There are lingering traces in the American constitutional system of the older theory that there are inalienable rights which government may not absorb. But these rights are really not inalienable because they can be taken away by constitutional amendment. There is no theoretical limit upon the power of the ultimate majorities which create civil government.

There are only practical limits. They are restrained by inertia, and by prudence, even by good will. But ultimately and theoretically they claim absolute authority as against all foreign states, as against all churches, associations, and persons within their jurisdiction.

The victory of the civil power was not achieved everywhere at the same time. Spasmodically, with occasional setbacks, but in the long run irresistibly, the state has attained supremacy. In the feudal age the monarch was at no time sovereign. The Pope was the universal lawgiver, not only in what we should call matters of faith, but in matters of business and politics as well. As late as the beginning of the Seventeenth Century, Pope Paul V insisted that the Doge of the Venetian Republic had no right to arrest a canon of the church on the charge of flagrant immorality. When, nevertheless, the canon was arrested, the Pope laid Venice under an interdict and excommunicated the Doge and the Senate. But the Venetian Government answered that it was founded on Divine Right; its title to govern did not come from the church. In the end the Pope gave way, and "the reign of the Pope," says Dr. Figgis, "as King of Kings was over."

It was as a result of the loss of its civil power that the Roman Church evolved the modern doctrine of infallibility. This claim, as Dr. Figgis points out, is not the culmination but the (implicit) surrender of the notions embodied in the famous papal bull, *Unam Sanctam*. The Pope could no longer claim the political sovereignty of the world; he then asserted supreme rights as the religious teacher of the Catholic communion. "The Pope, from being the Lord of Lords, has become the Doctor of Doctors. From being the mother of states, the Curia has become the authoritative organ of a teaching society."

6. *The Dissolution of a Sovereignty*

Thus there has gradually been dissolving the conception that the government of human affairs is a subordinate part of a divine government presided over by God the King. In place of one church which is sovereign over all men, there are now many rival churches, rival states, voluntary associations, and detached individuals. God is no longer believed to be a universal king in the full meaning of the word king, and religious obedience is no longer the central loyalty from which all other obligations are derived. Religion has become for most modern men one phase in a varied experience; it no longer regulates their civic duties, their economic activities, their family life, and their opinions. It has ceased to have universal dominion, and is now held to be supreme only within its own domain. But there is much uncertainty as to what that domain is. In actual affairs, the religious obligations of modern men are often weaker than their social interests and generally weaker than the fiercer claims of patriotism. The conduct of the churches and of churchmen during the War demonstrated that fact overwhelmingly. They submitted willingly or unwillingly to the overwhelming force of the civil power. Against this force many men claim the right of revolution, or at least the right of passive resistance and conscientious objection. Sometimes they base their claims upon a religious precept which they hold sacred. But even in their disobedience to Caesar they are forced to acknowledge that loyalty in the modern world is complex, that it has become divided and uncertain, and that the age of faith which was absolute is gone for them. However reverent they may be when they are in their churches, they no longer feel wholly assured when they listen to the teaching that these are the words of the ministers of a heavenly king.

23

Gerald Gurin, Joseph Veroff, and Sheila Feld

People Who Have Gone for Help

Societies throughout history have set up institutions to provide comfort and aid for their troubled members. In the past, this function was usually performed by religious institutions: the oracle, the priest, the witch doctor were often invested with responsibility for the care and healing of the sick in body or spirit. Their approaches to therapy differed, depending upon the nature of their religious doctrines. The persons who sought their help—practicing widely diverse rites and ceremonies, trusting in totally different powers—had in common with one another the faith that the counsel of these various religious leaders would be effective in helping them establish personal equilibrium. Such leaders, of course, did not always rise from the ranks of churchmen. At various periods, other kinds of individuals were invested with healing powers. "Expert" insight into human nature has been attributed to politicians, scholars, physicians, and others. These men were often credited with having powers of healing as reliable and effective as those attributed to religious leaders.

Modern society is characterized by the multiplicity of resources that share this therapeutic function and by their growing professionalization. Furthermore, there has been a formal expansion of the functions of more traditional professions to include the psychological counselor role. Thus, included among contemporary professional counselors are clergymen, psychiatrists, psychologists, lawyers, marriage counselors, physicians, vocational guidance workers, social workers, and others.

Excerpted from *Americans View Their Mental Health* by Gerald Gurin, Joseph Veroff, and Sheila Feld, © 1960 by Basic Books, Inc., Publishers, New York, reprinted by permission of the publisher. The three authors are social psychologists at the University of Michigan.

279

. . .

The discussion centers around the responses to the following set of questions:

> Sometimes when people have problems like this, they go
> someplace for help. Sometimes they go to a doctor or a minister.
> Sometimes they go to a special place for handling personal problems
> —like a psychiatrist or a marriage counselor, or a social agency or
> clinic. . . .
> How about you—have you ever gone anywhere like that for advice
> or help with a personal problem?
> What was that about?
> Where did you go for help?
> How did you happen to go there?
> What did they do—how did they try to help you?
> How did it turn out—do you think it helped you in any way?

. . .

In our sample, 345 respondents reported that they have gone some-where for help with a personal problem. In this group there are undoubtedly some for whom this act represented a last resort, a last attempt to forestall despair. Others, of course, may have acted as they did for far less drastic reasons. In either case, we cannot treat this decision as a casual choice among alternatives. A person who goes for help with a personal problem is, in a sense, revealing at least two assumptions that he has made about his situation: first, that he is faced with a personal problem that distresses him; and second, that he cannot solve this problem by himself or by the help and advice of family or friends.[1] We assume that either of the latter choices would be preferable if they were available and were considered as potentially helpful.

Once having recognized a personal problem that cannot be solved by one's own resources, a person in trouble can choose among a number of alternatives if he wishes to seek further help. Some of these, however, may be only potentially, rather than actually, available: the person may not be aware of the existence of certain agents or agencies; he may be skeptical about some or unable to afford or not have ready access to others. We do not know why, ultimately, our respondents chose certain sources of help; we only have reports of the fact that they have done so.[2] But we hope to suggest some of the factors that may have influenced them, by inference from the social characteristics of the groups preferring particular sources and from the kinds of problems for which help was sought.

The professional persons approached for help by our respondents have been listed in the categories outlined in Table 1. The most frequently consulted source of help or advice was a clergyman—42 per

TABLE 1 SOURCE OF HELP USED BY PEOPLE WHO HAVE SOUGHT PROFESSIONAL HELP FOR A PERSONAL PROBLEM

Source of Help	
Clergyman	42%
Doctor	29
Psychiatrist (or psychologist): private practitioner or not ascertained whether private or institutional *	12
Psychiatrist (or psychologist) in clinic, hospital, other agency; mental hospital	6
Marriage counselor; marriage clinic	3
Other private practitioners or social agencies for handling psychological problems	10
Social service agencies for handling nonpsychological problems (e.g., financial problems)	3
Lawyer	6
Other	11
Total	—
Number of people	(345)

* Actually only six people specifically mentioned going to a private practitioner. This category should thus be looked upon as representing in the main those people who said "psychiatrist" without specifying that he was part of a mental hygiene agency.

cent—followed by a doctor—29 per cent (physicians who were not specifically designated as psychiatrists are referred to here as doctors). Thirty-one per cent of the group went to some practitioner or agency subsumed under the heading of "mental health professionals," including psychiatrists, psychologists, marriage counselors, and other private practitioners or institutions that are set up to handle psychological problems. Eighteen per cent specifically mentioned having gone to a psychiatrist or psychologist [3] (6 per cent reported seeing a psychiatrist attached to a clinic, hospital, or other agency; 12 per cent either just referred to a psychiatrist or, in a few instances, specifically mentioned a private psychiatrist). Another 6 per cent mentioned that a lawyer was asked to give help with a personal problem (most of these cases involved counsel associated with divorce proceedings).

Eleven per cent of the responses were coded as using "other sources of help." A content analysis of these "other sources" disclosed that only three responses were directly associated with an agency for mental health rehabilitation, all of these being Alcoholics Anonymous. Five of the remainder referred to consultation with teachers in connection with a child's problems; ten responses referred to nurses or visiting nurses; eight people named policemen or judges as being helpful with personal problems. None of these people, of course, are set up to be psychological counselors. But we feel it is legitimate to include them because, like lawyers, they are associated with situations that may potentially cause intense psychological distress—school problems, health problems, problems with the law—and they have been viewed as having the ability to help with a personal problem and have been asked for such help.[4]

In summary, we find that most of the respondents who went for help in times of personal distress chose a resource that offered, as *one* of its functions, psychological guidance. But it is interesting that those institutions explicitly created for this function alone—such as psychiatry, clinical psychology, social work—were less often consulted than those for which psychological guidance is not a major function—clergymen and physicians in general. It might be contended that clergymen and physicians are more numerous than psychiatric specialists and therefore more available. On the other hand, the greater use of nonpsychiatric specialists may indicate a lack of readiness in the general population to consult mental health professionals in times of crisis, or a lack of knowledge about the availability or effectiveness of such professionals.

To infer what reasons people might have for choosing particular sources of help, we have related the sources of help they chose to the kinds of problems they were interested in solving (Table 2). There are slight differences among the kinds of problems that were brought to clergymen, physicians, and psychiatrists. People who consulted clergymen mention marriage problems more often than those who went to physicians or psychiatrists; those who went to psychiatrists were more likely to do so about problems with a child or a personal adjustment problem than those who chose either of the other sources; and physicians are more likely than the other two professions to be confronted with nonpsychological situational problems. In general, however, the three professions seem to be consulted for very similar reasons and are presented with very similar patterns of personal problems; the differences among them are not so striking as we might have expected.

In attempting to understand why the content of the problems that are referred to physicians, ministers, and psychiatrists are so similar, it should be remembered that we are dealing here with answers to a question that focused on personal problems. We are not dealing, therefore, with all problems that people have faced in their lives that may have had psychological implications and for which they received help. The results—that the contents of the problems for which physicians, ministers, and psychiatrists are consulted are very similar—concern only those problems already defined in personal, psychologically relevant terms. If we were to consider all problems having potential psychological implications, whether or not people defined them in those terms, we might expect to find greater differences in the content of the problems referred to ministers, physicians, and psychiatrists. Specifically, we would expect to find that problems defined in broadly personal or interpersonal terms would be more likely to be handled by psychiatrists than problems not cast in these terms.

TABLE 2 RELATIONSHIP OF SOURCE OF HELP USED TO THE PROBLEM AREA (FIRST-MENTIONED RESPONSES ONLY)

Problem Area	Source of Help						
	Clergy	Doctor	Psychiatrist *	Marriage Counselor	Other Psychological Agencies	Non-psychological Agencies	Lawyer
Spouse; marriage	46%	36%	35%	92%	50%	10%	61%
Child; relationship with child	8	8	20	8	39	10	8
Other family relationships	5	6	4	—	6	—	8
Other relationship problems; type of relationship problem unspecified	8	3	2	—	—	—	8
Job or school	5	2	2	—	—	—	—
Adjustment problems in self (nonjob)	18	22	30	—	5	—	—
Psychological reaction to situational problems	5	6	7	—	—	10	—
Nonpsychological situational problems	2	15	—	—	—	60	15
Nothing specific; can't remember	3	—	—	—	—	—	—
Not ascertained	—	2	—	—	—	10	—
Total	100%	100%	100%	100%	100%	100%	100%
Number of people †	(130)	(89)	(46)	(12)	(18)	(10)	(13)

* Here and in all subsequent tables this category includes both people who mentioned seeing a "psychiatrist" or a "psychiatrist at a hospital."

† Does not include 27 people who mentioned "other" sources of help.

. . .

It is one thing to seek help, and another thing to find it. Although most of the people who received professional counsel felt that it helped them to solve their problems, one out of every five reported that it failed to do so.

. . .

People who went for help with marriage problems were most likely to assert that they did not benefit from it (Table 3); similarly, those who localized the source of the problem either in another person or in a relationship were most likely to report the same kind of failure (Table 4). Together, these findings suggest that individuals who expe-

TABLE 3 Relationship Between Area of Problems and Perception of Helpfulness of Therapy (First-Mentioned Responses Only)

How Much Therapy Helped	Area of Problem							
	Marriage	Child	Other Family	Other Relationship	Job	Adjustment (Self)	Situations Involving Others	Nonpsychological Situational Problems
Helped, helped a lot	48%	58%	56%	73%	67%	74%	50%	62%
Helped (qualified)	13	16	25	—	16	14	28	14
Did not help	32	13	—	20	11	7	11	14
Don't know	1	5	—	—	—	3	—	—
Not ascertained	6	8	19	7	6	2	11	10
Total	100%	100%	100%	100%	100%	100%	100%	100%
Number of people *	(143)	(38)	(16)	(15)	(18)	(58)	(18)	(29)

* Does not include ten people for whom the area of the problem was not ascertained.

rienced marital difficulties and attributed them either to their spouses or to some defect in the relationship were least amenable to help in working out their problems. In contrast, those who sought help for a personal adjustment problem (Table 3), as well as those who perceived their problems arising from some defect in themselves (Table 4), claimed more often than any other group in either comparison that therapy had helped them. We may conclude that individuals who recognize that some change in themselves is required to alleviate their difficulties are most likely to believe that professional counsel has helped them.

From these findings one might expect that sources of help that handle marriage problems in which the defects were perceived in the spouse or in the relationship itself would be perceived to have been the least effective. And furthermore, sources of help that handle problems in which the defect was perceived in the person himself would be seen as most effective.

As we saw in Table 2, marriage counselors almost exclusively handle marriage problems where the defect is perceived either in the relationship or in the other person. Of all sources of help, the marriage counselors are perceived as least effective (Table 5). The number of cases is small, but the differences are striking.

We hoped to be able to discover the kinds of criteria people employed to measure therapeutic benefits and whether these criteria differed according to the source that was consulted. Although most of

TABLE 4 RELATIONSHIP BETWEEN NATURE AND LOCUS OF PROBLEMS AND PERCEPTION OF HELPFULNESS OF THERAPY (FIRST-MENTIONED RESPONSES ONLY)

How Much Therapy Helped	Nature and Locus of Problem				
	Personal Psychological Reaction to Situational Problem	Personal Problem with Defect in Self	Defect in Other	Interpersonal Problem with Defect in Relationship or Unspecified	Impersonal
Helped, helped a lot	65%	73%	47%	55%	56%
Helped (qualified)	19	14	14	13	15
Did not help	4	10	29	24	9
Don't know	—	2	2	1	—
Not ascertained	12	1	8	7	10
Total	100%	100%	100%	100%	100%
Number of people *	(26)	(73)	(86)	(105)	(41)

* Does not include 13 people for whom the nature and locus of the problem was not ascertained.

TABLE 5 RELATIONSHIP OF SOURCE OF HELP USED TO PERCEPTION OF HELPFULNESS OF THERAPY (FIRST-MENTIONED RESPONSES ONLY)

How Much Therapy Helped	Source of Help						
	Clergy	Doctor	Psychiatrist	Marriage Counselor	Other Psychological Agencies	Non-psychological Agencies	Lawyer
Helped, helped a lot	65%	65%	46%	25%	39%	60%	62%
Helped (qualified)	13	11	13	8	33	20	15
Did not help	18	13	24	67	17	20	15
Don't know whether it helped	—	1	6	—	—	—	—
Not ascertained	4	10	11	—	11	—	8
Total	100%	100%	100%	100%	100%	100%	100%
Number of people *	(130)	(89)	(46)	(12)	(18)	(10)	(13)

* Does not include 27 people who mentioned "other" sources of help.

our respondents could not describe explicitly how therapy had helped them, they gave responses generally relevant to this question, and these could be classified into distinct categories (Table 6). The more specific of these were the 12 per cent who said they were comforted by the help they received, 14 per cent who said they were changed person-

TABLE 6 Perception of Ways in Which Therapy Helped

Type of Help	
Helped in terms of comfort, ability to endure problem	12%
Helped in terms of cure, change in respondent or relationship	14
Helped by working with other person in relationship	8
Helped by breaking, or by being given support for breaking, relationship (e.g., divorce)	6
Helped in nonpsychological aspect of problem	12
Helped by talking, advice; not ascertained how this helped	27
Helped in other ways	6
Not ascertained	15
Total	100%
Number of people *	(260)

* Includes only people who said therapy helped.

ally by the experience, 8 per cent who said that the therapy helped another person close to them, and 6 per cent who said that they had received support for breaking up a relationship (mainly by divorce). Twenty-seven per cent indicated having been helped by talking or getting advice, without specifying why this talk or advice had been helpful. Fifteen per cent of those who claimed to have been helped gave no indication at all of how their situations had been improved.

Are particular sources of help associated with certain ways of perceiving therapeutic benefits? This relationship is presented in Table 7. Because only 260 of our help-seeking respondents claim to have been helped, we shall limit this investigation to the three most common sources of help—physicians, clergymen, and psychiatrists—to keep our samples large enough for meaningful analysis.

In most cases, clergymen were appreciated for their ability to offer comfort or, more vaguely, for their capacity to give advice. Both of these benefits were ascribed to clergymen proportionately more often than to either physicians or psychiatrists. These results, taken together, substantiate the assumption that clergymen serve as emotional supporters. Physicians, whose help was frequently perceived as consisting of advice, in addition were thought to have effected cures in a relatively large number of cases. Psychiatrists were viewed as having helped by bringing about a change in the respondent and, less frequently, in another person; but a large proportion of people who visited psychiatrists could give no indication of a specific way in which therapy had helped them. These findings suggest that, although there may be a fairly clear idea among the public of the kinds of problems psychiatrists handle—i.e., defects in the self—there is not a concomitant clarity about what psychiatrists do to solve these kinds of problems; the aura of mysticism, connected to powers of spiritual healing, may still prevail to some extent, in the public conception of psychiatry.

TABLE 7 RELATIONSHIP BETWEEN PERCEPTION OF WAYS IN WHICH THERAPY HELPED AND
USE OF CLERGYMAN, DOCTOR, AND PSYCHIATRIST

Ways in Which Therapy Helped	Source of Help		
	Clergyman	Doctor	Psychiatrist
Comfort; ability to endure	23%	9%	7%
Cure; change in respondent or relation-ship	7	26	22
Changed other	10	6	15
Breaking relationship	9	4	—
Nonpsychological aspect	4	12	4
Advice	34	24	15
Other	5	7	11
Not ascertained	8	12	26
Total	100%	100%	100%
Number of people *	(100)	(68)	(27)

* Includes only people who said therapy helped.

It appears that people who go for help are in most cases not seeking
any change in themselves but rather are looking for comfort, reassurance, and advice. This serves to clarify a number of the findings we
have presented: that only a minority of the people who went for help
defined their problems as a defect in the self; that more people have
gone to ministers and physicians than to psychiatrists with their
problems; that people are less satisfied with the help received from
psychiatrists than they are with the help that clergymen and physicians have given.

. . .

Generally speaking, respondents from all educational levels make
about equal use of clergymen as a resource for help in handling their
personal problems. Religious counsel evidently plays as important a
role at one educational level as it does in another, once people have
decided that they need help with their personal problems.

Religion and church attendance/ Table 8 shows the relationship
between church attendance and source of help, presented separately
for Protestants and Catholics. We would anticipate that regular attenders—whether Catholic or Protestant—would indicate that they
sought help from clergymen to a greater extent than low church-
attenders, and so they have. Aside from this difference, there are no
major differences in the patterns of help sought between Protestants
who were low church-attenders and those who were regular church-
attenders. Furthermore, Catholics and Protestants who are regular
church-attenders are strikingly similar in the sources of help they
turned to. This result was surprising. One might have expected
Catholics to have turned to clergymen to a greater extent than Protes-

TABLE 8 RELATIONSHIP OF CHURCH ATTENDANCE AND RELIGION TO SOURCE OF HELP USED

Source of Help	Protestants		Catholics	
	Regular Attenders *	Low Attenders †	Regular Attenders *	Low Attenders †
Clergyman	54%	33%	52%	28%
Doctor	28	32	28	22
Psychiatrist	14	20	18	6
Marriage counselor	1	6	1	6
Psychological agency	12	8	4	17
Nonpsychological agency	4	5	1	6
Lawyer	7	8	3	11
Other	12	7	12	28
Total	—	—	—	—
Number of people ‡	(103)	(122)	(69)	(18)

* Refers to people who attend church once a week or more frequently.
† Refers to people who attend church less than once a week.
‡ Does not include 33 people whose religion or frequency of church attendance was not ascertained, or who had other types of religious affiliation.

tants, but this did not appear to be true. Although, as we indicated in the preceding chapter, religious Catholics go for help more often than religious Protestants do, there are no differences among those who do go for help in the particular resources chosen.

The only group which tends to show a pattern for help-seeking which is generally different from the others is the low-attending Catholic group. But here we are again faced with a small number of cases, and the differences that do appear—the lower use of psychiatrists and the higher use of nonpsychological resources in the low-attending Catholic group—probably reflect the lower educational level of that group.

Income/ [Additional data show] the relationship between income and the source of help used by people who went for help. We again find confirmation of the central theme of Hollingshead and Redlich's report of psychiatric treatment in New Haven. The wealthier respondents are more likely than the poorer ones to turn to psychiatrists with personal problems. The relationship is an extremely striking one. Among the respondents with the lowest incomes ($2,000 a year or less), only 5 per cent consulted a psychiatrist. In the three middle-income ranges—$2,000 to $7,000 a year—the percentage of respondents using psychiatrists is 12 to 15 per cent, with no major variations among these three groups themselves. But of the group that earns the second highest income in the table—$7,000 to $10,000 a year—almost a quarter (24 per cent) report having consulted a psychiatrist. Finally, this figure almost *doubles* for respondents in the highest income group, of which 47 per cent saw a psychiatrist.

NOTES ——

1. We will talk about these 345 cases as if they were all individuals who went for help voluntarily. We realize this may involve a slight distortion, for some of these people may have been coerced into seeking help—e.g., schools often insist upon parents taking their children to a professional if they are "problems." However, only a handful of respondents indicated any such coercion.

2. We must remember that we are dealing with *reported* sources of help, and that the public terminology is loose. A general practitioner, for instance, may have been referred to incorrectly as a "psychiatrist," while a psychiatrist may have been simply designated as a "doctor."

3. Since only 6 people mentioned going to a "psychologist," and the public image of psychologists and psychiatrists tends to be confused, we have grouped those who mentioned psychologists with those who mentioned psychiatrists. It should also be noted that, although these figures represent the responses to only one question in the interview, there was only one case where a respondent mentioned seeing a psychiatrist without referring to it in response to this particular question. This 18 per cent figure, then (2 per cent of the total population we sampled), represents the total number of people that we interviewed who mentioned going for some psychiatric help at some point in their lives.

4. Another twelve respondents mentioned informal sources of help such as friends, relatives, or bosses, although the question was specifically directed toward professional sources. These people—3 per cent of the total number who said they went to professional help with a personal problem—represent a certain degree of unreliability of response to this, as to any other survey question. In terms of assessing the number of people in the country who have at some time gone for professional help with a personal problem, this figure is very likely counterbalanced by people who did go for help but did not report this to the interviewer.

24

Rodney Stark
and Charles Y. Glock

Churches as
Moral Communities

            In this chapter we shall shift our attention from individual criteria of religious commitment to examine the character of the relationships which church members establish with their churches. The church can be a central institution in a person's life absorbing much of his energy and providing a primary source of his friendships and social contacts. Or, a person's attachments to the church may be merely nominal counting little in the total context of his life. Religious thinkers through the ages have affirmed the ideal that a church should be "a community of believers," as exemplified by the Christian churches of the first and second centuries. In such an ideal community members are united by strong and intimate interpersonal bonds. Groups in which such close social relations exist constitute what social scientists call a "primary group," because of the importance for the individual of his ties to such groups. Charles H. Cooley, who first introduced the term "primary group" in his 1909 book, *Social Organization,* spoke of the "wholeness" that characterizes such groups.[1] "Perhaps the simplest way of describing this wholeness is by saying that it is a 'we'; it involves the sort of sympathy and mutual identification for which 'we' is the natural expression."[2]

A criterion of the ideal church, then, is that it function as a primary group. In turn, a criterion for the ideal church member is that he be related to his church by bonds of friendship and affection. Gerhard Lenski has identified this kind of attachment of church members to their churches as *communal involvement.*[3]

From Rodney Stark and Charles Y. Glock, *American Piety,* Berkeley, Calif.: University of California Press, 1968, pp. 163–173, by permission of the publisher. Rodney Stark and Charles Y. Glock are sociologists at the University of California, Berkeley.

But it has long been recognized that these ideals are frequently, and perhaps typically, not fulfilled either by churches or by church members in actual practice. Indeed, the fact that churches have drifted away from this "authentic" state has been a central concern of religious reformers throughout the centuries. Perhaps the majority of dissident religious movements have aimed to establish a religious group that would approach the ideal of community.

What has come to be called "church-sect theory" represents an effort by social scientists to describe and account for this friction between the ideal and the actual. Briefly, this body of theory postulates that social forces acting upon religious organizations are such that they are almost invariably transformed from moral communities (sects) into more formal and less intimate organizations (churches). We have elsewhere questioned the utility of limiting the classification of religious bodies to sects and churches.[4] However, it remains that religious bodies do differ in these ways, and that individual members differ greatly in the extent to which they are tied to their churches by bonds of friendship.

It must be recognized that the ideal of communal involvement applies at two levels of analysis. On the one hand we may speak of the extent to which a church constitutes a primary group. We may also speak of the extent to which the church serves as a primary group for any individual member, whether or not it does so for most of its members.

At the level of the church we have in mind a continuum. At one pole is a church whose membership might be called a religious audience, at the other is a church whose membership constitutes a religious community. A church's membership represents a religious audience when it is composed of persons who gather periodically to participate in worship, but no network of interpersonal relations binds them together. Thus, they resemble other audiences, such as those that gather in movie theaters or in sports stadia. The polar type at the other end of this continuum is characterized by bonds of interpersonal relationships that unite the participants. This is the religious community in which participants know one another and share much more than the transitory proximity of being in an audience.

Whether or not a church tends to be a religious audience or a religious community it is possible for individual members to participate either as part of an audience or as members of a community. Although most members in a church may lack all interpersonal ties to other members, a minority could still maintain primary relations within the congregation. Conversely, although the majority may constitute a primary group, a minority could simply remain unrelated strangers. In subsequent volumes we shall examine the importance of communal involvement for other aspects of human behavior. For the present, our concern is to measure and describe the extent to which modern churches approach or fall short of this ideal.

We shall begin by examining the extent of friendship among church members. Respondents were asked:

Of your five closest friends, how many are members of your congregation or parish?

Table 1 shows the extent to which contemporary Christian denominations are united by friendship. The overwhelming majority of Christians report that most of their five best friends are not members of their church congregation. While 29 percent of the Protestants said at least three are members of their congregation, 36 percent of the Catholics said this. Furthermore, 36 percent of the Protestants and 34 percent of the Catholics reported that none of their five best friends were members of their congregation. Roughly speaking the overall Christian picture is one of thirds: a third have most of their friends in their congregation, a third have some friends, and a third have none.

But various Protestant bodies greatly depart from this general pattern. The Congregationalists, Methodists, Episcopalians, Presbyterians, and Lutherans have far less than a third of their members who have most of their friends in their church, and greatly exceed a third in the number with no friends. Indeed, 50 percent of the American Lutherans and 49 percent of the Congregationalists said *none* of their best friends belonged to their congregation. At the other extreme, 67 percent of the sect members and 49 percent of the Southern Baptists reported that most of their best friends were in their congregation. Indeed, 30 percent of the sect members and 20 percent of the Southern Baptists said that *all* of their five best friends were in their congregation!

Clearly American Christians differ greatly in the extent to which they are tied to their church congregations by bonds of friendship. But just as clearly the denominations differ greatly in the proportions of their members who are so tied. Examining the various denominations it is obvious that some resemble religious audiences while others come closer to the ideal of being religious communities. It is not possible to say absolutely just what proportion of a congregation ought to have how many friends from the congregation in order for the group to be called a true community or a primary group. Obviously it is not necessary that all be friends of all. For the sake of comparison, we shall adopt several relatively arbitrary but reasonable standards. If we can consider a person to be imbedded in a religious community if at least two of his five best friends are members of his church, then it seems clear that the small Protestant sect groups come rather close to the ideal of being religious communities—80 percent of their members restrict their friendship to fellow congregants to this extent. Among

TABLE 1 Congregational Friendship (Church-Member Sample) "Of five best friends, how many belong to your congregation?"

	Congregational	Methodist	Episcopalian	Disciples of Christ	Presbyterian	American Lutheran	American Baptist	Missouri Lutheran	Southern Baptist	Sects	TOTAL Protestant	Roman Catholic
Number:	(151)	(415)	(416)	(50)	(495)	(208)	(141)	(116)	(79)	(255)	(2,326)	(545)
Percentage who answered:												
Three to five	18	24	20	42	23	20	40	25	49	67	29	36
Two	11	17	19	10	19	14	13	15	11	13	16	14
One	22	16	21	12	18	15	12	19	14	7	16	14
None	49	43	39	36	39	50	31	40	23	9	36	34
No answer	0	0	1	0	1	1	4	1	3	4	3	2

the major denominations the Southern Baptists are closest to this ideal with 60 percent of their members having at least two of their five best friends in their congregations. The Disciples of Christ, American Baptists, and Roman Catholics manage a bare majority of members who meet this standard of communal involvement. The least communally involved denomination is the Congregational Church with only 29 percent meeting our criterion of involvement. Thus, Christian churches range from religious audiences to religious communities and within all denominations the communal involvement of individual members varies greatly.

We have thus far examined the extent to which persons are bound to their churches by ties of friendship and the extent to which they limit their friendship to their fellow congregants. We shall now examine a somewhat more general measure of communal involvement: the extent to which persons limit their organizational participation to the church. . . . church members vary greatly in the number of church activities and organizations in which they take part. While the sheer amount of organizational participation a person gives to his church is an important measure of his commitment, this can be substantially qualified by what portion of his total organizational participation is in the church. For example, one person may only take part in two church activities, while another takes part in four. But if the first person has no other organizational involvements, while the person with four church activities is also active in ten secular organizations it follows that the first person is much more organizationally immersed in church than is the second. On the one hand, the church is the only outlet for the organizational activity of some persons, while for others the church is only one of many such outlets. This variety of communal involvement cannot be judged solely on the basis of the extent of organizational participation in the church. Thus, we must examine participation in both church and secular organizations.

All respondents were asked to complete the following battery of items on their participation in secular organizations.

> Now we would like to know something about the organizations
> and clubs you belong to. Below are listed various kinds of
> organizations. In the blank in front of each kind of organization,
> write in the number of organizations like this to which you belong.
> If none, mark 0.
>
> —— FRATERNAL GROUPS, such as Elks, Eagles, Masons, Knights of
>   Columbus, Eastern Star, and women's auxiliaries to groups
>   like this, etc.
>
> —— SERVICE CLUBS, such as Lions, Rotary, Zonta, Jr. Chamber of
>   Commerce, etc.

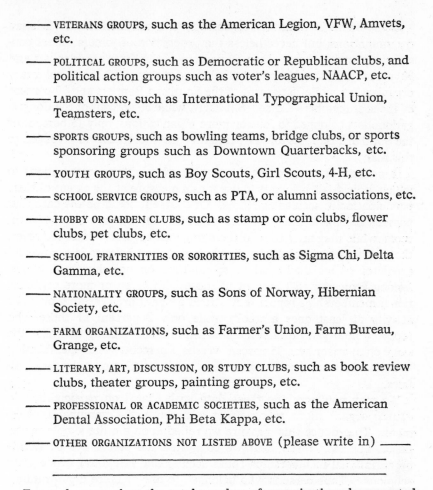

—— VETERANS GROUPS, such as the American Legion, VFW, Amvets, etc.

—— POLITICAL GROUPS, such as Democratic or Republican clubs, and political action groups such as voter's leagues, NAACP, etc.

—— LABOR UNIONS, such as International Typographical Union, Teamsters, etc.

—— SPORTS GROUPS, such as bowling teams, bridge clubs, or sports sponsoring groups such as Downtown Quarterbacks, etc.

—— YOUTH GROUPS, such as Boy Scouts, Girl Scouts, 4-H, etc.

—— SCHOOL SERVICE GROUPS, such as PTA, or alumni associations, etc.

—— HOBBY OR GARDEN CLUBS, such as stamp or coin clubs, flower clubs, pet clubs, etc.

—— SCHOOL FRATERNITIES OR SORORITIES, such as Sigma Chi, Delta Gamma, etc.

—— NATIONALITY GROUPS, such as Sons of Norway, Hibernian Society, etc.

—— FARM ORGANIZATIONS, such as Farmer's Union, Farm Bureau, Grange, etc.

—— LITERARY, ART, DISCUSSION, OR STUDY CLUBS, such as book review clubs, theater groups, painting groups, etc.

—— PROFESSIONAL OR ACADEMIC SOCIETIES, such as the American Dental Association, Phi Beta Kappa, etc.

—— OTHER ORGANIZATIONS NOT LISTED ABOVE (please write in) ——

For each respondent the total number of organizations he reported belonging to in this battery was computed. The figures were quite amazing. Surveys of a nationwide sample of American adults typically find that about 50 percent say they belong to no voluntary organizations.[5] In our sample of church members only 16 percent said they belonged to no such groups. Similarly, while only about 12 percent of Americans in general report belonging to three or more such organizations, 49 percent of these church members had this number of organizational affiliations. Clearly, church members are active "joiners" in contrast with the general public. Of course, at least for Protestants, membership in a church congregation is itself an act of joining and thus our respondents are preselected for their likelihood to belong to organizations. In addition, of course . . . church members are likely to be middle and upper class persons and past studies have shown that organizational participation of all kinds is predominately a middle and upper class activity.

Membership in voluntary organizations is common in all Christian denominations, but nevertheless the proportion of joiners differs considerably among them. Thus, 91 percent of the Congregationalists and 90 percent of the Methodists belonged to one or more voluntary organization, while 75 percent of the Southern Baptists and 70 percent of the sect members did so. Similarly, while 56 percent of the Congregationalists belonged to four or more organizations, only 15 percent of the Southern Baptists and 17 percent of the sect members belonged to this many.

Our reason for computing the number of voluntary organizations to which individuals belong is to use it as a measure of the extent of their participation in secular activities. Of course it could be the case that persons belong to many secular organizations but are not active in them, while they are active in their religious organizations. However, the number of organizations to which a person belongs is a powerful predictor of his likelihood to spend time on non-church activities. Among Protestants 90 percent of those with seven or more organizational memberships report they attend a non-church meeting or other activity at least once a week, while only 2 percent of those who reported no organizational membership did so. Among Catholics the same comparison was 95 percent versus 4 percent. Thus membership is quite likely to engender participation in secular organizational affairs.

We may now combine these data with [data] on participation in church organizations to construct a measure of Communal Involvement. To produce this measure we relied upon a quite simple procedure. For each respondent we computed the percentage of all his organizational memberships (both secular and religious) which were religious.[6] Thus persons who belonged to one or more organizations, none of which were religious, were scored as 0 percent on the Index of Communal Involvement. Similarly, persons could score as high as 100 percent if all of their memberships were in religious organizations.

Table 2 shows that church members differ greatly in the proportions of their total memberships which are religious. While 50 percent of the Episcopalians and 47 percent of the Congregationalists include no church groups in their organizational life, only 18 percent of the Southern Baptists and 22 percent of the sect members hold exclusively secular memberships. On the other hand, only 7 percent of the Congregationalists and 10 percent of the Episcopalians reported that 60 percent or more of their organizations were religious, while 43 percent of the Southern Baptists and 41 percent of the sect members did so. Indeed, 16 percent of the Southern Baptists, 17 percent of the Missouri Lutherans, and 22 percent of the sect members completely limited their organizational participation to church groups. Overall, 19 per-

TABLE 2 Communal Involvement (Church-Member Sample) Proportion of total number of organizational memberships which are religious

	Congregational	Methodist	Episcopalian	Disciples of Christ	Presbyterian	American Lutheran	American Baptist	Missouri Lutheran	Southern Baptist	Sects	TOTAL Protestant	Roman Catholic
Number:	(148)	(396)	(387)	(48)	(468)	(188)	(135)	(103)	(70)	(227)	(2,170)	(460)
Percentage who answered:												
60% or more	7	14	10	31	17	21	22	27	43	41	19	9
40% to 59%	12	18	9	29	19	20	23	17	62	24	18	10
10% to 39%	34	29	31	19	31	27	29	25	13	13	27	24
0% *	47	39	50	21	33	32	26	31	18	22	36	57

* No respondent scored between 1% and 9%.

cent of the Protestants find 60 percent or more of their organizational outlets in religion, while 9 percent of the Catholics do so.

Thus, whether it is measured in terms of bonds of friendship or in terms of the extent to which persons concentrate their organizational activities within the church, communal involvement produces marked differences among the Christian bodies. The more liberal denominations such as the Congregationalists, Methodists, and Episcopalians tend to constitute religious audiences. Their members are typically not bound to their religious congregation by personal friendships. Furthermore, in these more liberal bodies not only are members less likely to take part in church activities, but their church activities make up a relatively small proportion of their organizational outlets. In the most conservative bodies, however, such as the Southern Baptists and the various sects, the churches tend to function as primary groups composed of persons who restrict their friendships and their organizational activities to their congregations.

Émile Durkheim's conception of a church as a moral community is inapplicable to many contemporary Christian denominations. Today, to speak of churches as communities is also to speak of theologically conservative churches.

NOTES

1. New York: Charles Scribner's Sons.

2. *Ibid.,* p. 23.

3. Gerhard Lenski, *The Religious Factor* (Garden City, N.Y.: Doubleday, 1961), especially pp. 21–22.

4. Charles Y. Glock and Rodney Stark, *Religion and Society in Tension* (Chicago: Rand McNally, 1965), ch. 13. See also the theoretical discussion in Stephen Steinberg, "Reform Judaism: The Origin and Evolution of a 'Church Movement,'" *Journal for the Scientific Study of Religion,* V, No. 1 (1965), pp. 117–129, and the extremely important paper by Benton Johnson, "On Church and Sect," *American Sociological Review,* XXVIII, No. 4 (1963), pp. 539–549.

5. For a summary see: Bernard Lazerwitz, "Membership in Voluntary Associations and Frequency of Church Attendance," *Journal for the Scientific Study of Religion,* II, No. 1 (1962), pp. 74–84.

6. Two hundred and thirty-six persons who belonged to no organizations, either secular or religious, were excluded from the data.

QUESTIONS FOR DISCUSSION

1. Gurin and his associates indicate that persons who seek help from clergy regarding personal problems report more or less success depending upon

the nature of their problems. What do you think this means for the larger question of "religion and societal integration"?

2. If, as Lippmann argues, the authority of religious organizations has broken down, where can that "lost" authority be found? Does he mean that churches have *no* authority?

3. The findings of Stark and Glock on the differential degree to which church members are organizationally "involved" can have at least two interpretations: (1) persons who are most involved in church do not want to get involved in secular organizations; (2) persons who are not involved in secular organizations use the church as a substitute. To what extent is reality reflected in either or both of these interpretations?

4. Can you picture the kind of research necessary to determine: (1) if various individuals are integrated into their society, and (2) whether "religion" is involved?

ADDITIONAL READING

Berger, Peter L. *The Sacred Canopy.* Garden City, N.Y.: Doubleday, 1967. Borrowing from Durkheim but blending several other perspectives also, Berger discusses religion's role as "reality definer" and what happens, therefore, when religions offer competing definitions of reality.

Durkheim, Émile. *Elementary Forms of Religious Life.* Translated by J. W. Swain. London: George Allen and Unwin, Ltd., 1915. Paperback edition now available through The Free Press, New York. An undisputed classic in sociology of religion, this monograph presents a very disputed theory regarding the "ever present" origins and societal nature of religion. It does so, however, in a manner that poses the issue of religion's role in societal integration.

Glock, Charles Y., and Rodney Stark. "Religion and the Integration of Society," in *Religion and Society in Tension.* Chicago: Rand McNally, 1965. Here is an earlier attempt by these authors to take up a question they address in their selection in this chapter.

Hammond, Phillip E. "Secularization, Incorporation, and Social Relations," *American Journal of Sociology* 72 (September 1966), 188–194. In a context tangential to what is ordinarily regarded as churchly, this empirical research is an attempt to evaluate some Durkheimian notions about integration and religion's role in it.

Chapter IX

Nonformalized
Religion in
American
Society

It is a peculiar trait of the Western world to equate "religion" with "church." Much of what people regard as sacred is experienced outside of organized religion, and most persons will concede that a wide variety of events—from the birth of a child to the elegance of a mathematical equation—can evoke a sense of awe, of inspiration, or even, as Freud termed it, of "holy dread." But if Western man, especially American man, has most of these experiences patterned for him by and mediated through the church, it is nevertheless the case that significant portions of his religious life occur "outside" the religious organization. Just as there are nonreligious aspects of the church, so are there nonchurch aspects of religion in American society. The selections in this chapter treat this subject by dealing with the "sacralization" of the political arena, arguing that Americans do not regard political life as just another activity, but to some significant degree they transpose it into a sacred endeavor. As Durkheim put one aspect of it, if society "happens to fall in love with a man and if it thinks it has found in him the principal aspirations that move it, as well as the means of satisfying them, this man will be raised above the others and, as it were, deified." *

Of course, deification of men is different from the deification of social patterns and positions that men might observe and occupy. At issue is the degree to which sacredness is institutionalized, and one of the great theoretical questions is why Western society tended to institu-

---

* Émile Durkheim, *Elementary Forms of the Religious Life*, J. W. Swain (tr.) (London: George Allen and Unwin, Ltd., 1915), p. 243.

tionalize so many of its sacred aspects in and around "churches."
The first essay in this chapter, Conrad Cherry's "American Sacred
Ceremonies" (Selection 25), discusses two specific instances of "deification," arguing that they were not merely glorifications of particular,
respected men, but, more importantly, they were occasions for worshipping authentically sacred American ideals. These sacred American
ideals, when seen as more or less systematized or integrated, constitute an American "civil religion," with its "saints," places of worship,
high holy days, and so forth. Existing alongside but not contradicting
"church" religion, this civil religion has been a strategic element in
American society since the beginning.

Without question, the earliest years of the American experience
permitted—perhaps encouraged—the development of this civil theology. As Willard L. Sperry (Selection 10) indicates, nearly from the
beginning America was committed to pluralism and thus a "separation" of church and state. In this chapter's second reading (Selection
26), the church historian Jerald C. Brauer goes on to demonstrate
more of the development of the civil religion by citing the observations
of early nineteenth century European visitors to America. The "faith"
people had in democracy, the celebration by churches of this American
experiment, the assumption by many that America's purposes were
God's purposes were seen clearly by these visitors during the 1800s.
Some came to inquire, others to scoff, but none could ignore how religion "spilled out" of churches and into everyday political life.

Churches, then, were not the only social structures affected. The
nation was becoming ethnically heterogeneous (Gaustad, Selection 11)
and increasingly urbanized (Olmstead, Selection 12), which meant
that religious organizations must—if they were to be maintained at all
—amend their particularities to bring them more into line with mosaic
America. But in substantial measure, the civic religion had a life of
its own. *One* of the ways this separate life is observed is discussed by
Bayless Manning in "The Purity Potlatch . . ." (Selection 27). Referring to a process of "moral escalation," the author, a professor of law,
sees American political officials as engaged in a competition not only
for office but also for crowns of virtue. Political campaigns thus become alternating claims of moral righteousness, with politicians
expected to symbolize the highest standards of rectitude.

Nonformalized religion appears in arenas other than politics, of
course. Science, family life, even corporations contain elements of
ritual, priesthood, unquestioned values. And persons may respond to
these things in ways that can clearly by called "religious." Durkheim
argued that a people's commonality—their "collective conscience"
or "moral density"—would find religious expression; in this chapter
we are raising the question of the degree to which these religious expressions are found in America outside of formal churches.

25

Conrad Cherry

American Sacred Ceremonies

Students of American culture have been sensitive to the religious meaning of American civic ceremonies. A classic example is Lloyd Warner's analysis of Memorial Day celebrations as religious cults for the war-dead. And in a recent issue of *Christianity and Crisis*, Roger Shinn has sketched the flight of Apollo XI as an instance of modern man's ritualization of life, the television camera allowing wide participation in actions of the astronauts that were both scientific-functional and liturgical-expressive.[1] Such occasions of public ritual have also been recognized as clues to their larger religious context, as expressions of a national religious faith. For the most part, however, analysts of American religion have not given serious attention to American sacred ceremonies since they have viewed with jaundiced eye the national religion ritualized in these ceremonies. The American national religion has been charged with offenses ranging from sentimental piety and theological naïveté to idolatrous chauvinism.

Lately, new studies of the national religion have suggested that these charges usually spring from a truncated perspective. In particular, Robert Bellah in his article "Civil Religion in America" and Sidney Mead in his "The 'Nation with the Soul of a Church'" have argued that a shortsightedness has plagued our observation of the American civil religion.[2] First of all, we have too readily identified this religion with the most banal forms of American religiosity, with the shallow piety of the "American way of life." We have failed to recognize that if the civil religion has indeed encouraged an idolatrous worship of middle-class values, some of its leading spokesmen have directed the attention of Americans to a transcendent God who brings all human values under judgment. If the national faith has issued in "cookie prayers" in the public schools, it has also been expressed in solemn

This essay, especially prepared for the present volume, is reprinted by permission of the author. Conrad Cherry is a member of the Department of Religious Studies at Pennsylvania State University.

occasions when American citizens dedicate themselves to high human ideals. Secondly, the label "common denominator religion" has distorted the origins and nature of the civic faith. The national religion simply cannot be explained as the reduction of Judaism and Christianity to their bare essentials. It is a distinctive religious tradition which draws upon American history for its revelatory events and personages, treats official documents like the Declaration of Independence and the Gettysburg Address as sacred scriptures, and embodies itself in American civic institutions. Although the civil religion has borrowed heavily from the symbolism and mythology of Judaism and Christianity and has found an institutional haven in church and synagogue, its commonality has been created not by its borrowed elements but by the unfolding American experience itself. Finally, the civil religion's long and complex history has been overlooked because of our preoccupation with its appearance during the surge of piety in the 1950s.

In brief, Bellah and Mead have in different ways clearly pointed to the American civil religion as a phenomenon that deserves the same kind of careful, dispassionate study we have accorded other religions. This paper will deal with the ceremonial expression of the civil religion as a revealing object of attention for the historian. If, as Émile Durkheim and others have claimed,[3] public ritual is the way in which societies periodically quicken and sustain their belief systems, the American sacred ceremony should yield for the social scientist the lively and efficacious religious sentiments that have gone into the making of the national experience. The sacred ceremony should also provide some answers to puzzling questions that are still being raised about the nature and function of the civil religion. Brief analyses of two American ceremonies will serve as the primary empirical bases for our reflections.

I

At fifty minutes past noon on the Fourth of July, 1826, Thomas Jefferson died at Monticello. Only a few hours later, in Quincy, Massachusetts, John Adams followed Jefferson into death. Americans of the time could scarcely be expected to treat lightly the deaths of these two fathers of Independence on the fiftieth anniversary of the Declaration. For nineteenth-century Americans, God moved wondrously through the course of human history, and most wondrously of all through American history. President John Quincy Adams expressed a uniform sentiment when he declared that the deaths of these two men on such an auspicious occasion was "Heaven directed" and furnished "a new seal" to the belief that the nation was under the special care of Providence.

John Adams' last words were, "Thomas Jefferson still survives." As Merrill Peterson has said, Adams' last words were to be his most significant.[4] It was Jefferson, revered as the defender of the supremacy of the popular will and as the proponent of the rights of man, rather than Adams, remembered as too much the restrainer of the popular will and too much the believer in institutions, who would survive as a symbol of republican liberty. But at the time Americans blended their grief for the two Founding Fathers.

Jefferson's own directions for his burial were followed: he was laid to rest at Monticello without ostentatious pageantry. And for more than a century the conviction that no monument of stone could possibly do justice to the fame of Jefferson would hold sway over the American will. Not until 1938 was ground broken for the Jefferson Memorial in Washington, and not until 1943 was that Roman Temple dedicated to his memory.[5] But the bias against stone monuments and Jefferson's own preference for inelaborate funerals did not deter elegant monuments of words or great public ceremonies during the weeks following his death.

During those weeks the people of Richmond, Virginia, turned out in droves to participate in a mock funeral procession, and at a meeting of the American Philosophical Society the president's chair, once occupied by Jefferson, was draped in black. In Boston, American patriots gathered to listen to an oration by Daniel Webster that ran for two and one-half hours. Thirty thousand people joined services in Baltimore's Howard Park where the guest of honor was Charles Carroll, the last surviving signer of the Declaration of Independence. To describe these ceremonies simply as "acts of hero-worship" would be to skim the surface of their meaning. The orations during the ceremonies did certainly pay tribute to Jefferson and Adams, even to the point of apotheosis. But in elevating the two leaders to a place in the American pantheon, the speeches also celebrated principles and aspirations shared by a nation. The ceremonies looked back to 1776 as an event wrought by the hand of God and dwelt upon the two deaths in 1826 as occurrences that hallowed that event for the future. "In this most singular coincidence," said one interpreter, "the finger of Providence is plainly visible! It hallows the Declaration of Independence as the Word of God, and is the bow in the Heavens, that promises its principles shall be eternal, and their dissemination universal over the Earth." [6] The encomia raised across the land in 1826 echoed the same themes: the new Republic was a nation elected by Providence to demonstrate to the world the inherent right of democratic liberties; the sacred scripture which preserved that trust was the Declaration of Independence; and the paradigmatic events by which Americans could interpret the meaning of their destiny under God were the Revolution and the achievement of Independence.

The summer of 1826 was one of the most dramatic instances in which Americans appropriated their national heritage by means of sacred ceremonies. Less dramatic occasions would continue to provide Americans opportunities to sanctify their heritage, pledge themselves anew to American ideals, and look forward to the spread of those ideals. Sacred civic ceremony has not passed into oblivion in the present age, an age so highly touted for its secularity and abhorrence of religious ritual. In June, 1968, Americans participated in an elaborate ritual for a fallen leader.

The differences between the ritual occurring after the death of Robert Kennedy and that which arose after the deaths of Jefferson and Adams are striking. A sense of fulfillment in death surrounded the passing of Adams and Jefferson: after all, these two had not only reached old age but had also attained the highest office in the land. In the ceremonies of 1826, therefore, a rejoicing mixed with the mourning, the holiday atmosphere of Independence Day was permitted with untroubled conscience to pervade the solemn occasions. A contrasting emotional climate was created by witnessing a man stopped short of the peak of his political influence and his bid for the presidency and by the haunting impression that the Kennedys seemed fated to meet violent deaths. But the contrast between the two ceremonial events is accounted for, as well, by the divergent dispositions of the nation. The ritual acts of 1826 presented "the spectacle of a whole people blending their grief 'in the funeral trains of their rival chieftains.'" This was "a fitting symbol of the Era of Good Feelings" in the nation—an era that had already ended in American politics but which could still be captured momentarily by sacred ceremony. The nation could still unite around a republican faith that transcended the divisions of party and ideology.[7] The late 1960s are so far removed from the Era of Good Feelings that only the most naïve of us could possibly assume that the ritual response to Robert Kennedy's death called up a faith that really united—even momentarily—a deeply divided America. In fact, the murder of Kennedy by one overcome by a fanatical loyalty seemed only further tragic proof that America was profoundly divided by reactions to crises both at home and abroad.

Such contrasts are extremely important and we shall return to them, but for the moment note must be taken of what the Kennedy funeral had in common with the ceremonies of 1826.

The solemn ritual commenced on June 7th when hundreds of thousands of Americans waited outside St. Patrick's Cathedral to pay their last respects. Millions more were able to assume a kind of presence there through their television sets. By way of television they participated in the funeral the next day, followed the funeral train at its points of passage to Washington, and witnessed the burial at the locus of so much American sacred ceremony, Arlington National Cemetery.

The funeral itself was obviously a religious affair; it was "religious" in the sense in which most Americans think of that term. It was, after all, a Roman Catholic funeral mass. But it was, at the same time, a civic-religious ceremony designed to address Americans regardless of their denominational persuasions. The funeral liturgy appealed to the doctrines of hope, resurrection and a heavenly reward for a life well-lived. Senator Edward Kennedy, quoting from and commenting on a speech by his brother, offered a different kind of affirmation in the face of death as he called upon his fellow citizens to remember Robert Kennedy as one who dedicated himself to the ideals of peace and justice.

It was the eulogy offered by Archbishop Terence J. Cooke that epitomized the civic-religious nature of the funeral. The part of the funeral liturgy which affirms eternal life was cited at the beginning and at the close of the Archbishop's eulogy, providing the frame for the substance of the address. The greater part of the eulogy, however, placed Robert Kennedy in the context of an American dream and was a challenge to Americans to prevent the waste of Kennedy's life by fulfilling that dream. The qualities admired in Kennedy, the Archbishop said, are the best qualities of the nation. "We admire the ability to identify so that Negro people spoke of him as one of ours. We admire his vision in confronting the problems of poverty and civil rights." But it was a dream that he had for America that evoked this admiration and enlisted his followers: "a dream of an America purged of prejudice, assuring freedom for all her citizens, a land of truly equal opportunity." And the proper response to this man's tragic death, the Archbishop continued, is to occupy ourselves with his vision of the American task. "Our sense of shame and discouragement tears alone will not wash away," he said. "Somehow by the grace of God, and with the strength that still lies deep within the soul of America, we must find the courage to take up again the laborious work to which Senator Kennedy devoted all his energies, the building of a great and honorable nation. Especially in this hour we must keep faith with America and her destiny and we must not forsake our trust in one another. . . . We have always believed in our national destiny marked by unity in lofty ideals. We believe that our country came into existence to secure the blessings of freedom, equality and peace for ourselves and those who will come after us." [8]

Archbishop Cooke's words indicate not only a different emotional climate from that of 1826; they bespeak as well a different interpretation of the national heritage. The orations of 1826 focused on independence and self-government as the providentially bestowed heritage of America and looked to the day when democratic principles would spread across the face of the globe. Cooke's eulogy and other addresses of the occasion dwelt on an unrealized national promise—the promise that all citizens are entitled to full participation in their society—and looked to the day when equal opportunity would spread across the nation itself. Yet the two ceremonial events have much in common. Both are what Lloyd Warner has called national "cults of the dead"—cults in which the living are united with the dead, the living are united with one another, and all are united with God and what are believed to be his purposes for the nation.[9] Both ceremonies reiterate the belief that God has in store—has always had in store—for this nation a special destiny for which the supreme sacrifice has been often made and to the fulfillment of which all Americans must dedicate themselves. Both rites appeal to their participants as American citizens rather than as members of one of the traditional denominations. And both elevate American leaders to the status of sainthood or martyrdom as a way of dramatizing the national ideals which the leaders are believed to embody.

American history is, of course, replete with leaders who have been canonized in the national memory and in sacred ceremony as exemplars of American ideals and as particular bearers of America's destiny under God. Together with the birthdays of Washington and Lincoln, Memorial Day, presidential inaugurations, Thanksgiving and similar occasions, national ceremonies for fallen leaders form the ritual expression of the American civil religion.

II

What, then, can be discerned about the civil religion in its ceremonial expressions?

First of all, *American sacred ceremonies invoke the archetypal themes and myths that have had continuous popular appeal to the American people. A comparative historical study of these themes and myths in their cultic context would reveal both the unifying and the divisive functions of the American mythology.*

A central theme around which many other convictions in the civil religion cluster is the theme of American destiny under God. This is the belief raised to prominence in the ceremonies of 1826, and it is at the center of Archbishop Cooke's reflections on the life and death of Robert Kennedy. The belief that America is a New Israel elected by God to carry out his historical designs and serve as an example for the nations has been a preponderating conviction of the American people from the colonial settlements to the present. It has become, over the years, such a pervasive conviction in the national life that it has passed into the "realm of motivational myths."[10] That is, it has come to provide a religious outlook on history and its purpose, and by having found a place in the feelings and choices as well as in the ideas of

American citizens, it has become a spring of their action. Historians and theologians have long recognized that this powerful myth of American election has decisively shaped our foreign relations as well as our internal developments, that it has served as a stimulus of creative American energy in such tasks as the winning of the frontier and as a source of American self-righteousness in foreign relations.[11] Particular note has been taken of the way in which the mysterious, undeserved election by a transcendent God was transformed into a "manifest," deserved election as the nation grew more and more self-assured.[12] Yet an examination of the theme of American destiny under God in its cultic context and in terms of its relation to the other beliefs and to the social roles of the civil religion is an enterprise that still awaits us. Such an examination would disclose the fact that the motivating myths of the civil religion can contribute to both the unity and the diversity of the nation.

A crucial question to be raised about the civil religion is whether it invents national unity where there is only diversity. Are the national themes celebrated in ritual capable of uniting a pluralistic society? Is it really the case that Americans share common sentiments and attain religious unity in their sacred ceremonies? It is clear that in July 1826 the greater part of the nation was able to transcend divisions of party and achieve—even if the achievement were short-lived—a rededication to shared ideals. A nation fifty years young could find in Independence Day an opportunity to rejoice in the freedoms guaranteed by the Republic, could count on the relatively unhampered cultivation of those freedoms, and could look forward to the spread of democratic principles across the world as a saving light to all men. It is equally clear that in June 1968 the nation was in no position to achieve such a harmonious rededication or such a sanguine outlook on the future. Torn by racial crises at home and by controversy over American actions abroad, the nation discovered that the celebration of the themes of the civil religion could divide as well as unite; it discovered that Kennedy's death occasioned renewed pledges to justice, peace and democratic freedom but also stirred some citizens to despair further of such principles as authentic parts of the American heritage.

The clearest index of the capacity of the *same theme* both to unify and to divide the nation is found in the civic ceremonies during the American Civil War. James Silver, in his study of the role of religion in the Confederacy, has shown how Confederate war propaganda relied heavily on the time-tested motifs of the national faith. "Because of the limited industrial resources of the South," Silver says, "the success of the Confederacy depended on the degree of intestinal fortitude developed by the man in the street and on the farm. He needed to identify himself as a member of God's chosen people and his country as a fulfillment of the destiny of history."[13] The same was true, *mutatis mutandis*, of Union war propaganda: Northern industrial strength was complemented by an appeal to the Union cause as the pursuit of the national destiny under God. We are aware of the way in which President Lincoln lifted his vision beyond the sectional religion of both North and South to the God who brought both sections under judgment and of how similar visions were attained by a number of clergymen on both sides of the Mason-Dixon line.[14] But such visions were atypical of the time. The typical scene was the great gathering at the First Presbyterian Church in New Orleans on the first of many fast days called by President Davis. There Benjamin Morgan Palmer, minister of the church and leading champion of the Confederate cause, directed the people's attention to a providential destiny beckoning the South. The South was called to preserve the basic American principle of self-government, Palmer said, a principle repudiated by Yankee infidels. Or picture as typical the service held in Plymouth Church in Brooklyn after word had spread of the firing on Fort Sumter. Henry Ward Beecher assured the congregation that Northern war efforts would serve as the very instruments of God himself as He struggled to preserve America as the "chosen refuge of liberty for all the earth." [15] Throughout the war years, the motifs of the civil religion were turned on the lathe of sectionalism. Sacred ceremony fortified each section in the conviction that it was pursuing the authentic American mission under God, that its ideals preserved the fundamental principles of American government, that its military was the advance guard of the New Israel crossing the Red Sea of war.

The divisive role of American sacred ceremonies and their mythologies, a role maximized during the Civil War, indicates that the American civil religion is not a monolithic phenomenon but is, at best, a national religious point of view, which narrower points of view may share with varying degrees of tension. In other words, the civil religion itself is composed of a number of different "sects" or "denominations" divided from one another according to regional, ideological, ethnic and socio-economic lines. Certainly the myths, symbols and sources of revelation of the civil religion are sufficiently continuous and uniform to constitute an isolable religion that has operated vigorously in the American public sphere. And on occasions like those following the deaths of Jefferson and Adams, public ceremonies are capable of uniting diverse representative groups of the national faith. Yet the robe of the civil religion is no more seamless than the robe of Christ. And, as the career of the civil religion during the Civil War demonstrates, the garment may certainly be torn asunder.

There is a second feature of the civil religion that appears in the study of that religion's ceremonies, viz., *the complex relation between the civil religion and the religious denominations in America.* Robert Bellah chose the inauguration of John Kennedy as an example of the differentiation between the civil religion and the denominations. In that ceremony distinct denominational beliefs did not intrude. In his inaugural address Kennedy avoided the articulation of any specifically Roman Catholic doctrine or references to Jesus Christ and the Church. Participation in the ceremony was invited through appeal to such beliefs as "the rights of man" that come from the "hand of God." A similar, but less absolute, differentiation occurred in the funeral for Robert Kennedy. There specifically Christian doctrines were articulated, but the eulogies of both Senator Edward Kennedy and Archbishop Cooke dwelt mostly on civil religious themes. The upshot of the ceremonial differentiation between the civil religion and other American religions is that an American may be a Methodist, a Conservative Jew or a Roman Catholic and at the same time participate in the celebration of the civil religion—but without insisting that the civil religion be expressed in specifically Methodist, Jewish or Catholic terms.

Although this differentiation between the civil religion and other American religions has found its defenders throughout American history, only recently has it become a real option in the national life. Only after Protestantism lost its powerful grip on the public life of the nation did the civil religion begin to extricate itself from Protestant custody. There were important exceptions to the hegemony that Protestantism exercised over the civil religion in the past. One thinks of Rabbi Isaac M. Wise's objections to nineteenth-century Protestantism's monopolistic claims on the national public life and his own articulation of national religious themes in a mode that transcended divisions between Jews and Christians.[16] For the most part, however, during the nineteenth century and well into the twentieth, leading spokesmen for the civil religion couched its beliefs in terms that were unmistakably Protestant. Sacred ceremonies celebrated the hope for the spread of an "American Christian civilization," a Christian civilization that was inclusive enough to embrace the diverse Protestant denominations but seldom large enough to include Roman Catholics.[17]

In addition to those religious groups which have been excluded from the civil religion by a Protestant hegemony, there are those groups and individuals who have intentionally excluded themselves. The most obvious instances are the sects, like the Jehovah's Witnesses, which have spurned patriotic symbols and declined participation in American sacred ceremonies. One must also add those clergy and scholars within the Christian and Jewish mainstreams who have been quite vocal in their insistence that any civil or national religion is a banal, watered-down version of their prophetic faith, as well as those deeply involved in an ecumenical movement that intends to cross both national and cultural barriers. The pressing question at this point is whether the sects, the critics, the ecumenical movement have seriously weakened the appeal of the civil religion to the American masses. To my knowledge, there exists little hard data that would allow us to answer this question with real confidence. There is some information available, however, and it indicates that the civil religion is being celebrated on an increasingly wider national scale. Religious groups which previously prided themselves on their rejection of the American "culture religion" are finding ways of ceremonially appropriating that religion according to their own modes of ritual. One illustration must suffice.

During the week following the burial of President Kennedy, Oliver Graebner distributed a questionnaire to 230 pastors of Missouri Synod Lutheran churches across the United States. The purpose of the questionnaire was to discover the actions of the congregations during the weekend of the death and burial of the President. It inquired into such matters as sermon topics and the pastors' assessment of the impact of the total weekend upon the people. The answers revealed a fairly wide diversity of response but the composite picture was, in Graebner's words, "one of active involvement by the majority of pastors and congregations in a national tragedy; of deep concern for understanding the religious significance of a crisis." A very high percentage of the congregations responded directly and sympathetically to Kennedy and national ideals they believed were represented by him. Many of the sermons disregarded the Missouri Synod Lutheran principle of Biblical exegesis and spoke directly to the topic of the death of the President. About 20 per cent of the sermons were eulogies or bordered on eulogy. And although few of the pastors indicated any feeling of consonance with the Roman ritual at Kennedy's funeral, they did attest that they and their congregations could, through the medium of their own worship services, engage in solemn ceremony dedicated to a fallen national leader. This overall reaction on the part of the Missouri Synod churches is especially significant when measured against the fact that ninety per cent of the respondents had voted for Nixon and that they represented a church that has struggled to speak from within its biblical and doctrinal tradition rather than from within the American cultural context as such. Graebner interpreted the reaction as the sign of a decided Americanization of the church, of a shift from a former position of nonentanglement with the national or political scene to a position of deep involvement in the culture.[18] It also indicates a shift to active participation in the ceremonies of a civil religion that eulogize national leaders and celebrate national themes.

This questionnaire was, of course, too close to Kennedy's death to suggest any long-range effects of the tragedy on the denomination, and its results must be partly explained by the fact that the whole of the nation was literally overwhelmed by a tragedy covered repetitiously and in its minutest details by the mass media. Yet it is a significant enough instance to illustrate the continued appeal of the persons and themes of the civil religion and to demonstrate how the national faith may be celebrated by denominations which treasure the distinctiveness of their own religious traditions. And, I must say, it confirms my own suspicion that the vociferous criticism of the American civil religion has been confined largely to the academy without much effect on the denominations or the masses of American citizens. Freed from narrower definitions and celebrations of the past, the civil religion seems to have worked its way even farther into the public life of the nation and has increased the breadth of its appeal to Americans of many different denominational persuasions.

Still another aspect of the civil religion is discernible in its sacred ceremonies, viz., its *two-fold relation to the values and stated purposes of American society. It has, in other words, offered both uncritical religious sanction and prophetic criticism of the culture.*

The civil religion's complacent sanctification of American society has received considerable attention since the mid-1950s. There is no denying this as one side of the civil religion. It is now a sociological and historical truism that any religion which becomes a vital part of its culture is inclined to maintain the status quo of that culture. When the motifs of the national faith are invoked, therefore, it is frequently for the sake of uncritical endorsement of American values and tasks. As Sidney Mead has pointed out, while Americans have rather consistently viewed themselves as bearers of a special destiny under God, "God, like Alice's Cheshire Cat, has sometimes threatened gradually to disappear altogether or, at most, to remain only a disembodied and sentimental smile." [19] American sacred ceremonies are rife with the invocation of a sentimental God without judgment who smiles innocuously on American undertakings. The Memorial Day ritual which sweeps rural and small city America in the spring of every year has become almost exclusively a collection of ceremonies which extol American war efforts and indiscriminately sanction American actions abroad. Sponsored by local chapters of the VFW and the American Legion, Memorial Day rites call down the blessing of God on all things American, purify every American action abroad with references to the spilled blood of American soldiers, and engage in that curious paradox of glorifying American liberties while at the same time undermining the personal freedom to dissent from and criticize particular national commitments.[20] But one need not turn to the most chauvinist ceremonies to discover the civil religion's uncritical validation of the nation. Following the deaths of Jefferson and Adams, narrow jingoism did not characterize the ceremonies, and the American experiment in self-government was viewed as an enterprise performed on behalf of mankind. Yet an aura of Jeffersonian innocence pervaded the ceremonies, a sense that the nation had landed itself squarely in the Garden before the Fall. Certainly there was no feeling manifest that the nation then deserved, or would deserve in the future, an outbreak of the wrath of an offended God.

Other American sacred ceremonies indicate, however, that the civil religion need not be insensitive to the limitations and shortcomings of the nation, that religious expressions of national ideals need not be uncritical ones. The classic example of the nation's being brought under the severest critical review according to the motifs of the civil religion is Lincoln's second inaugural address. Lincoln, who identified with no particular religious denomination, did adhere to the position that this nation was God's "almost chosen people," and in his second inaugural he pointed vividly to the wrath of God visited upon his people in the form of a basically incomprehensible war. Robert Bellah notes how the theme of the "rights of man from the hand of God" functions in the inaugural address of President Kennedy as a revolutionary lever, an instrument for political and social change.[21] A critical perspective on the nation is also present in the funeral for Robert Kennedy. Archbishop Cooke's reference to the American destiny of freedom was not simply an attempt to lift the sights of Americans beyond the immediacy of a tragic event; it also called attention to the discrepancy between American ideals and American realities. Cooke's eulogy faced up to the contrast between the promise of American liberty and the prejudice and unequal opportunities still afflicting the nation.

The twofoldness of the civil religion's relation to American society characterizes the relation of most religion to its cultural context. The history of religion in the West, as Peter Berger says, has been the story of religion as both a "world-maintaining" and a "world-shaking" force. Religion has functioned as both a sanctifier of the "precarious formations" of human culture and as a relativizer of those cultural formations *sub specie aeternitatis*.[22] Yet we have assumed that the American civil religion has performed only the former function, that as a "culture faith" it has been altogether world-maintaining and culture-sanctifying. And we have assumed further that the churches must be counted on as the preservers of prophetic religion, as the depositories of world-shaking and culture-relativizing religious forces. The sacred ceremonies of the civil religion suggest the dubiety of these assumptions. The "hallmark of the prophetic posture" can and does emerge in the civic ceremonies when devotees of the civil religion are made aware of the tension between national ideals and national actualities.[23] This is not to deny that the civil religion, like any religion which enjoys the fruits of its culture, is always more than a little inclined to sanction blindly dominant cultural values and cover national vices with a pious façade. Instead, one must deny that this has been the *only* function of the civil religion, and one must raise the question whether *any* religion has been immune from falls into provincialism. Both the "priestly" and the "prophetic" roles of religion have been ably performed by church and civil religion alike.

NOTES ─────────────────────────────────

1. W. Lloyd Warner, "An American Sacred Ceremony," *American Life: Dream and Reality* (Chicago: University of Chicago Press, 1962), pp. 5–34. Roger L. Shinn, "Apollo as Ritual," *Christianity and Crisis,* Aug. 4, 1969, p. 223. Cf. the reactions to Lindbergh's flight as celebrations of both a technological and a liturgical event, discussed in John William Ward, *Red, White and Blue* (New York: Oxford University Press, 1969), pp. 21–37.

2. Robert N. Bellah, "Civil Religion in America," *Daedalus* (Winter 1967), pp. 1–21. Sidney E. Mead. "The 'Nation with the Soul of a Church,'" *Church History,* September, 1967, pp. 262–283.

3. Émile Durkheim, *The Elementary Forms of the Religious Life,* J. W. Swain (tr.) (London: George Allen and Unwin, Ltd., 1915), pp. 464 and 475.

4. Merrill D. Peterson, *The Jefferson Image in the American Mind* (New York: Oxford University Press, 1960), p. 3. For many of my remarks on Jefferson and the ceremonies after his death I am heavily indebted to Professor Peterson's book, especially the Prologue and Chapter Eight.

5. *Ibid.,* pp. 420–442.

6. *Ibid.,* p. 6.

7. *Ibid.*

8. All quotations are from a transcript of the eulogy furnished by the office of Archbishop Cooke.

9. Warner, *op. cit.,* p. 32.

10. The phrase is Sidney Mead's, *The Lively Experiment* (New York: Harper & Row, 1963), p. 75. Cf. Russel B. Nye, *This Almost Chosen People* (East Lansing: Michigan State University Press, 1966), pp. 164–165.

11. There is a wealth of historical literature dealing with the American sense of destiny, but see especially Nye, *op. cit.;* Edward M. Burns, *The American Idea of Mission* (New Brunswick, N.J.: Rutgers University Press, 1957); Perry Miller, *Errand into the Wilderness* (Cambridge, Mass.: Belknap Press, 1956); Albert K. Weinberg, *Manifest Destiny* (Gloucester, Mass.: Peter Smith, 1958); Reinhold Niebuhr and Alan Heimert, *A Nation So Conceived* (New York: Charles Scribner's Sons, 1963); Ernest Lee Tuveson, *Redeemer Nation* (Chicago: University of Chicago Press, 1968). For a theological critique of the self-righteousness growing out of the sense of American election see Reinhold Niebuhr, *The Irony of American History* (New York: Charles Scribner's Sons, 1952). For a secular critique of the impact of this mythology on American foreign policy see J. William Fulbright, *The Arrogance of Power* (New York: Random House, 1966), pp. 3–22.

12. See H. Richard Niebuhr, *The Kingdom of God in America* (New York: Harper & Row, 1959), p. 179.

13. James W. Silver, *Confederate Morale and Church Propaganda* (New York: W. W. Norton, 1967), p. 25.

14. See William J. Wolf, *The Religion of Abraham Lincoln* (New York: Seabury Press, 1963); and William A. Clebsch, "Christian Interpretations of the Civil War," *Church History*, June, 1961, pp. 212–222.

15. Benjamin M. Palmer, *National Responsibility Before God, A Discourse Delivered on the Day of Fasting, Humiliation and Prayer,* June 13, 1861 (New Orleans: Price-Current Steam Book & Job Printing Office, 1861). Henry Ward Beecher, "The Battle Set in Array," in J. R. Howard (ed.), *Patriotic Addresses* (New York: Fords, Howard & Hulbert, 1889), pp. 269–288.

16. See Isaac M. Wise, "Our Country's Place in History," a lecture delivered before the Theological and Religious Library Association of Cincinnati, Jan. 7, 1869.

17. The close identification of a view of America's providential role in history and a liberal Protestant interpretation of the Kingdom of God was a vital part of the foreign missions impulse in the late nineteenth and early twentieth centuries. For an illustration of this identification see Washington Gladden, *The Nation and the Kingdom: Annual Sermon Before the American Board of Commissioners for Foreign Missions* (Boston, 1909).

18. Oliver E. Graebner, "Pastor and People at Kennedy's Casket," in Richard D. Knudten (ed.), *The Sociology of Religion: An Anthology* (New York: Appleton-Century-Crofts, 1967), pp. 315–325.

19. Mead, *The Lively Experiment*, p. 152.

20. My own analysis of Memorial Day rites as chauvinist expressions of the civil religion is contained in an article, "Two American Sacred Ceremonies: Their Implications for the Study of Religion in America," to be published in 1970 in *American Quarterly*.

21. Bellah, "Civil Religion in America," p. 4.

22. Peter L. Berger, *The Sacred Canopy* (Garden City, N.Y.: Doubleday & Co., 1967), pp. 97 and 100.

23. This definition of the "hallmark of the prophetic posture," employing the insights of A. N. Whitehead, is offered by Sidney Mead in his article "Reinterpretation in American Church History," in Jerald C. Brauer (ed.), *Reinterpretation in American Church History* (Chicago: University of Chicago Press, 1968), p. 181.

26

Jerald C. Brauer

Images of Religion in America

Two key motifs dominate the various [nineteenth century] European images of religion in America, and both were discerned by De Tocqueville when he stated, "Upon my arrival in the United States, the religious aspect of the country was the first thing that struck my attention; and the longer I stayed there, the more did I perceive the great political consequences resulting from this state of things, to which I was unaccustomed." [1]

That to which he and all other Europeans were unaccustomed was religious liberty or separation of church and state. The other surprise for which he was unprepared was the extent to which this condition of separation worked an opposite effect from that anticipated. He was struck by the centrality of the religious life for the people and for the mores, and he perceived gradually that it had tremendous political consequences. All sensitive visitors made these same observations throughout the nineteenth century.

The first motif, religious liberty, did not receive as much space or emphasis in the various pictures of America. It was always stated, and an effort was made to point out how utterly strange this was for a European. In some sense, this was an unavoidable fact. Europeans had lived through fifteen hundred years of church establishment, so they could think of no other form in which the church could be embodied. At most, they had wrestled with the idea of a gentleman-like establishment in which there would be a minimal toleration for other groups.

Several observers sketched out how this condition came to prevail, but most were content merely to state the bald fact of religious liberty as part of the great American experiment. Philip Schaff, a clergyman, if it is legitimate to count him as a European observer, briefly outlined

From "Images of Religion in America," *Church History*, **30** (March 1961), 2–16, by permission of the author and publisher. Jerald C. Brauer is Dean of the Divinity School, University of Chicago.

the development of religious liberty in America when, in the 1850's, he presented in Germany a series of lectures on America. It was in this early picture of the American scene that he first made clear the fact that there was no option open to Congress except religious liberty. All church historians built on his subsequent statement that Congress was "shut up" to the course of religious liberty.

However, it was not the massive fact of religious liberty itself that struck the European observers. They were far more impressed with its consequences. Visitors came prepared for the worst. A few, such as Mrs. Trollope, found it without searching, but all fair-minded and shrewd observers discovered things totally unexpected. What they discovered became the center of their picture of religion in the American scene; and for some it became the key to understanding the totality of American life. They discovered that religious liberty did not undercut financial support of the churches, destroy a sufficient clergy, breed atheism among the masses, or subvert the moral foundations of the nation. On the contrary, they observed that under the conditions of religious liberty the American experiment produced a people and a culture, including politics, in which religion and morality were absolutely central.

Francis Grund spoke eloquently and typically for many European observers when he said: "Religion has been the basis of the most important American settlements; religion kept their little community together, religion assisted them in their revolutionary struggle; it was religion to which they appealed in defending their rights, and it was religion, in fine, which taught them to prize their liberties. It is with the solemnities of religion that the Declaration of Independence is yet annually read to the people from the pulpit, or that Americans celebrate the anniversaries of the most important events in their history. It is to religion they have recourse whenever they wish to impress the popular feeling with anything relative to their country; and it is religion which assists them in all their national undertakings. The Americans look upon religion as a promoter of civil and political liberty; and have, therefore, transferred to it a large portion of the affection which they cherish for the institutions of their country." [2]

He then pointed to the role of morality and its relation to Christianity by stating that "the deference which the Americans pay to morality is scarcely inferior to their regard for the Christian religion, and is considered to be based upon the latter. The least solecism in the moral conduct of a man is attributed to his want of religion, and is visited upon him as such." [3]

A number of Europeans who noted the unusually close connection between morality and politics in American life were driven to ask the question why. The fact of religious liberty appeared to provide one answer; however, that in itself was not sufficient. In theory, it should have driven religion completely out of American life and undercut all general morality. Something was operative that blocked the theory and produced an opposite result.

Two primary factors were given credit for the reversal of theory. The first, the removal of religion from the political realm, was skillfully developed by both De Tocqueville and Francis Grund. The second, the Puritan strain of religious consciousness, was alluded to by several authors but, unfortunately, never fully developed. De Tocqueville emphasized equality in American life as a deciding factor in helping religion maintain its decisive role in American society. Equality does help to explain how there was a decided shift from religion as a political requirement to religion as a social requirement in the American scene.

De Tocqueville also pointed out that, in America, religion aided in the struggle for independence and helped bring the new society into existence; therefore, it was closely allied to the central habits of the nation.[4] It helped to produce the conditions that resulted in religious liberty and came to appreciate this as the most advantageous of all arrangements. Even a Roman Catholic clergy in America concurred in this judgment. But this, in itself, cannot account for the phenomenal success of religion in America.

Probably the formative factor is that by losing its life as an establishment, religion in America gained both its religious and its political life. By seeking first its spiritual good, all other things were added unto it.[5] So argue Grund and De Tocqueville. They grant that religion exercises but little direct influence on laws and on the details of public opinion in America, but by concentrating on the manners and mores of the community and of domestic life, it regulates the state. This was the way it appeared to the early nineteenth-century European observer, and it was undoubtedly so.

This achieved several distinct advantages for the churches, the Europeans argued. For example, it raised the doctrines of Christianity above the ebb and flow of political arguments and political parties. Law could and would be changed, parties would ascend and fall, but Christianity retained its stronghold in the public mind, unshaken by the vicissitudes of party political strife. By embracing separation of church and state in a democratic society, religion was enabled to live in a new situation and to assume a leading role in the whole of social and political life.

One of the ways religion achieved this eminence was through its inculcation of morality in individuals and in society. Most Europeans were astonished by the fact that under the conditions of separation of church and state and under the prohibition of religious tests for public federal offices, there was a powerful unwritten law pervasively at work.[6] All candidates had to exhibit impeccable personal moral lives, insofar as that could be discerned, and no candidate could deny the importance of religion for the public welfare. Such a requirement was impossible of achievement in European religious establishments.

Grund makes quite clear that in America "private virtue oversteps the highest qualifications in the mind" for public office or simply for general acceptance in the public mind.[7] Only the person practicing certain ethical standards derived from the contemporary Protestant pietistic interpretation of Christianity is truly trustworthy in society. Suddenly, religion has shifted ground—it is no longer directly a political necessity; it is a necessity for the welfare of society. Also, in America, society is prior to and more fundamental than the state; therefore, a social necessity is more powerful or influential than that which is simply a political necessity.

It is recognized by the Europeans that this state of affairs presents a number of difficulties, but, on the whole, they are pleased by what they see—religion and morality flourish and the experiment in political liberty proceeds with orderliness in achieving remarkable progress in a short time. Religion provided the necessary tradition and stability which made the democratic experiment possible. Most of the observers did not doubt this. The lack of inherited responsibilities, of the balance wheel of the aristocracy, and of the multiform institutions of state and society had to be remedied by some force or institutions in American life. Religion played that role. By removing it from political life, it could become the unitive, stable force undergirding all social life.

So religion in America became instrumental in nature and indispensable for the national welfare. It could do this because it had full freedom to indulge in doctrinal disputes within its own circle while, at the same time, all groups were busily engaged in disseminating basic Christian morality throughout the new, young nation. Most European purveyors of images expressed sentiments comparable to De Tocqueville when he said that the many aspects in America "differ in respect to the worship which is due from man to his Creator, but they all agree in respect to the duties which are due from man to man. Each sect adores the Deity in its own peculiar manner, but all the sects preach the same moral law in the name of God." [8]

It is this morality that soon became the common law of the land, and to dispense with that "would not only shake the foundation of society, but eventually subvert the government." [9] It was not only the New England divines and the frontier missionaries [10] who thought that religion was essential for the maintenance of the republic, but sophisticated European scholars and travelers came to the same conclusion. Perhaps all of them were so astonished at the continued successes and stability of the brash young republic that they had to affirm supernatural causes. However, their observations were probably correct purely on sociological and political grounds.

Irreligion could not be tolerated. Under the law it had to be, and was, legally permissible, but an openly avowed agnostic had little chance to win office and influence people.[11] Even the doubter had to admit the public importance of religion, then he too would be trustworthy. What the foreign observers did not detect was the ongoing struggle in the American scene between those who insisted on grounding such morality in revealed truth and those who insisted that it was available through reason and human experience. Neither denied the centrality and necessity of the commonly accepted moral code, but they disagreed violently on its source and maintenance. Most European observers, including De Tocqueville, assumed the necessity and role of revelation as conveyed through the historic churches.

Thus, there early developed the amalgamation of the Christian faith and its morality with the democratic faith of the American people. So closely were these fused in history that they produced what contemporary historians call the American faith. It was widely held by the American people throughout the nineteenth century and well into the present century. Virtually all Americans then and many Americans now would agree with Grund's sentiment when he said: "Change the domestic habits of the Americans, their religious devotion, and their high respect for morality, and it will not be necessary to change a single letter of the Constitution in order to vary the whole form of their government. The circumstances being altered, the same causes would no longer produce the same effects; and it is more than probable, that the disparity which would then exist between the laws and the habits of those whom they are destined to govern, would not only make a different government desirable, but absolutely necessary, to preserve the nation from ruin." [12]

The images of religion in America further developed the implications of religious liberty by asserting that an additional consequence was a more thoroughly churched nation. Because ministers were on their own and congregations had to seek their own financial support, they had to produce or die. Strangely enough, most European commentators thought highly of this. There were more ministers, more churches, and more people in churches. What was lacking in quality, some thought, was made up in quantity. Furthermore, this situation compelled the minister to deal directly with the people. By the very nature of the situation, the ministers could not ignore their people or their needs. Hence, religion in America is concerned with not only the future life but very much with the life of people here and now. Herein is to be found one of the several bases for activism in the American churches.

Unfortunately, no European observer plumbed a similar depth in analyzing the role of the religious heritage or the nature of Christian experience in accounting for the triumph of religion under the conditions of religious liberty. All mention it in passing, so it becomes a part of the image, but at best it remains only a streak of light in the foreground.

In commenting on the moral vigor of the American people, W. L. George credited this to the Puritan tradition through which America "created in her own mind an aristocracy of God-fearing men and women. She still tends to estimate people according to their morals." [13] Hugo Munsterberg also recognized that religion never could have shifted from being a political requirement to becoming a social obligation unless there had been a "deep religious consciousness living in the people . . . a religiously inclined population." [14] He traces this strain to the New England Puritans. Perhaps church historians should not expect too much at this point. Europeans generally recognized the importance of the religious forces; they did not bother to analyze them.

On the other hand, De Tocqueville exhibited his superior perceptive powers in posing several basic questions concerning the role of religion under democracy and religious liberty. These questions are again being posed by W. Herberg, S. Mead, H. R. Niebuhr, and a number of other historians. It is remarkable that De Tocqueville raised them so early in the nineteenth century. However, he did not raise these simply as questions; he made certain observations concerning the state of religion in America and he deduced certain conclusions based on particular assumptions concerning equality and democracy. In some of these he proved wrong both for his own day and for the future. In other comments, he demonstrated a rare capacity to diagnose correctly the directions in which Christianity in America would move.

De Tocqueville was correct in noting the paradoxical consequences of equality in a democratic society and in discerning certain reflections of this in religious life. Equality led to the simultaneous tendencies to the elevation of human reason in the autonomy of the individual and to the prohibition of autonomous thought by the opinions and the will of the majority. He shrewdly pointed out the consequences of the latter for Christianity in America, but he did not discern the former operating along with it.

In a remarkable way, he developed the concept of the unquestioned basis of religion for American culture. Because Christianity gave birth to Anglo-American society, it is fused with all the habits of the nation. Removed from the political sphere, it has not been subject to the basic inquiry of society.[15] Nobody has to defend it nor dare attack it. It is believed without discussion; therefore, many of its moral insights are taken for granted by all society and form the basis of that society.

Hence, Christianity is held, either implicitly or explicitly, by the vast majority of individuals in American society.

De Tocqueville then correlates this insight with his views on the consequence of equality for majority opinion. If equality drives each man to assert the sufficiency of his own reason against external principles of authority, and if he finds the exercise of his reason sufficient to meet his practical daily needs, he still requires some final court of appeal in which he can test his reason. Ultimately, he argues, a democratic society will locate this in the will of the majority. Common opinion becomes the arbiter and judge. Because the majority of the people hold the Christian faith, or at least its morality, implicitly or explicitly, this majority provides the unquestioned basis guaranteeing its acceptance by the members of society. To go against public opinion on this matter would be a foolish act in the American democratic society.

With keen insight De Tocqueville notes certain derivative elements in the image of religion in America. For one thing, he points out that just as Americans adopt many theories on philosophy, morals, and politics on public trust, without inquiry, so too "religion herself holds sway there, much less as a doctrine of revelation than as a commonly received opinion." [16] Furthermore, he is convinced that this is known and understood by the American clergy, who never take on any but absolutely necessary conflicts with the opinions of the majority. The result is that religion retains the full support of public opinion. [17]

De Tocqueville foresees basic difficulties for American society on this point when he says: "Faith in public opinion will become a species of religion there, and the majority its ministering prophet." Several of these predictions appear to be actualized in the American religious scene if the generalizations concerning organization men are at all applicable to the churches. A vast number of complicating factors have intervened between De Tocqueville's age and ours; nevertheless, the American faith in faith, the identification of American morality with the Christian faith, the public acceptance of this general religiousness—all of these derive, in part, from the factors which he outlined. The ease with which Protestant evangelical-pietistic Christianity merged into and became identified with the American faith rests in part upon the prevalence of equality in the American scene. Its influence was felt both in politics and in religion.

In one important aspect, De Tocqueville's picture of religion in America and its future was incorrect. He was convinced that in a democratic society where equality of conditions prevails, an instinctive disbelief in the supernatural will occur. Men will look to themselves, to their reason, and their experience to judge things aright; thus, they will develop a suspicion of all modern prophets, will "not easily give credence to divine missions" and certainly would establish no new religions.[18] He was undoubtedly correct in observing a new emphasis placed upon human reason and experience as an arbiter in all matters, including religious affairs. This did have vast consequences for Protestantism in America and did, at times, conflict with the other factor, public opinion, as the final arbiter. But it did not prevent the appearance of new religions, nor did it discourage the activity of modern prophets or heap abuse on special divine missions. On the contrary, nineteenth-century American Protestantism produced several new religions with their own modern prophets with special divine missions. Revelation was encountered in many ways through many forms and believed by large numbers of people.

Several things produced consequences in a direction opposite to that anticipated by De Tocqueville. First, the molding power of public opinion in religion was stronger than even he had observed and anticipated. It actually outweighed or gave form to the new-found emphasis on individual reason and experience. The latter did not undercut the possibility of founding new religions because reason could not operate easily beyond the bounds made possible by public opinion. Thus, as he observed, religion, including modern prophets, really went unquestioned. The bounds of the religiously possible were never really discussed at depth or with consistency by the new-found instrument of reason. Where it was tried, in early nineteenth-century deism, it ran aground against public opinion rallied by the churches.

Also, solitary reason had sufficient problems to handle in all other aspects of life without tackling the ultimate questions of religion. It exercised itself on politics, economics, personal and national survival, on the frontier, on education, and on a host of other issues. As De Tocqueville pointed out, all cultures have an unquestioned bedrock on which they build. They cannot raise questions pertaining to every aspect of life. Involved in a vigorous effort to subdue the wilderness and to plant a society, the democratic citizen had neither the time nor the inclination to question the nature and role of revelation in religion. In fact, he found it necessary to leave it unquestioned. So, there were many examples of religious prophets acclaimed, divine missions believed in, and several new religions established. These forces plus the religious heritage of the American people coalesced to produce a strange combination of the free exercise of reason and a basic anti-intellectualism which has since marked Christianity in America. This one key aspect of the image of religion in America was apparently missed by the most astute of all observers.

Thus, a wide variety of European observers painting their images of religion in America developed as their two central and coordinate themes, religious liberty and the beneficial consequences of this for both political and religious life in America. As they worked out these two themes, they developed generalizations that are almost identical with the standard interpretations employed by church historians today. But they did not complete their pictures with these two themes. Almost all European visitors were equally struck by the sheer activity in the American churches and the full participation of the laity. This, too, was quite unlike their European experience. Mrs. Trollope detested the hustle and bustle of the clergy and laity alike and concluded it was hardly dignified or worthy of the Christian religion. Almost all other observers were impressed by this activism and sought reasons to explain it.

No single observer presented a coherent and consistent explanation. They usually pointed to the reality and supplied several comments. It is possible, however, to piece together a fairly convincing explanation drawn from a variety of insights provided by Grund, Munsterberg, Raeder, De Tocqueville and others. None of them sought an explanation in the nature of the religious faith professed by believers. Perhaps they thought this was the preserve of the church historians. All of them agreed that American society *in toto* was marked by a tumultuous activity and "incessant excitement" that "gives to the Americans an air of busy inquietude, for which they have often been pitied by Europeans; but which . . . constitutes their principal happiness."[19] The churches simply participate in this restless activity and seek to employ it to their ends.

To carry out this activity and to achieve their goals of action, Americans founded countless associations and organizations. In a society based on the equality of all individuals and not on the power of government, people have freedom to pursue their particular and collective goals; therefore they must band together to achieve these goals beyond the capacity of any individual. Thus, the whole of American society is engaged in associations to pursue a wide variety of goals. The churches are not an exception to this but the best example of it. Francis Grund and De Tocqueville noted the tremendous number of associations created by the churches, functioning both in and outside of the churches to achieve the moral goals of religion as understood and practiced in America. The churches themselves are such associations under the system of religious liberty. It is this insight which Professor Mead has developed so persuasively in his analysis of the church in America as a denomination, a new form over against the older church or sect concepts.

If the churches themselves exist in America to achieve specific goals determined both by their nature and by the action they carry on, then churches are bound to exhibit activity beyond anything previously witnessed in Christian history. De Tocqueville is convinced that a further impetus to activism is given by the amalgamation of religion and patriotism in the American scene. This is but another facet of the unusual relation that exists between religion and society in America.

He refers to "missionaries of Christian civilization" who seek to preserve liberty by extending the sway of the Christian religion in the new
western states. These are the New Englanders and circuit riders, who
sought to Christianize the West, of whom De Tocqueville said that in
them, "you meet with a politician when you expect to find a priest." [20]

The churches reflected the activistic nature of society in their own
special ways. Munsterberg spoke for a number of other Europeans
when he commented on the this-worldly bent of the sermons. The
minister usually spoke on a topic of immediate concern to his members. The similes and metaphors were borrowed from every-day and
frequently from vulgar life. Anecdotes were freely used and given in
colloquial form. The whole purpose of the sermon appeared to be an
attempt to confront the person in the midst of his daily vexations,
problems, and possibilities. The sermon was geared for immediate
response and action in daily affairs.

Also the Europeans were aware of dimensions in churchly activity
not usually found in their home lands. Churches in America, on the
frontier, in villages, or in the cities, functioned as social clubs. They
carried on a wide variety of activities, such as meals, libraries, picnics,
raffles, social games, lecture circles, church clubs, schools for children,
and a host of other activities. To a European, much of this appeared
secular, or even ridiculous in the eyes of a Mrs. Trollope.

But most Europeans understood that the churches had "woven
themselves by countless threads into the web of daily life."
Consequently, they exemplified the activism of American society more
fully than any other institution, including politics. Europeans were
amazed at the achievement of this activistic spirit as it molded the
fundamental character of nineteenth-century American society. They
were particularly impressed and, at times, depressed by the pervasive-
ness of the American Sabbath day. Grund thought it the most democratic of all Christian institutions because all aristocratic distinctions
of birth or commercial achievement were leveled. He was surprised
by its hold on the American society. Europeans were equally astonished at the achievements of temperance work, Sunday school activity,
societies for moral reform, and the other benevolent associational
achievements in America. Truly, activism was a distinctive mark of
religion in America.

Revivalism also caught the attention of the Europeans, especially the
Continentals. They understood revivalism to be something unusual
and definitive about religion in America. Many of them wrote elaborate reports on camp meetings or on revivals in city churches.
Munsterberg saw it as a stimulation of the emotions that filled a void
in the lives of the masses. Deprived of the splendor of monarchial
celebrations, lacking the stimulation of Roman Catholic pomp and
drama, caught in a drab and hard life of complete or relative isolation,

revivalism provided people with relief from deadening reality. So spoke Munsterberg the psychologist.

De Tocqueville saw the sociological beyond the psychological in this segment of the image. He sensed that people endured hardship and deprivation on the frontier because they lived in perpetual hope. They were very much oriented toward the future achievement of their wants. He was pleased with the fact that people turned their attention away from promoting only their worldly welfare in the new world to a concern for their eternal welfare in the world to come. He was convinced that a most effective truce was worked out between these two drives, and he saw revivalism and the circuit rider as the forces that maintained the necessary balance between the two. It was in his discussion of revivalism that he noted the presence in American society of men filled with a prophetic enthusiasm unmatched in Europe. Here, too, he noted the emergence of peculiar sects on the American scene.

All European observers, therefore, counted revivalism as one of the basic motifs in the American religious image. Unfortunately, they offered little in the way of interpretation or analysis of the phenomenon. They did not seek to understand the nature of revivalism, its sources in the Christian faith and its development in the American scene. They alluded to the fact that it provided a means of winning people to the churches, but they never developed this insight that became so central in Professor Sweet's interpretation of revivalism. It is surprising that De Tocqueville did not attempt to understand it as a natural means through which a vast public could express its deepest feelings about religion—a great equalizer with a basic common denominator of experience. This would be a most fruitful line of inquiry to pursue within the context of De Tocqueville's framework of interpretation—the impact of equality on religious life in America.

A fourth facet of the images of religion in America is encountered in most of the European observations. The presence of limitless space with vast untouched resources is pointed up as a fundamental reality in American experience. These men knew nothing of a frontier hypothesis, but they were fully aware that the experiences of Europeans in a primeval forest did something to the Europeans and culture. Crevecoeur, who wrote most extensively on this, saw the experience as psychologically and physically transforming. He wrote of the creation of fear and uncertainty in the minds of those who face the endless forest with its unknown enemies. He also idealized it as the opportunity for a self-sustaining cleansing life that produced industry, honesty, and contentment.

De Tocqueville saw the frontier as an elemental fact in social experience—an opportunity to begin life over without first going through the horrors and excesses of revolution. The presence of a virgin continent to conquer provided the Americans with the necessary locale to attempt the great experiment of liberty and equality.

Both Europeans saw consequences for the religious life. The frontier made possible the development of every conceivable sect without creating open warfare in American society. Crevecoeur likens religious zeal to gunpowder in an enclosed situation in Europe where it inevitably explodes. In America, it evaporates in the limitless space or burns harmlessly in the open air. He was convinced that this situation promoted a healthy indifference that eliminated all nonessentials in religion and forced the teaching of the bare essentials. These sounded suspiciously like the basic moral virtues that all Europeans agreed undergirded American society.

The final touches on the images of religion in America are provided by a confluence of factors that are clearly interdependent and, perhaps, even interchangeable. Most Europeans noted that American life, including religion, was deeply colored by an anti-historical tendency, and at the same time it was oriented to the present and was perfectionistic. Again, De Tocqueville provides most of the insights, but others commented on these facts as well.

The Frenchman traced the presence of all these factors in American life primarily to equality, but he also understood that religion helped produce and reflected these qualities. Aristocracy, he argued, always upholds the position and place of given religions, and predisposes the mind to accept one particular faith. It holds tradition in highest esteem and is inclined to place intermediate powers between God and man. Thus it must employ history and the arts as media through which tradition is carried and through which mediation between God and man occurs. In America, for several reasons, democracy and equality did not undercut religion; however, they did simplify it and diverted attention from all mediation and secondary agents to the Supreme Power itself. Thus was produced a distinctive aversion to the past, to that which is ancient. Attention turned to the present, to man in his concrete situation. However, what he did not observe was the consequent humanizing of the divine through an unrelenting pressure to confine the divine to an ethical dimension.

A corollary of the anti-historical attitude was belief in the perfectibility of man. This arose from two primary sources and made its impact on every phase of life. Equality engendered a belief in the autonomy of individual reason. Experience proved that reason can be improved and developed in individuals and in society. Why should it not be capable of infinite improvement? Furthermore, as man tests, discards, and refines his goals and ideals, "an image of an ideal perfection, forever on the wing, presents itself to the human mind." This image undergoes refinement and improvement; hence, man himself must be "endowed with an indefinite faculty of improvement."

De Tocqueville made the point that religion in America never contradicted the basic ideals held by the majority of the public if those ideals did not undercut the faith; thus, it was only too easy for religious beliefs in the American scene to coalesce with the anti-historical, perfectionistic, present-oriented tendencies of public opinion. It is difficult to determine whether the particular form of religious belief present at that moment hastened the adoption of these ideas by the majority or whether these beliefs held by the majority reinterpreted the nature of the Christian faith as professed in America. This in itself would be an exciting problem for the church historian to pursue.

From this brief analysis of the images of religion constructed by non-clerical Europeans, it is obvious that through their special perspectives they noted most of the factors that church historians have since generalized as distinctively American. They achieved, to a remarkable degree, what recent church historians have called for. They developed insights and generalizations not based on the assumptions operative among European church historians. The reason is simple enough—though they reflected the habits and mores of European Christians, they did not carry the systematic and necessarily sophisticated theological assumptions of the church historians. This provided the observers both with sufficient continuity to seek to understand Christianity in America and with enough freedom to recognize and appreciate utterly strange and unusual developments.

Is it possible that they introduced the sociological perspective into the discipline of church history in America? Or, did they only inadvertently reflect that perspective as they sought to make sense of the peculiar developments of Christianity in America? In either case, their importance as interpreters cannot be underestimated. We are all indebted to them for calling our attention to the distinctiveness of the following elements in Christianity in America—religious liberty, the centrality of morality and success of the church under the system of separation, the universality of activism and revivalism, and the predominance of an anti-intellectual, anti-historical spirit coupled with a faith in the perfectibility of man.

Several of these insights, particularly as developed by De Tocqueville, never have been worked out adequately. For example, his conception of equality provides us with a point of departure for a much more sophisticated and subtle analysis of the success and continuance of revivalism in American life. If this were combined with a penetrating theological interpretation it would be most welcome. Also, sufficient use of De Tocqueville's generalizations on equality in relation to the autonomy of reason has not been made by church historians. The different ways this was worked out in relation to religion in the West and in the East would be most instructive. The Europeans remind us that present generalizations concerning American faith in general, the faith in faith, the domestication of Christianity by Americanism, "other-directed" Christians and the utilitarian activism of our churches, must seek their explanation in additional factors beyond modern technocracy and urbanization. We have not yet exhausted the implications of these European images for our interpretation of Christianity in America.

The obvious weakness of these observers is their greatest strength. They saw these factors apart from the nature of the religious faith and the historic community that nurtured and nursed it. They did not probe the sources of the particular religious experience out of which the Americans came; hence, their observations must always be placed in a wider context by the church historian. If the task of the American church historian is to analyze and to interpret the life of the Christian community in the American scene, he will find the insights of these European observers exceedingly provocative and stimulating. Nevertheless, he will not find in them a framework sufficiently broad and deep to make sense of the Christian community in America in terms both of its continuities and its discontinuities with the church universal. It is at this point that the creative task of the American church historian confronts our generation.

NOTES

1. A. De Tocqueville, *Democracy in America,* trans. H. Reeve (New York: J. E. H. G. Langley, 1841), I, 337.

2. F. J. Grund, *The Americans in Their Moral, Social, and Political Relations* (London: Longman, Rees, Orme, Brawn, Green & Longman, 1837), I, 294.

3. *Ibid.,* p. 295.

4. De Tocqueville, *op. cit.,* II, 68.

5. *Ibid.,* I, 342.

6. J. Bryce, *The American Commonwealth* (Chicago: C. H. Sergel & Co., 1892), II, 596. De Tocqueville, *op. cit.,* I, 332.

7. Grund, *op. cit.,* I, 297 f.

8. De Tocqueville, *op. cit.,* 331.

9. Grund, *op. cit.,* 298.

10. De Tocqueville, *op. cit.,* 335.

11. Grund, *op. cit.,* 281.

12. *Ibid.,* p. 307.

13. W. L. George, *Hail, Columbia!* (London: Chapman & Hall, Ltd., 1923), p. 112.

14. H. Munsterberg, *The Americans,* trans. E. B. Halt (New York: McClure, Phillip & Co., 1907), p. 500.

15. De Tocqueville, *op. cit.*, II, 6 f.
16. *Ibid.*, p. 12.
17. *Ibid.*, p. 28.
18. *Ibid.*, pp. 10–11.
19. Grund, *op. cit.*, I, 11.
20. De Tocqueville, *op. cit.*, I, 335.

27

Bayless Manning

The Purity Potlatch:
An Essay on Conflicts of
Interest, American Government,
and Moral Escalation

Particularly since 1953, when the issue exploded noisily with the nomination of Charles Wilson, president of General Motors, to be Secretary of Defense,[1] the Senate Armed Services Committee in confirmation hearings has invested hundreds of hours in enquiries into the personal fiscal affairs of nominees to posts in the Department of Defense. Major studies of conflicts of interests were conducted by public and private agencies in the late 50's.[2] Among the earliest official acts of President Kennedy was the appointment of a special three-men Advisory Panel on Ethics and Conflicts of Interest in Government, and the report of the Panel was made the basis for a special Presidential Message to the Congress on the subject.[3] In response to these events and the President's message, Congress in 1962 completely overhauled the federal conflict of interest laws,[4] but agitation for further revision, especially of the rules applicable to the lawmakers themselves, continues.[5] The executive agencies are pouring out new regulations on the matter.[6] At this writing, controversy rages in New York over alleged conflicts of interest on the part of state legislators, and a distinguished public commission has just produced, with much publicity, a new report calling for reforms.[7] A similar uproar is under way in Connecticut.[8]

Reflecting even more vividly the new station of conflicts of interests

---

From Bayless Manning, "The Purity Potlatch: An Essay on Conflicts of Interest, American Government, and Moral Escalation," *The Federal Bar Journal*, **24** (Summer 1964), 241–248, by permission of the author and the Federal Bar Association. Bayless Manning is Dean of the Law School at Stanford University.

in the public eye is the ever-growing list of political *causes célèbres* and career casualties centering upon it. Friends of the TVA and public power could not halt the Dixon-Yates contract, but disclosure of a possible conflict of interest on the part of one consultant to the Budget Bureau did the trick.[9] When the TFX contract was under determined assault in the fall of 1963, a similar attempt was made, the TFX opponents calling into question the former law firm association of the Undersecretary of Defense. In this instance the attack was not successful, but everyone knew that conflict of interest had enough fire power for the job if it could be made to go off. Public accusation of conflicts of interest in President Truman's White House circle gave the Republicans in 1952 a vote-winning opportunity to call for a clean-up of the "Mess in Washington." In 1953 the winds of the Wilson matter blew to gale proportions, and in addition the newly selected Chairman of the National Party suddenly resigned; in 1958 the Secretary of the Air Force left office under conflict of interest fire; and in 1958 the same slim dart found the heel of Sherman Adams, fleet of foot. In the brief time given to the Kennedy administration, at least one Defense Department resignation was suddenly filed because of indications of conflict of personal interests. And now, only a few months out in the Johnson administration, the name of the former secretary to the majority in the Senate is known to every newspaper reader in the country.

I do not summon these recollections out of relish for old dirt. Exactly the contrary. The significant feature of these nation-rocking exposés is that, so far as is known from the record, none of the men involved actually *did* anything demonstrably injurious to the public treasury or the public interest. None figured in an alleged Teapot Dome or anything resembling it. The charge was only that the combination of their economic circumstances and their offices did not *look* just right. The *worst* allegation that could be made against them was that they held an economic interest or received gifts that *might*, upon a certain set of assumptions about the conduct of their office and about human nature generally, tempt them in the future to act contrarily to the public interest in certain limited situations.

Now, that would seem to be pretty pale stuff for a populace hardened by frontier history, TV, and the drugstore magazine rack. Without rattling a teaspoon, any Thackeray heroine could accept as a topic for conversation so faint a hint of a statistical possibility of an unexecuted impropriety. Yet in our present political environment it is enough to force even the mightiest from office. Today all tremble at the charge "conflict of interest."

What has happened to bring about this phenomenon, to make the essentially subtle subject of conflicting interests so fascinating to the public? I believe the answer lies quite deep in the special character of American politics, and that it is worth digging out.

Moral Inflation in Our Politics—
the Potlatch

As a nation, we like our politics neat. The heroes still wear white hats, and the villains black ones; we do not like to get them mixed up, and we decidedly do not like the players to wear gray hats. A foreign observer noting this might conclude that the American must be a stupid fellow. How can he not know that men are complex, fail to understand that good and evil dwell in all men, and be incapable of summoning the maturity required to accept a world of grays for what it is? But the American is decidedly not a stupid fellow. He is perfectly aware that the fellowman whom he knows in his neighborhood, his office, his church, and his club is neither a distillate of perfidy unalloyed nor a crystal of virtue unblemished. It is not here that the American and the foreign observer differ. The difference lies rather in the American's unusual, perhaps unique, conception of what his political process is about.

We look to our political process not only to run the government, but also to perform other vitally important social and spiritual functions for us. In our Democracy we look to the political process to identify, produce, and articulate many of our ideals, our goals, our standards, our heroes, our examples for our society, for ourselves, and for our young. In substantial measure, the American looks upon his politics as a Morality Play. Our national political conventions every four years are massive comings together for spiritual mutual support and communion, revival meetings for endless reassertions of our national moral symbols and rededication to those elevating ideals. For just this reason, the Democratic and Republican conventions are almost identically devoid of programmatic content while new parties are soon rejected by the body electorate as redundant or, if organized around a program or position, as an incompatible foreign engraftment.

To the extent that our politics partake of the nature of a Morality Play, they have inevitably required, and generated, a set of theatrical conventions as arbitrary, and as acceptable, as those of any dramatic form. The vocabulary of our politics conforms to its role as a national Morality drama. That vocabulary is formal, dogmatic, simplified, symbolic, repetitive, and goal-setting; it is not descriptive and must not be thought of as being descriptive. And the actors in the political drama must, as in epic drama, appear as more than life-size, establishing, declaring, and appearing to live in accordance with, standards that are not of this world. We therefore demand ultimate moral pronouncements from our parties and our officials. We beatify or apotheosize our former Presidents, feeling the need for unifying national moral

norms and having no national established church to do the job or to
produce national saints. We are terribly concerned at a candidate's
divorce because we are worried about our own divorce rate, and
because in our Democracy we cannot be concerned about a king's
divorce.[10]

The foreign observer encountering our politics for the first time
deserves some sympathy; he cannot be expected to know that he is at
the theatre. At the *bunrakuza* he would not think it peculiar that the
audience seems not to detect the black-clad puppeteers. At Epidauros,
he would not complain at the watchers for not protesting that the
masks are wood, that the tall gods are men on clogs, and that Iphe-
genia is male. But at San Francisco and Atlantic City this summer, not
knowing what he is observing, he is apt to perceive, and perceiving
announce as discovery, that the party positions are more platitude
than platform, that the non-stop speeches mainly rehearse the virtues
of the national saints, the flag, freedom, and purity and denounce the
unprincipled character of the opposition party.

Thus we look to our elected officials for moral affirmations. This
does not mean, however, that the American voter thinks his Congress-
man a moral giant. Indeed, he often thinks of him not as a "government official"—a term of respect—but as a "politician"—a pejorative.
We are bewilderingly ambivalent in our split vision of our officials—as
religionists are apt to be about their priests. But when it comes to
official public pronouncements, this double image makes no difference.
When we are thinking of our officials in their role as public agents of
governance, respect and authority, we demand that they speak with
sobriety and uncompromising morality; when we suspect them of the
worst, we demand that they constantly reassure us that they know
where morality lies, and are dedicated to it. In either view of the
matter, the public official in the United States must in his public
dialogue take his stand foresquare and often for Absolute Rectitude.
If presidents, senators, congressmen, and governors suspect that this
world cannot be operated on such a simplified basis, they are expected
to keep their suspicions to themselves—and they generally do.

Some would remark that this is a strange way to run a government.
Perhaps it is. But the United States has turned in a record of governmental accomplishment over the past 175 years that is unapproached
in world history, and in some measure, at least, its achievements are
attributable to its insistence upon an elevated moral vision of itself
and its officials—an insistence upon a moral reach that exceeds the
practical grasp. Central to our political history has been the conviction that political man can be good, or made good, that reform is
worthwhile, and that problems can be solved if addressed with faith
and energy. To the observer from many other cultures, all this seems
Americanly naïve, amusing and, if not downright juvenile, at least

unrealistic; and he has sometimes been moved to leap to his feet to declare his low opinion of simplistic success and his preference for sophisticated failure. But whatever the merits or demerits of the American way of doing politics, the present point is simply to note that this is the character of American politics, and that it substantially affects the problem at hand—conflicts of interest.

For a major consequence of this special character of our politics is that in matters touching public morality we are inflation-prone.

So long as our extraordinary Two-Party Non-System blesses us with a massive majority committed to an ideological center, American elections are won and lost in a very few ways only. The main avenues to success are two—public dissatisfaction with a major irritant, such as a depression or unpopular war (these sorespots are always called "issues" in our political parlance) is one, and personal charisma is the other. When a candidate and a party have both, as Roosevelt did in 1932 and Eisenhower did in 1952, they win overwhelmingly. When these are not present—and they seldom are for the local candidate, and cannot be manufactured—the next most effective approach in the American political environment is to interpret the contest in terms of the great Morality Play. The opposition, and especially the Ins, must be made to be personal scoundrels and dishonest men; that they might be proven to be incompetent or inert is not enough; they must be shown to have been morally delinquent—deficient in patriotism, domestic habits, or fiscal responsibility. One may not always win with this argument, even when there are some supporting facts for the charges, but it offers the most promising strategy and is therefore regularly tried. Conversely, of course, the political spokesman must himself project a spotless purity, dazzling to the eye. What follows is something like a duel in public—a purity duel between the political contestants.

All public duels are substantially of the same character in every society. The theme of the duel is some personal attribute or skill highly prized by the society. It may be physical courage and personal honor-pride as in Scott and Dumas; it may be one's command over magic as in Southwestern Indian medicine-man duels; or it may be, as in the calypso singing duels, the divine gift of lyric creativity. In the Alaskan Tlingit potlatch, the virtue at stake is spirituality and generosity coupled with bravado and display. The duelists in the potlatch take alternate turns in destroying those things that are of most value to them, the winner gaining great community prestige by reducing himself to material ruin.

All such duel systems are inflation-prone. They tend to escalate. It is difficult for any participant to spot when he is a notch below his opponent; it is difficult for both participants to recognize a standoff; and it is difficult to get either participant to begin to climb down. If the participants were not playing in public, they would often find it possible to limit their engagement with each other. In the case of the potlatch, they could maintain their self-respect and their property as well. But when the duel is fought out in public view, and when the prize of power and position hinges on the public's estimate of who won the contest, escalation and rigidity are inevitable.

And thus it is with morality duels in American politics. Like bomb-rattling, virtue-rattling escalates. To permit a moral march to be stolen on you is exceedingly dangerous. When in the 1952 controversy over the Nixon campaign fund, candidate Eisenhower prescribed the "hound's tooth" standard, Nixon produced his "Checkers" performance. The next move was up to Stevenson. He responded with objective irrelevance but symbolic political relevance by publishing a list of his personal assets.[11] Since then, the practice has slowly begun to spread, and if one political candidate publicly lists his personal holdings it is very difficult for his opponent not to do the same. If there ever was a rational reason why this should be done, that reason is soon overtaken by the better reason that one must do it to stay in the purity potlatch. When the ante goes up, one must at least match it.

In a somewhat different form, the same process may be seen typically at work in the practice of the Senate Armed Services Committee to require Defense Department appointees coming before it to dispose of their stockholdings in companies doing business with the Pentagon. The rule is announced as an Absolute Principle. The Committee is fond of expressing its concern not only with actual conflicts of interest between the public duties of Defense Department officials and their personal stockholdings, but with the appearances in the matter; "Caesar's wife" appears often in the transcripts of the hearings. And, nearly always, a small shareholding is treated as being as offensive as a large one, a minor Defense Department contractor as being as dangerous as a major one.[12] No senator is anxious to take a public stand in favor of anything less than Absolute Purity—however small the practical risks involved might be. Further, there is the matter of precedent. Interrogations on stockholdings by government officials were almost unknown before the Wilson controversy in 1953. But once the issue was brought out, it became difficult for any committee member to retire it again. As a consequence, every Defense Department nominee since 1953 has had to run the gauntlet of the Committee's enquiry and suffer its Draconian divestment rule. There is considerable evidence that no one on the Committee likes the situation, but no one knows how to change it. This political susceptibility to moral escalation explains in part out present national fascination with conflicts of interest.

This is not the whole explanation, however. Throughout American history it has often been possible to fetch up evidence of casual, if not fraudulent, standards of public trust on the part of government officials. In the last century, a Vanderbilt could refuse to contribute to campaign funds on the ground that it was cheaper to buy the legislator after he was elected. Overt bribery was, if not common, at least not uncommon. And it was generally assumed and understood (as it still is in many countries and a few places in the United States) that men who live the political life somehow line their bank accounts in the process. The situation in the United States today is quite different. Though some may find it surprising, the fact is that in this country we are currently living in an era of unexampled honesty in public adminis- tration. Evolution of modern administrative techniques for fiscal control, development of a professional sense in the civil service, virtual elimination of the spoils system, spread of competitive bidding, in- crease in public education, enrichment of the economy, and other basic shifts in the national political organism have reduced blatant pecula- tion of federal funds almost to the vanishing point. By now the governmental record is much better than that of private business in coping with the problem of the dishonest employee.[13] World War II and the Korean War saw no great procurement rackets of the kind that were spawned by the Civil War, the Spanish-American War, and, to a lesser degree, World War I. When it is considered that the Department of Defense alone has dispensed some 686 billion dollars since the end of World War II, that federal, state, and municipal budgets currently aggregate over 200 billion dollars per year, and that there are over 9,000,000 people on government payrolls, excluding the uniformed military, the record for administrative integrity achieved by modern American governments almost passes belief.

The general improvement in governmental fiscal responsibility poses something of a problem to American political practitioners. How can the Outs convincingly demonstrate the perfidy of the Ins when thieves, grafters, and suborners stubbornly refuse to reveal themselves to be actively at work in the In-administration? There are only two avenues open. One is to blow up isolated instances of impropriety so that they appear as illustrations of massive, pervasive hidden corruption. This is attempted regularly. The other avenue is more subtle. If the facts will not make out a case of moral deficiency by accepted standards, the standards must be escalated to a point where facts can be found that *will* make out a deficiency; and the public must be educated to be horrified by the resulting new sins in substantially the same degree that they were horrified by the old. This process is constantly going on about us.

As the old government briber-contact man—the fixer—has faded into history, the operator who for pay steers an outsider around the bu- reaucratic labyrinth of Washington comes to be called by the vaguely invidious tag "Five Per Center," and soon earns a place in the public mind close alongside Albert Fall. The public understands the fixer, but how many know what it is that makes the Five Per Center such a menace? When it proves difficult to find a suborned Commissioner, it may be discovered that one has received "*ex parte* communications" and should therefore be put in the stocks. What part of the public understands what this new sin is? If bribery cannot be shown, perhaps the public can be persuaded that it is as bad for the government employee to receive Christmas presents. If government officials are fired in disgrace at once *either* for taking a bribe *or* for accepting a gift, how long can the public be expected to distinguish between the two transactions? And if instances cannot be found where an official has diverted public moneys to his own pocket, coals can be heaped on the head of the official who *might* someday be tempted to divert public moneys to his pocket because his personal economic interests and those of the government *might* someday conflict.

In the public mind, to receive a gift or to have a conflict of interest has by now been equated with venality; a government official in a position of conflicting interests is a kind of a crook. What else is the public to conclude when Senate committees in confirmation proceedings, the Congress through legislation, the executive by regulations, and the Supreme Court [14] in chorus denounce in the most absolute terms the public vice of conflicting interests? And when no modulating or qualifying voice can be heard in our ethotropic political environment?

The process by which yesterday's peccadillo becomes today's enormity has been sketched here metaphorically. Such transitions in public attitudes are not consciously brought on by master manipulators of American political psychology. The change comes about unconsciously, over time, and as a result of millions of signal impulses and receptions in the political interplay. And the change is fully as attributable to shifts in what the populace will listen to as to what new broadcasts are beamed to them. Moreover, those who are broadcasting political communications—officials, candidates, commentators, courts, scholars—are themselves among the listeners and indeed are apt to be ineffective politically if they are not. This blurring between the communicator and the receptor means that the political communicator does not need consciously to plan and manipulate his output; as a member of his own audience, he almost automatically transmits what they are willing, or want, to listen to. A more formal description of the change that has brought conflicts of interest to the front page of the newspapers would give greater emphasis to the role of audience reaction and dilute the implication that those in active political life have consciously arranged the evolution.

But the substance remains the same. Conflicts of interest have become a modern political obsession in this country, first, because American politics is highly susceptible to morality escalation and, second, because we are living in an era of unparallelled honesty in public administration when we can afford the luxury of worrying about public harms before they happen.

NOTES

1. The incident is reviewed in *Conflict of Interest and Federal Service*, 97–98.

2. *Staff of Subcomm. No. 5, House Comm. on the Judiciary, 85th Cong., 2d Sess., Report on Federal Conflict of Interest Legislation*, pts. *I & II* (Comm. Print. 1958); *Conflict of Interest and Federal Service; Harvard Business School Club of Washington, D.C., Businessmen in Government* (1958).

3. The members of the Panel were Judge Calvert Magruder of the United States Court of Appeals for the 1st Circuit, Dean Jefferson B. Fordham of the University of Pennsylvania Law School, and the present author. The President's message was sent to the Congress on April 27, 1961. 107 Cong. Rec. 6835 (1961).

4. 76 Stat. 1121 (1962), effective January 21, 1963. For analysis of the new statute, see Perkins, *The New Federal Conflict-of-Interest Law*, 76 Harv. L. Rev. 1113 (1963) and Manning, *Federal Conflict of Interest Law* (1964).

5. See this symposium, *infra*.

6. For an elaborate recent example, see the new regulations of the Department of Justice, 28 Fed. Reg. 7698 (1963).

7. *The New York Times*, March 9, 1964, p. 1, col. 1. See also *id.*, Apr. 26, 1964, p. 46, col. 3, and p. 47, col. 1.

8. As has often been the case, the Connecticut explosion was set off by alleged improprieties in the administration of the State highway program.

9. United States v. Mississippi Valley Generating Co., 364 U.S. 520 (1961).

10. It may be that all men are monarchists and that they differ only in the method for choosing their monarchs.

11. *The New York Times*, Sept. 29, 1952, p. 1, col. 8. A skilled practitioner recently provided us an instructive example of this kind of symbolic communication in his campaign to turn out unnecessary lights in the house where he lives—the White House. The money saved is insignificant, of course, and the rationalist is therefore tempted to dismiss or condemn the affair as cynical or hypocritical. I believe this reaction to be quite wrong. No one was misled or meant to be misled. "Lights Out" was a form of direct political communication, a formalized and readily graspable goal-setting statement by a protagonist in a stylized dramatic setting. It was a means of saying, "I, too, am worried about the cost of government, and shall try to do some-

thing about it," and, as such, is no more and no less to be criticized than the same sentence delivered in a speech. ("Actions speak louder than words" is true in two quite different senses.) Of course the proposition asserted could itself be true or false, sincere, or hypocritical; but that is so regardless of the technique of communication chosen.

12. See, for example, the failure of the *de minimis* argument in the confirmation hearings on the appointment of Mr. Dudley Sharp discussed at *Conflict of Interest and Federal Service*, 105.

13. Compare, for example, the rate of occurrence of embezzlement by employees of private banks with that of government employees holding fiscal responsibilities. Though it is difficult to be statistical, most observers would agree that fraud, kickbacks, and inside deals are more common features of the corporate, union, and business world than they are of modern government in the United States—not because standards in the former are so low, but because they are so high in the latter.

14. United States v. Mississippi Valley Generating Co., 364 U.S. 520 (1961).

QUESTIONS FOR DISCUSSION

1. What are the social structures through which Americans *learn* their nonformalized religion?
2. Does nonformalized religion *compete* with formalized religion for persons' loyalty, time, and money?
3. What range of responses do churches give to civic religion? For example, is the antidemocratic nature of much of fundamentalist Protestantism related to its incomplete "Americanization"?
4. What are the various churches' relationships with America's moral life if, as Durkheim contended, it is a *"single* moral community" that is united by religion?

ADDITIONAL READING

Bellah, Robert N. "Civil Religion in America," *Daedalus* (Winter 1967). Reprinted in Donald R. Cutler (ed.), *The Religious Situation, 1968.* Boston: Beacon Press, 1968. A widely cited—and excellent—depiction of America's civil "theology," using Presidential inaugural addresses as the main source of sacred text.

Fuller, Lon. *The Morality of Law.* New Haven: Yale University Press, 1964. A natural law position but quite different from the traditional one inasmuch as it articulates a "democratic" or procedural point of view rather than a "revealed" or substantive point of view.

Hammond, Phillip E. "Commentary on Civil Religion in America," in Donald R. Cutler (ed.), *The Religious Situation, 1968.* Boston: Beacon Press,

1968. Raises the question of how Americans are socialized to the civic religion and how decisions at times of conflict are rendered in terms of it.

Herberg, Will. *Protestant, Catholic, Jew.* Garden City, N.Y.: Doubleday, 1955. The best known effort to describe the "religion" of America, contending that the three traditions have so adopted "religion-in-general" that they are but alternative ways of being American.

Lerner, Max. "The Constitution and the Court as Symbols." *Yale Law Journal,* 46 (1937). A classic statement out of the realist school of jurisprudence arguing that Americans regard their Constitution as sacred and its interpreters as nine high priests.

Warner, W. Lloyd. *American Life: Dream and Reality.* Rev. ed. Chicago: University of Chicago Press, 1962. Chapter One, "An American Sacred Ceremony," argues that Memorial Day represents the celebration by Americans of their common identity, heritage, and destiny.